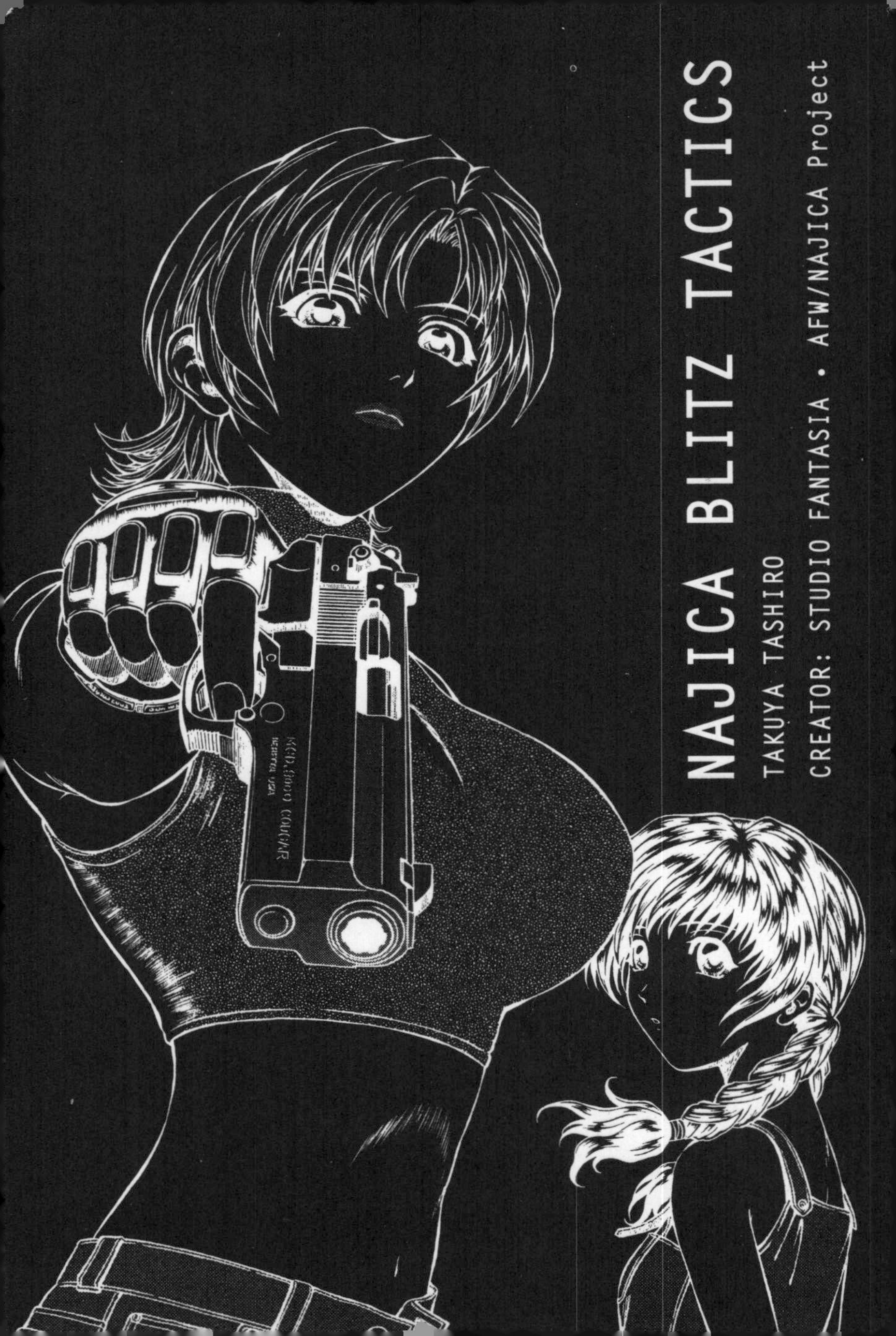
NAJICA BLITZ TACTICS
TAKUYA TASHIRO
CREATOR: STUDIO FANTASIA • AFW/NAJICA Project

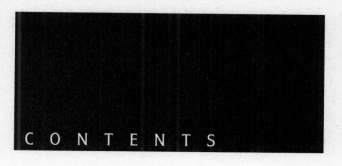

C O N T E N T S

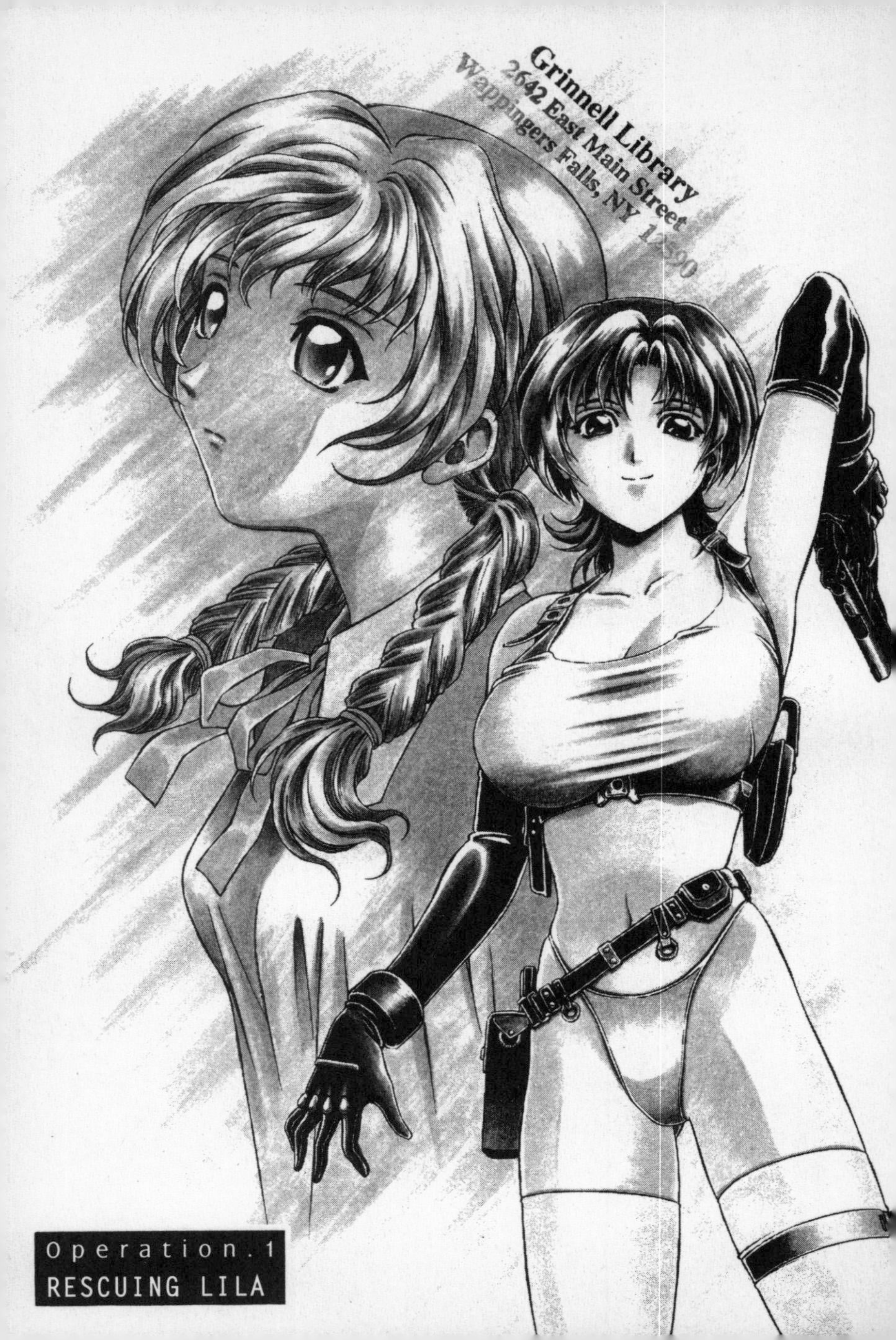
Operation.1
RESCUING LILA

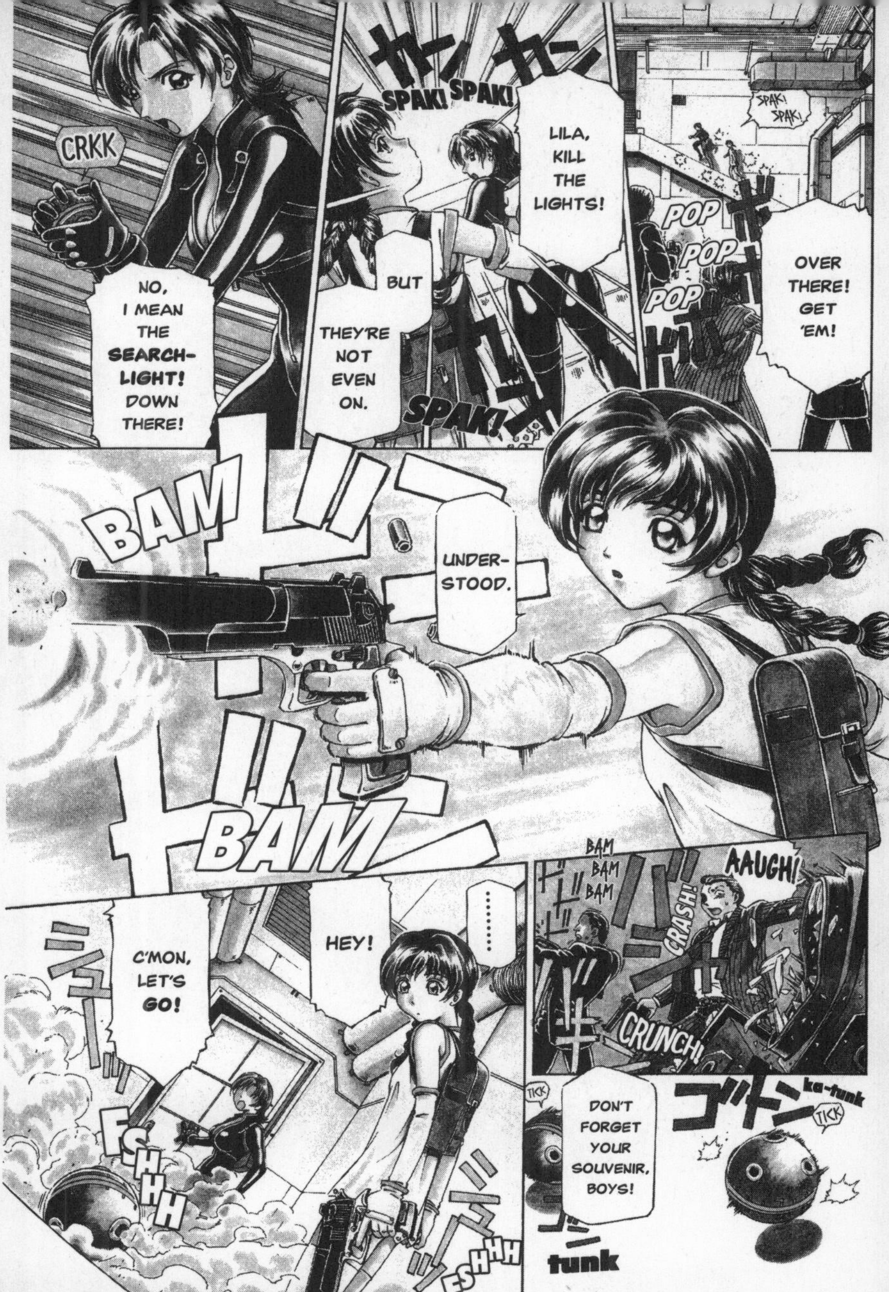
SPAK! SPAK!
POP
POP
POP
OVER THERE! GET 'EM!
SPAK! SPAK!
LILA, KILL THE LIGHTS!
BUT
THEY'RE NOT EVEN ON.
SPAK!
CRKK
NO, I MEAN THE SEARCH-LIGHT! DOWN THERE!
UNDER-STOOD.
BAM
BAM
BAM BAM BAM
AAUGH!
CRASH!
CRUNCH!
TICK
ka-tunk
TICK
DON'T FORGET YOUR SOUVENIR, BOYS!
tunk
......
HEY!
C'MON, LET'S GO!
FSHHH
FSHHH

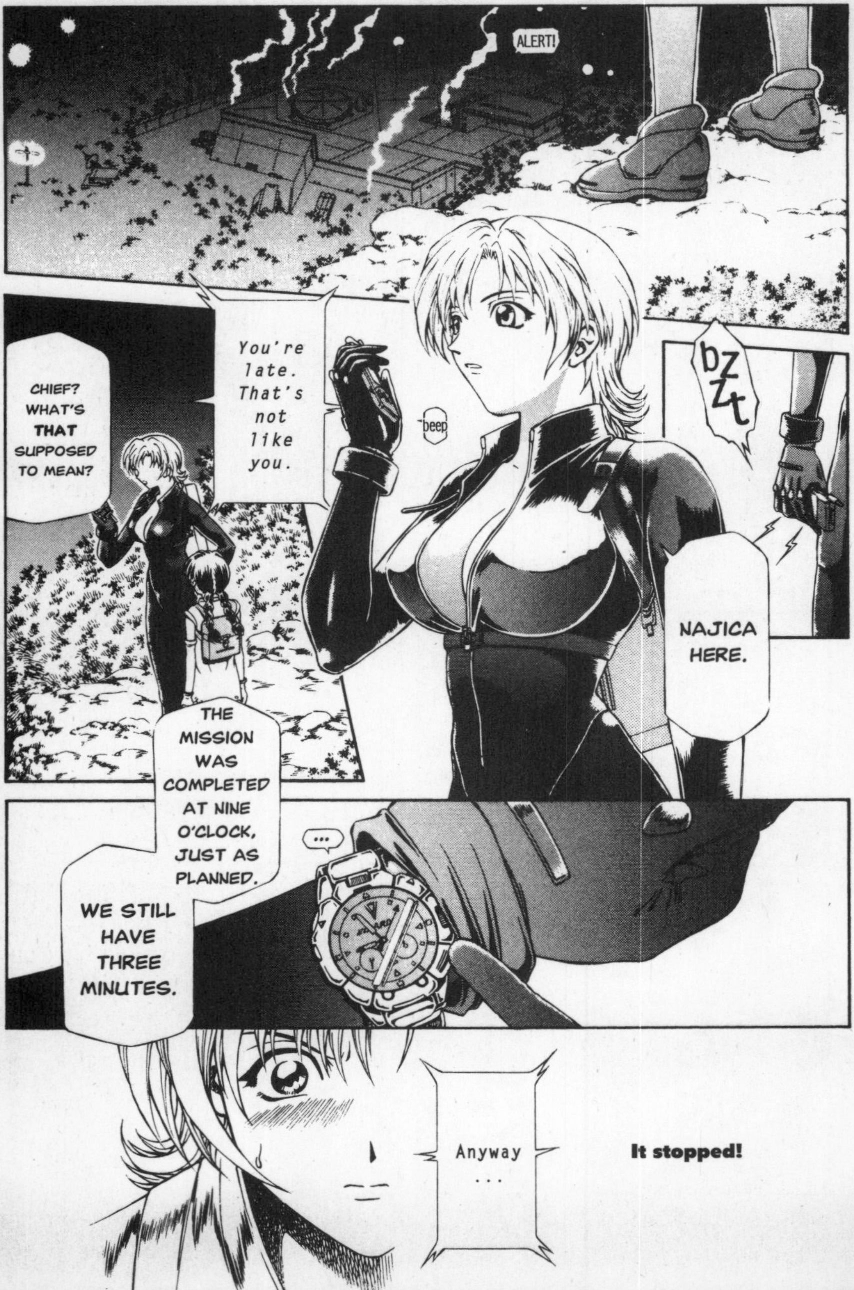
ALERT!
bzzt
NAJICA HERE.
beep
You're late. That's not like you.
CHIEF? WHAT'S THAT SUPPOSED TO MEAN?
THE MISSION WAS COMPLETED AT NINE O'CLOCK, JUST AS PLANNED.
...
WE STILL HAVE THREE MINUTES.
It stopped!
Anyway ...

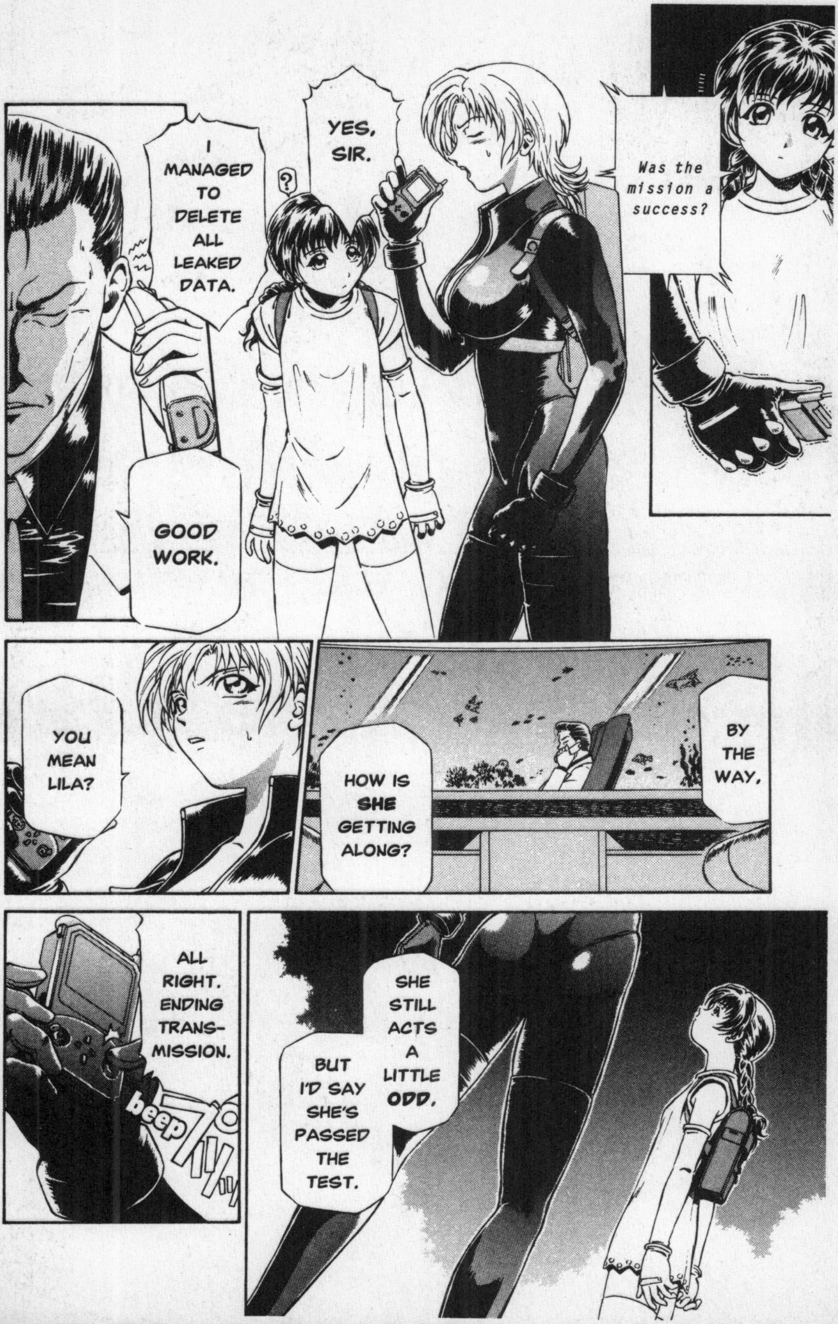
Was the mission a success?
YES, SIR.
?
I MANAGED TO DELETE ALL LEAKED DATA.
GOOD WORK.
BY THE WAY,
HOW IS SHE GETTING ALONG?
YOU MEAN LILA?
SHE STILL ACTS A LITTLE ODD.
BUT I'D SAY SHE'S PASSED THE TEST.
ALL RIGHT. ENDING TRANS-MISSION.
beep

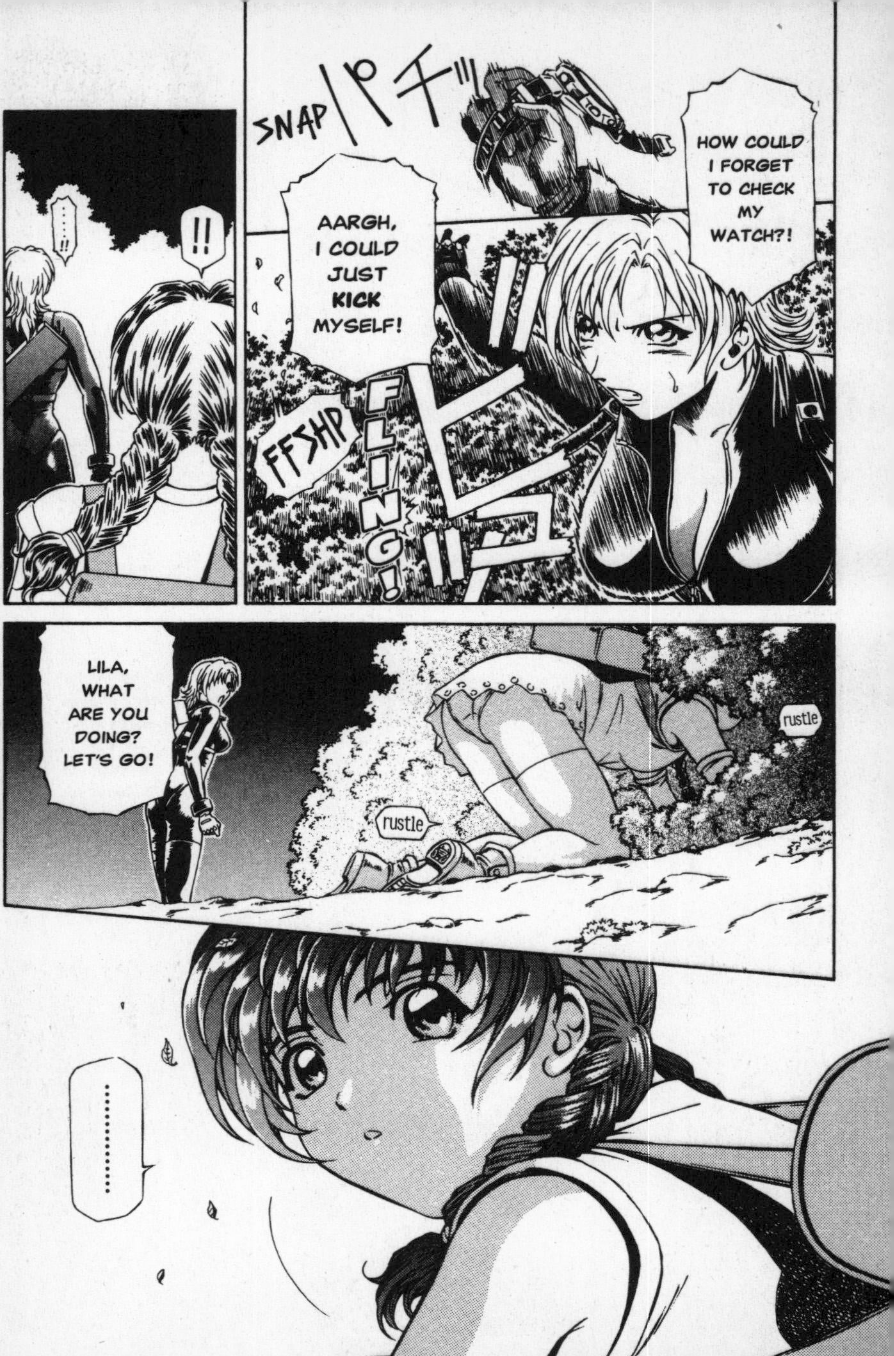
HOW COULD I FORGET TO CHECK MY WATCH?!
SNAP
AARGH, I COULD JUST KICK MYSELF!
FLING!
FFSHP
!!
...!!
LILA, WHAT ARE YOU DOING? LET'S GO!
rustle
rustle
......

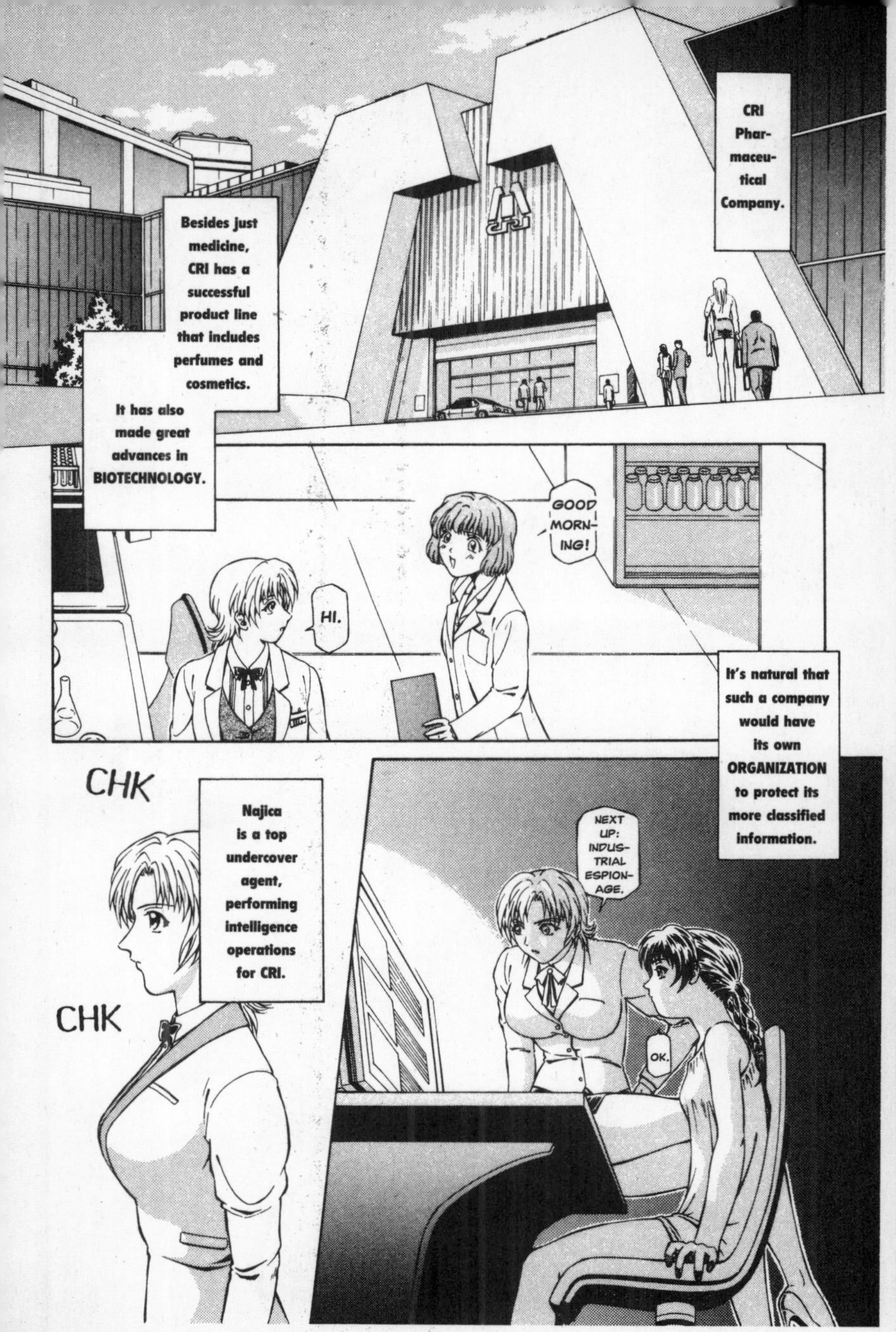
CRI Pharmaceutical Company.
Besides just medicine, CRI has a successful product line that includes perfumes and cosmetics.
It has also made great advances in BIOTECHNOLOGY.
GOOD MORNING!
HI.
It's natural that such a company would have its own ORGANIZATION to protect its more classified information.
NEXT UP: INDUSTRIAL ESPIONAGE.
OK.
CHK
Najica is a top undercover agent, performing intelligence operations for CRI.
CHK

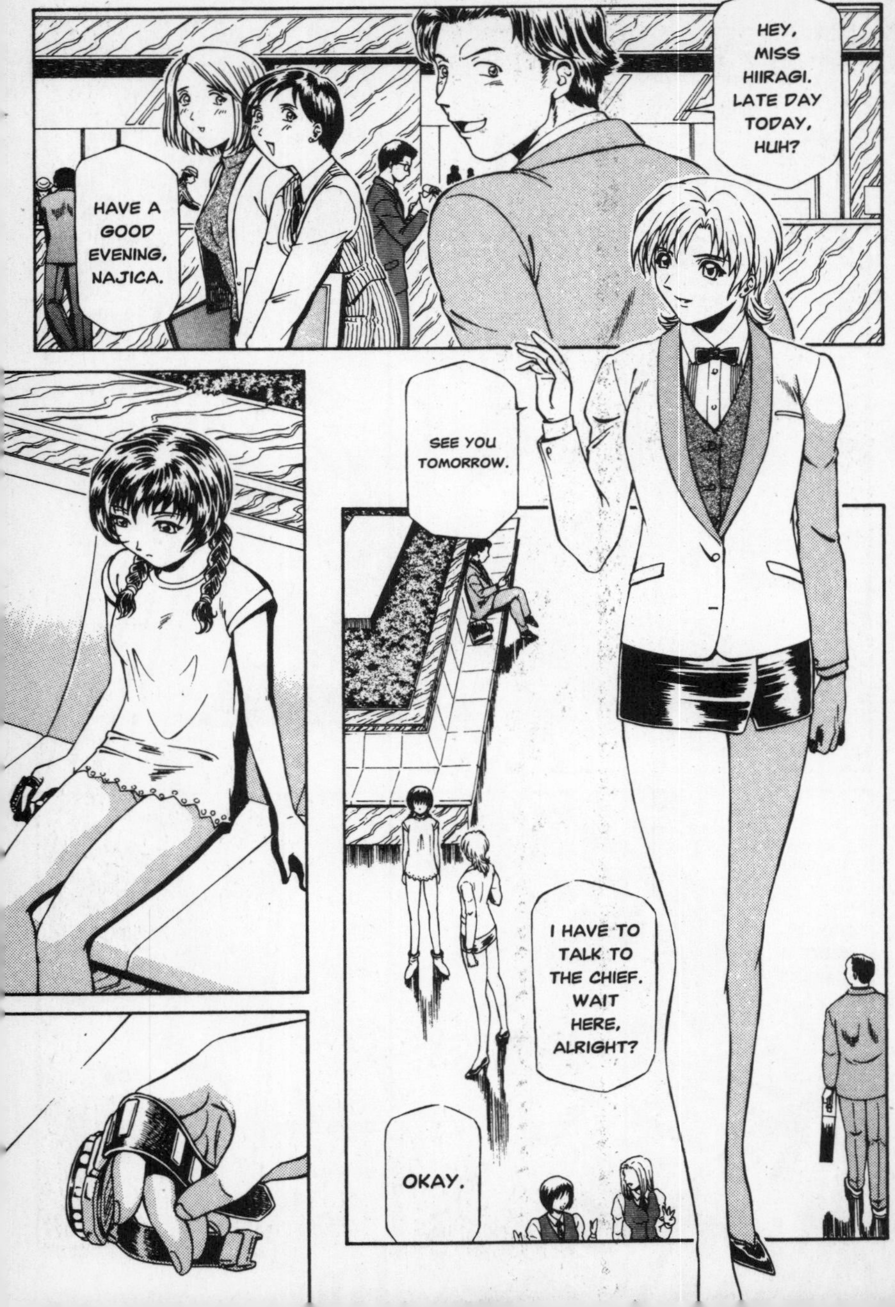
HEY, MISS HIIRAGI. LATE DAY TODAY, HUH?
HAVE A GOOD EVENING, NAJICA.
SEE YOU TOMORROW.
I HAVE TO TALK TO THE CHIEF. WAIT HERE, ALRIGHT?
OKAY.

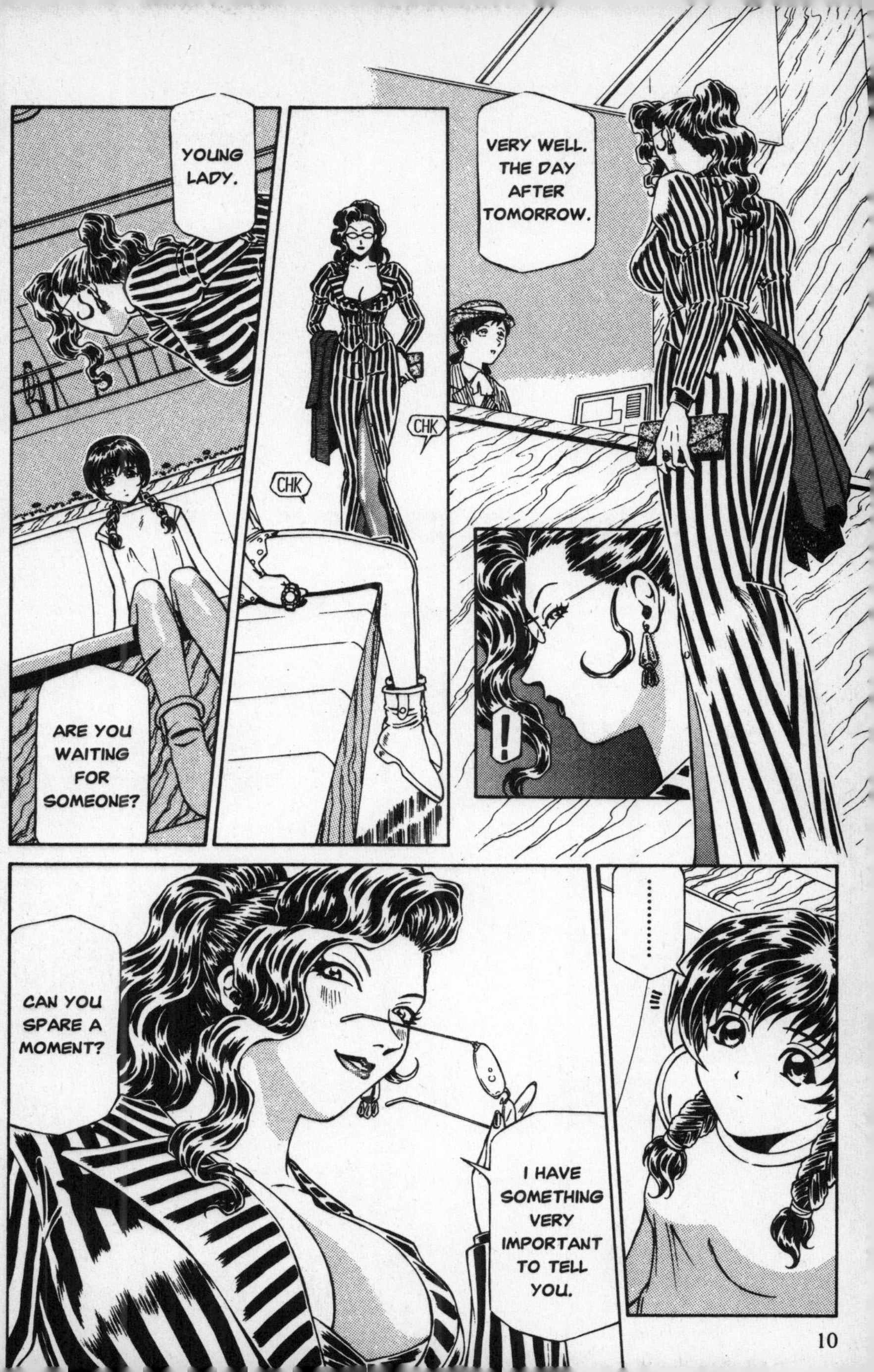
VERY WELL. THE DAY AFTER TOMORROW.
!
CHK
CHK
YOUNG LADY.
ARE YOU WAITING FOR SOMEONE?
......
CAN YOU SPARE A MOMENT?
I HAVE SOMETHING VERY IMPORTANT TO TELL YOU.

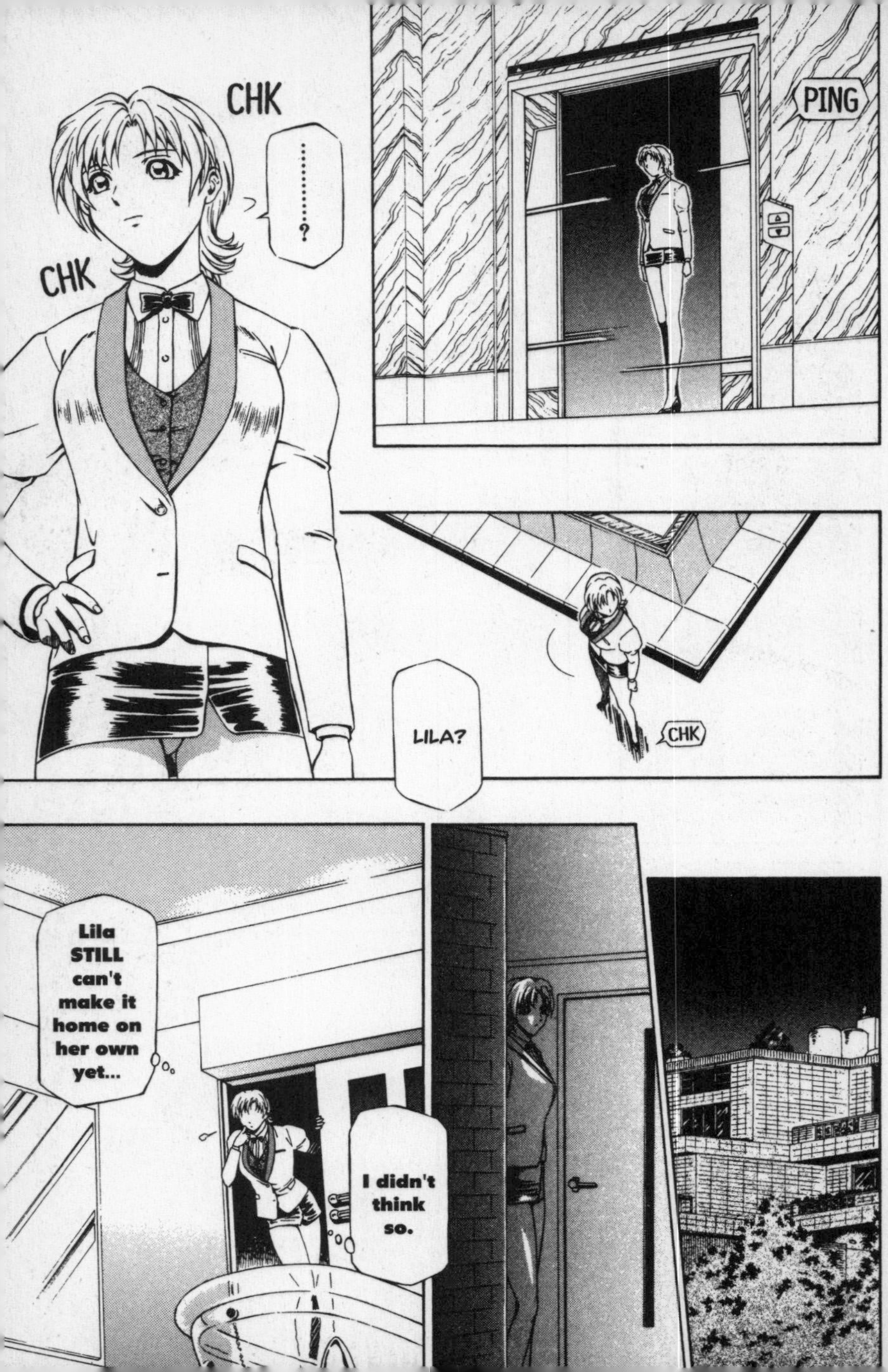
PING
LILA?
CHK
CHK
......?
CHK
Lila STILL can't make it home on her own yet...
I didn't think so.

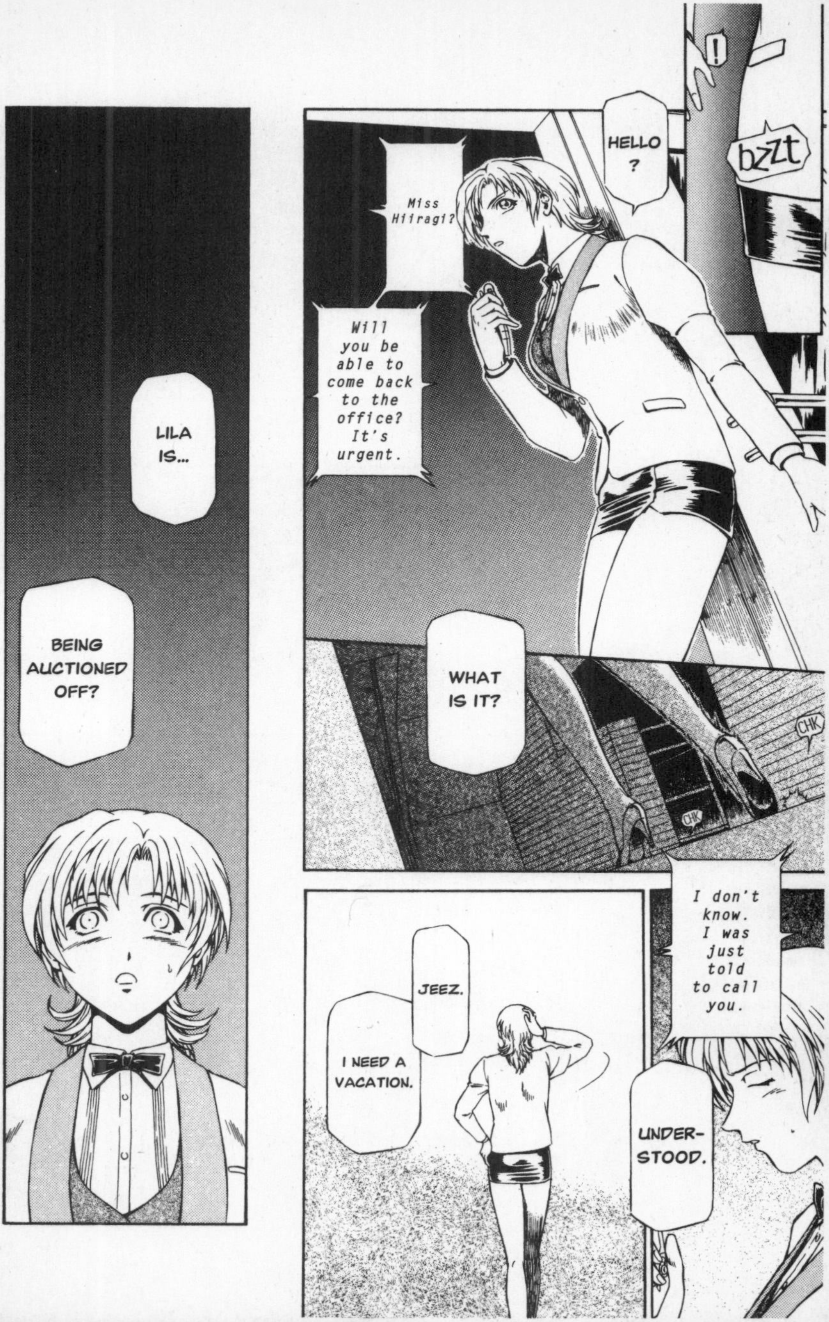

!
bzzt
HELLO ?
Miss Hiiragi?
Will you be able to come back to the office? It's urgent.
WHAT IS IT?
CHK
CHK
I don't know. I was just told to call you.
UNDER-STOOD.
JEEZ.
I NEED A VACATION.
LILA IS...
BEING AUCTIONED OFF?

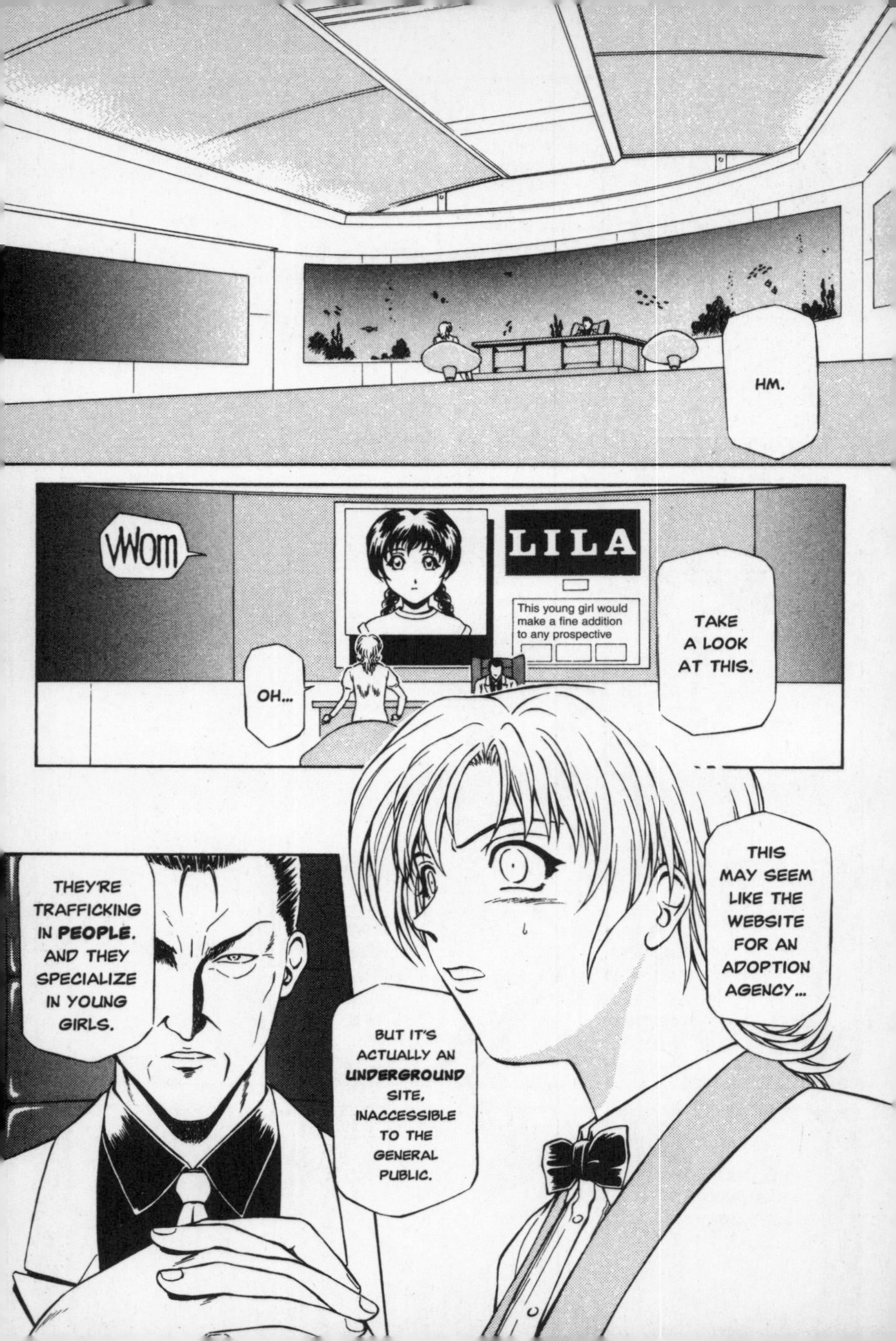
HM.
TAKE A LOOK AT THIS.
LILA
This young girl would make a fine addition to any prospective
VWOM
OH...
THIS MAY SEEM LIKE THE WEBSITE FOR AN ADOPTION AGENCY...
BUT IT'S ACTUALLY AN UNDERGROUND SITE, INACCESSIBLE TO THE GENERAL PUBLIC.
THEY'RE TRAFFICKING IN PEOPLE. AND THEY SPECIALIZE IN YOUNG GIRLS.

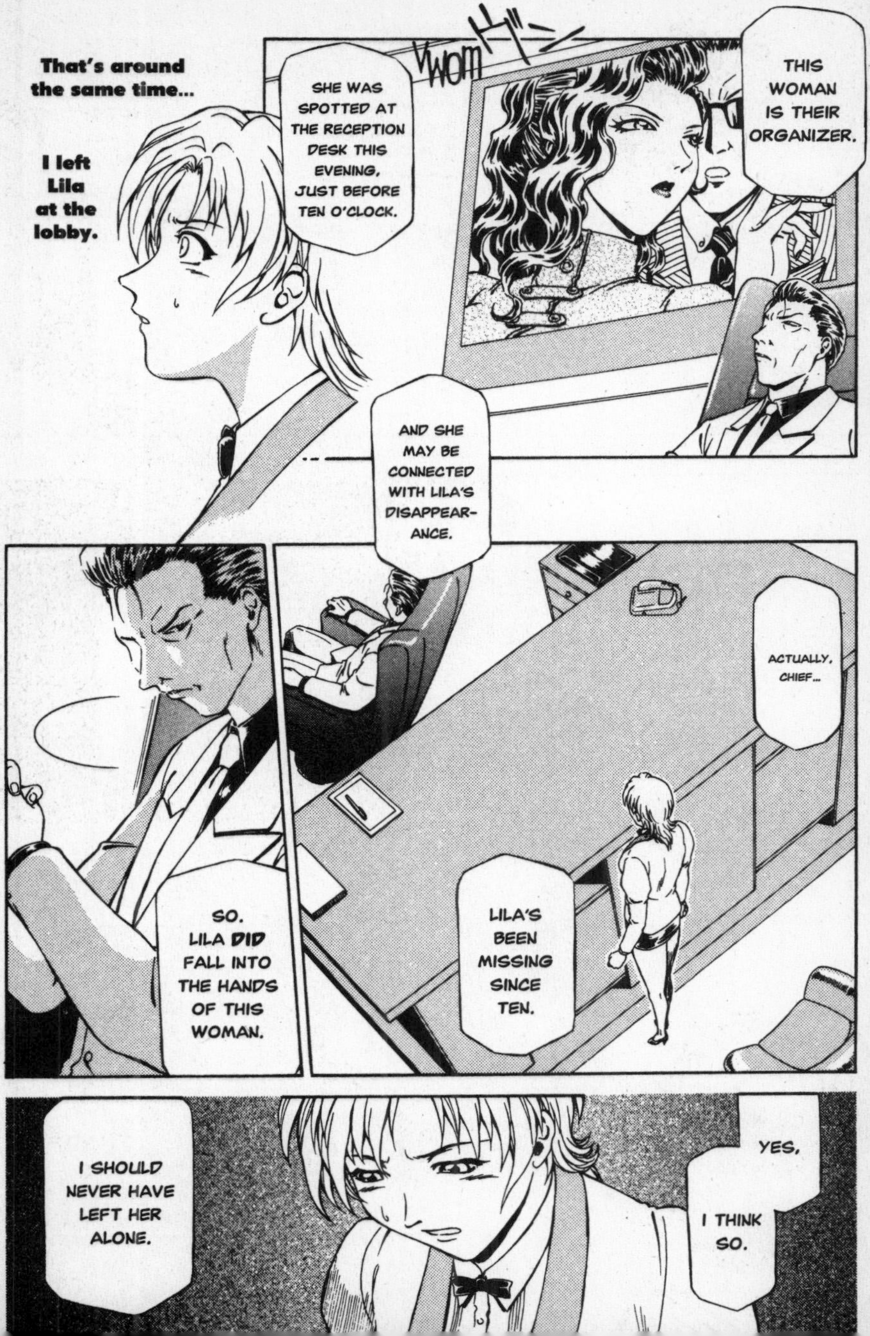

THIS WOMAN IS THEIR ORGANIZER.
VWOM
SHE WAS SPOTTED AT THE RECEPTION DESK THIS EVENING, JUST BEFORE TEN O'CLOCK.
That's around the same time...
I left Lila at the lobby.
AND SHE MAY BE CONNECTED WITH LILA'S DISAPPEARANCE.
ACTUALLY, CHIEF...
LILA'S BEEN MISSING SINCE TEN.
SO. LILA DID FALL INTO THE HANDS OF THIS WOMAN.
YES,
I THINK SO.
I SHOULD NEVER HAVE LEFT HER ALONE.

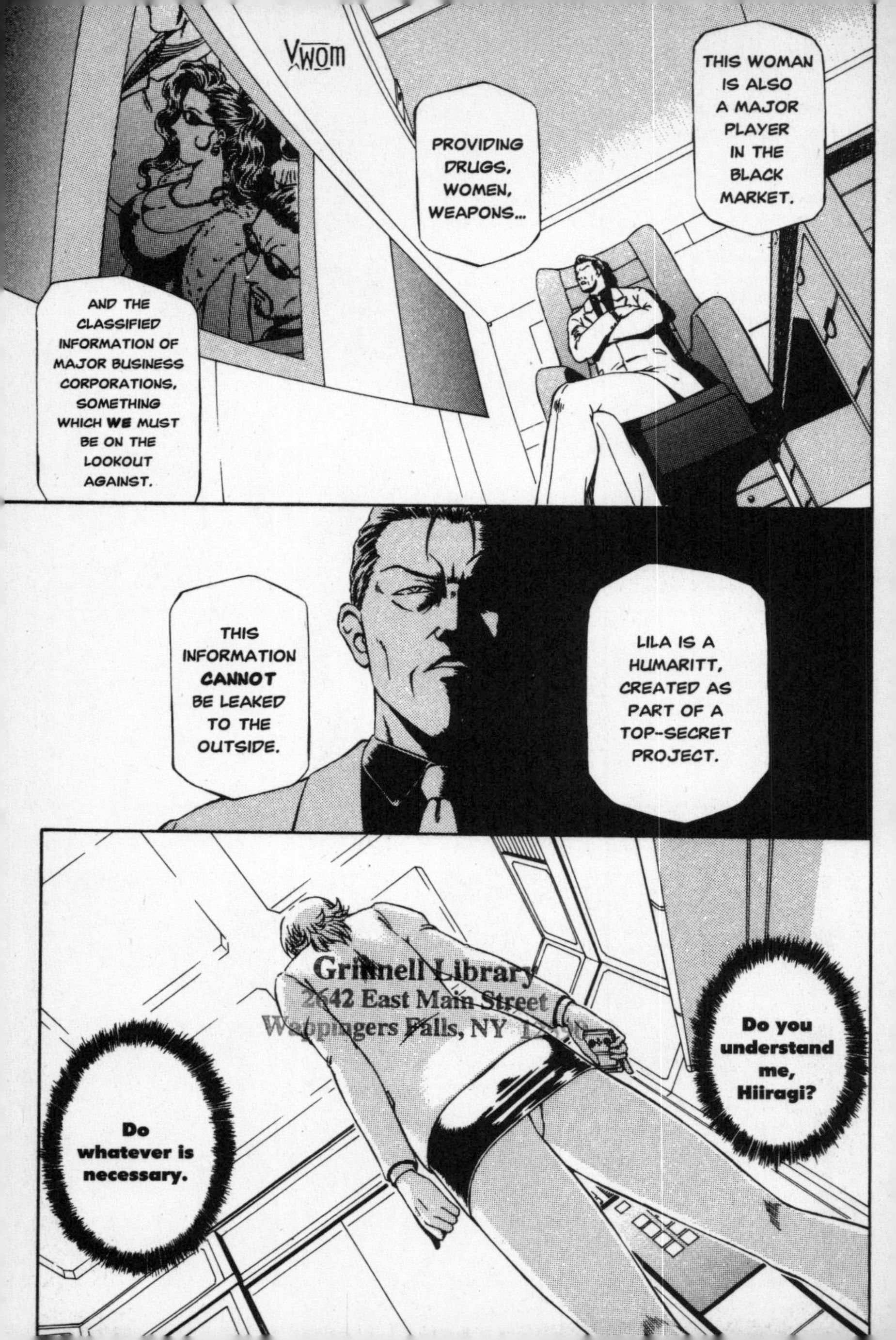
THIS WOMAN IS ALSO A MAJOR PLAYER IN THE BLACK MARKET.
PROVIDING DRUGS, WOMEN, WEAPONS...
VWOM
AND THE CLASSIFIED INFORMATION OF MAJOR BUSINESS CORPORATIONS, SOMETHING WHICH WE MUST BE ON THE LOOKOUT AGAINST.
LILA IS A HUMARITT, CREATED AS PART OF A TOP-SECRET PROJECT.
THIS INFORMATION CANNOT BE LEAKED TO THE OUTSIDE.
Do you understand me, Hiiragi?
Do whatever is necessary.

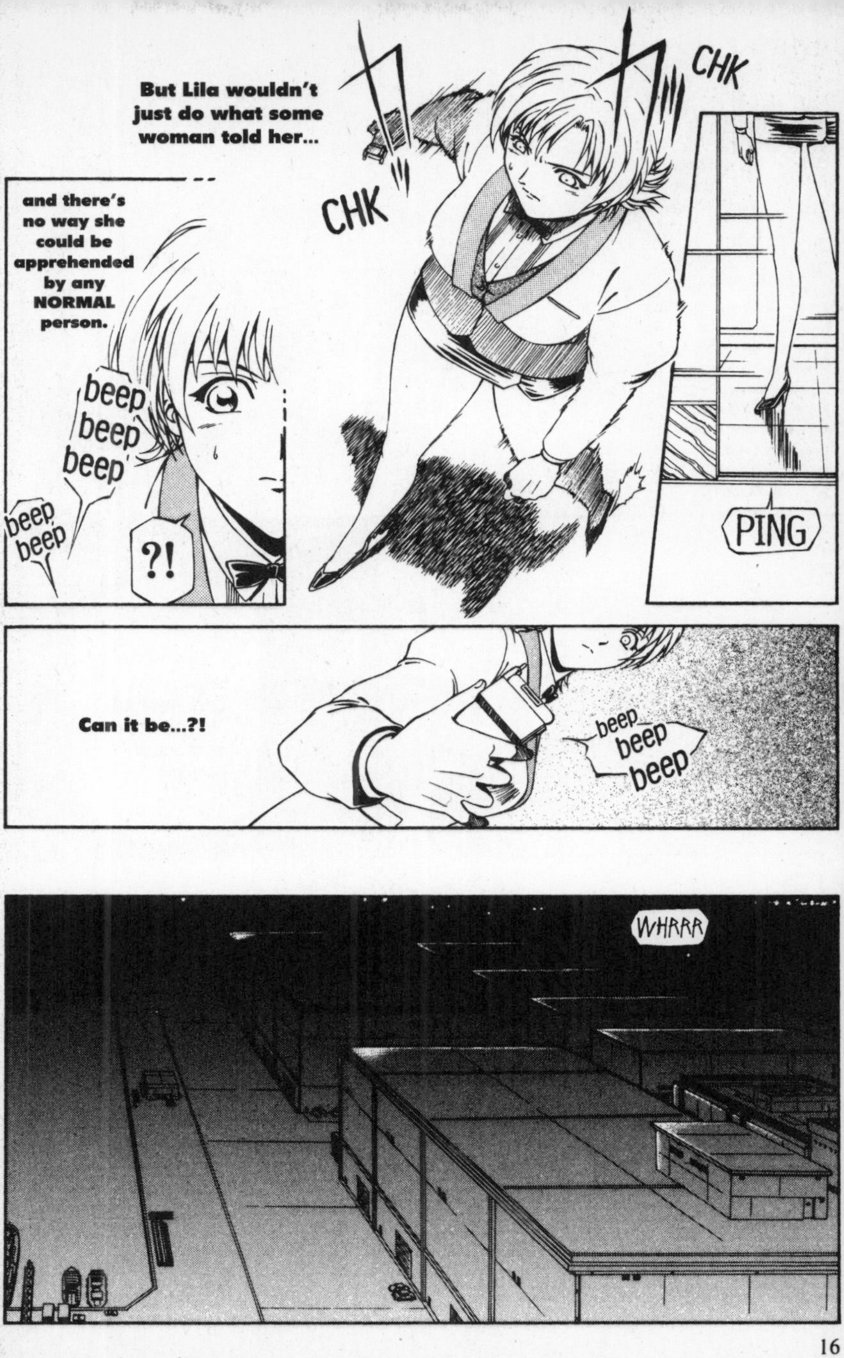
PING
CHK
CHK
But Lila wouldn't just do what some woman told her...
and there's no way she could be apprehended by any NORMAL person.
beep beep beep
beep beep
?!
Can it be...?!
beep beep beep
WHRRR

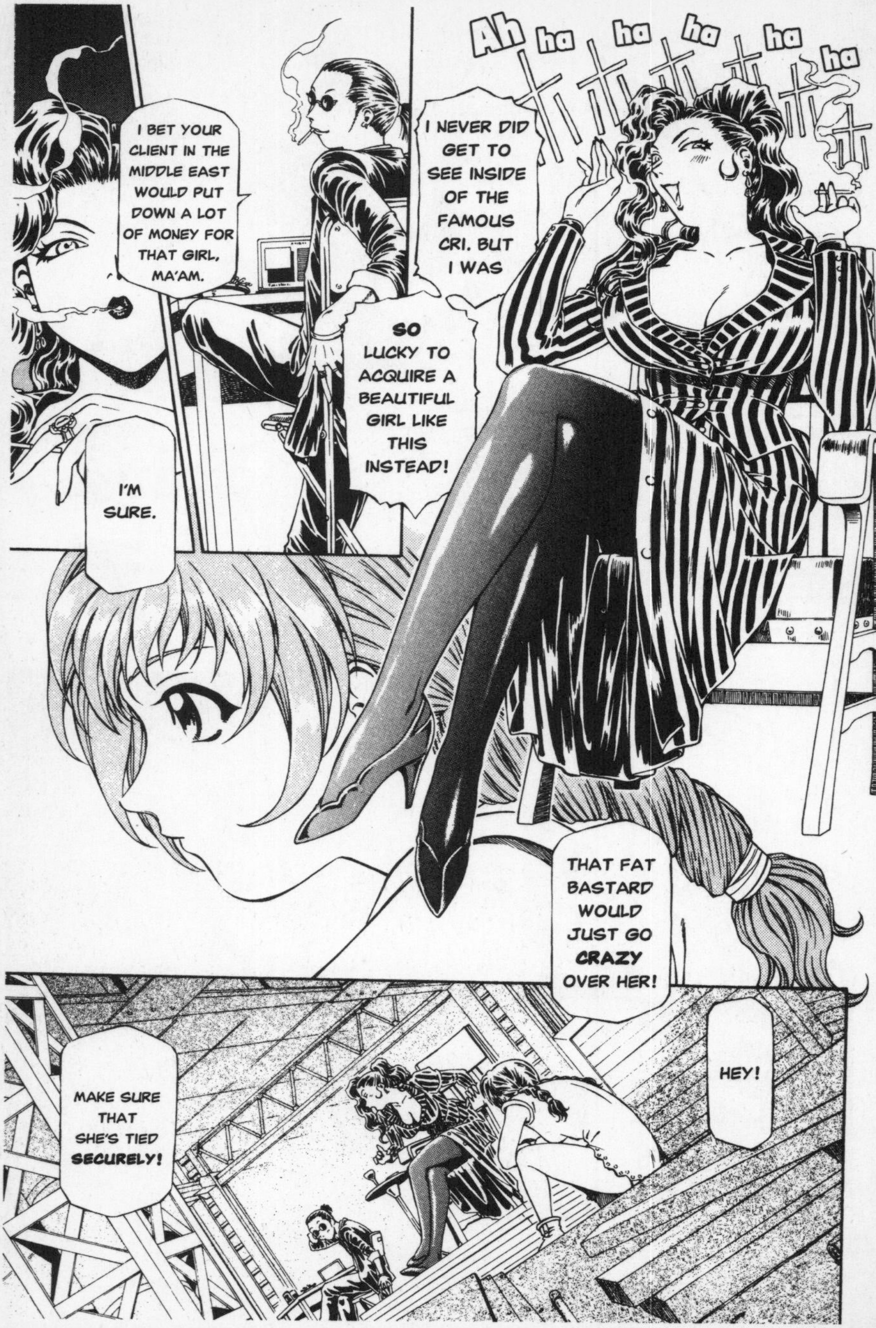
Ah ha ha ha ha ha
I NEVER DID GET TO SEE INSIDE OF THE FAMOUS CRI. BUT I WAS
SO LUCKY TO ACQUIRE A BEAUTIFUL GIRL LIKE THIS INSTEAD!
I BET YOUR CLIENT IN THE MIDDLE EAST WOULD PUT DOWN A LOT OF MONEY FOR THAT GIRL, MA'AM.
I'M SURE.
THAT FAT BASTARD WOULD JUST GO **CRAZY** OVER HER!
HEY!
MAKE SURE THAT SHE'S TIED **SECURELY**!

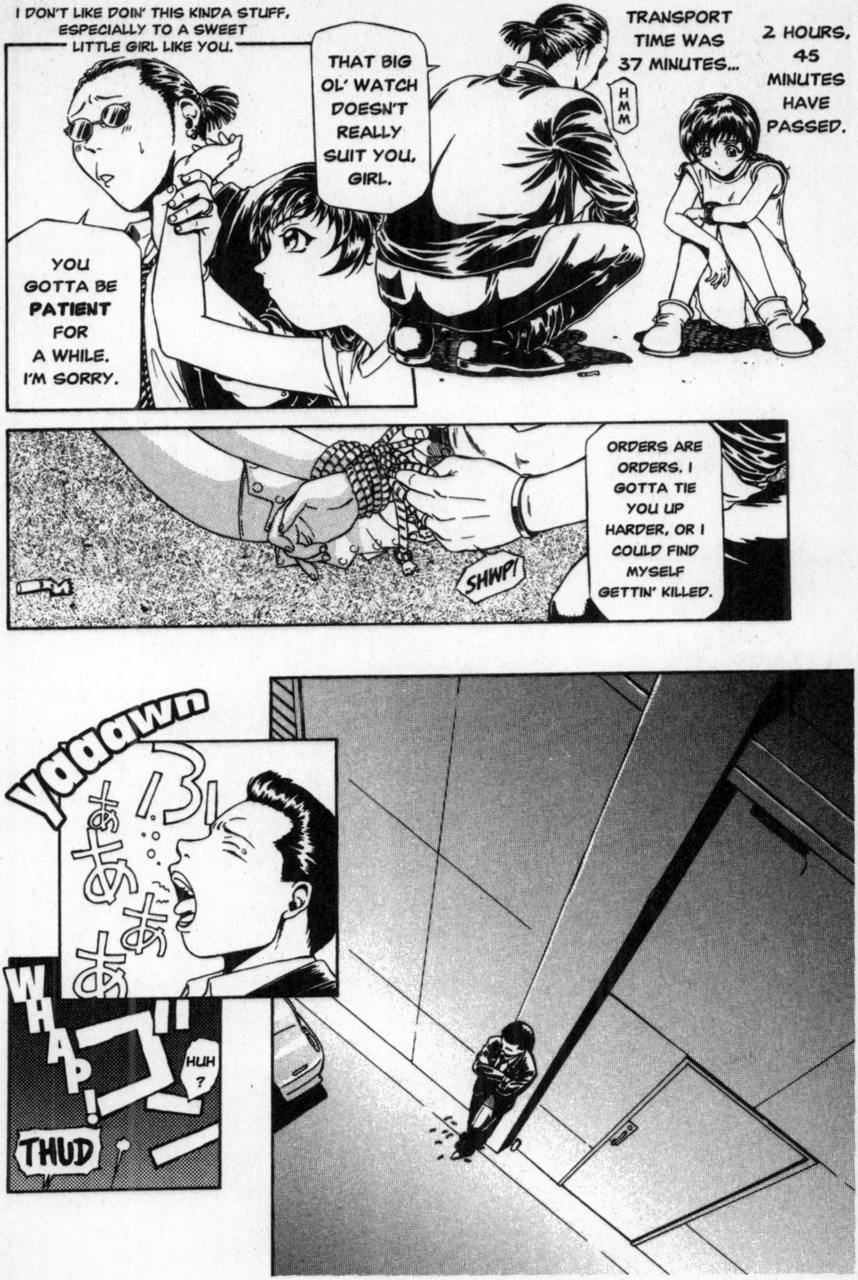
2 HOURS, 45 MINUTES HAVE PASSED.
TRANSPORT TIME WAS 37 MINUTES...
HMM
THAT BIG OL' WATCH DOESN'T REALLY SUIT YOU, GIRL.
I DON'T LIKE DOIN' THIS KINDA STUFF, ESPECIALLY TO A SWEET LITTLE GIRL LIKE YOU.
YOU GOTTA BE **PATIENT** FOR A WHILE. I'M SORRY.
ORDERS ARE ORDERS. I GOTTA TIE YOU UP HARDER, OR I COULD FIND MYSELF GETTIN' KILLED.
SHWP!
YAAAWN
ふぁあああ
WHAP!
ゴ
HUH?
THUD

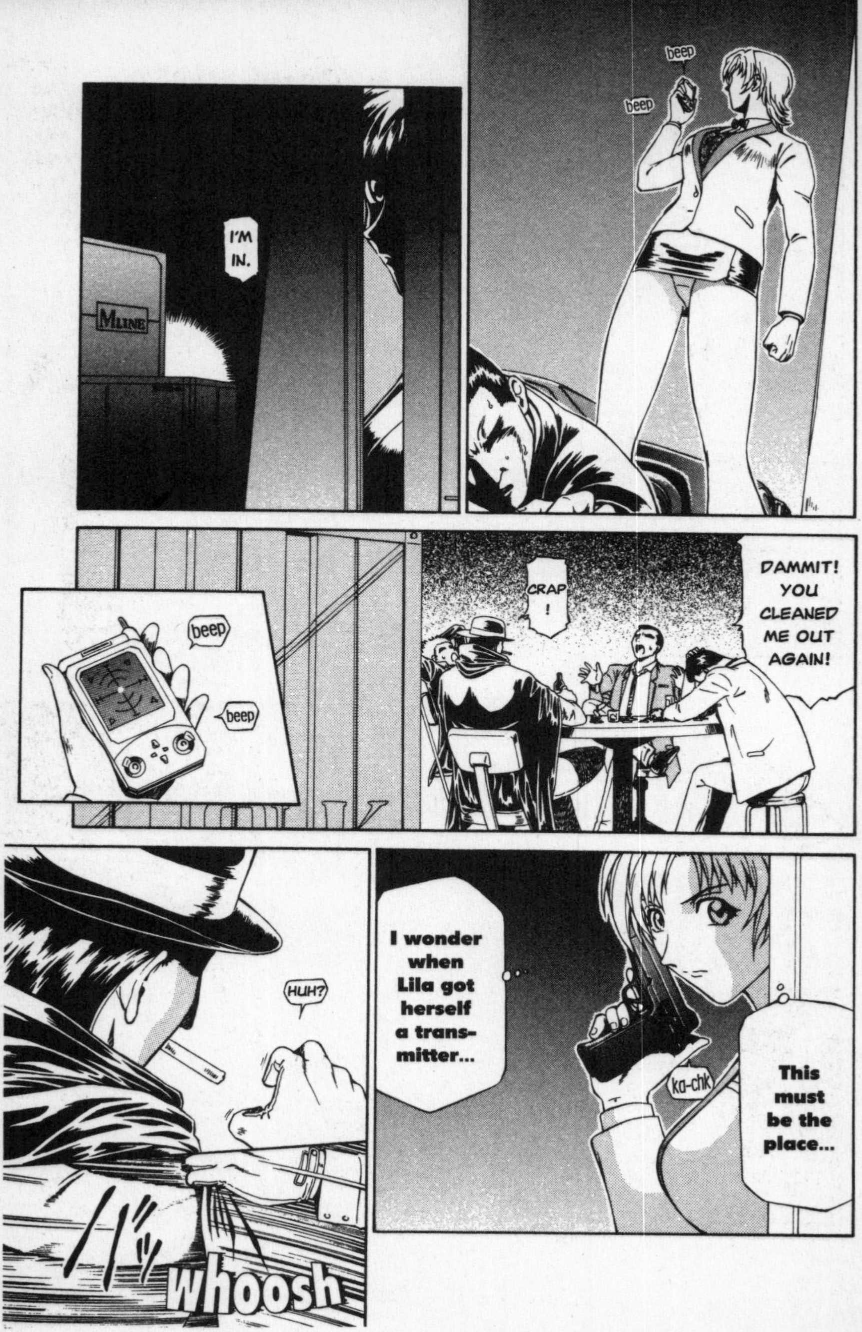
beep
beep
I'M IN.
DAMMIT! YOU CLEANED ME OUT AGAIN!
CRAP!
beep
beep
I wonder when Lila got herself a transmitter...
ka-chk
This must be the place...
HUH?
whoosh

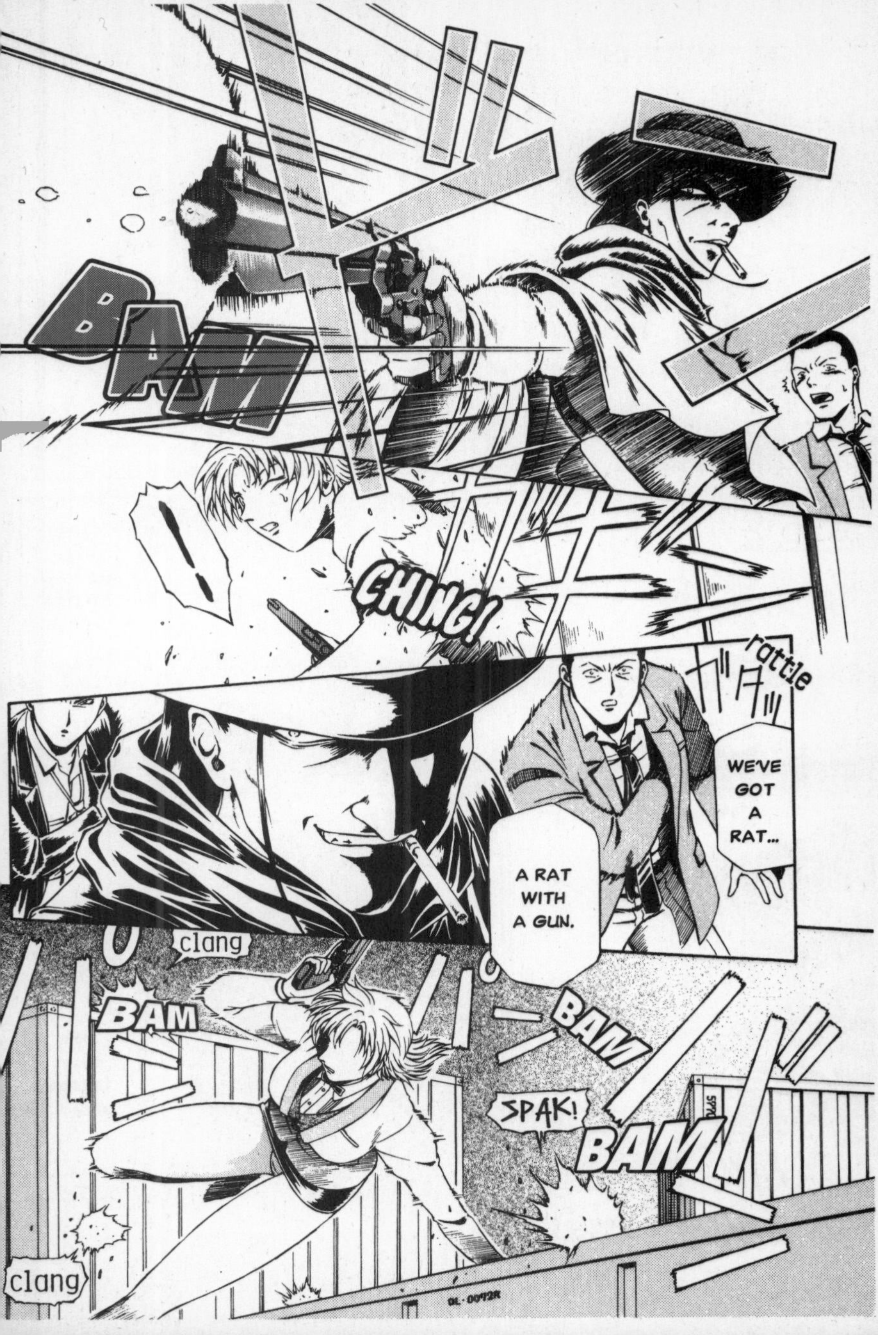
BAM
!
CHING!
rattle
WE'VE GOT A RAT...
A RAT WITH A GUN.
clang
BAM
BAM
SPAK!
BAM
clang

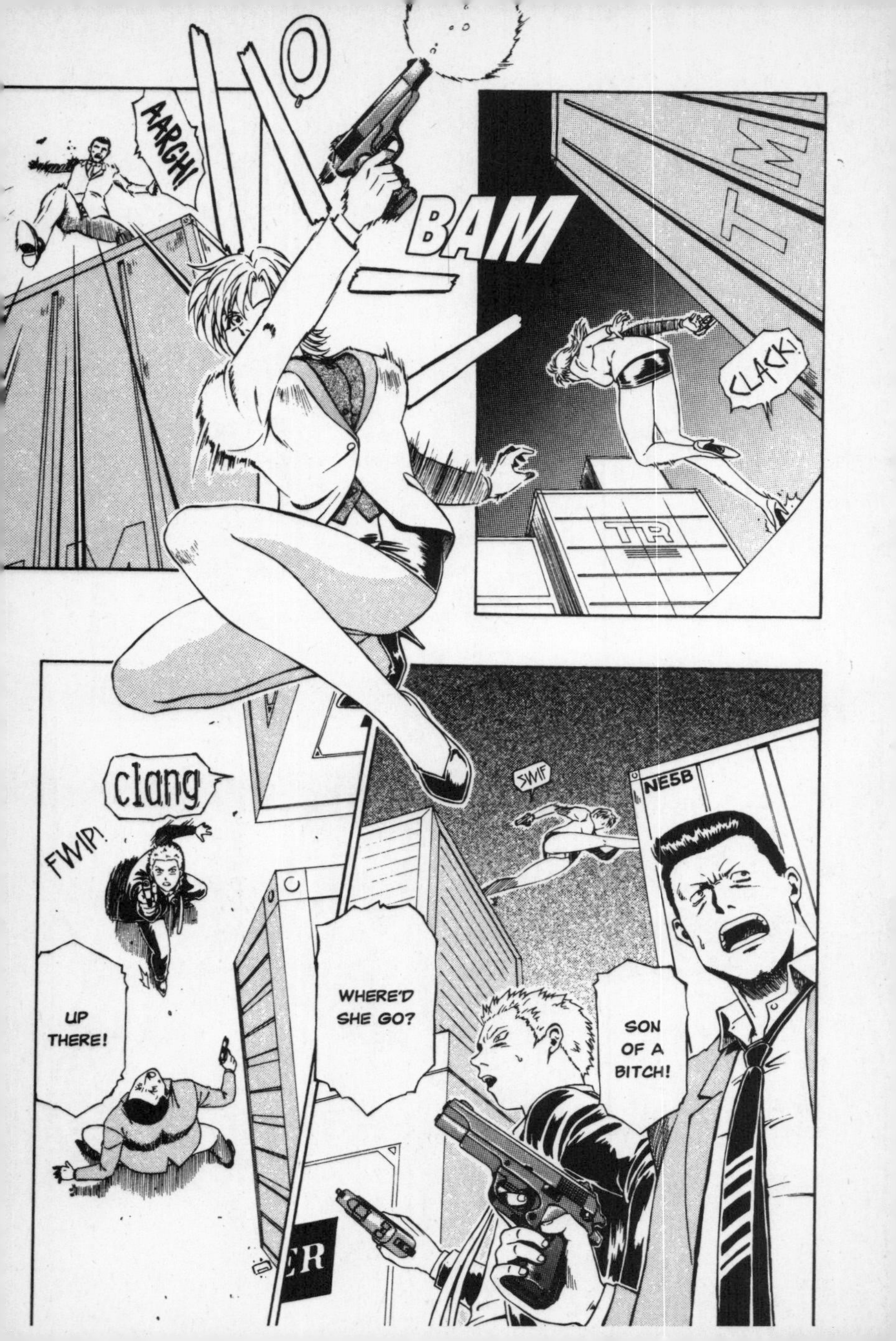
CLACK!
BAM
AARGH!
NE5B
SON OF A BITCH!
WHERE'D SHE GO?
clang
FWIP!
UP THERE!
ER

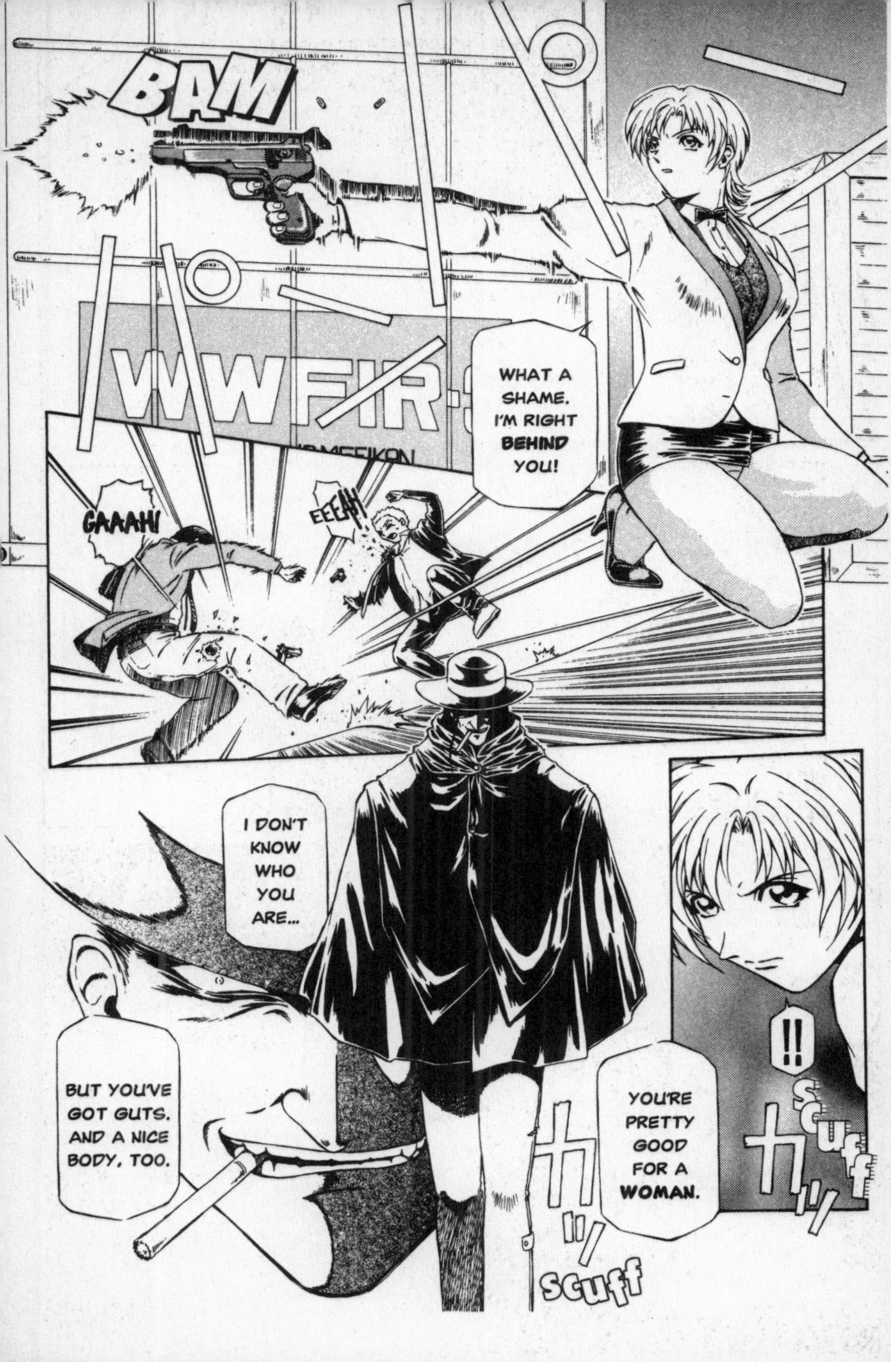
BAM
WHAT A SHAME. I'M RIGHT BEHIND YOU!
EEEAH
GAAAH!
!!
scuff
YOU'RE PRETTY GOOD FOR A WOMAN.
I DON'T KNOW WHO YOU ARE...
scuff
BUT YOU'VE GOT GUTS. AND A NICE BODY, TOO.

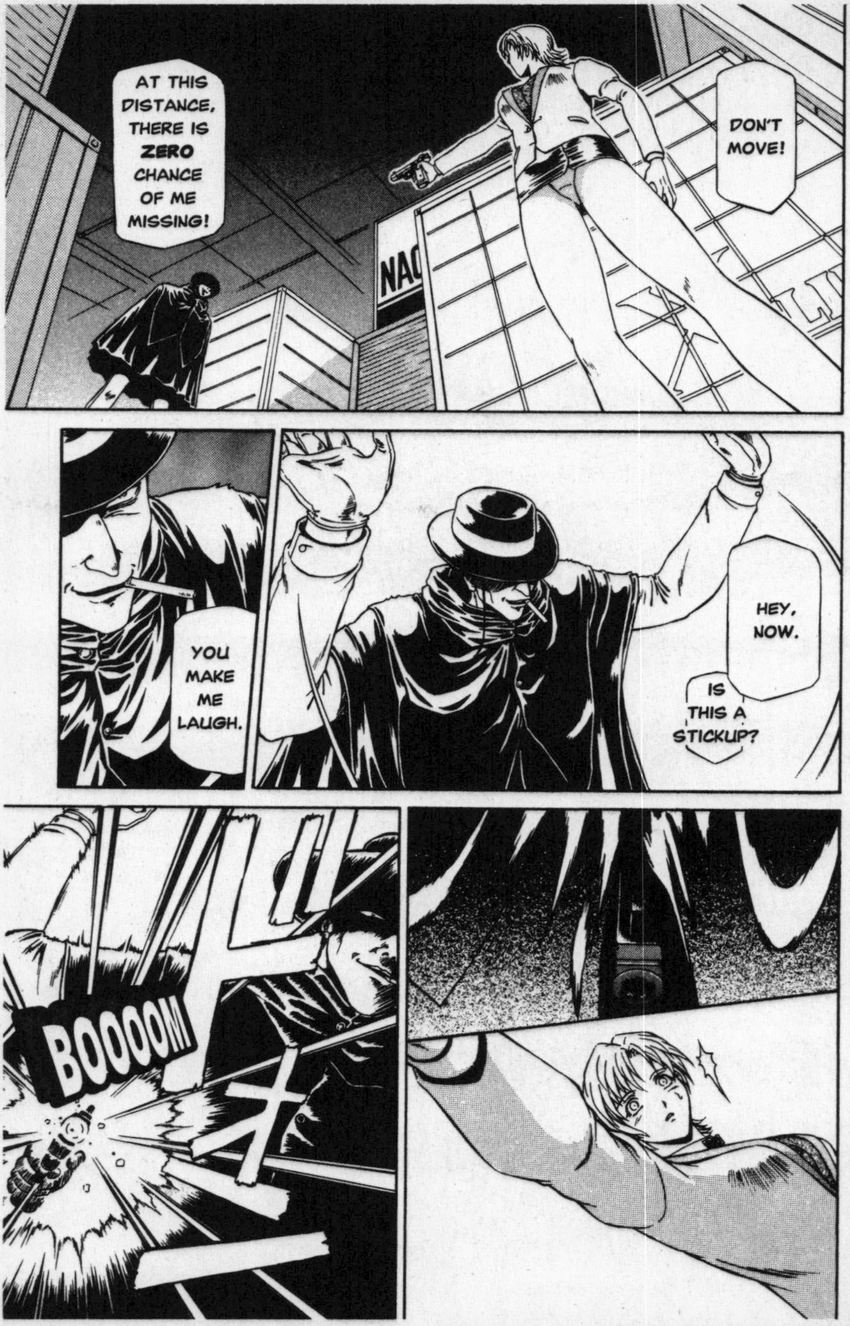
DON'T MOVE!
AT THIS DISTANCE, THERE IS **ZERO** CHANCE OF ME MISSING!
HEY, NOW.
IS THIS A STICKUP?
YOU MAKE ME LAUGH.
BOOOOM

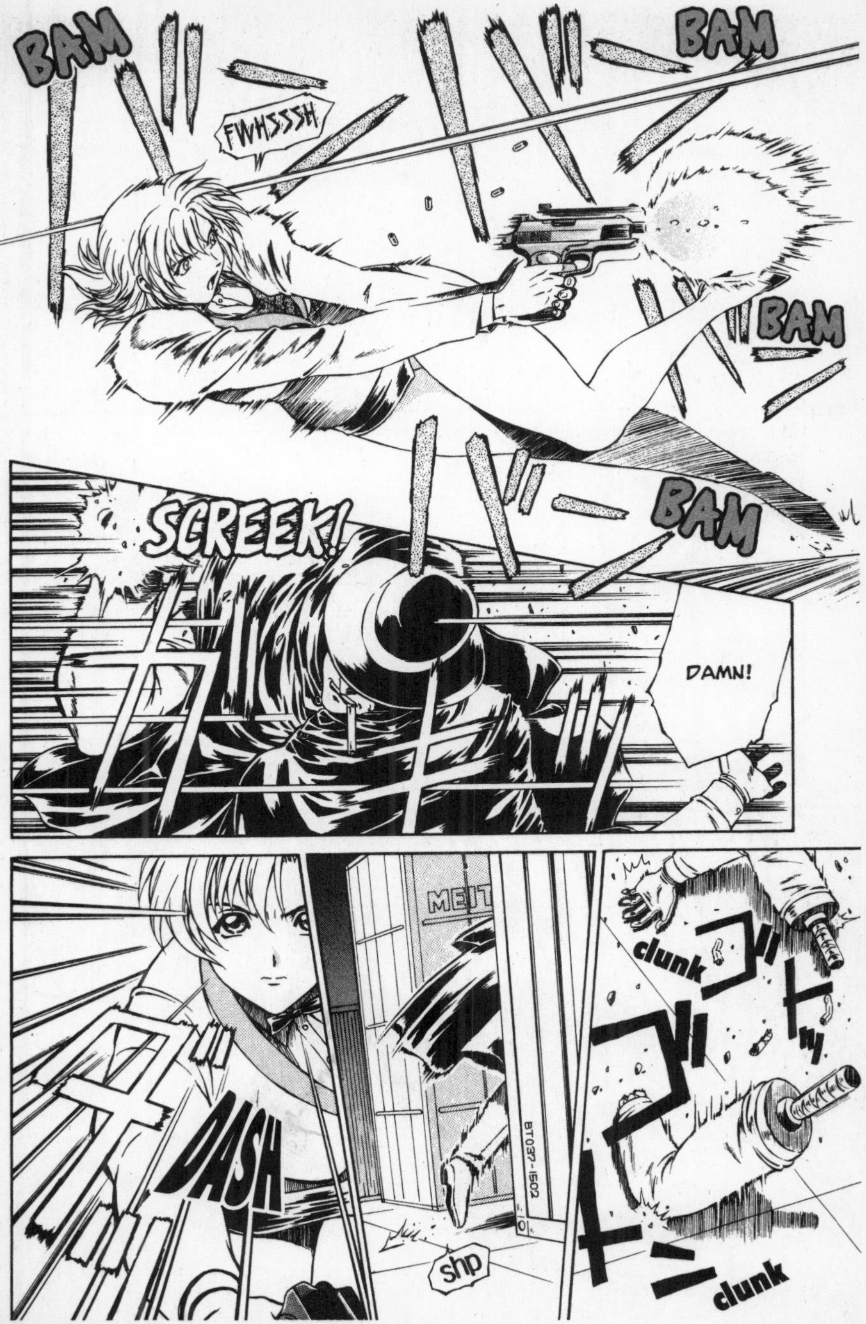
BAM
BAM
FWHSSSH
BAM
BAM
DAMN!
SCREEK!
clunk
clunk
BT037-1502
shp
DASH

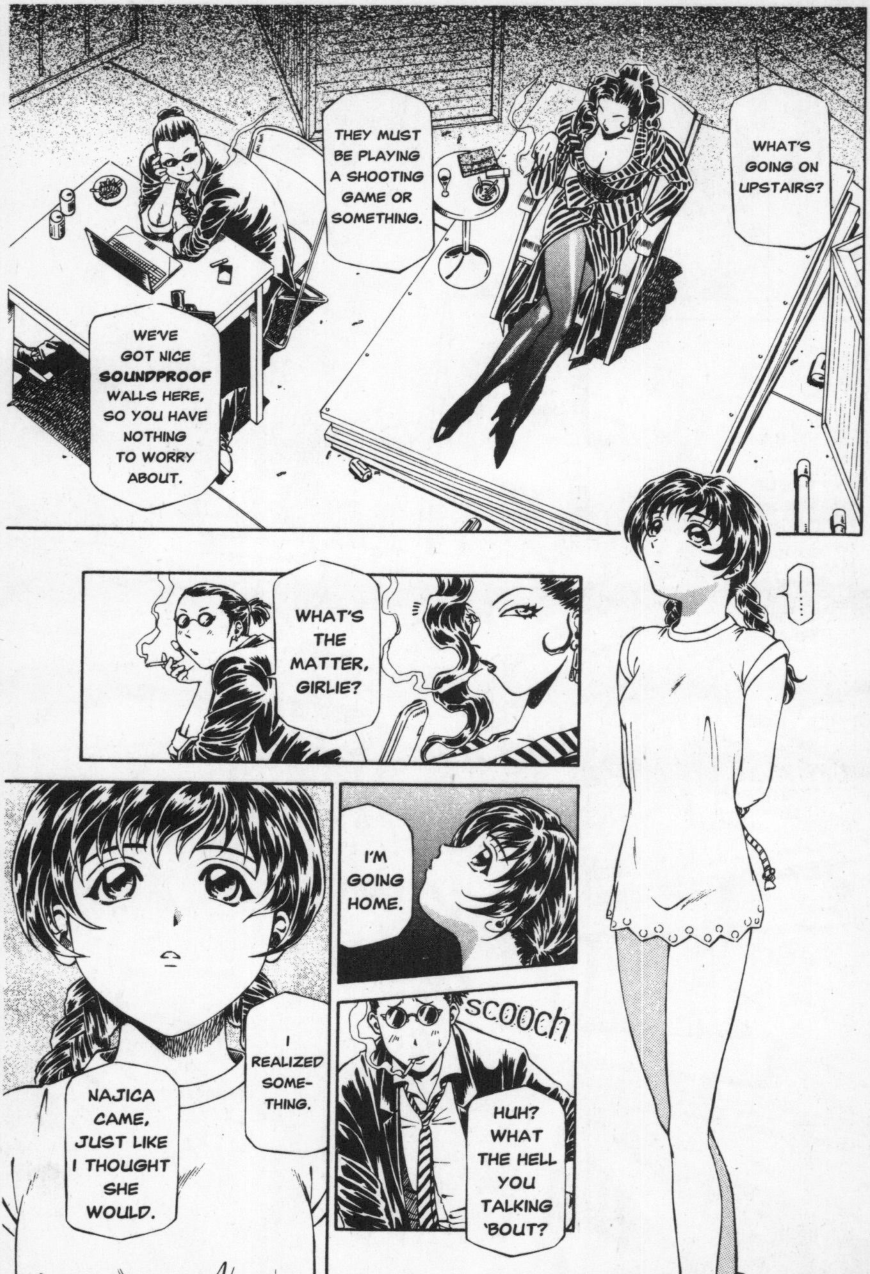
WHAT'S GOING ON UPSTAIRS?
THEY MUST BE PLAYING A SHOOTING GAME OR SOMETHING.
WE'VE GOT NICE **SOUNDPROOF** WALLS HERE, SO YOU HAVE NOTHING TO WORRY ABOUT.
—....
WHAT'S THE MATTER, GIRLIE?
I'M GOING HOME.
SCOOCH
HUH? WHAT THE HELL YOU TALKING 'BOUT?
I REALIZED SOME-THING.
NAJICA CAME, JUST LIKE I THOUGHT SHE WOULD.

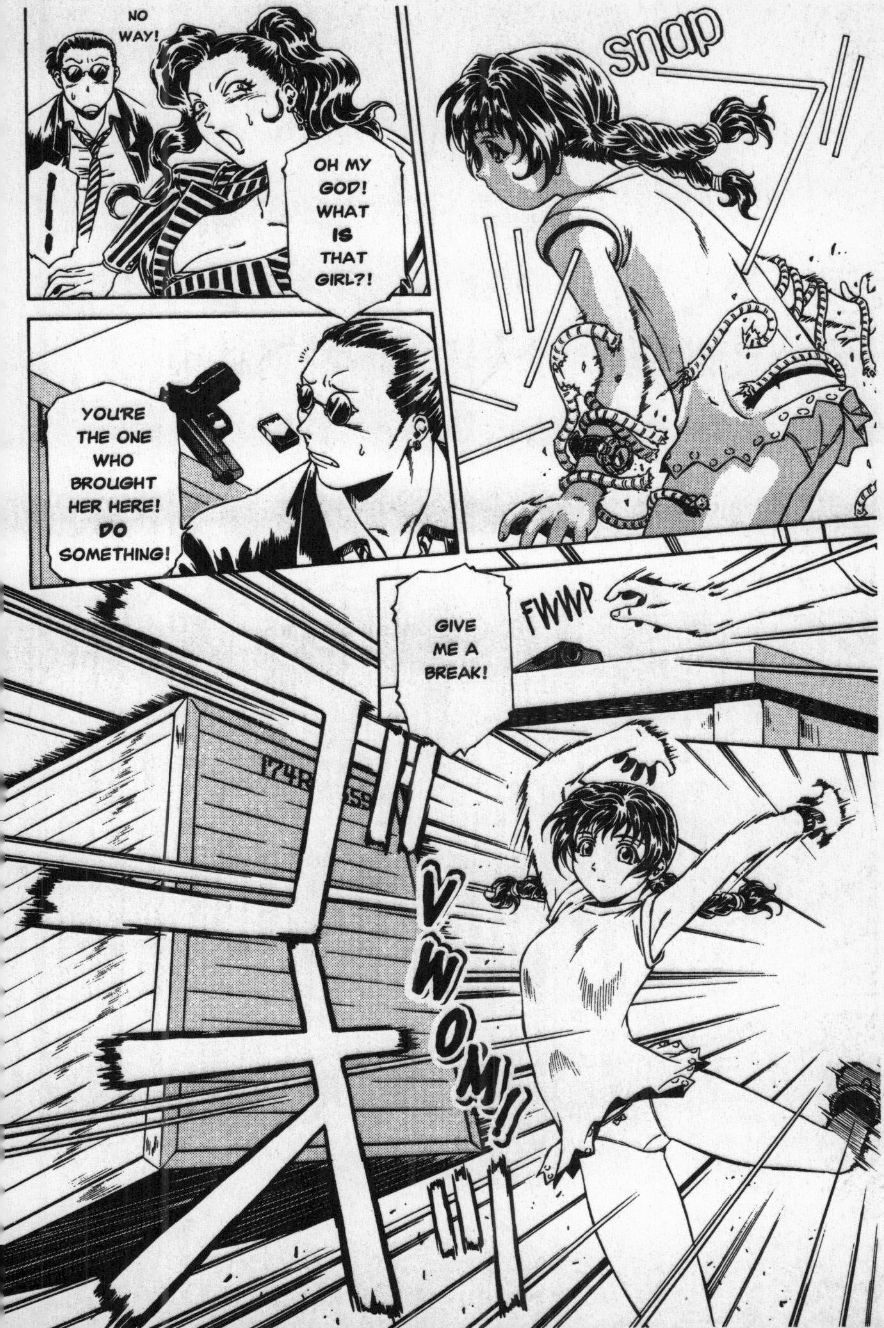
snap
NO WAY!
OH MY GOD! WHAT IS THAT GIRL?!
YOU'RE THE ONE WHO BROUGHT HER HERE! DO SOMETHING!
FWWP
GIVE ME A BREAK!
VWOM!!

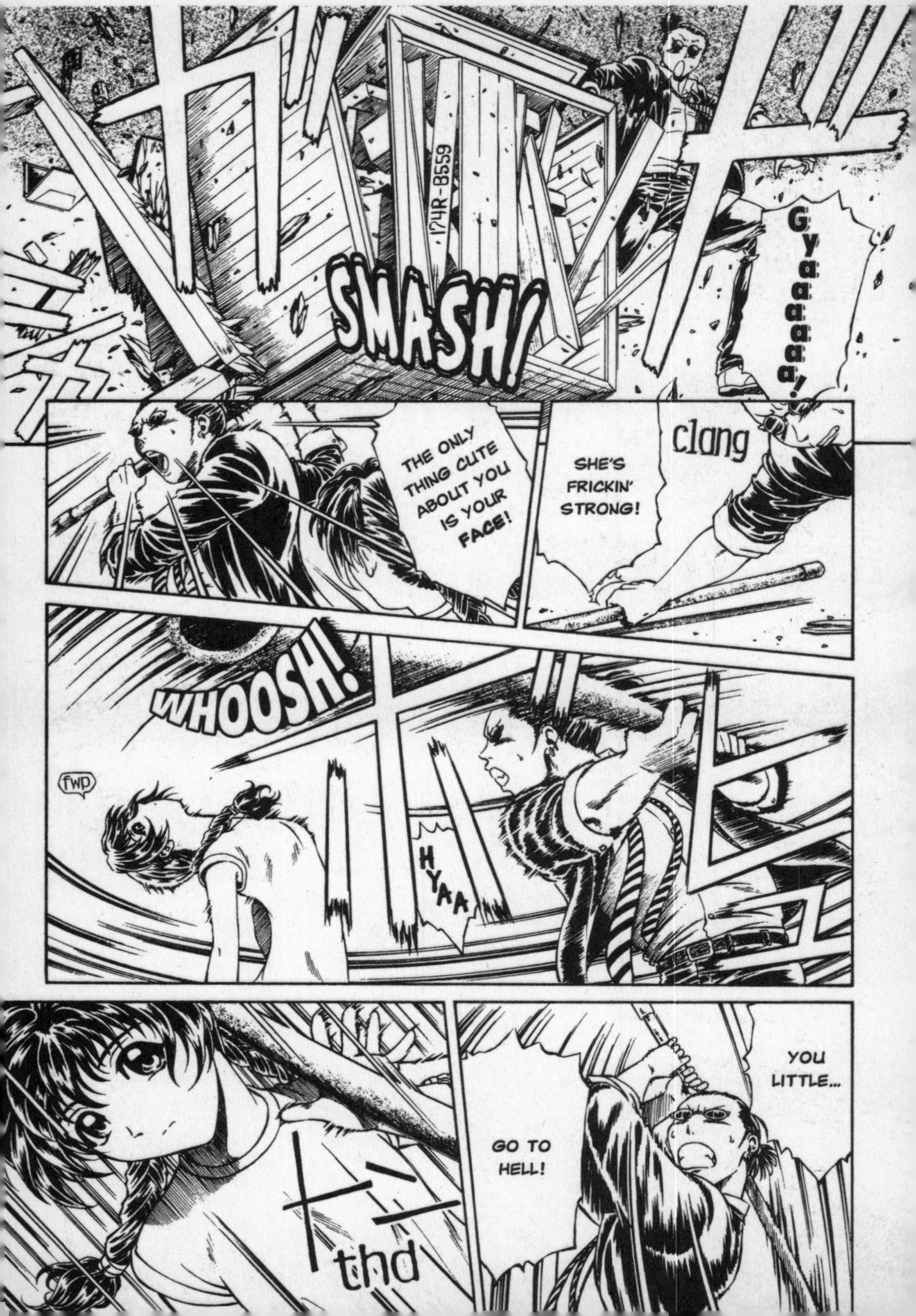
Gyaaaaaa!
174R-B559
SMASH!
clang
SHE'S FRICKIN' STRONG!
THE ONLY THING CUTE ABOUT YOU IS YOUR FACE!
WHOOSH!
HYAA
fwp
YOU LITTLE...
GO TO HELL!
thd

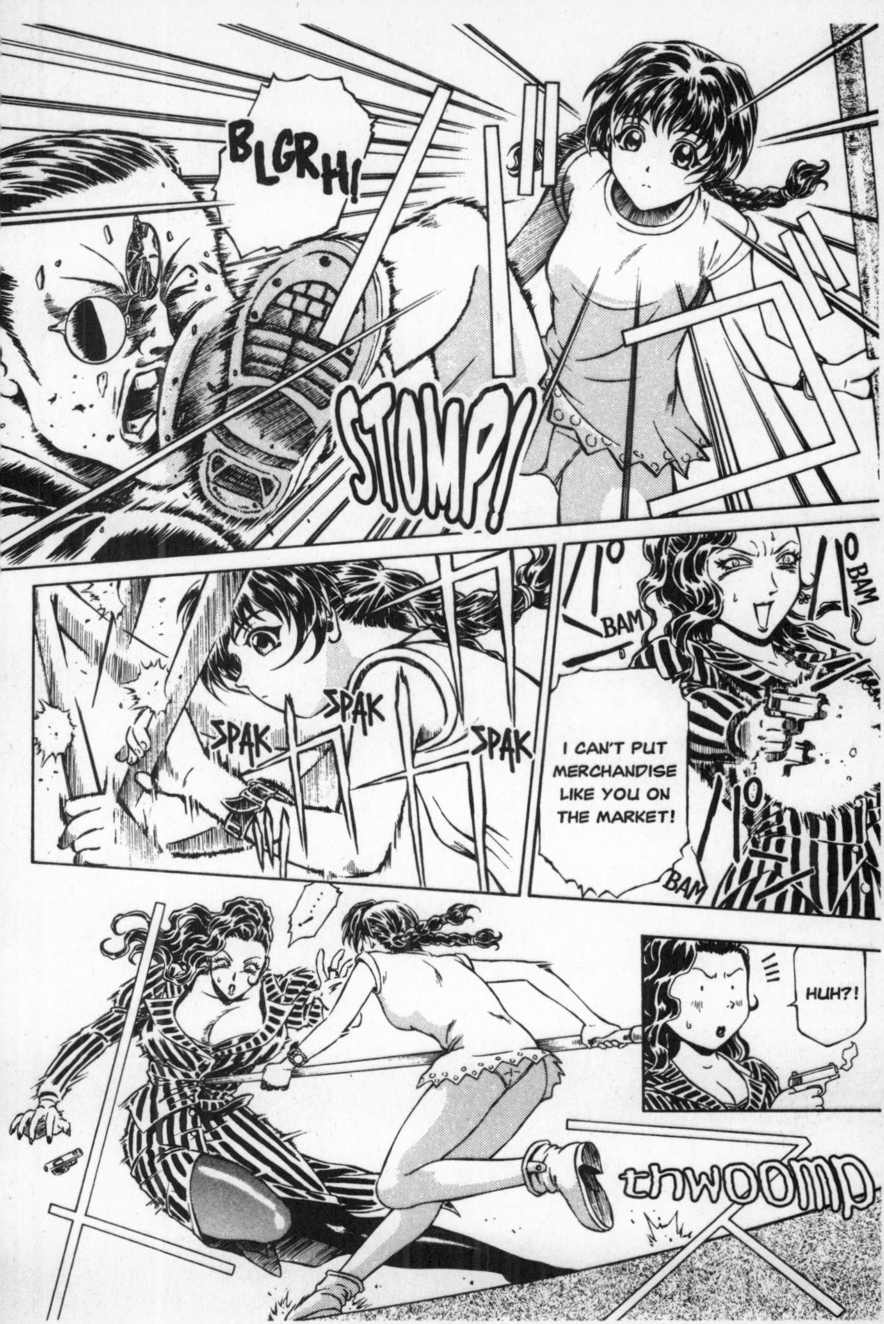
BLGRH!
STOMP!
BAM
BAM
I CAN'T PUT MERCHANDISE LIKE YOU ON THE MARKET!
BAM
SPAK
SPAK
SPAK
HUH?!
...
thwoomp

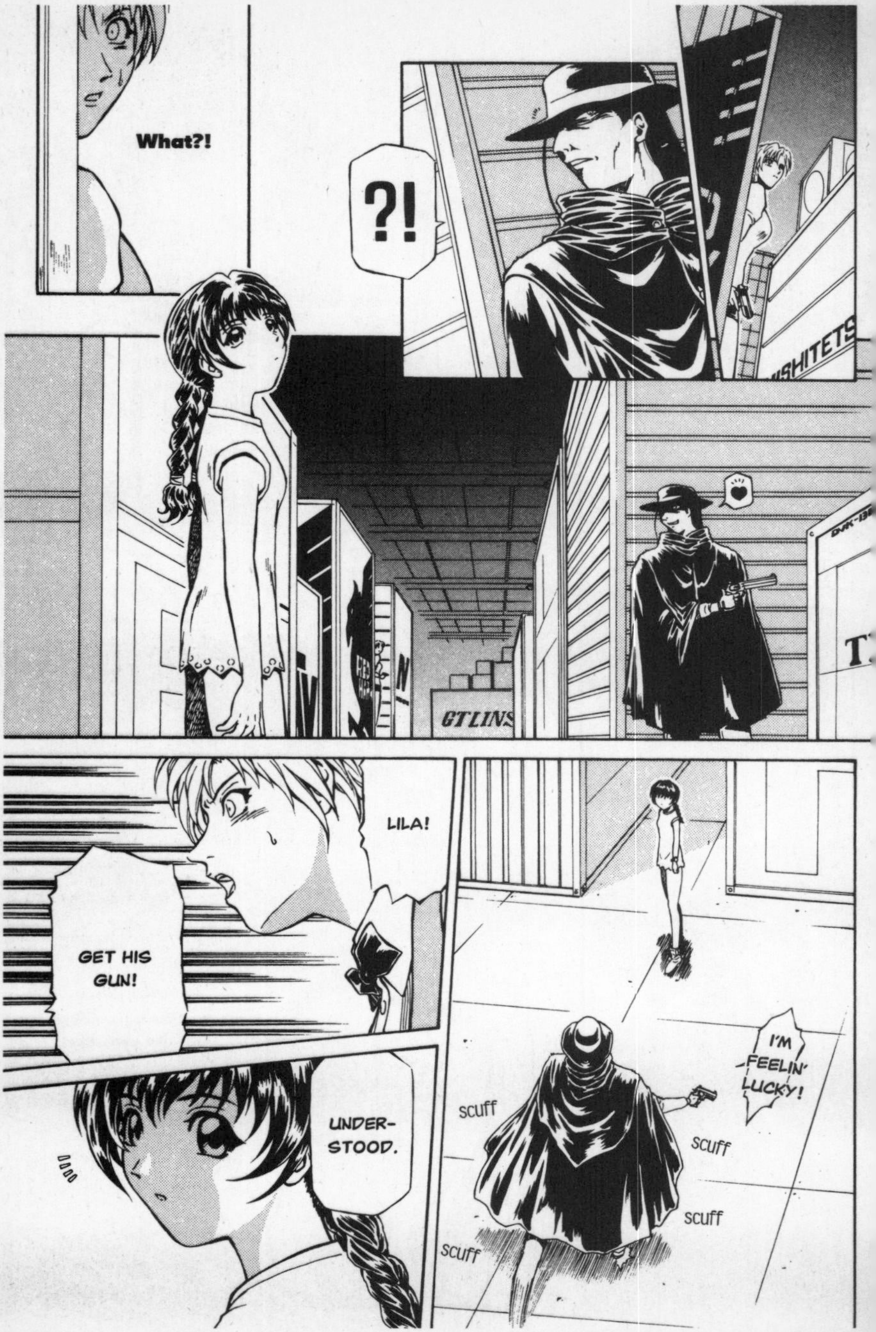
?!
What?!
I'M FEELIN' LUCKY!
scuff
scuff
scuff
scuff
LILA!
GET HIS GUN!
UNDER-STOOD.

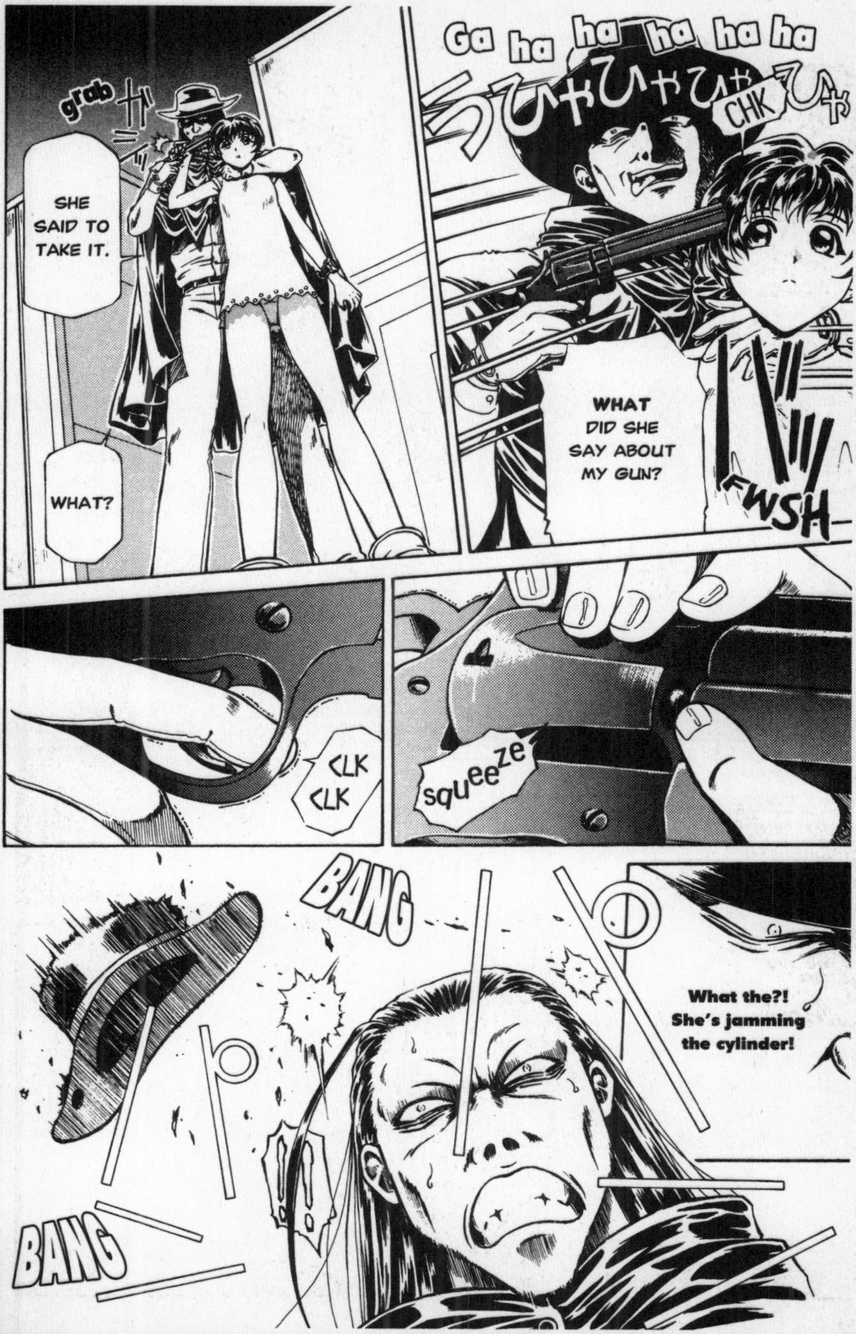
Ga ha ha ha ha ha
うひゃひゃひゃひゃ
CHK
WHAT DID SHE SAY ABOUT MY GUN?
FWSH
grab
SHE SAID TO TAKE IT.
WHAT?
squeeze
CLK CLK
What the?! She's jamming the cylinder!
BANG
BANG

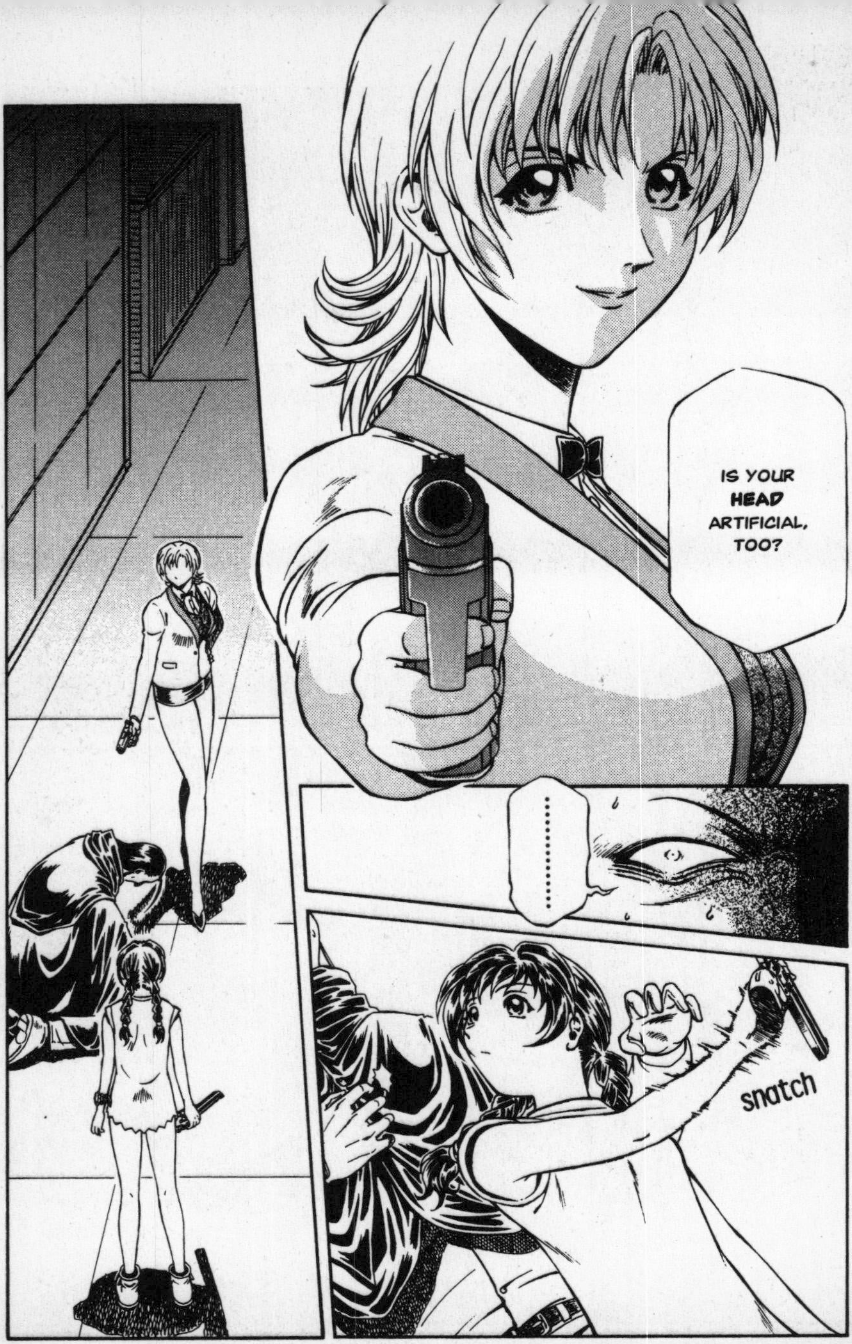
IS YOUR HEAD ARTIFICIAL, TOO?
......
snatch

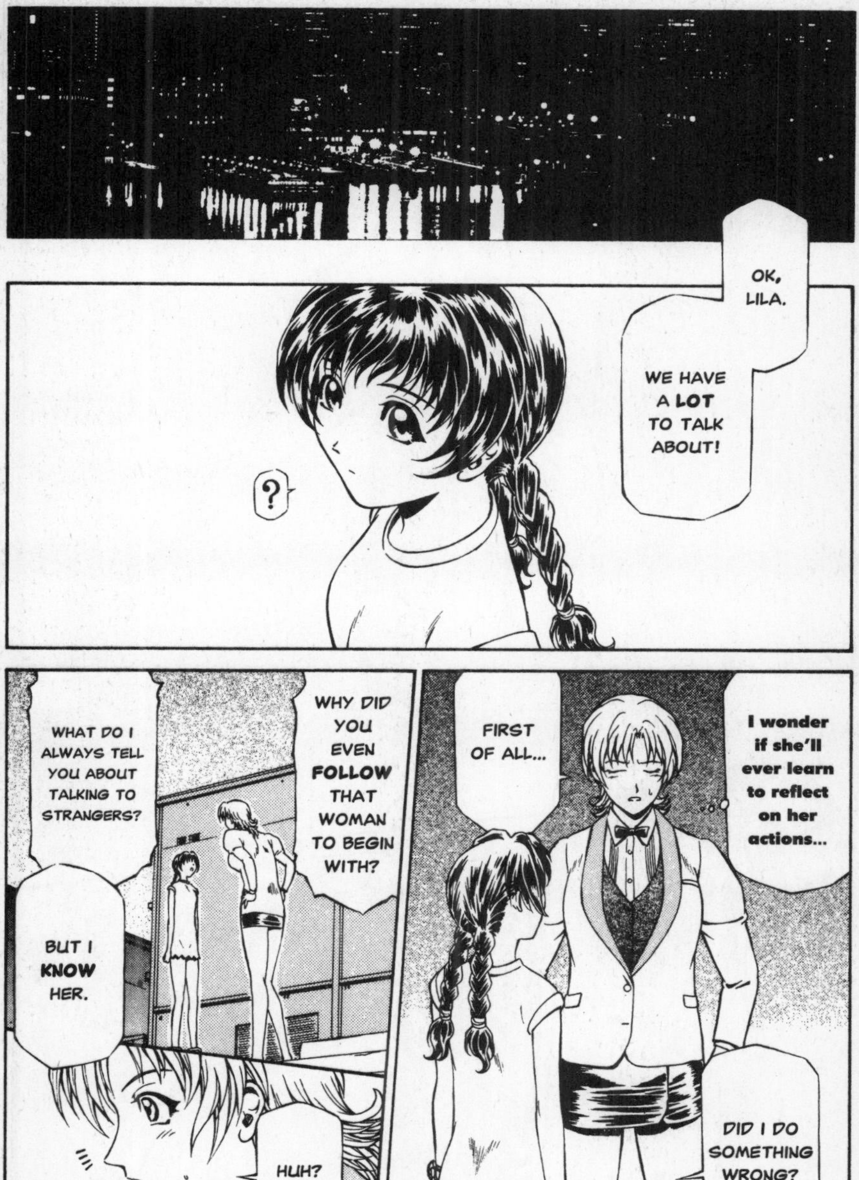
OK, LILA.
WE HAVE A LOT TO TALK ABOUT!
?
I wonder if she'll ever learn to reflect on her actions...
FIRST OF ALL...
DID I DO SOMETHING WRONG?
WHY DID YOU EVEN FOLLOW THAT WOMAN TO BEGIN WITH?
WHAT DO I ALWAYS TELL YOU ABOUT TALKING TO STRANGERS?
BUT I KNOW HER.
HUH?

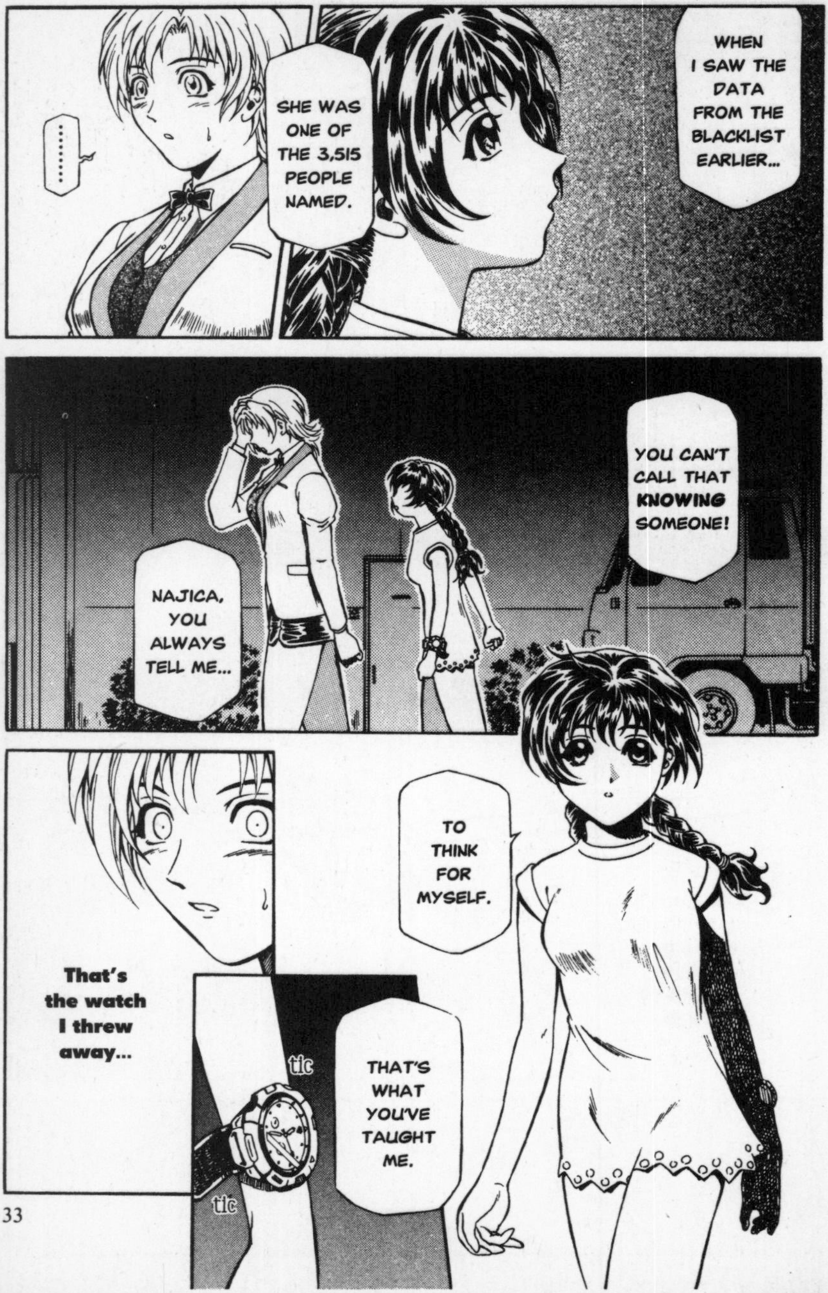
WHEN I SAW THE DATA FROM THE BLACKLIST EARLIER...
SHE WAS ONE OF THE 3,515 PEOPLE NAMED.
....
YOU CAN'T CALL THAT **KNOWING** SOMEONE!
NAJICA, YOU ALWAYS TELL ME...
TO THINK FOR MYSELF.
THAT'S WHAT YOU'VE TAUGHT ME.
tic
tic
That's the watch I threw away...

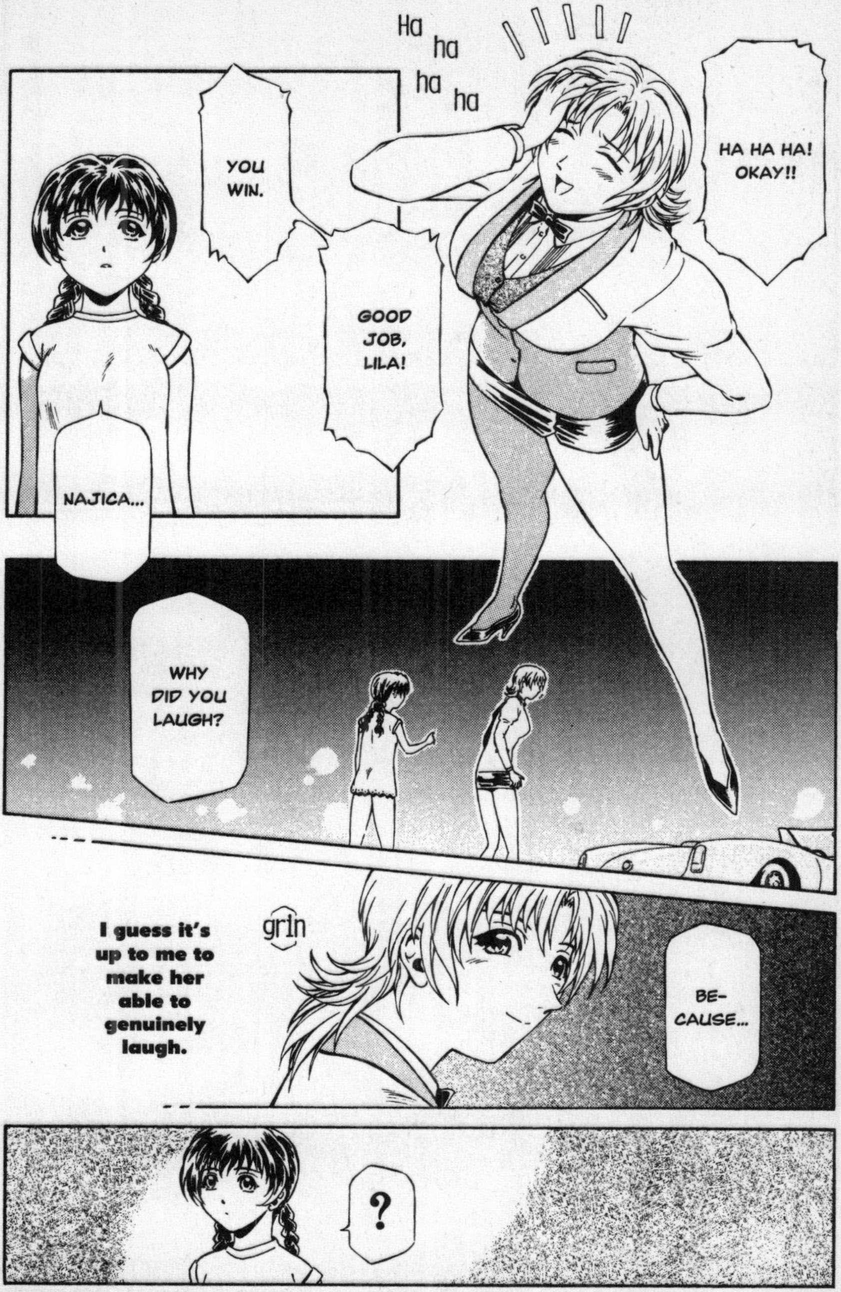
Ha ha ha ha
HA HA HA! OKAY!!
YOU WIN.
GOOD JOB, LILA!
NAJICA...
WHY DID YOU LAUGH?
BE-CAUSE...
grin
I guess it's up to me to make her able to genuinely laugh.
?

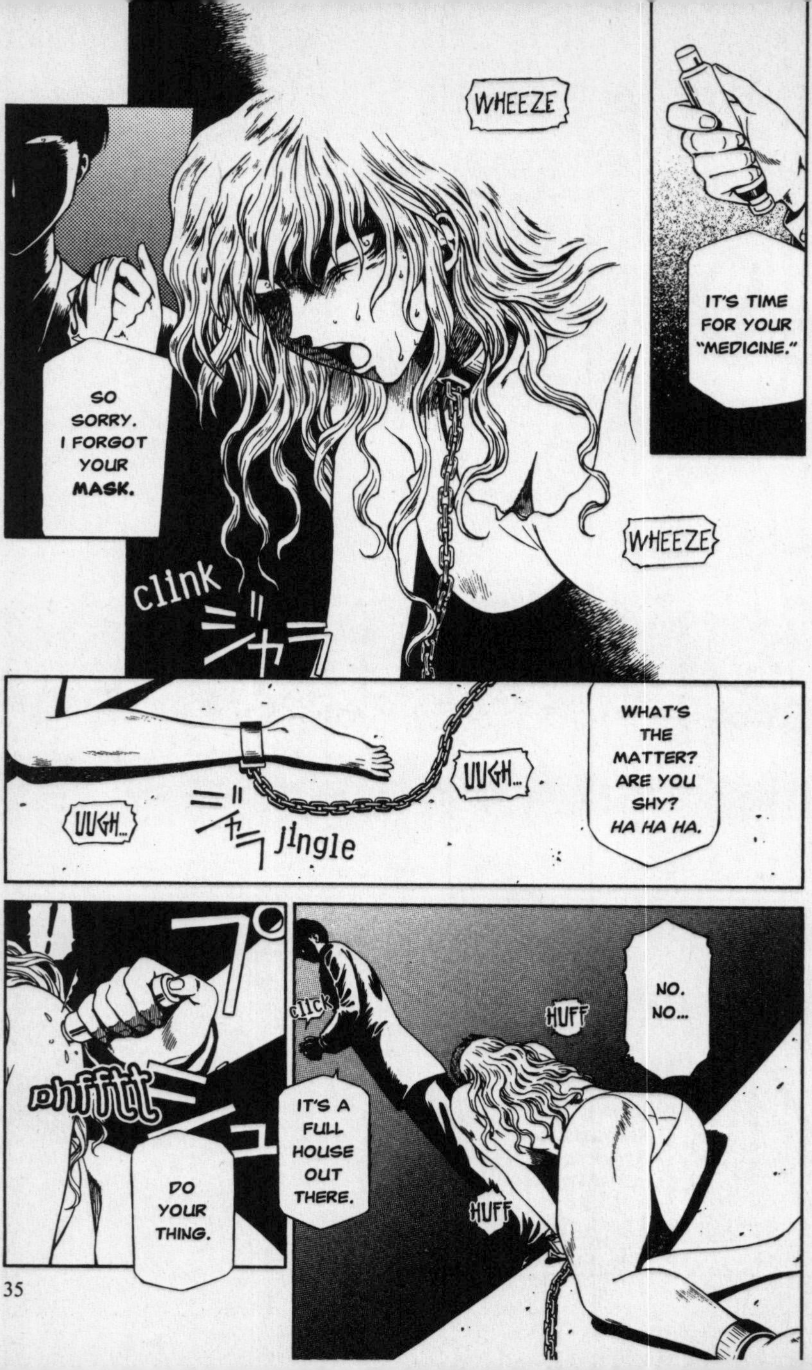
IT'S TIME FOR YOUR "MEDICINE."
WHEEZE
WHEEZE
clink
ジャラ
SO SORRY. I FORGOT YOUR MASK.
WHAT'S THE MATTER? ARE YOU SHY? HA HA HA.
UUGH...
UUGH...
ジャラ
jingle
NO. NO...
HUFF
click
IT'S A FULL HOUSE OUT THERE.
HUFF
!!
プ
phffttt
シュ
DO YOUR THING.

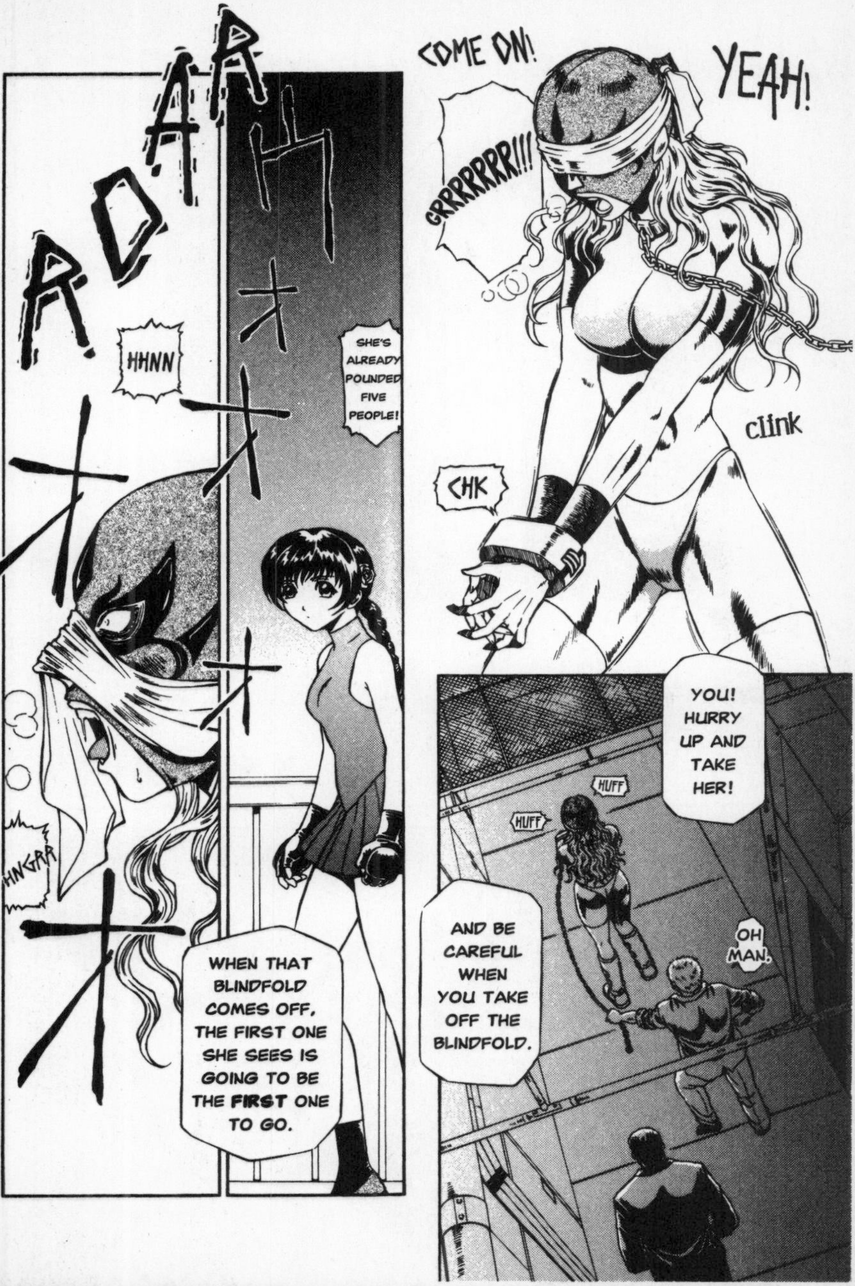
COME ON!
YEAH!
GRRRRRRR!!!
clink
CHK
YOU! HURRY UP AND TAKE HER!
HUFF
HUFF
AND BE CAREFUL WHEN YOU TAKE OFF THE BLINDFOLD.
OH MAN.
SHE'S ALREADY POUNDED FIVE PEOPLE!
WHEN THAT BLINDFOLD COMES OFF, THE FIRST ONE SHE SEES IS GOING TO BE THE **FIRST** ONE TO GO.
ROAR
HHNN
HNGRR

Operation.2
FIGHT CLUB

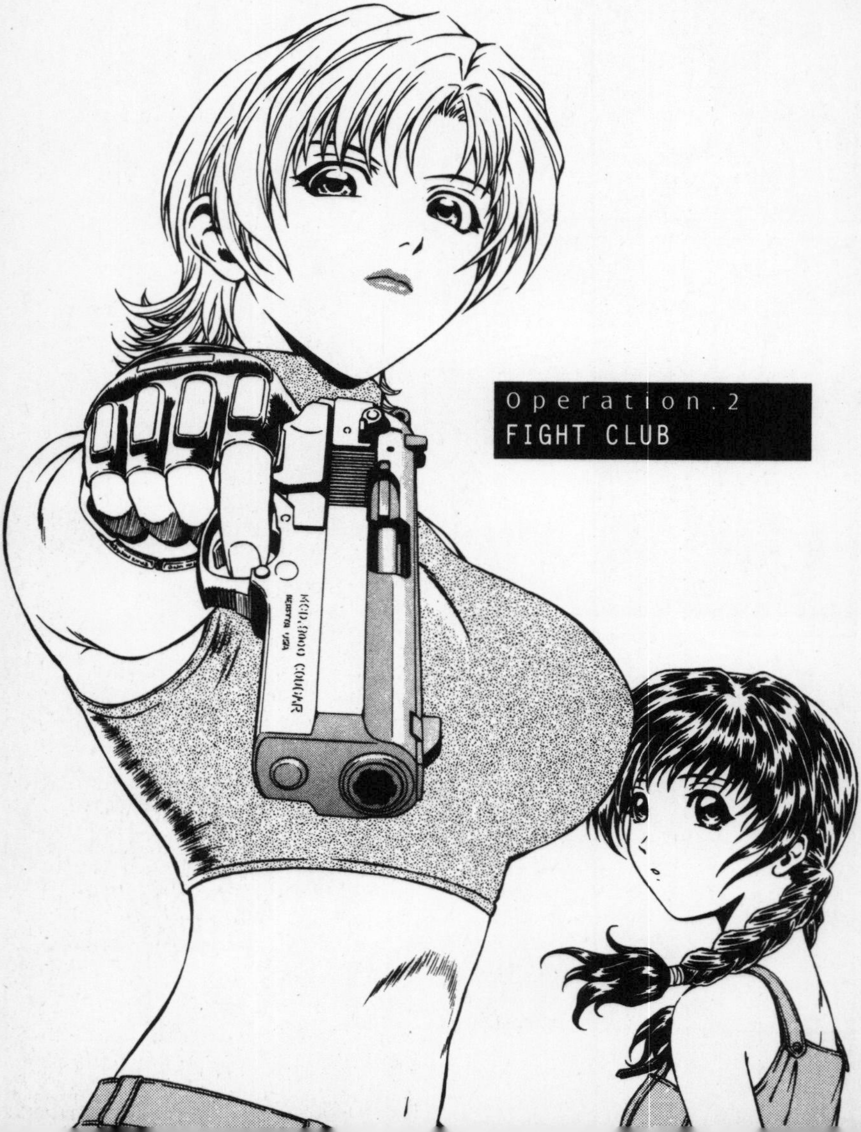

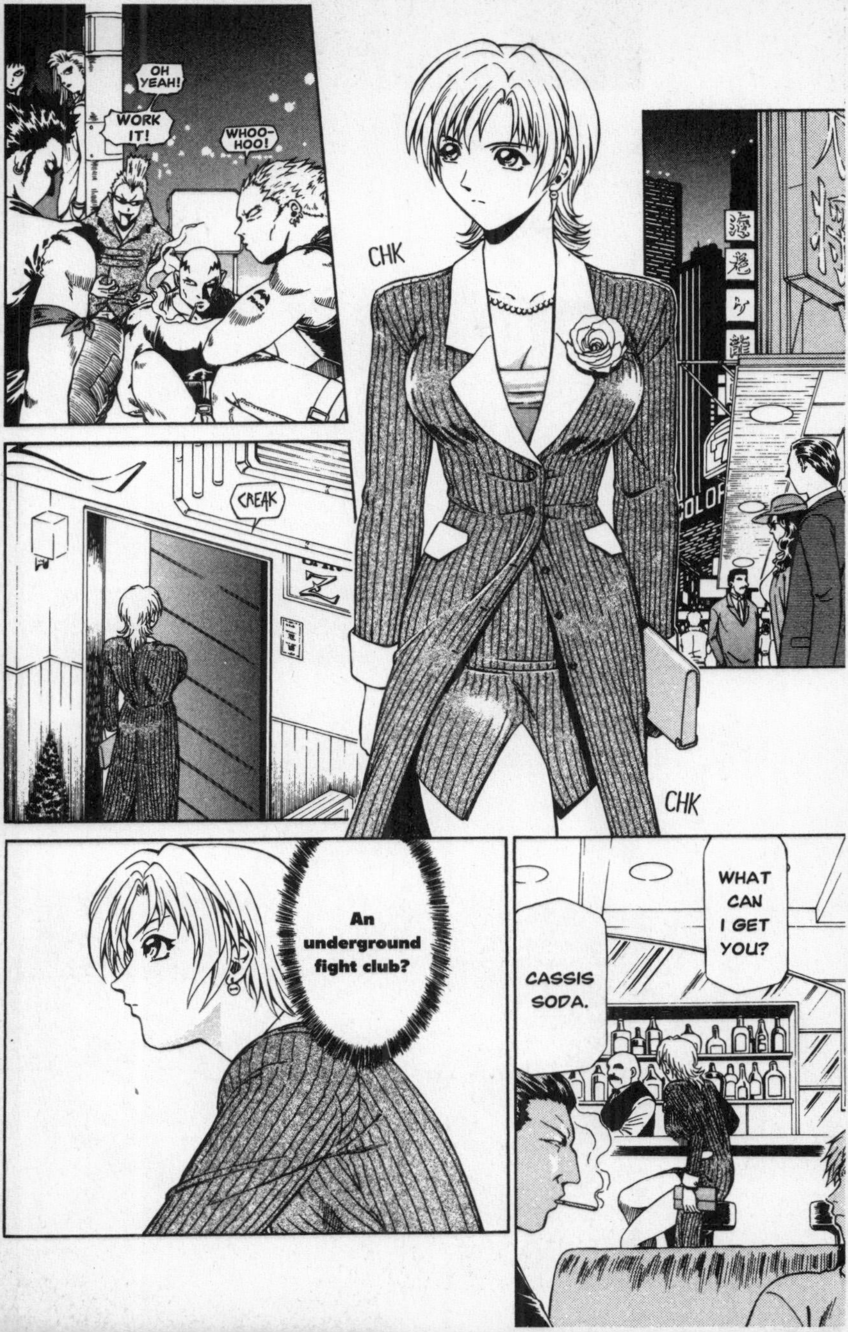
CHK
CHK
OH YEAH!
WORK IT!
WHOO-HOO!
CREAK
WHAT CAN I GET YOU?
CASSIS SODA.
An underground fight club?

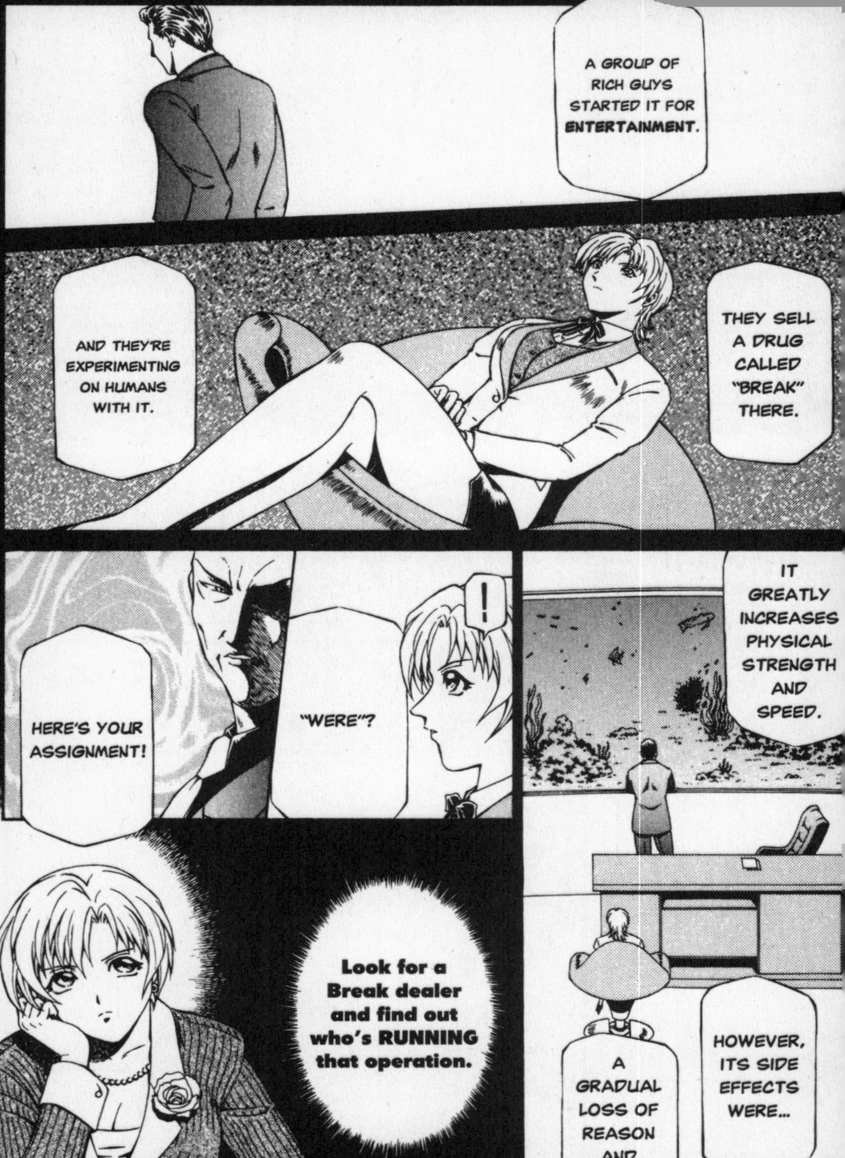

A GROUP OF RICH GUYS STARTED IT FOR ENTERTAINMENT.
THEY SELL A DRUG CALLED "BREAK" THERE.
AND THEY'RE EXPERIMENTING ON HUMANS WITH IT.
IT GREATLY INCREASES PHYSICAL STRENGTH AND SPEED.
HOWEVER, ITS SIDE EFFECTS WERE...
A GRADUAL LOSS OF REASON AND JUDGMENT.
!
"WERE"?
HERE'S YOUR ASSIGNMENT!
Look for a Break dealer and find out who's RUNNING that operation.

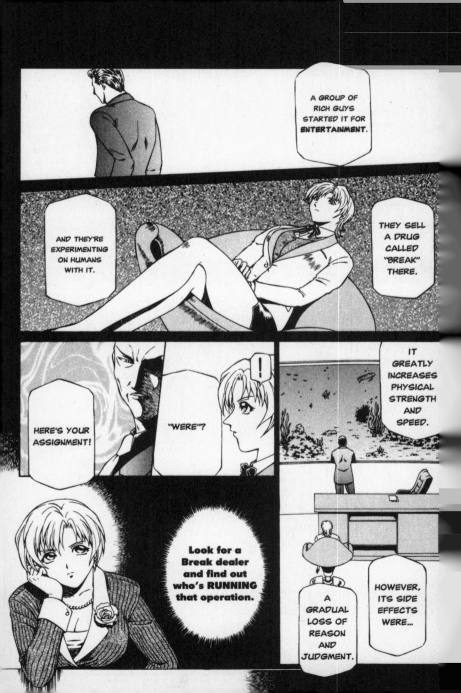

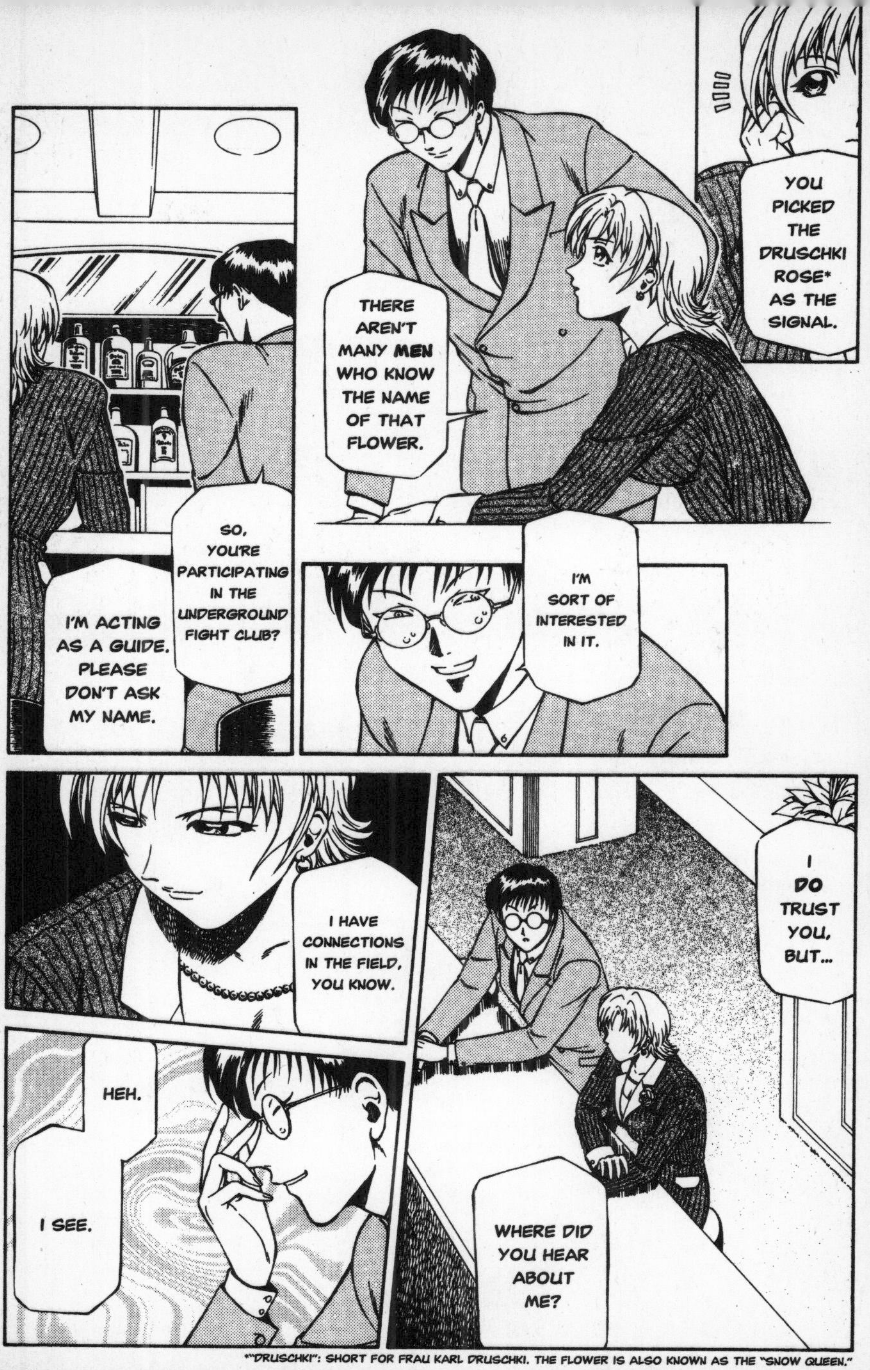
YOU PICKED THE DRUSCHKI ROSE* AS THE SIGNAL.
THERE AREN'T MANY MEN WHO KNOW THE NAME OF THAT FLOWER.
I'M SORT OF INTERESTED IN IT.
SO, YOU'RE PARTICIPATING IN THE UNDERGROUND FIGHT CLUB?
I'M ACTING AS A GUIDE. PLEASE DON'T ASK MY NAME.
I DO TRUST YOU, BUT...
WHERE DID YOU HEAR ABOUT ME?
I HAVE CONNECTIONS IN THE FIELD, YOU KNOW.
HEH.
I SEE.

*"DRUSCHKI": SHORT FOR FRAU KARL DRUSCHKI. THE FLOWER IS ALSO KNOWN AS THE "SNOW QUEEN."

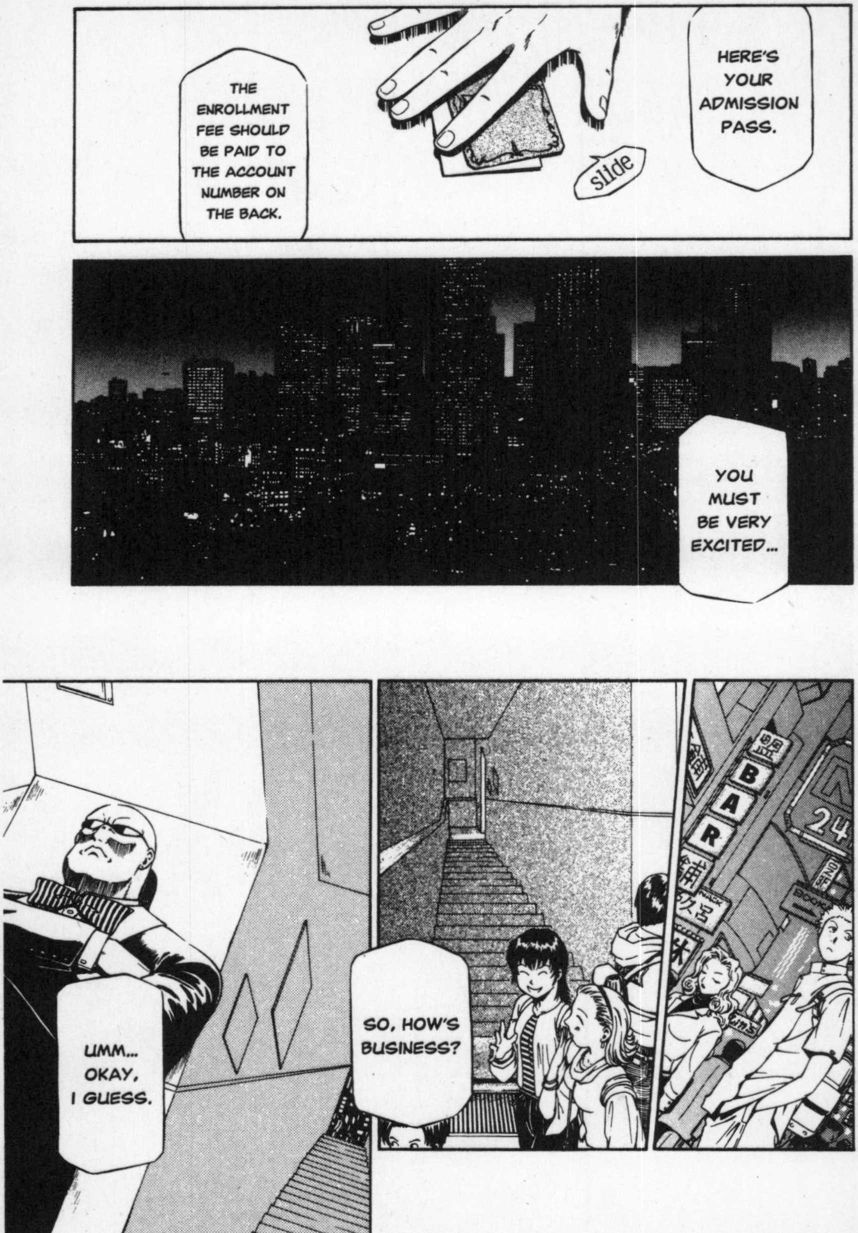
HERE'S YOUR ADMISSION PASS.
slide
THE ENROLLMENT FEE SHOULD BE PAID TO THE ACCOUNT NUMBER ON THE BACK.
YOU MUST BE VERY EXCITED...
BAR
24
SO, HOW'S BUSINESS?
UMM... OKAY, I GUESS.

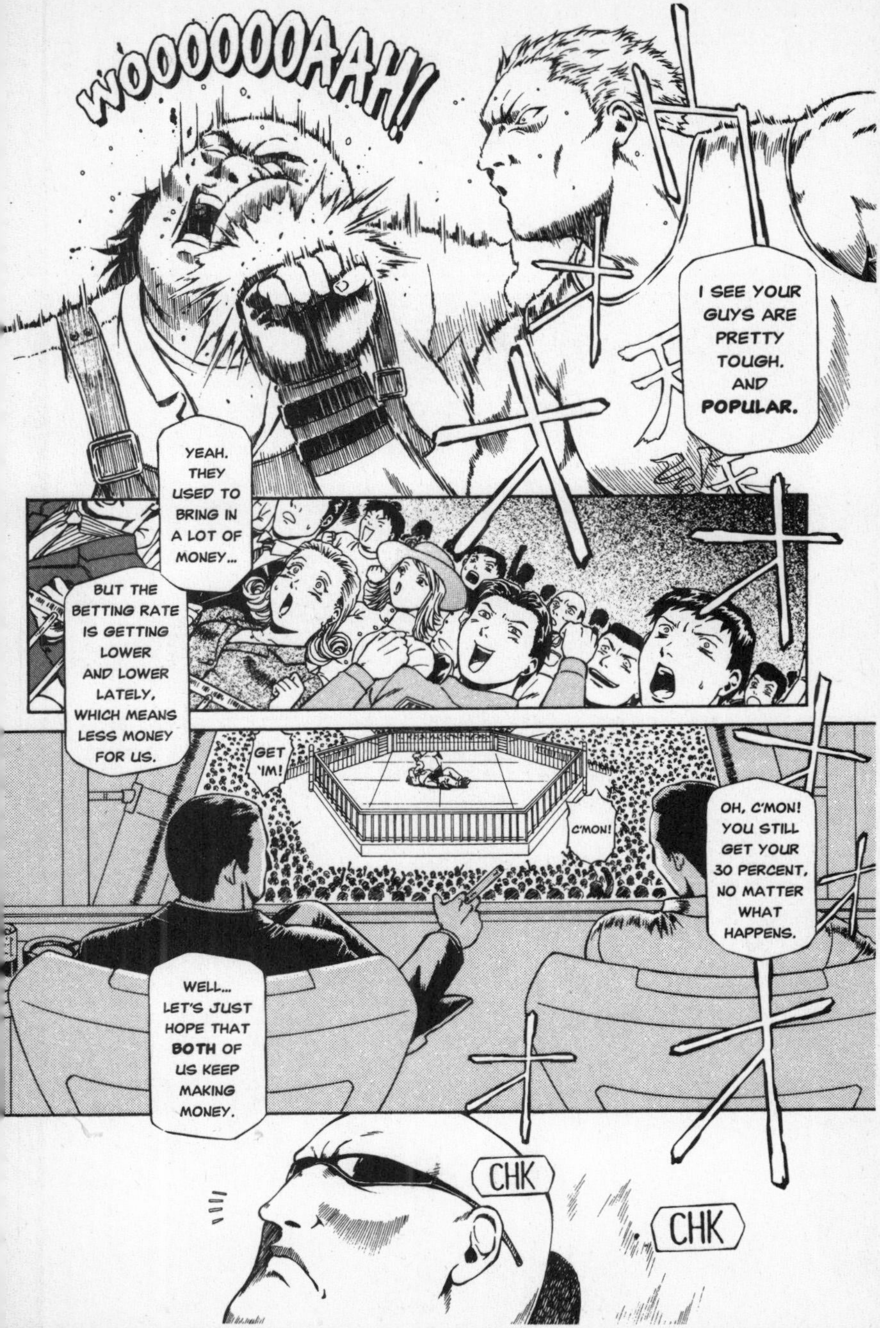
WOOOOOOAAH!!
I SEE YOUR GUYS ARE PRETTY TOUGH. AND **POPULAR.**
YEAH. THEY USED TO BRING IN A LOT OF MONEY...
BUT THE BETTING RATE IS GETTING LOWER AND LOWER LATELY, WHICH MEANS LESS MONEY FOR US.
OH, C'MON! YOU STILL GET YOUR 30 PERCENT, NO MATTER WHAT HAPPENS.
C'MON!
GET 'IM!
WELL... LET'S JUST HOPE THAT **BOTH** OF US KEEP MAKING MONEY.
CHK
CHK

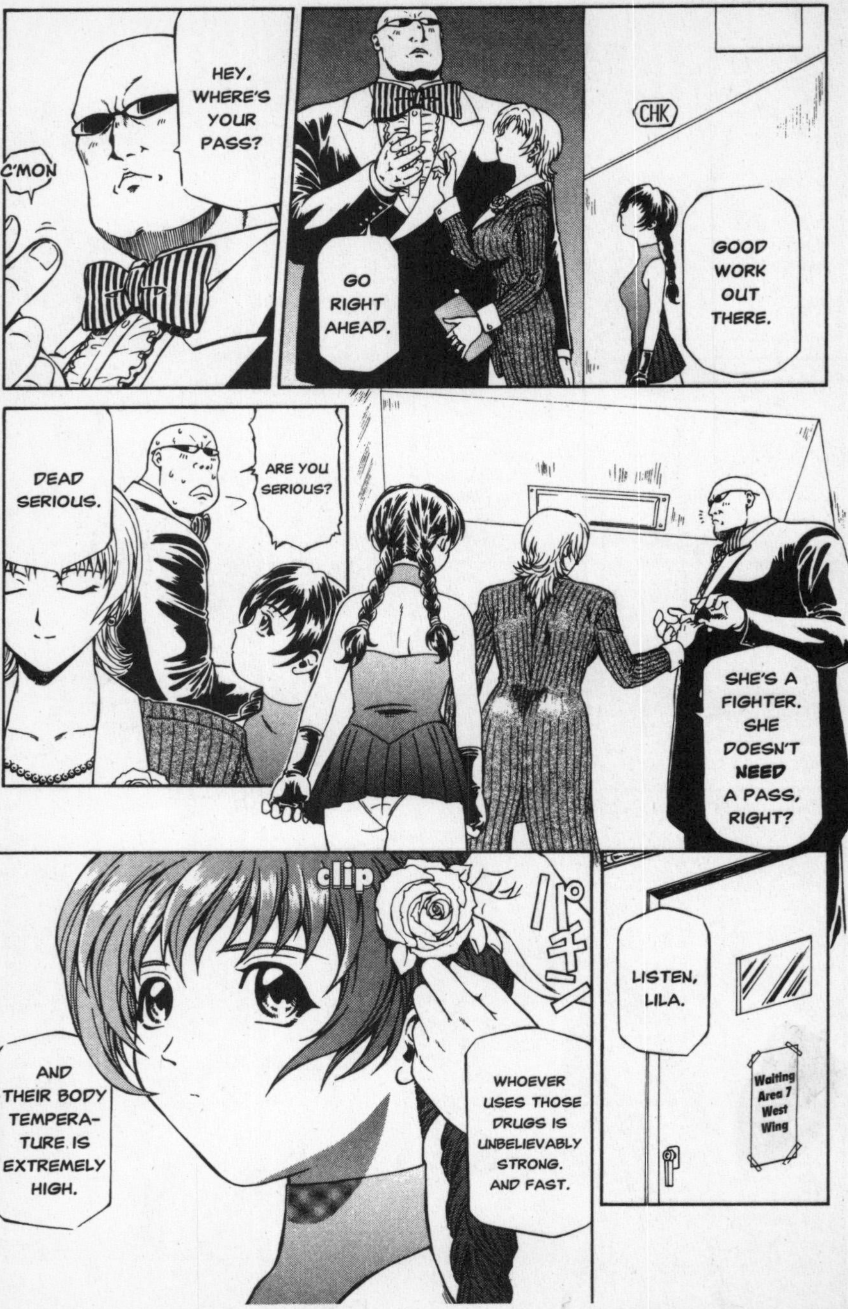
CHK
GOOD WORK OUT THERE.
GO RIGHT AHEAD.
HEY, WHERE'S YOUR PASS?
C'MON
SHE'S A FIGHTER. SHE DOESN'T NEED A PASS, RIGHT?
ARE YOU SERIOUS?
DEAD SERIOUS.
LISTEN, LILA.
Waiting Area 7 West Wing
clip
WHOEVER USES THOSE DRUGS IS UNBELIEVABLY STRONG. AND FAST.
AND THEIR BODY TEMPERA-TURE IS EXTREMELY HIGH.

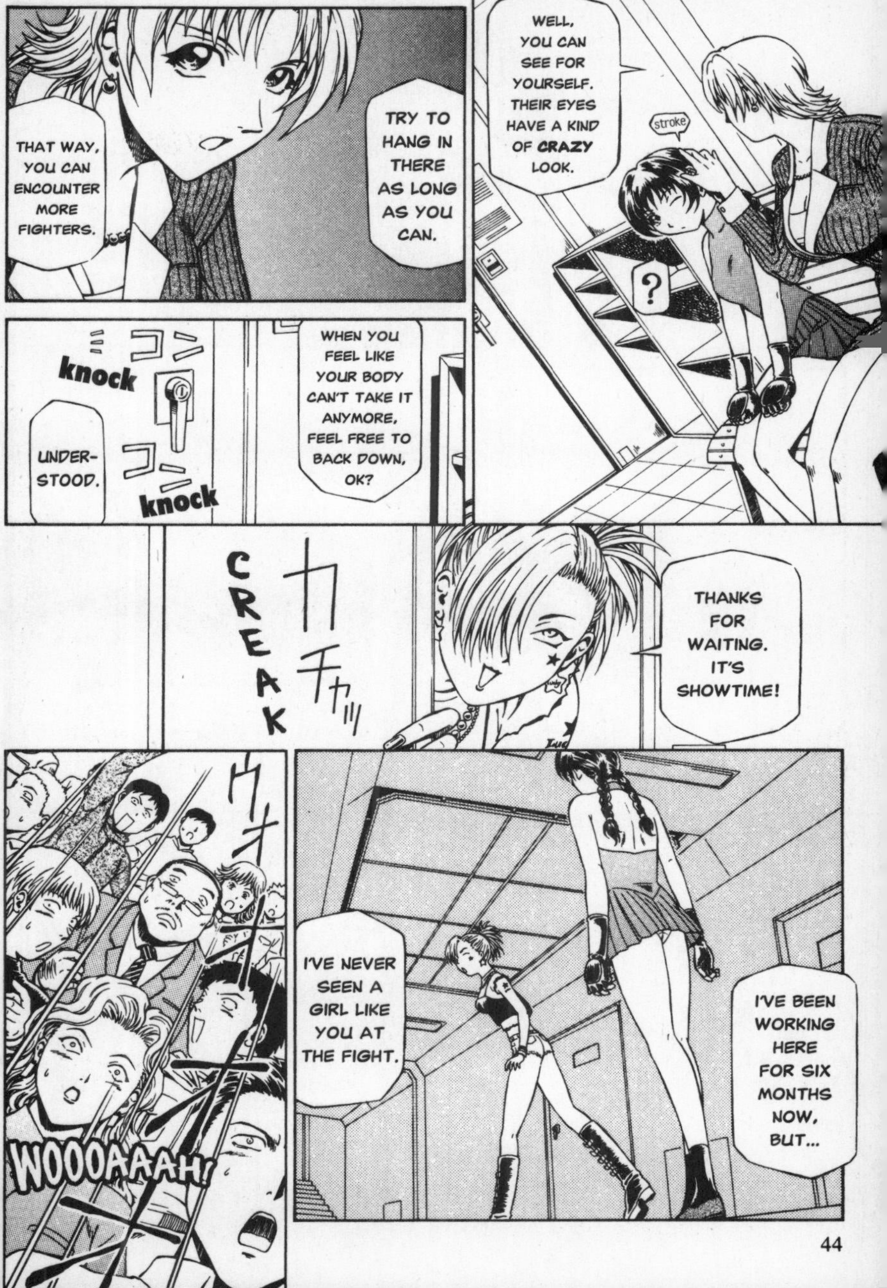
WELL, YOU CAN SEE FOR YOURSELF. THEIR EYES HAVE A KIND OF CRAZY LOOK.
stroke
?
TRY TO HANG IN THERE AS LONG AS YOU CAN.
THAT WAY, YOU CAN ENCOUNTER MORE FIGHTERS.
WHEN YOU FEEL LIKE YOUR BODY CAN'T TAKE IT ANYMORE, FEEL FREE TO BACK DOWN, OK?
knock
knock
UNDER-STOOD.
THANKS FOR WAITING. IT'S SHOWTIME!
CREAK
I'VE BEEN WORKING HERE FOR SIX MONTHS NOW, BUT...
I'VE NEVER SEEN A GIRL LIKE YOU AT THE FIGHT.
WOOOAAAH!

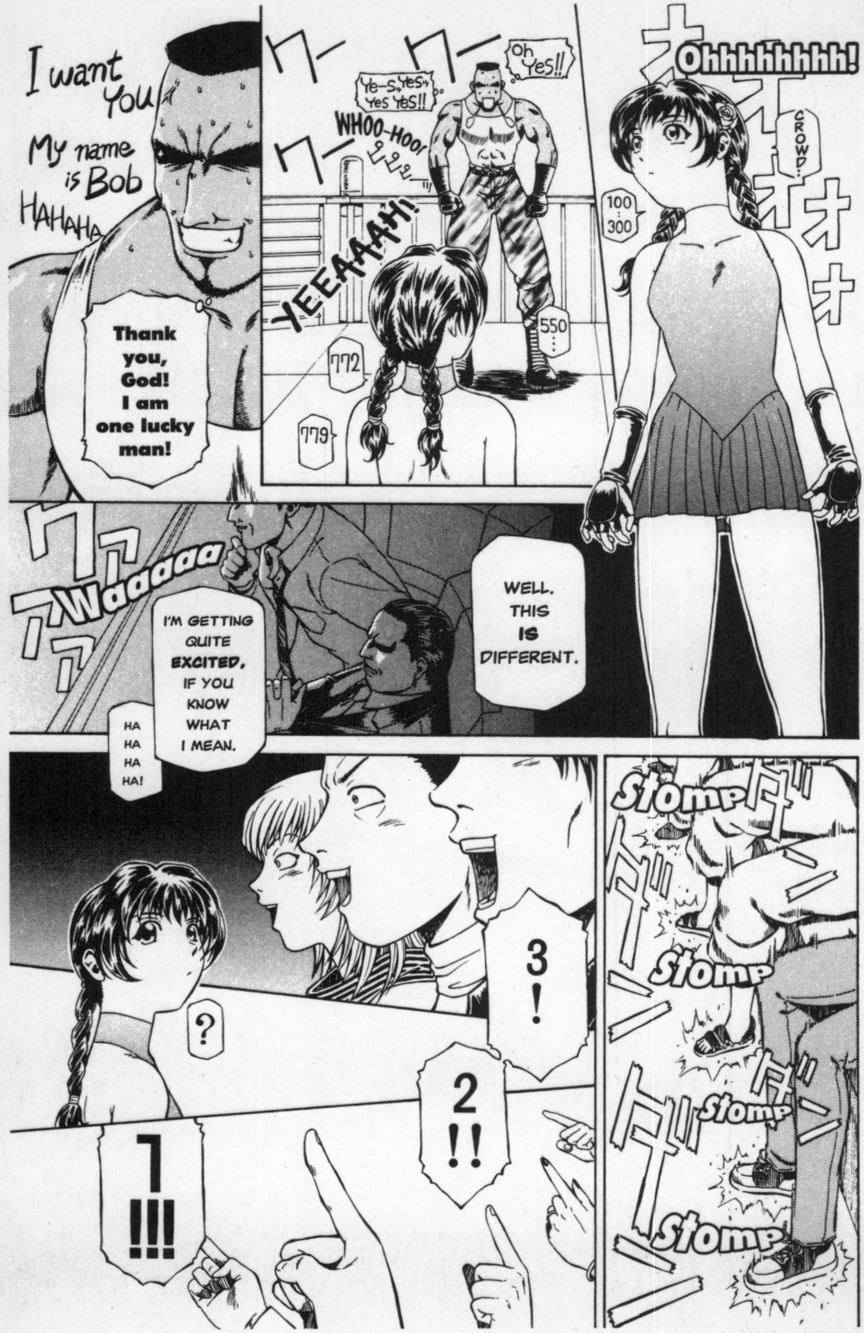
Ohhhhhhhh!
CROWD...
100
...
300
Oh Yes!!
Ye-s,, Yes,, Yes Yes!!
WHOO-HOO!
YEEAAAAH!
550
...
772
779
I want YOU
My name is Bob
HAHAHA
Thank you, God! I am one lucky man!
WELL. THIS IS DIFFERENT.
Waaaaa
I'M GETTING QUITE EXCITED, IF YOU KNOW WHAT I MEAN.
HA HA HA HA!
Stomp
Stomp
Stomp
Stomp
3 !
?
2 !!
1 !!!

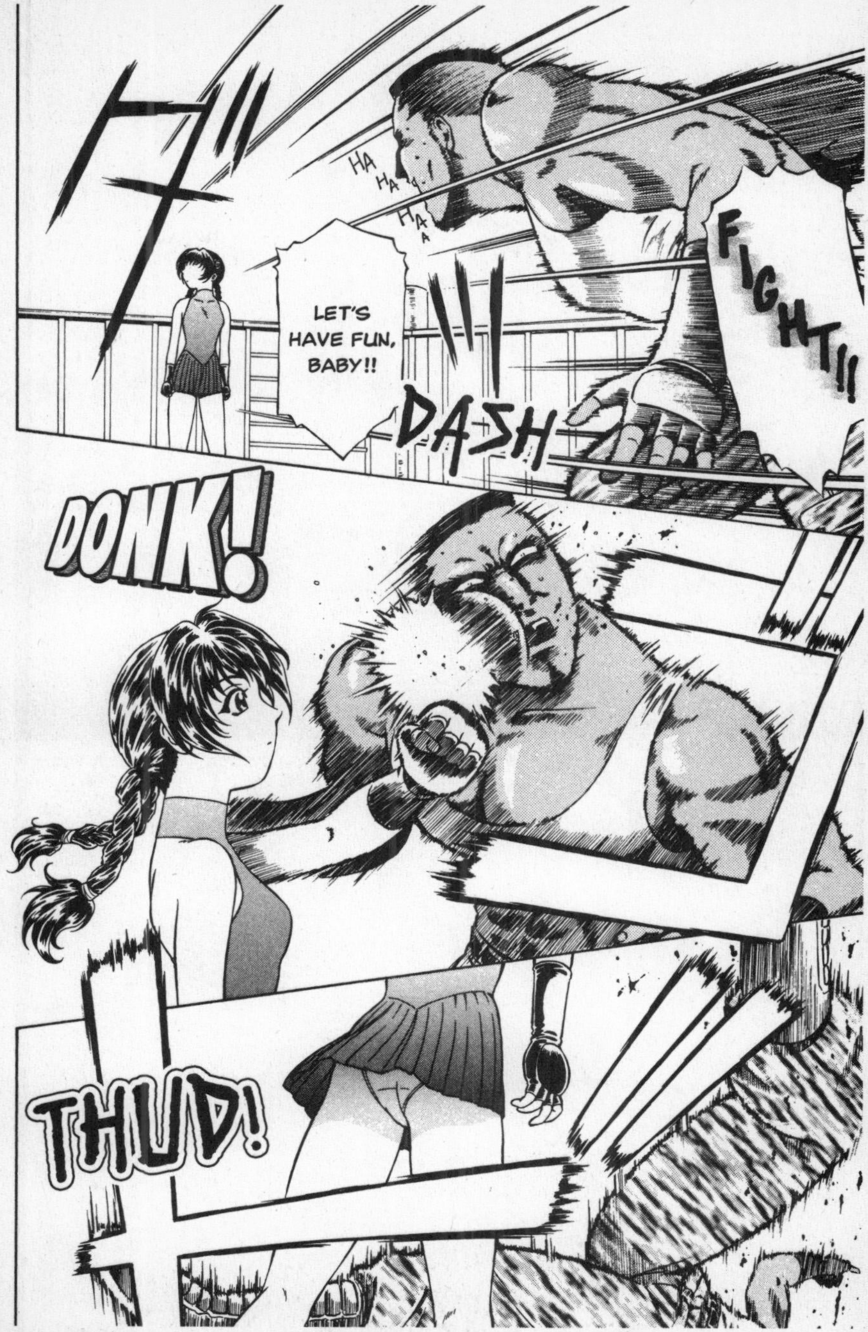
FIGHT!!
HA HA HA
LET'S HAVE FUN, BABY!!
DASH
DONK!
THUD!

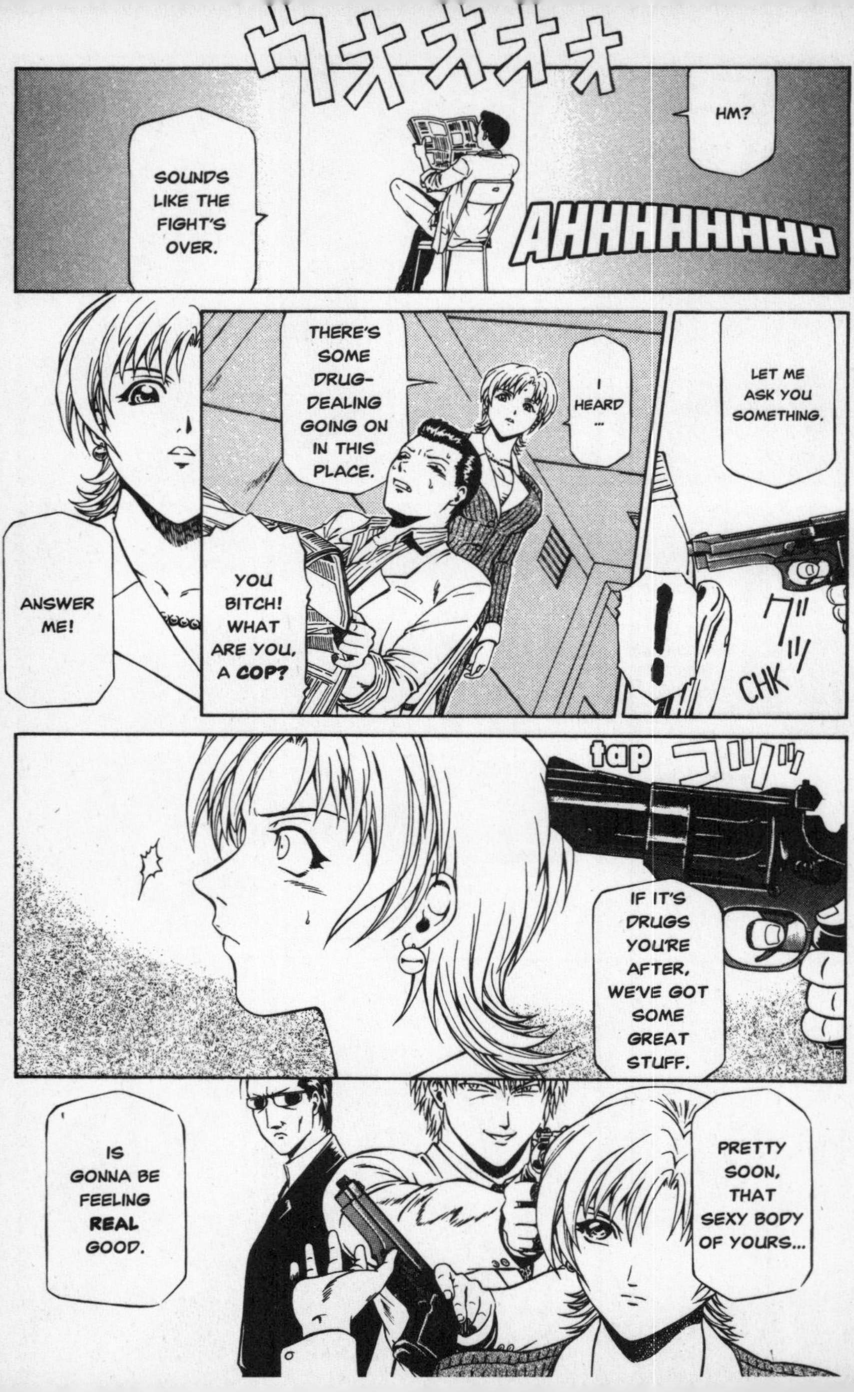

ウオオオオォ
HM?
AHHHHHHHHH
SOUNDS LIKE THE FIGHT'S OVER.
LET ME ASK YOU SOMETHING.
!
グッ
CHK
I HEARD...
THERE'S SOME DRUG-DEALING GOING ON IN THIS PLACE.
YOU BITCH! WHAT ARE YOU, A **COP?**
ANSWER ME!
tap
コツッ
IF IT'S DRUGS YOU'RE AFTER, WE'VE GOT SOME GREAT STUFF.
PRETTY SOON, THAT SEXY BODY OF YOURS...
IS GONNA BE FEELING **REAL** GOOD.

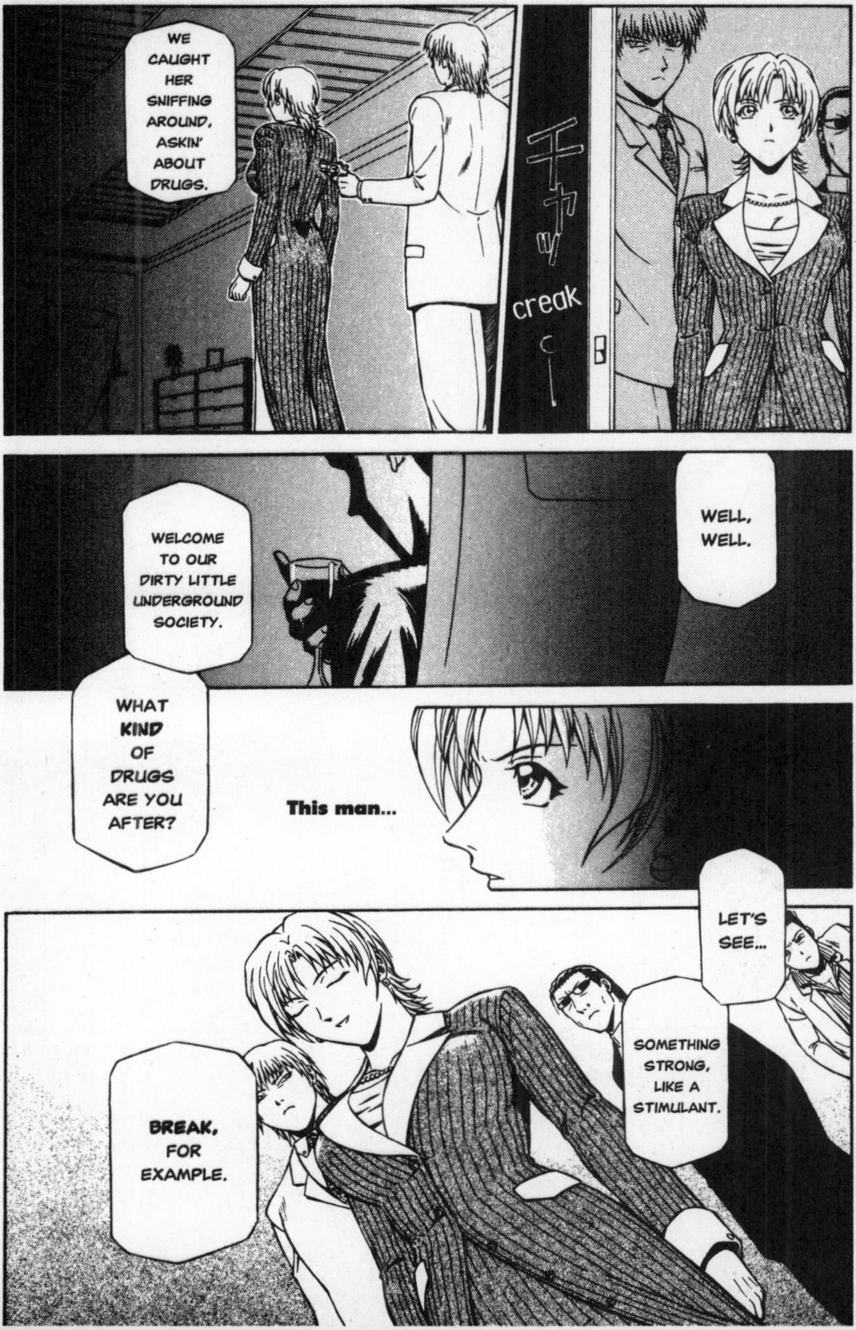
チャッ
creak
WE CAUGHT HER SNIFFING AROUND, ASKIN' ABOUT DRUGS.
WELL, WELL.
WELCOME TO OUR DIRTY LITTLE UNDERGROUND SOCIETY.
This man...
WHAT **KIND** OF DRUGS ARE YOU AFTER?
LET'S SEE...
SOMETHING STRONG, LIKE A STIMULANT.
BREAK, FOR EXAMPLE.

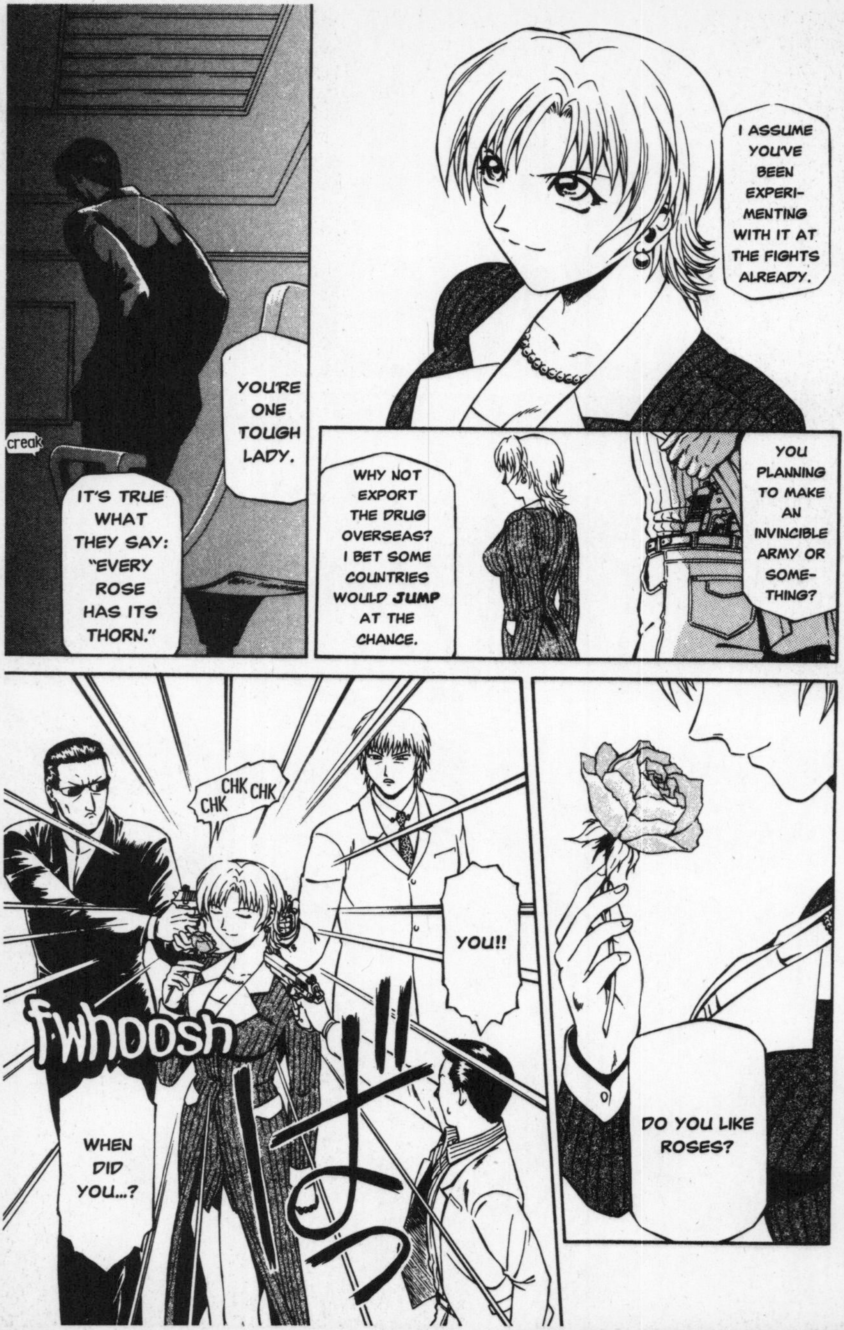

I ASSUME YOU'VE BEEN EXPERI-MENTING WITH IT AT THE FIGHTS ALREADY.
YOU PLANNING TO MAKE AN INVINCIBLE ARMY OR SOME-THING?
WHY NOT EXPORT THE DRUG OVERSEAS? I BET SOME COUNTRIES WOULD **JUMP** AT THE CHANCE.
YOU'RE ONE TOUGH LADY.
creak
IT'S TRUE WHAT THEY SAY: "EVERY ROSE HAS ITS THORN."
DO YOU LIKE ROSES?
CHK CHK CHK
YOU!!
fwhoosh
WHEN DID YOU...?

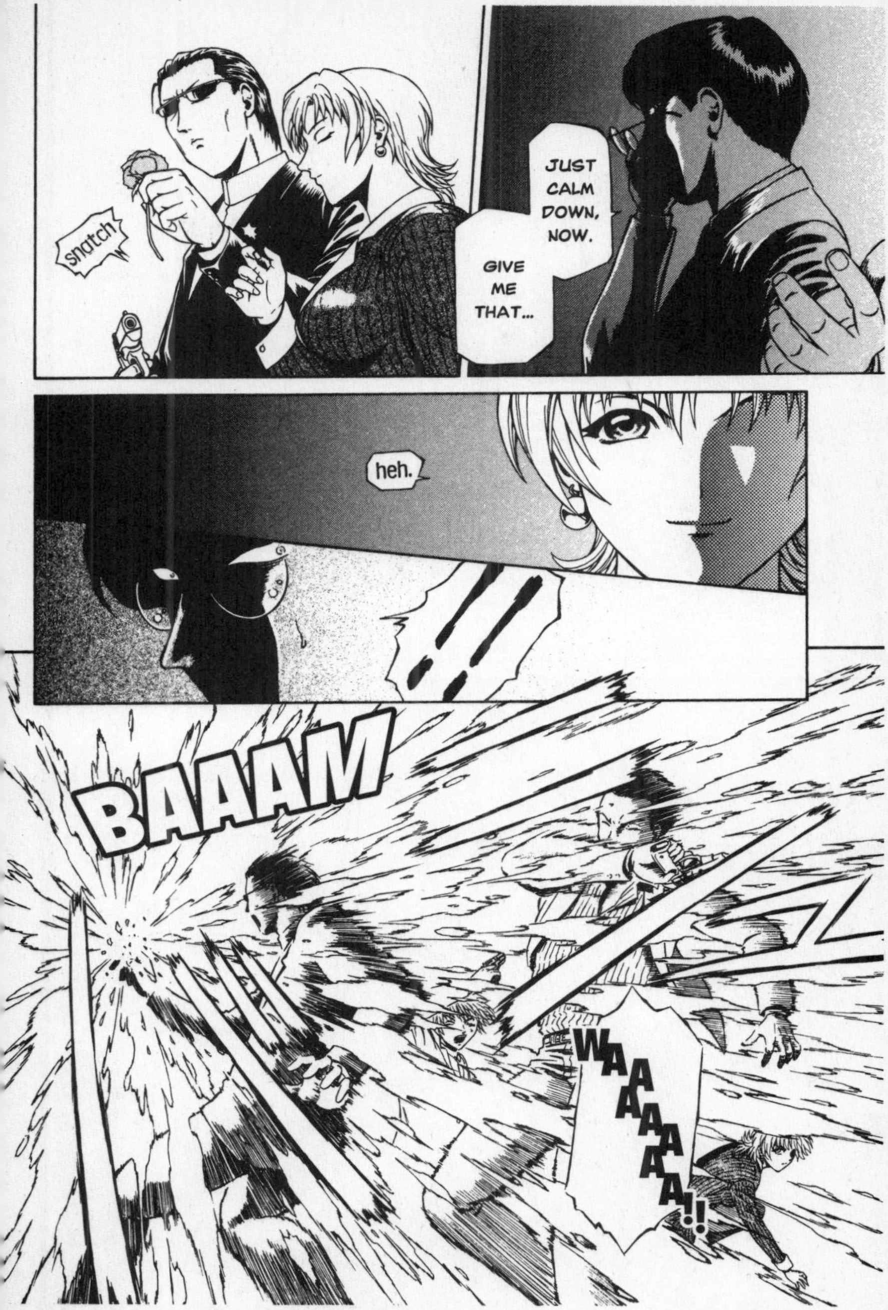
JUST CALM DOWN, NOW.
GIVE ME THAT...
snatch
heh.
BAAAAM
WAAAAAA!!

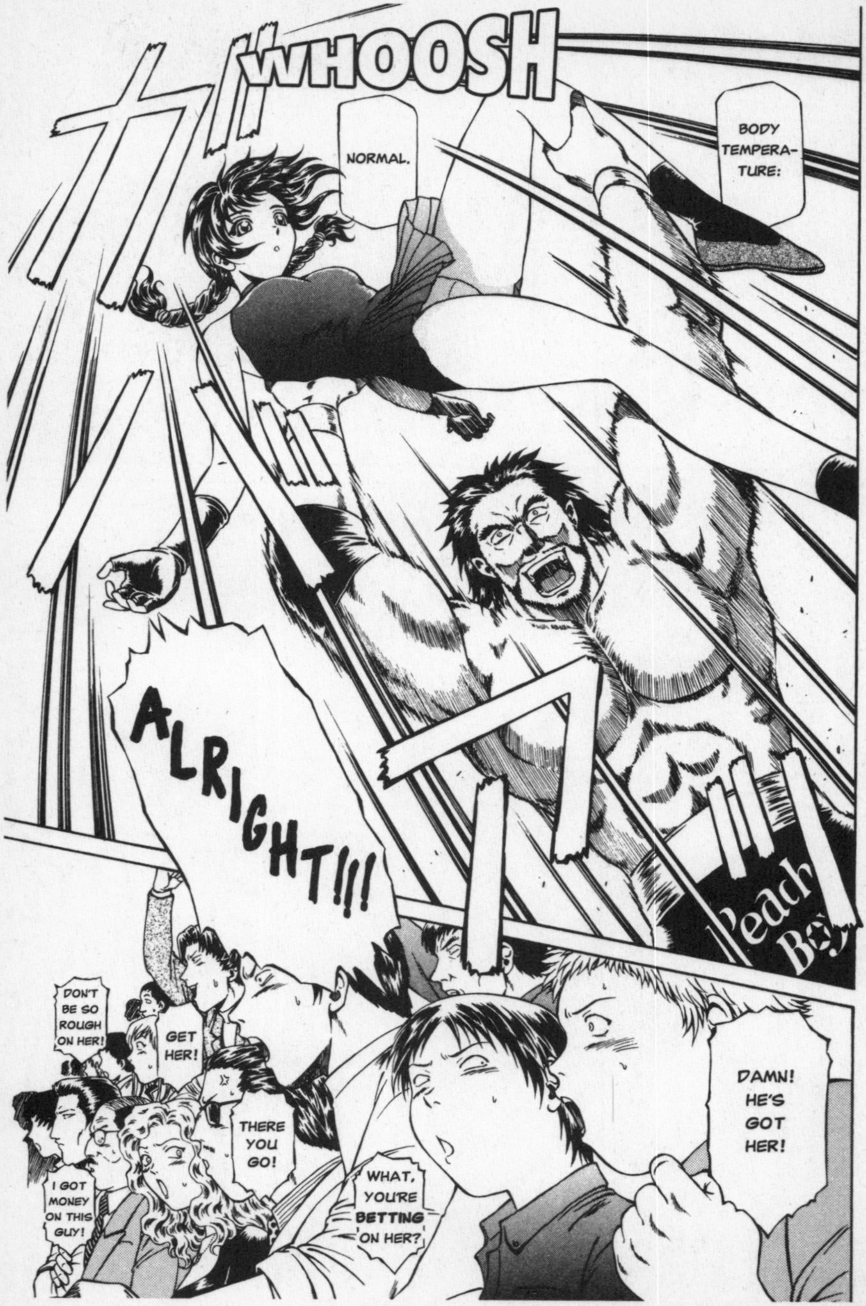
BODY TEMPERA-TURE:
WHOOSH
NORMAL.
ALRIGHT!!!!
DAMN! HE'S GOT HER!
WHAT, YOU'RE BETTING ON HER?
THERE YOU GO!
GET HER!
DON'T BE SO ROUGH ON HER!
I GOT MONEY ON THIS GUY!

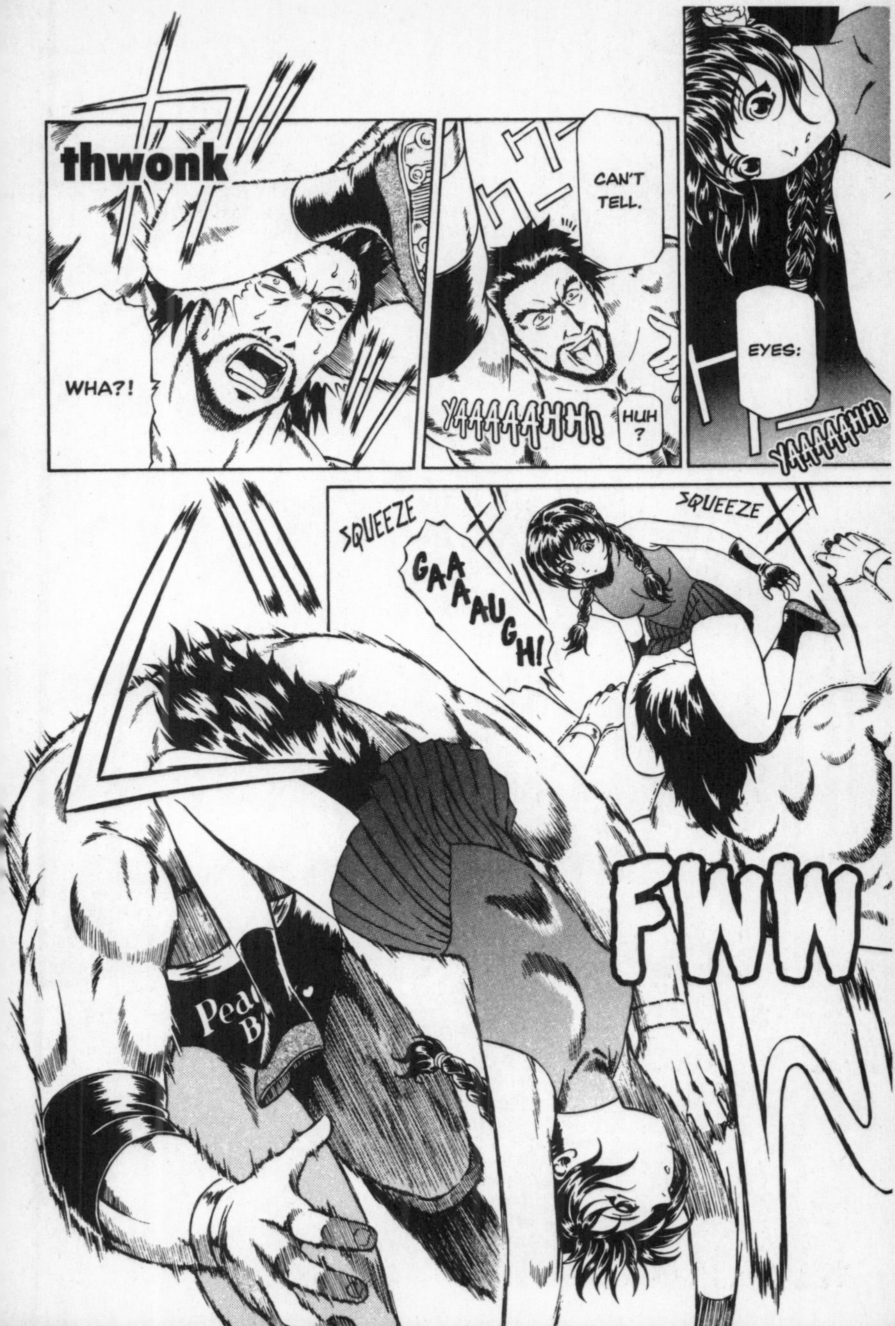
EYES:
YAAAAAHH!
CAN'T TELL.
YAAAAAAHH!
HUH ?
thwonk
WHA?!
SQUEEZE
GAAAAUGH!
SQUEEZE
FWW

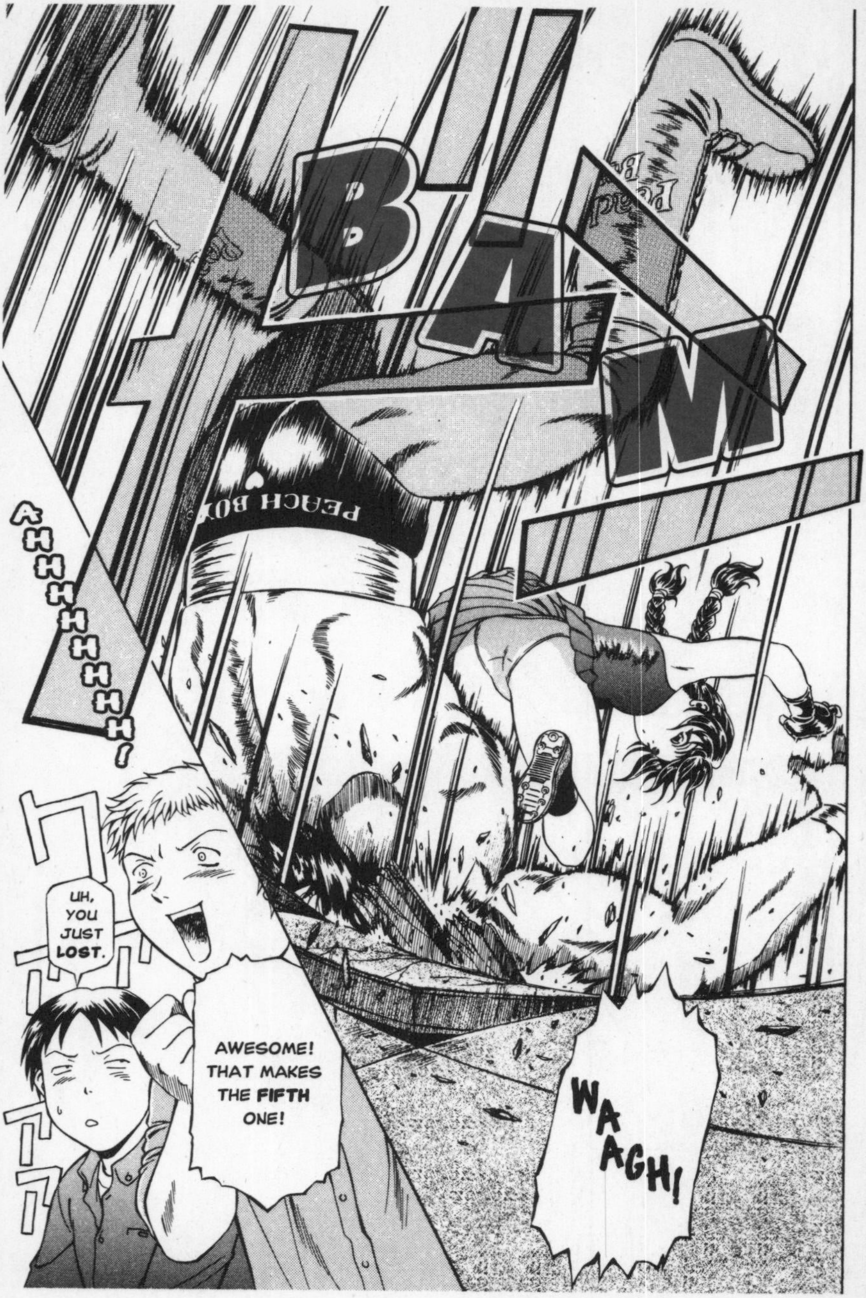
BAM
AHHHHHHHH!
WAAGH!
AWESOME! THAT MAKES THE FIFTH ONE!
UH, YOU JUST LOST.

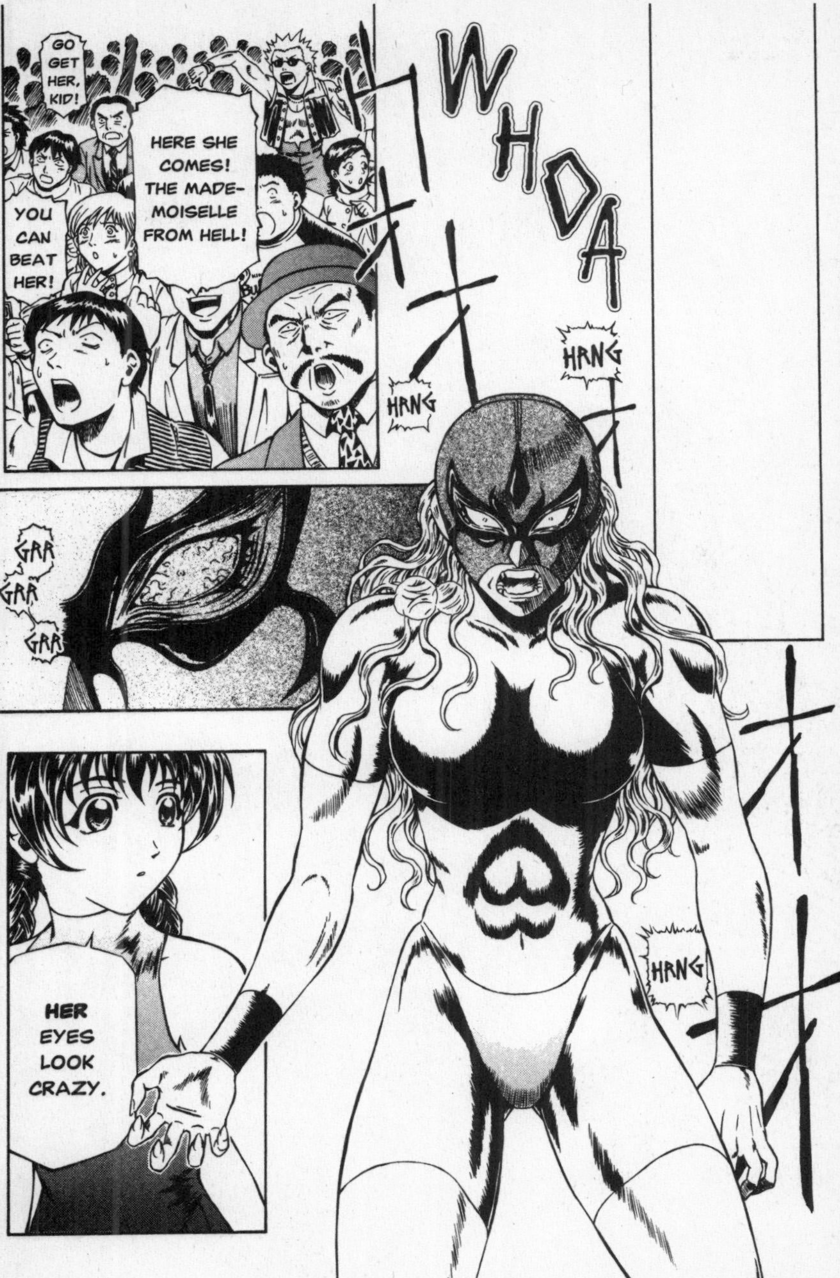

WHDA
HRNG
HRNG
HRNG
GO GET HER, KID!
HERE SHE COMES! THE MADEMOISELLE FROM HELL!
YOU CAN BEAT HER!
GRR
GRR
GRR
HER EYES LOOK CRAZY.

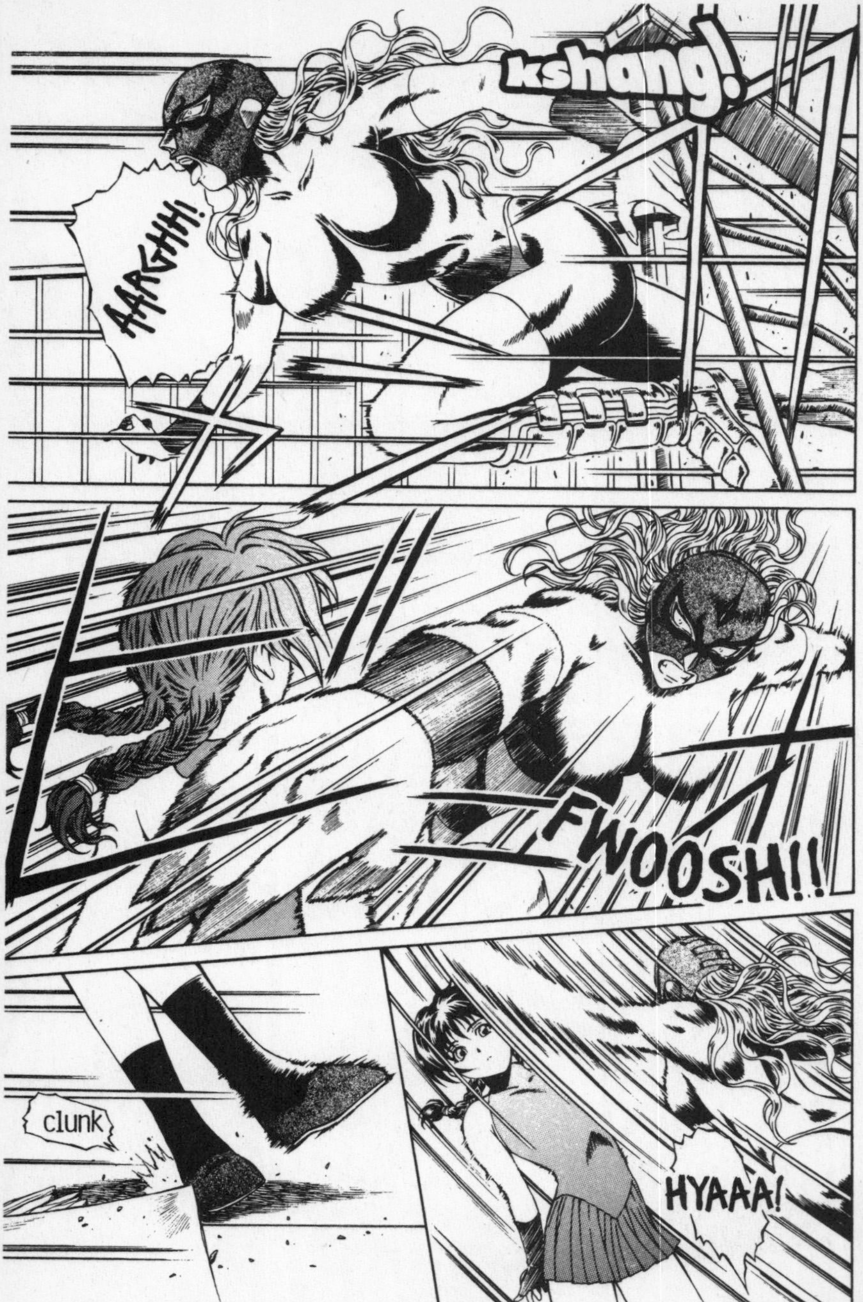
kshang!
AAAGHH!
FWOOSH!!
HYAAA!
clunk

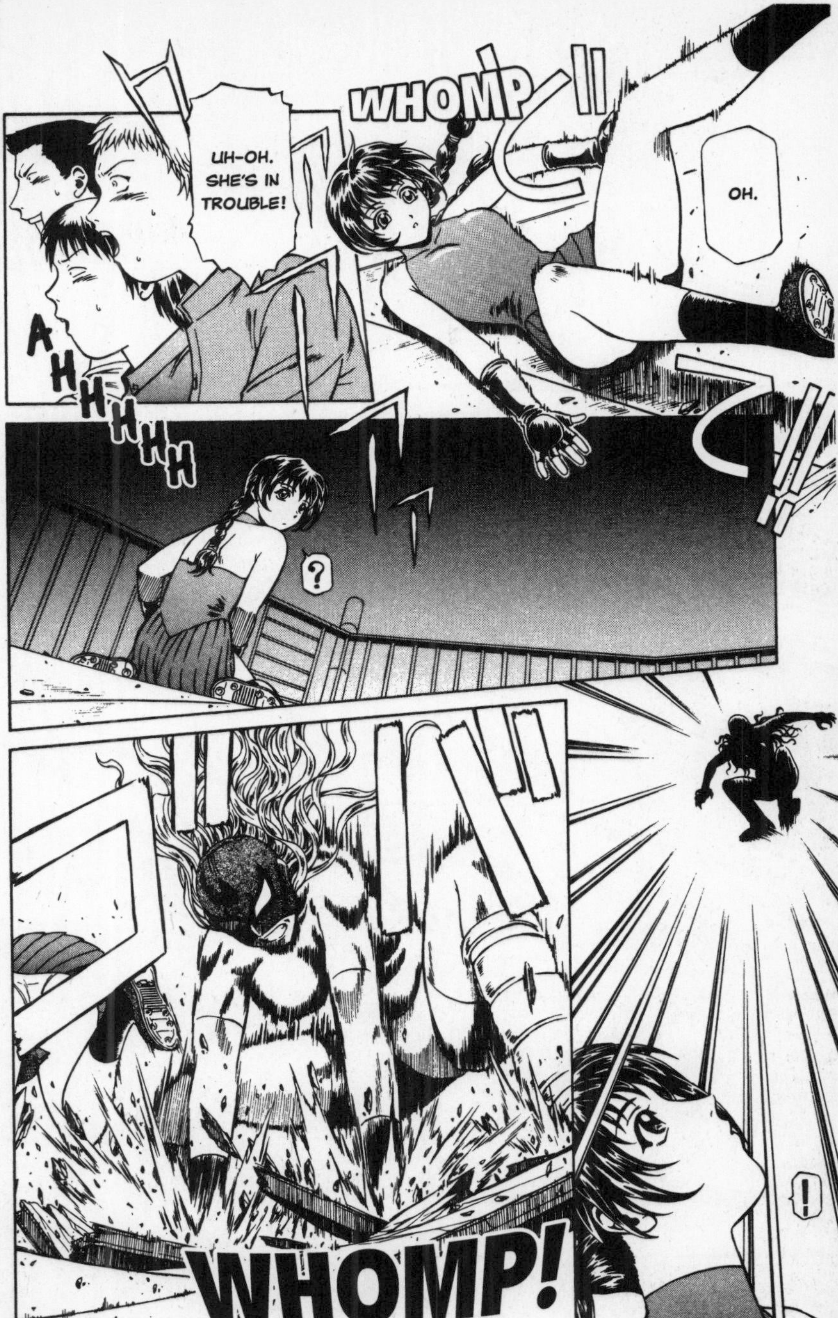
WHOMP
OH.
UH-OH. SHE'S IN TROUBLE!
AHHHHH
?
!
WHOMP!

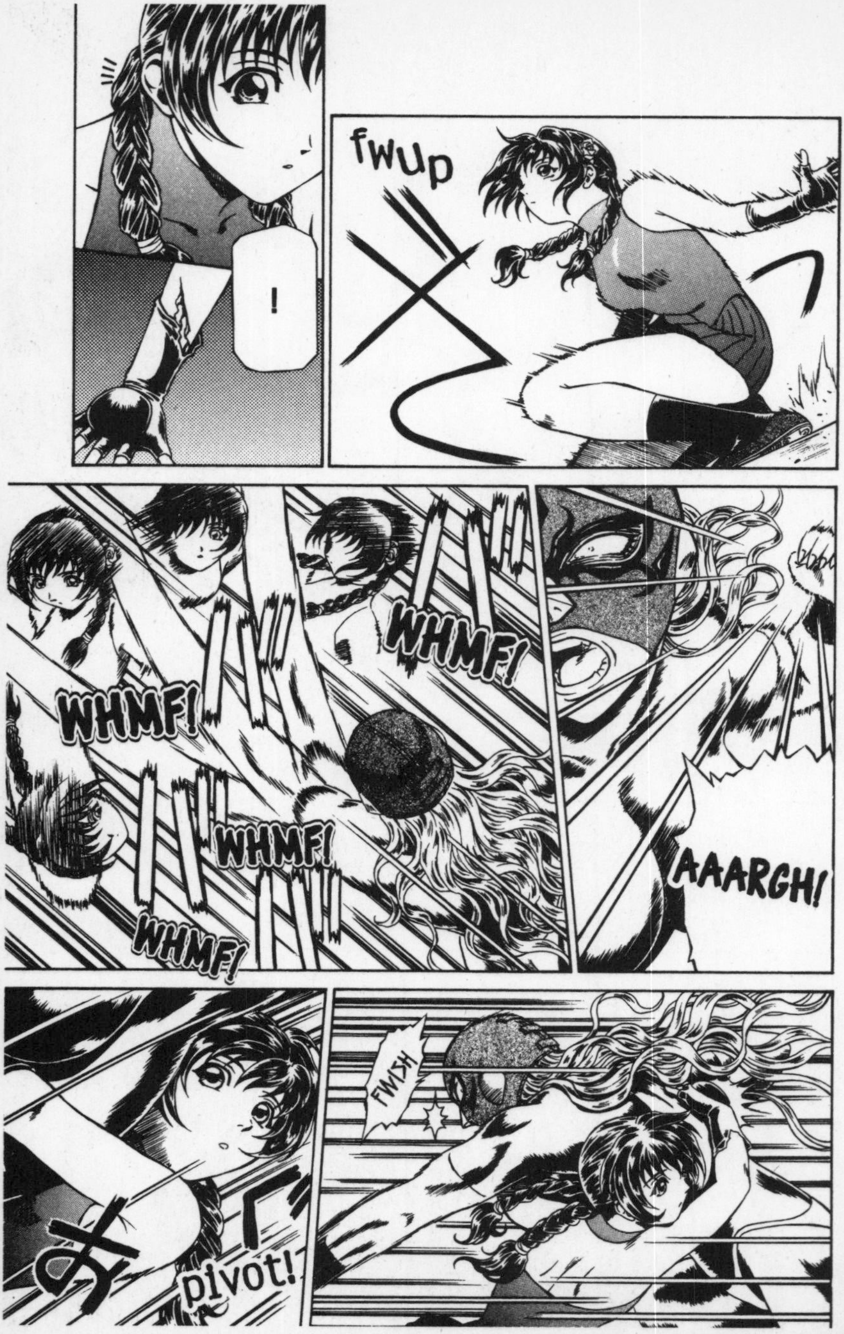
fwup
!
AAARGH!
WHMF!
WHMF!
WHMF!
WHMF!
FWISH
pivot!

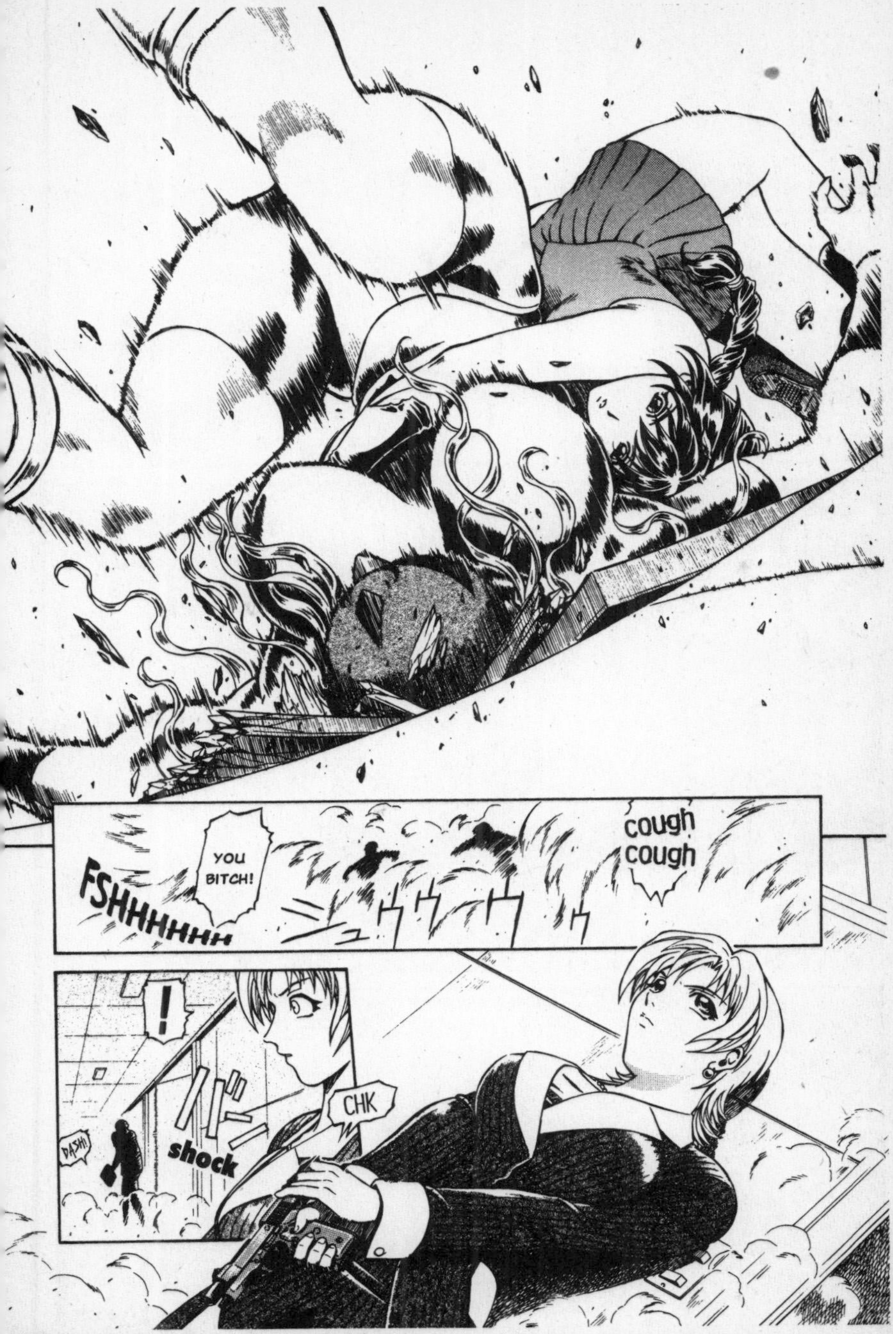
cough cough
YOU BITCH!
FSHHHHHHH
CHK
!
shock
DASH!

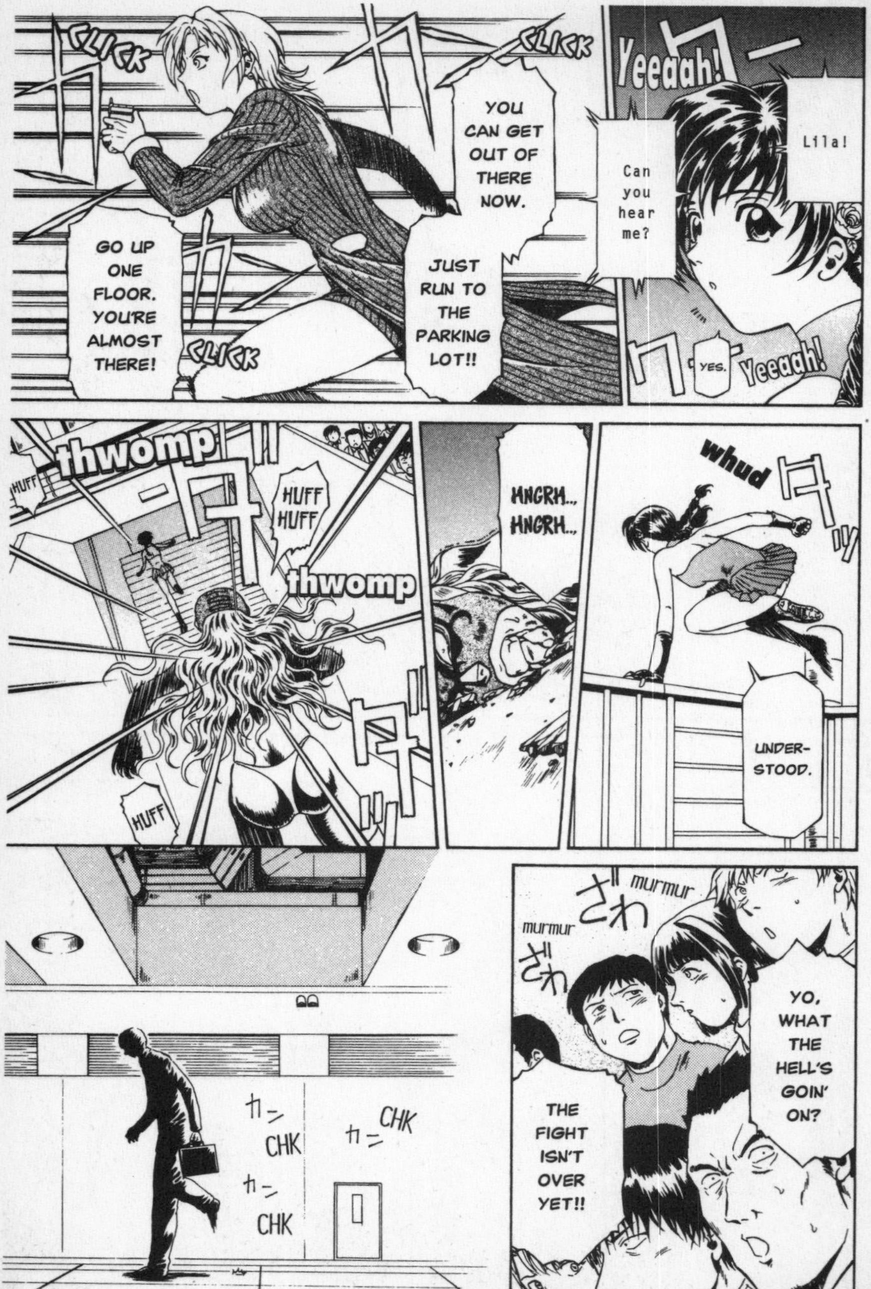
Yeeaah!
Lila!
Can you hear me?
YES.
Yeeaah!
CLICK
YOU CAN GET OUT OF THERE NOW.
JUST RUN TO THE PARKING LOT!!
CLICK
CLICK
GO UP ONE FLOOR. YOU'RE ALMOST THERE!
whud
UNDER-STOOD.
HNGRH.., HNGRH..,
thwomp
HUFF
HUFF HUFF
thwomp
HUFF
murmur
murmur
YO, WHAT THE HELL'S GOIN' ON?
THE FIGHT ISN'T OVER YET!!
CHK
CHK
CHK

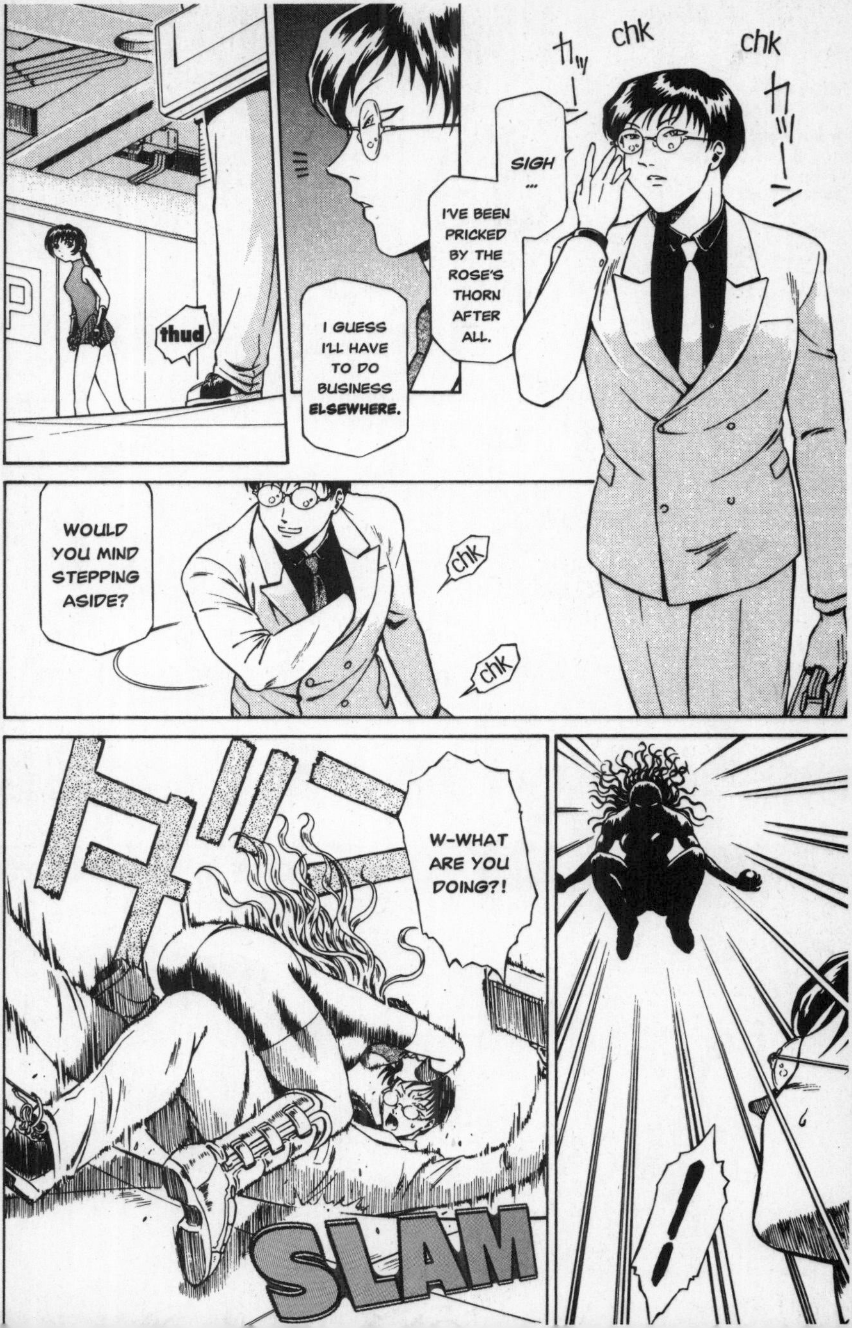
カッ
chk
chk
カッツーン
SIGH ...
I'VE BEEN PRICKED BY THE ROSE'S THORN AFTER ALL.
I GUESS I'LL HAVE TO DO BUSINESS ELSEWHERE.
thud
WOULD YOU MIND STEPPING ASIDE?
chk
chk
!
タッ
W-WHAT ARE YOU DOING?!
SLAM

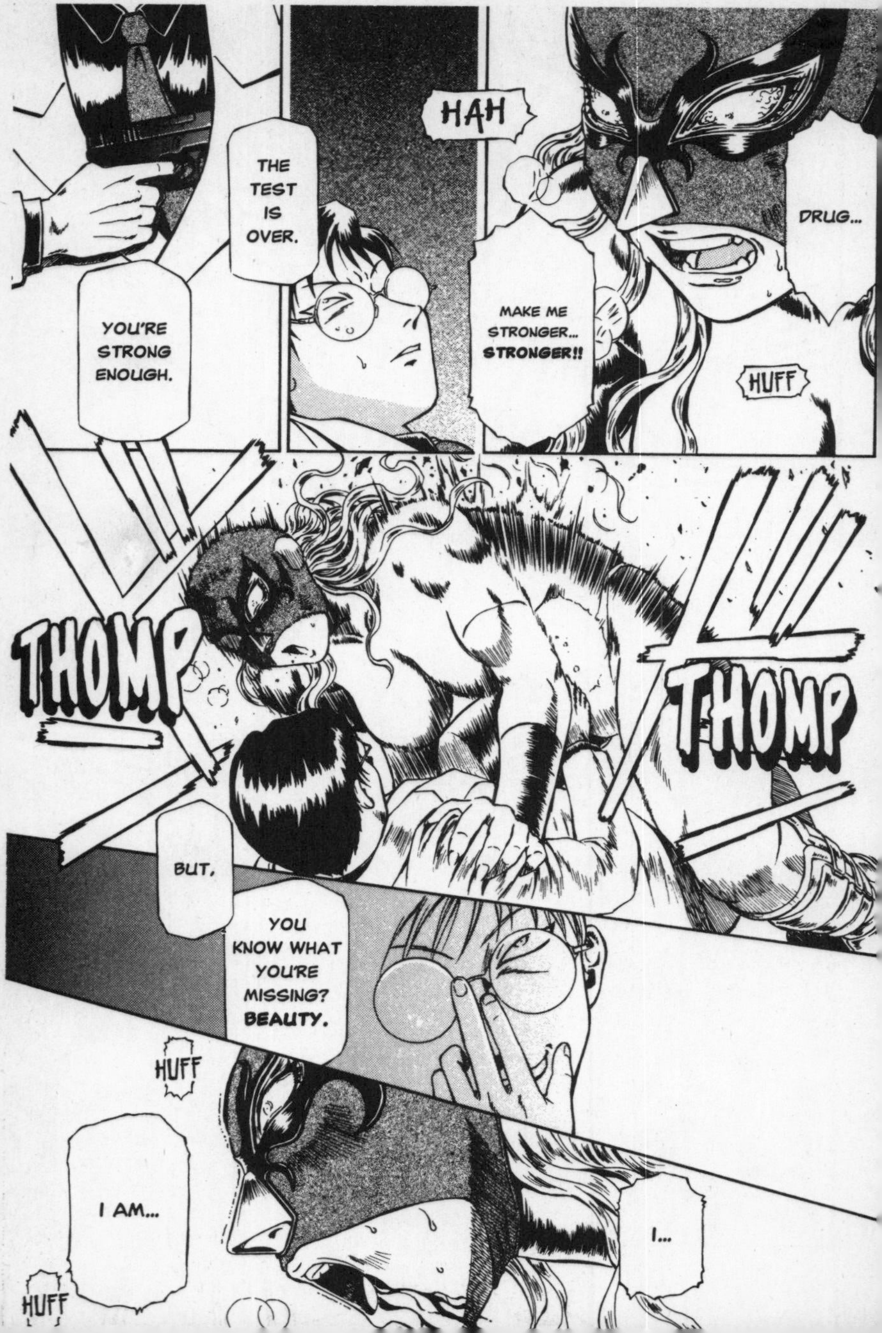

HAH
DRUG...
MAKE ME STRONGER... **STRONGER!!**
HUFF
THE TEST IS OVER.
YOU'RE STRONG ENOUGH.
THOMP
THOMP
BUT,
YOU KNOW WHAT YOU'RE MISSING? **BEAUTY.**
HUFF
I...
I AM...
HUFF

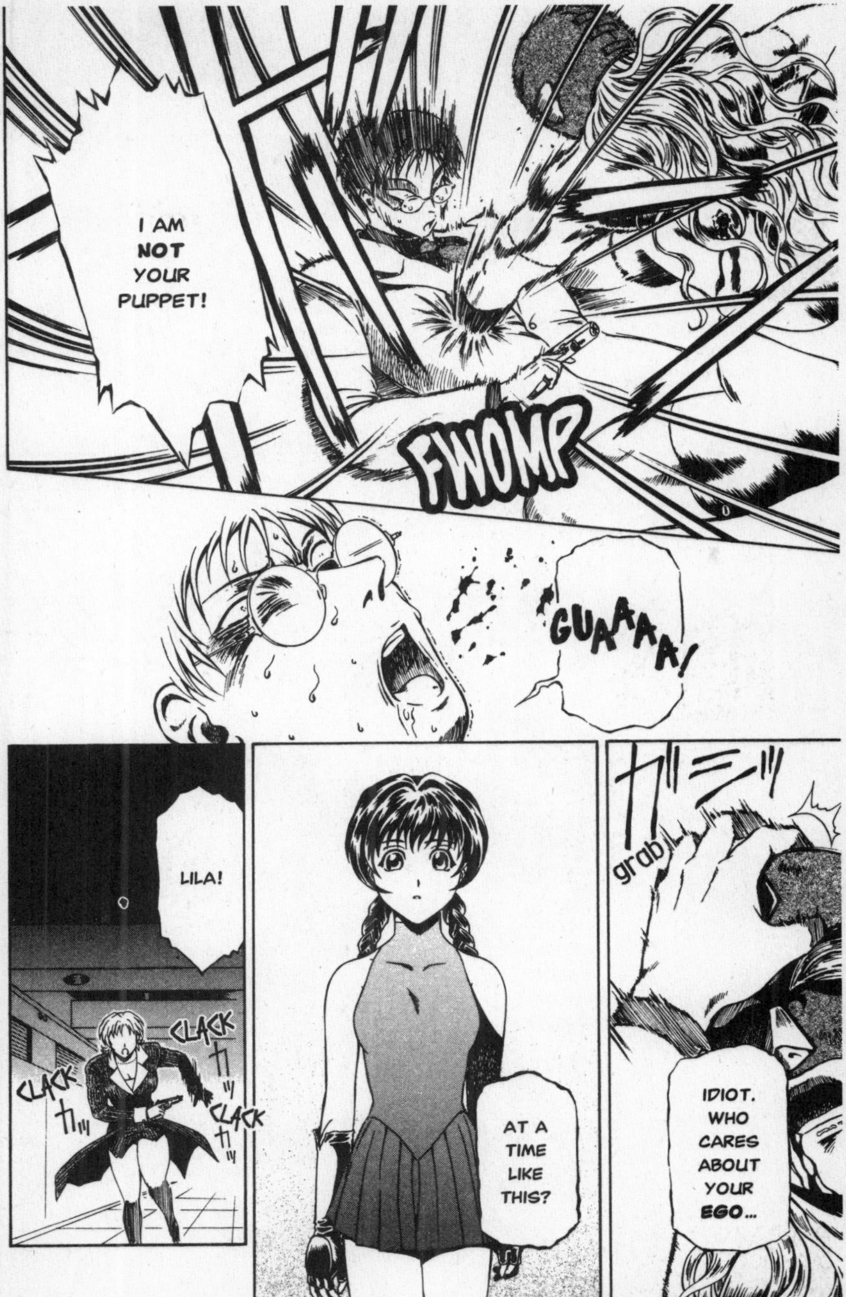
I AM NOT YOUR PUPPET!
FWOMP
GUAAAAA!
grab
IDIOT. WHO CARES ABOUT YOUR EGO...
AT A TIME LIKE THIS?
LILA!
CLACK
CLACK
CLACK

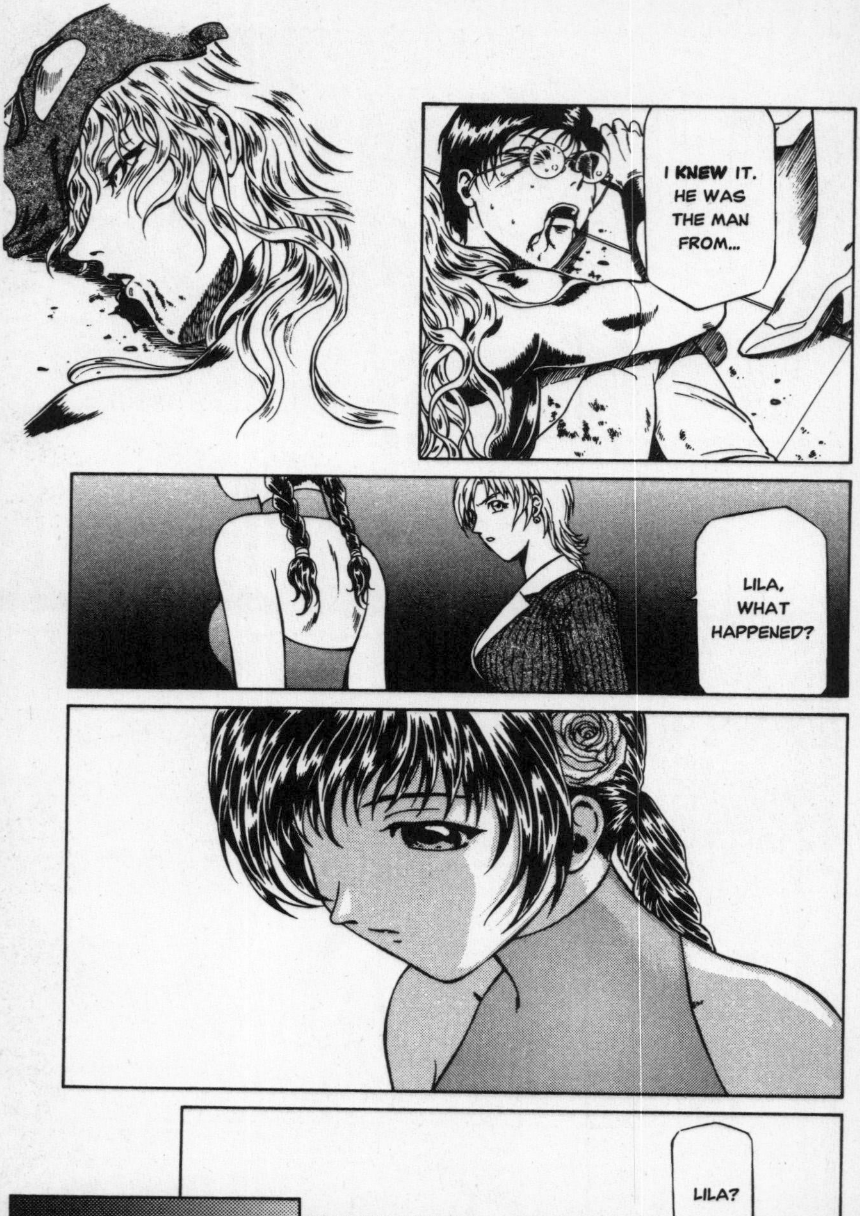
I KNEW IT. HE WAS THE MAN FROM...
LILA, WHAT HAPPENED?
LILA?

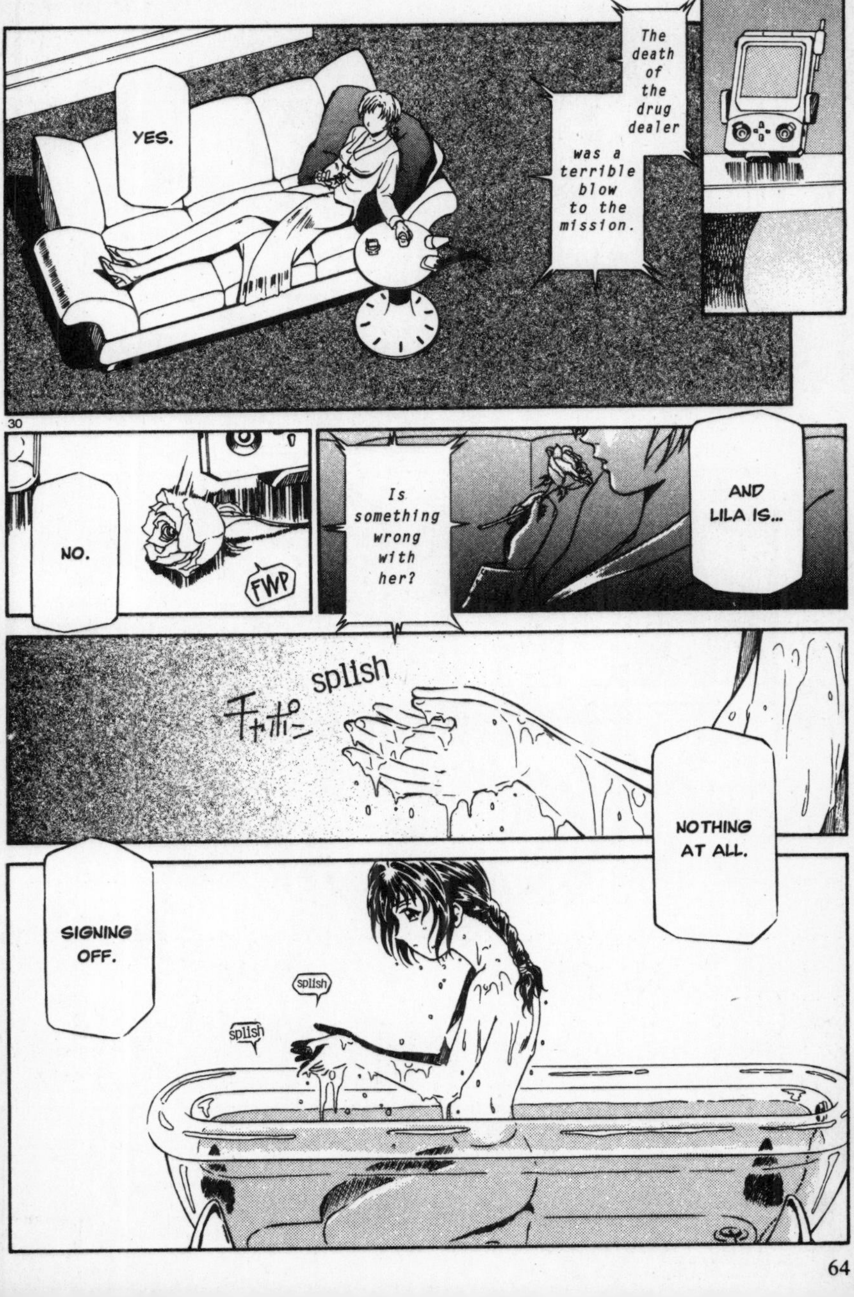
The death of the drug dealer was a terrible blow to the mission.
YES.
30
AND LILA IS...
Is something wrong with her?
NO.
FWP
splish
NOTHING AT ALL.
SIGNING OFF.
splish
splish

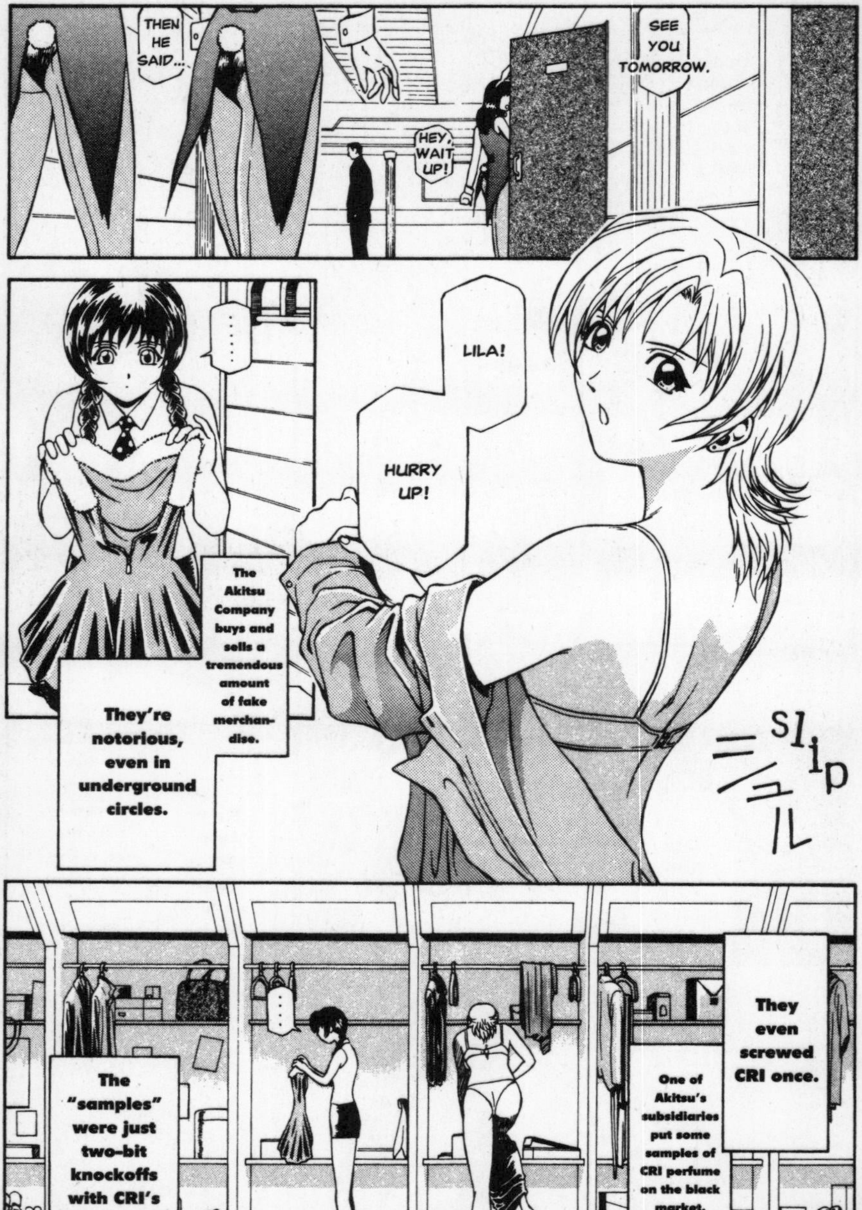
SEE YOU TOMORROW.
HEY, WAIT UP!
THEN HE SAID...
LILA!
HURRY UP!
slip
シュル
......
The Akitsu Company buys and sells a tremendous amount of fake merchandise.
They're notorious, even in underground circles.
They even screwed CRI once.
One of Akitsu's subsidiaries put some samples of CRI perfume on the black market.
...
The "samples" were just two-bit knockoffs with CRI's name on it.

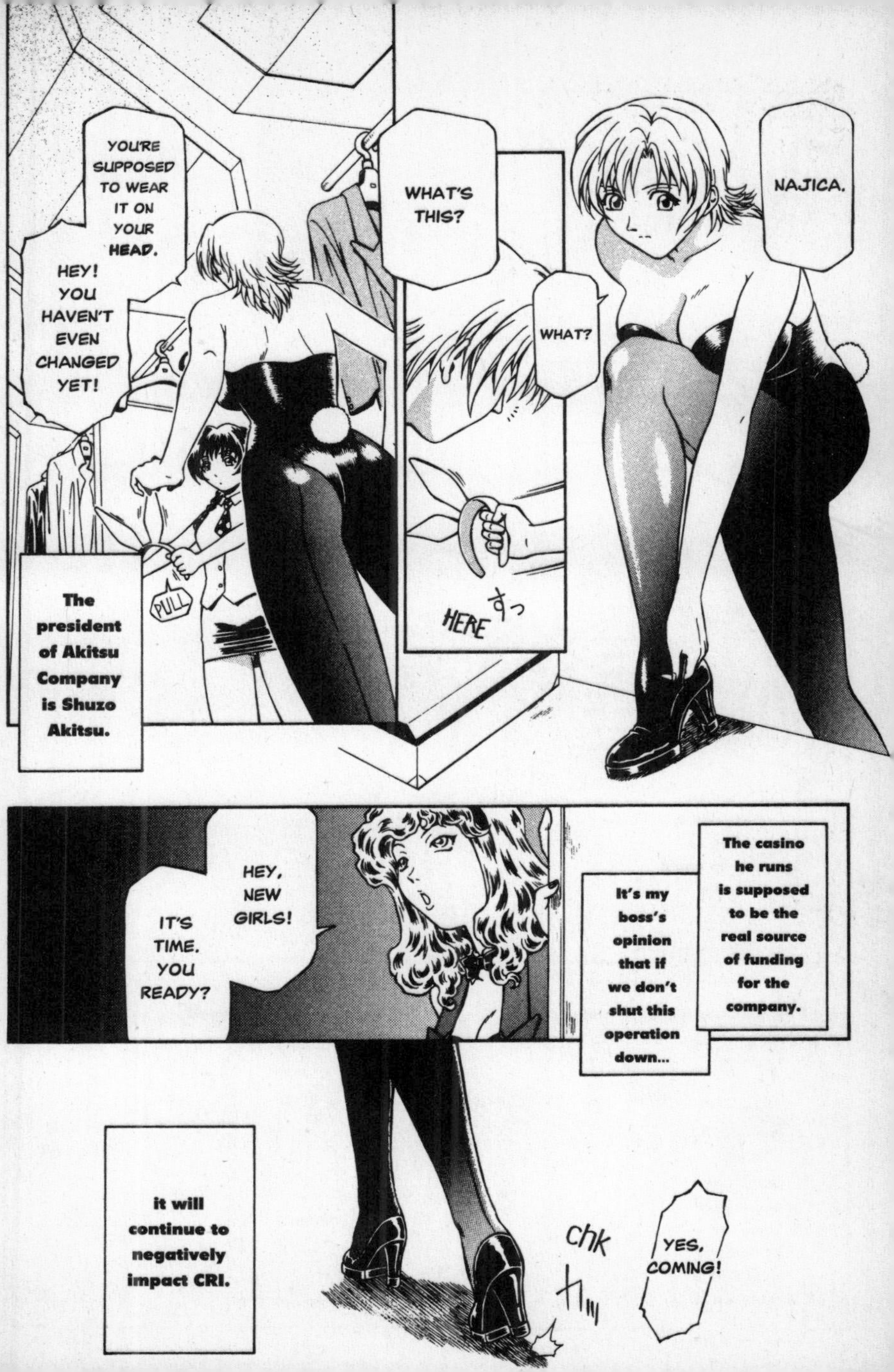
NAJICA.
WHAT'S THIS?
WHAT?
HERE すっ
YOU'RE SUPPOSED TO WEAR IT ON YOUR HEAD.
HEY! YOU HAVEN'T EVEN CHANGED YET!
PULL
The president of Akitsu Company is Shuzo Akitsu.
The casino he runs is supposed to be the real source of funding for the company.
It's my boss's opinion that if we don't shut this operation down...
HEY, NEW GIRLS!
IT'S TIME. YOU READY?
YES, COMING!
chk
it will continue to negatively impact CRI.

Operation.3
DESTRUCTION OF THE UNDERGROUND CASINO

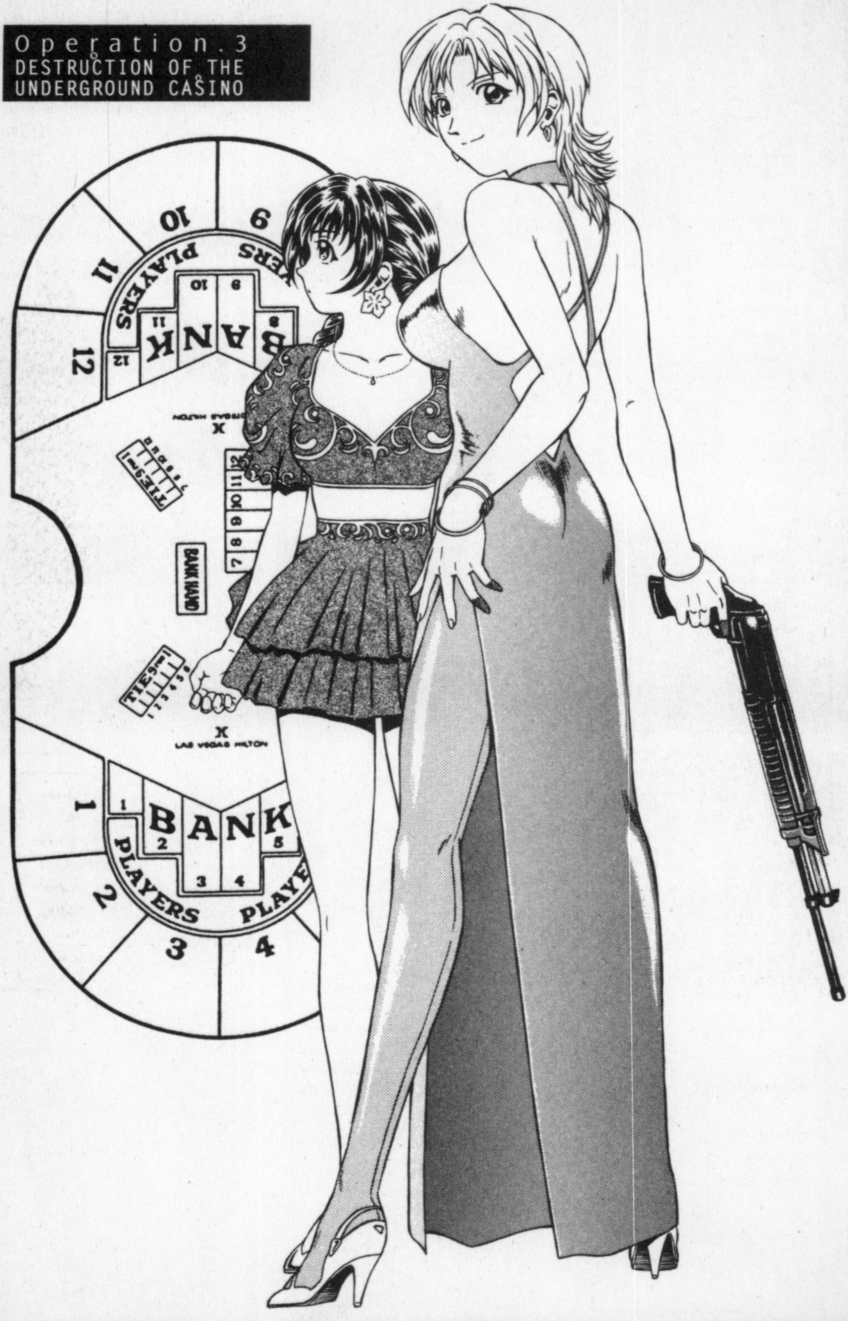
BANK
PLAYERS
BANK HAND
LAS VEGAS HILTON
TIE
BANK
PLAYERS

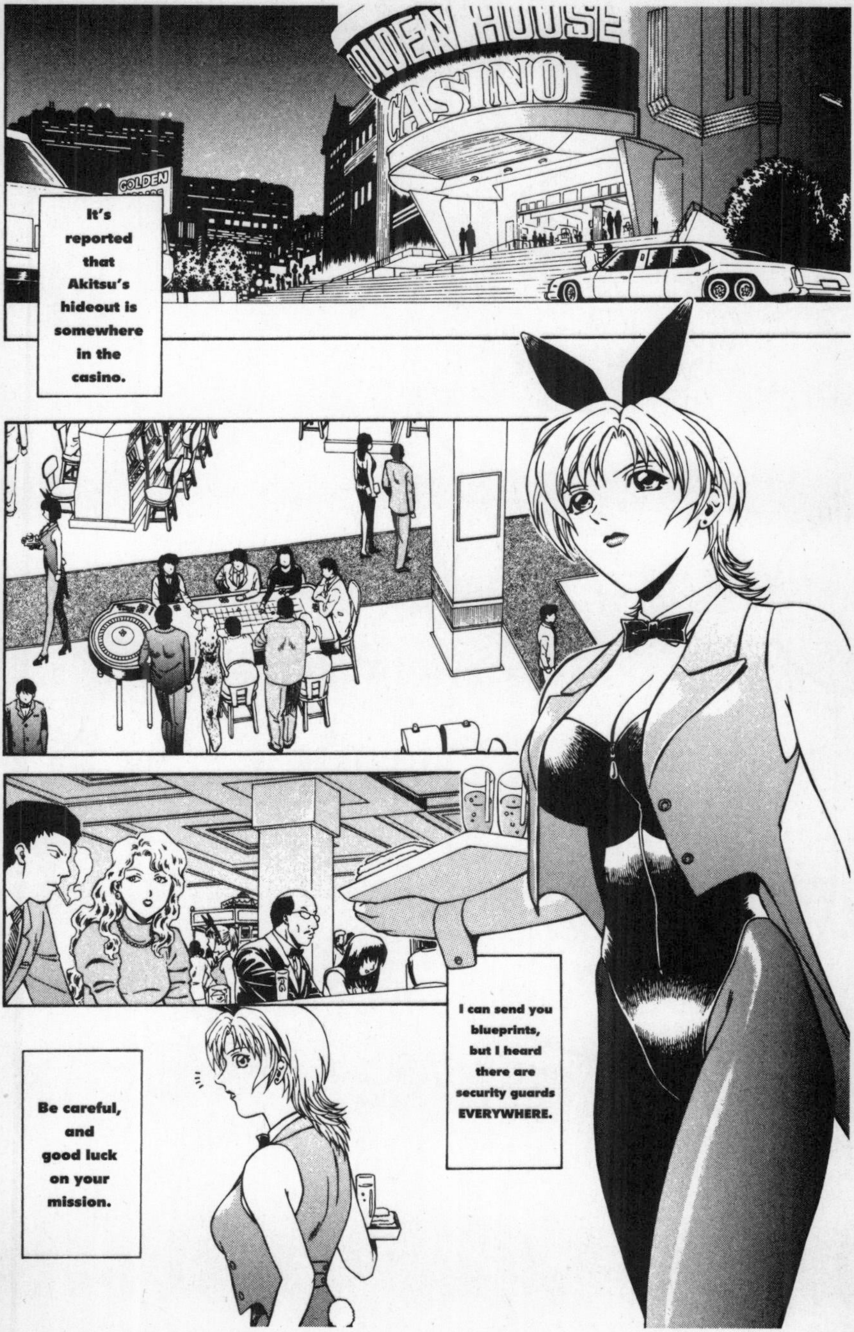
OLDEN HOUSE
CASINO
GOLDEN
It's reported that Akitsu's hideout is somewhere in the casino.
I can send you blueprints, but I heard there are security guards EVERYWHERE.
Be careful, and good luck on your mission.

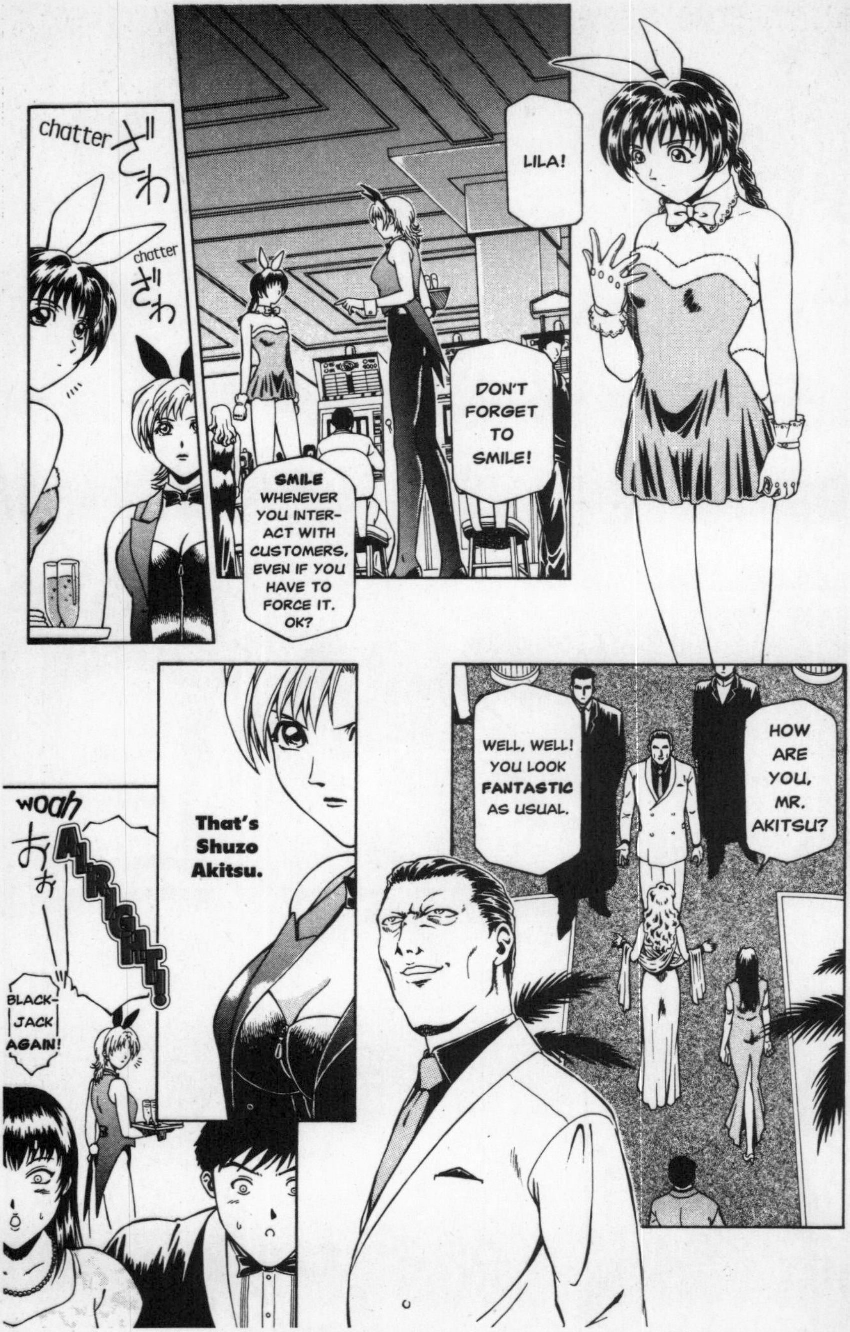
LILA!
DON'T FORGET TO SMILE!
SMILE WHENEVER YOU INTER-ACT WITH CUSTOMERS, EVEN IF YOU HAVE TO FORCE IT. OK?
chatter ざわ
chatter ざわ
HOW ARE YOU, MR. AKITSU?
WELL, WELL! YOU LOOK FANTASTIC AS USUAL.
That's Shuzo Akitsu.
woah おお
ALRIGHT!!
BLACK-JACK AGAIN!

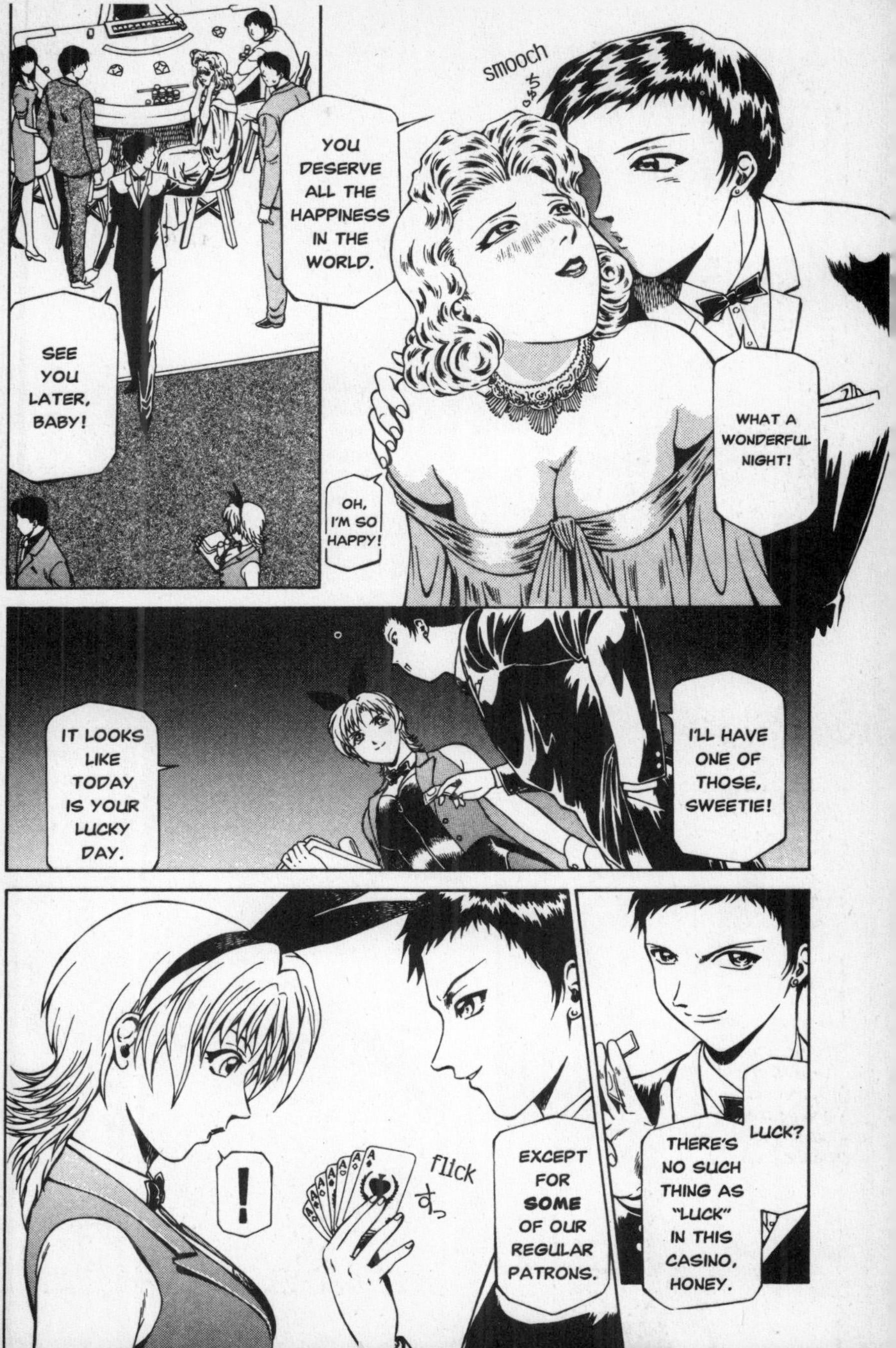
smooch
YOU DESERVE ALL THE HAPPINESS IN THE WORLD.
WHAT A WONDERFUL NIGHT!
OH, I'M SO HAPPY!
SEE YOU LATER, BABY!
I'LL HAVE ONE OF THOSE, SWEETIE!
IT LOOKS LIKE TODAY IS YOUR LUCKY DAY.
LUCK?
THERE'S NO SUCH THING AS "LUCK" IN THIS CASINO, HONEY.
EXCEPT FOR **SOME** OF OUR REGULAR PATRONS.
flick
すっ
!

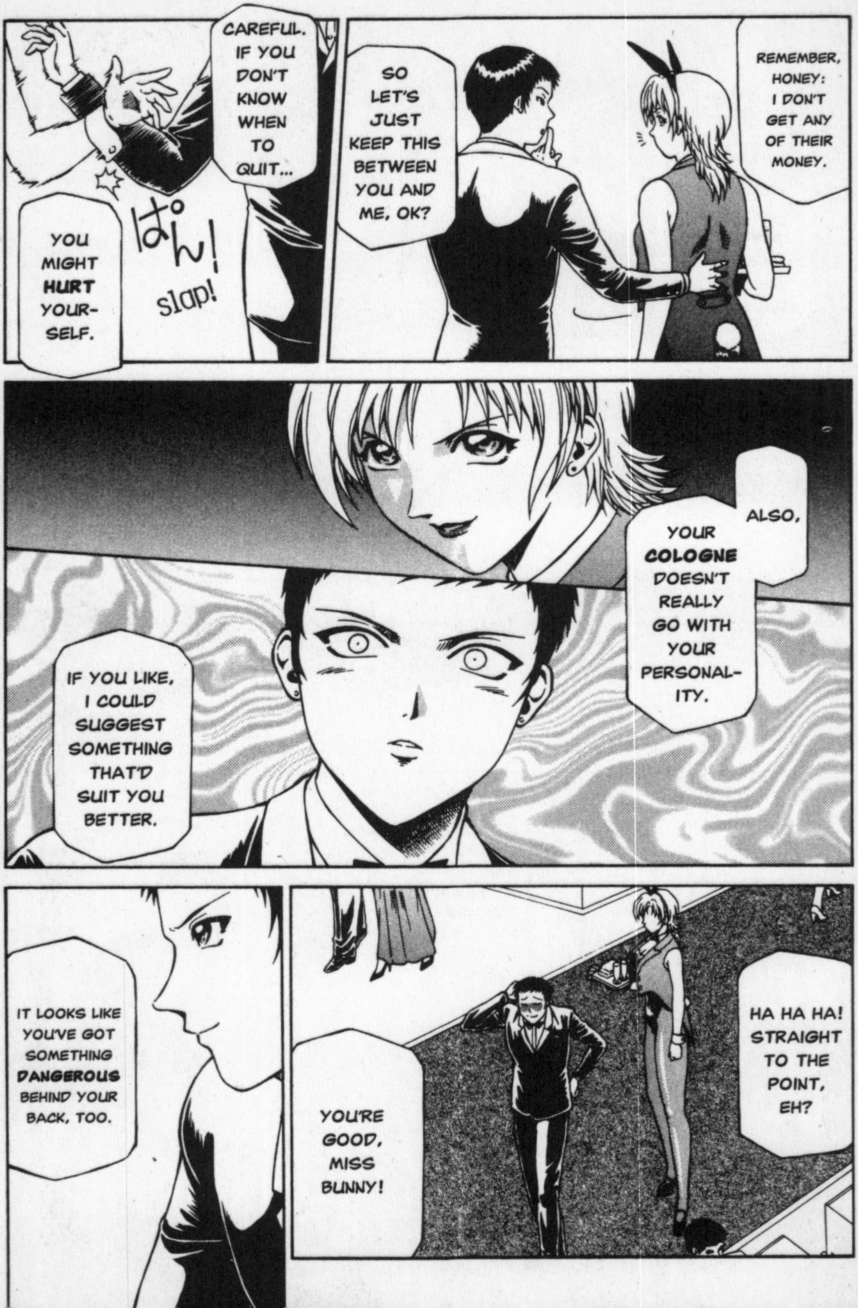
REMEMBER, HONEY: I DON'T GET ANY OF THEIR MONEY.
SO LET'S JUST KEEP THIS BETWEEN YOU AND ME, OK?
CAREFUL. IF YOU DON'T KNOW WHEN TO QUIT...
ぱん! slap!
YOU MIGHT **HURT** YOUR-SELF.
ALSO,
YOUR **COLOGNE** DOESN'T REALLY GO WITH YOUR PERSONAL-ITY.
IF YOU LIKE, I COULD SUGGEST SOMETHING THAT'D SUIT YOU BETTER.
HA HA HA! STRAIGHT TO THE POINT, EH?
YOU'RE GOOD, MISS BUNNY!
IT LOOKS LIKE YOU'VE GOT SOMETHING **DANGEROUS** BEHIND YOUR BACK, TOO.

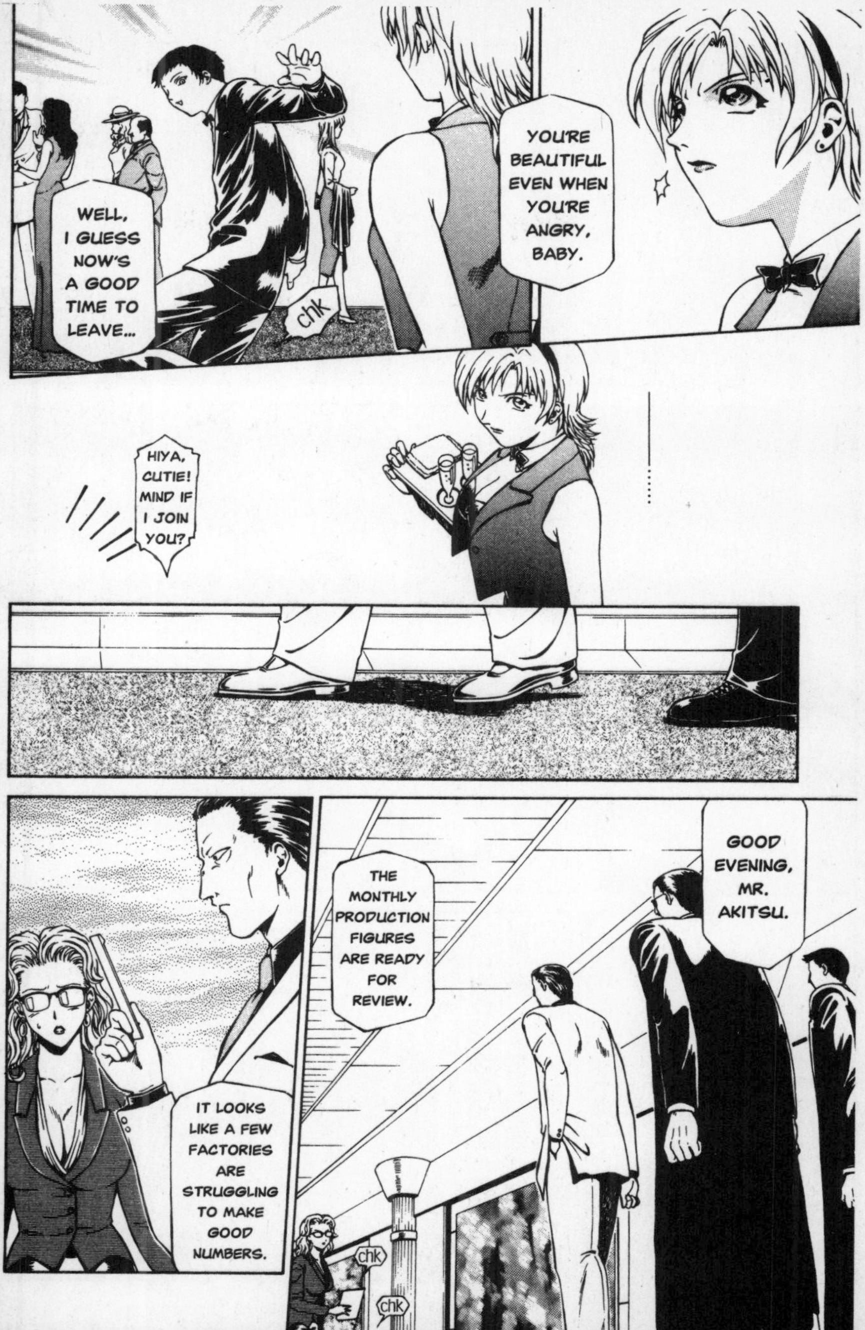
YOU'RE BEAUTIFUL EVEN WHEN YOU'RE ANGRY, BABY.
WELL, I GUESS NOW'S A GOOD TIME TO LEAVE...
chk
......
HIYA, CUTIE! MIND IF I JOIN YOU?
GOOD EVENING, MR. AKITSU.
THE MONTHLY PRODUCTION FIGURES ARE READY FOR REVIEW.
chk
chk
IT LOOKS LIKE A FEW FACTORIES ARE STRUGGLING TO MAKE GOOD NUMBERS.

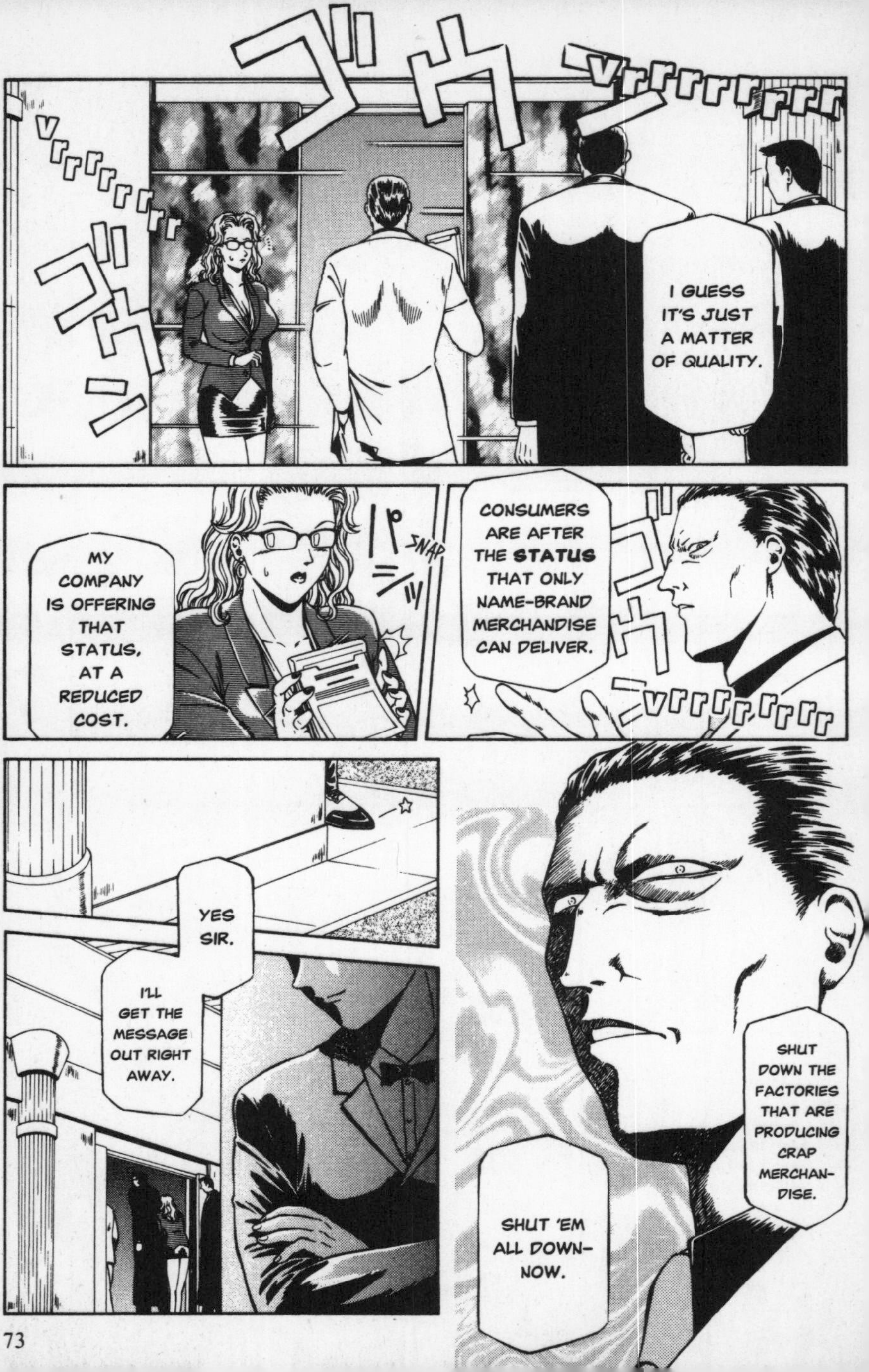
vrrrrrrrrr
vrrrrrrrrr
I GUESS IT'S JUST A MATTER OF QUALITY.
CONSUMERS ARE AFTER THE STATUS THAT ONLY NAME-BRAND MERCHANDISE CAN DELIVER.
vrrrrrrrrr
SNAP
MY COMPANY IS OFFERING THAT STATUS, AT A REDUCED COST.
SHUT DOWN THE FACTORIES THAT ARE PRODUCING CRAP MERCHANDISE.
SHUT 'EM ALL DOWN-NOW.
YES SIR.
I'LL GET THE MESSAGE OUT RIGHT AWAY.

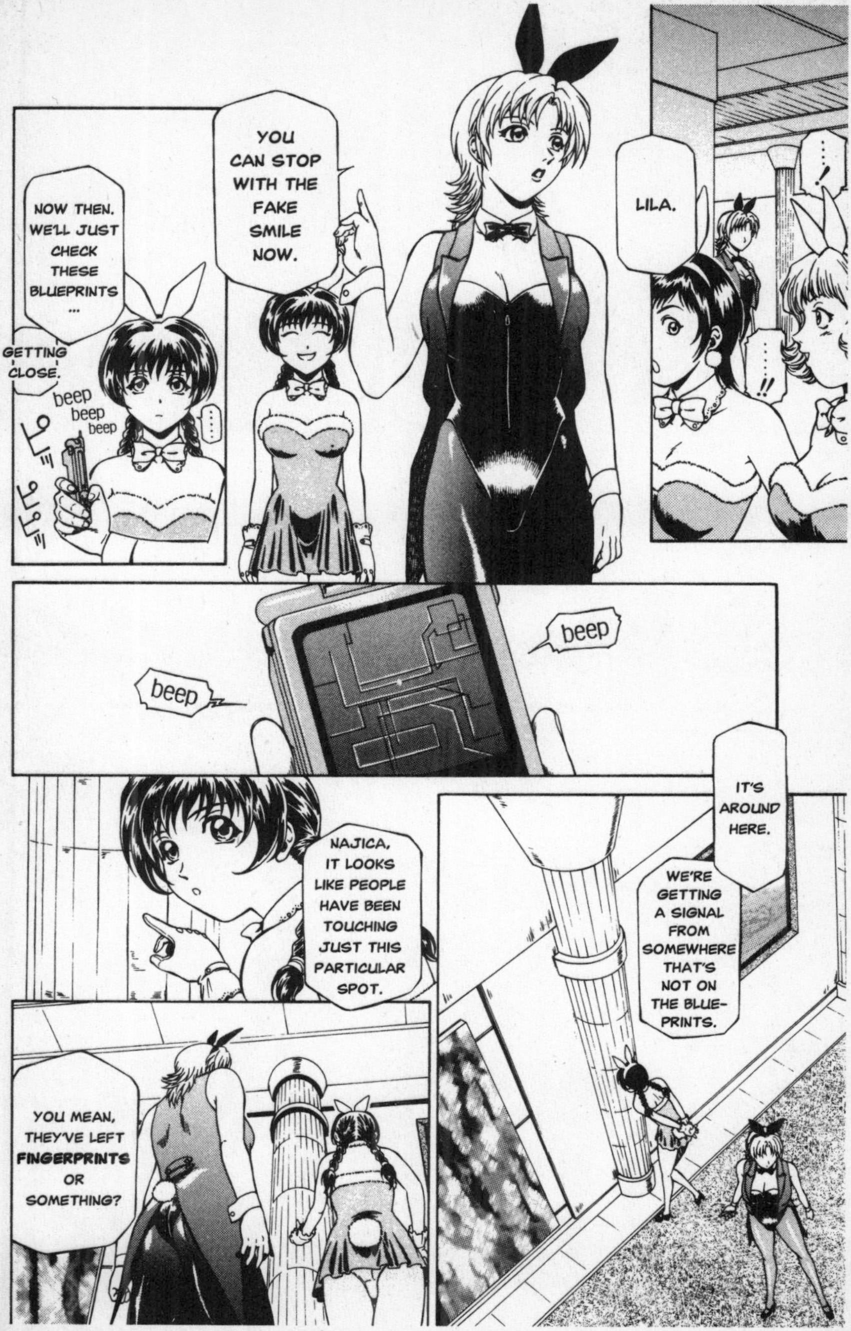
LILA.
......!
......!!
YOU CAN STOP WITH THE FAKE SMILE NOW.
NOW THEN. WE'LL JUST CHECK THESE BLUEPRINTS ...
GETTING CLOSE.
beep beep beep
......
beep
beep
IT'S AROUND HERE.
WE'RE GETTING A SIGNAL FROM SOMEWHERE THAT'S NOT ON THE BLUE-PRINTS.
NAJICA, IT LOOKS LIKE PEOPLE HAVE BEEN TOUCHING JUST THIS PARTICULAR SPOT.
YOU MEAN, THEY'VE LEFT **FINGERPRINTS** OR SOMETHING?

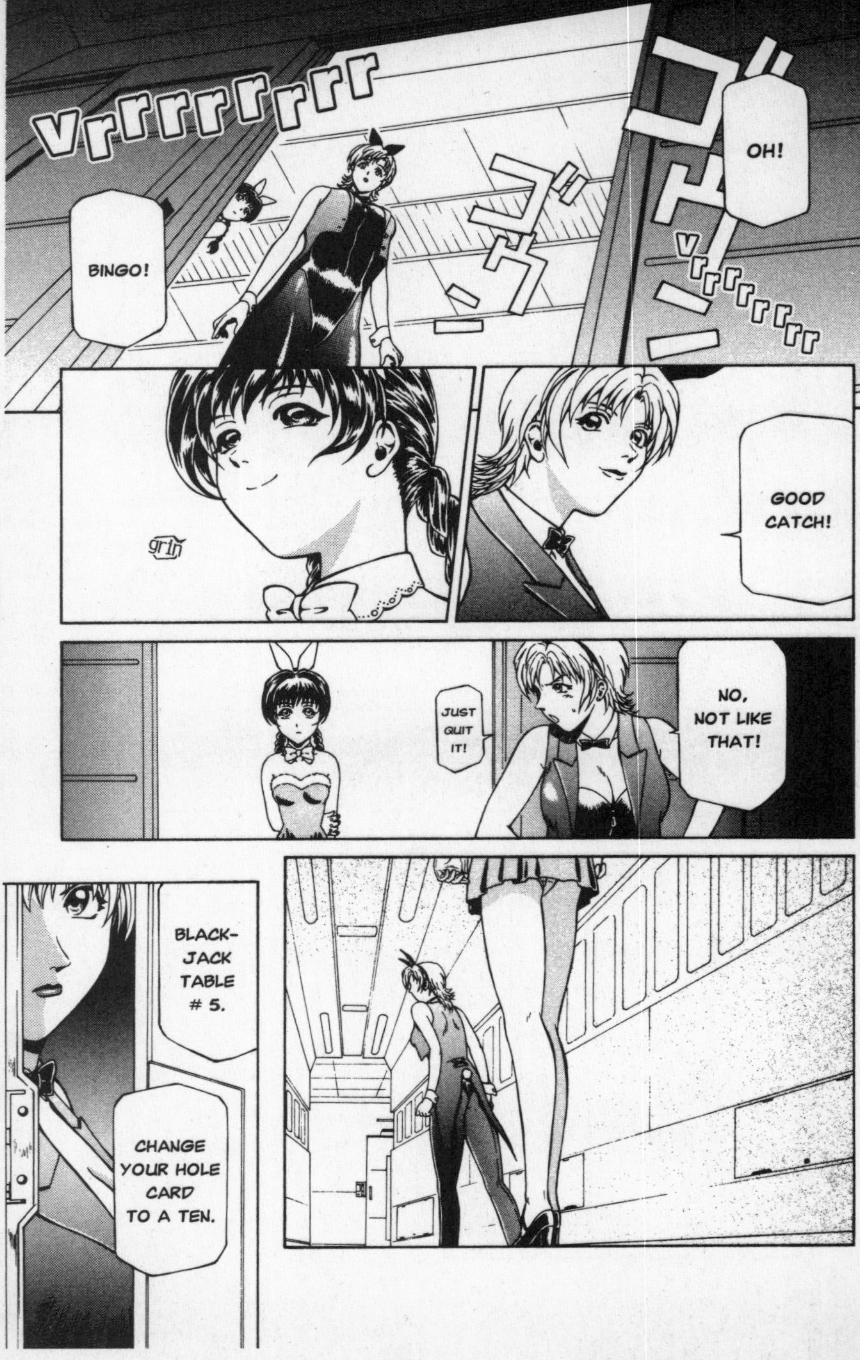
OH!
Vrrrrrrrrr
BINGO!
Vrrrrrrrr
GOOD CATCH!
grin
NO, NOT LIKE THAT!
JUST QUIT IT!
BLACK-JACK TABLE # 5.
CHANGE YOUR HOLE CARD TO A TEN.

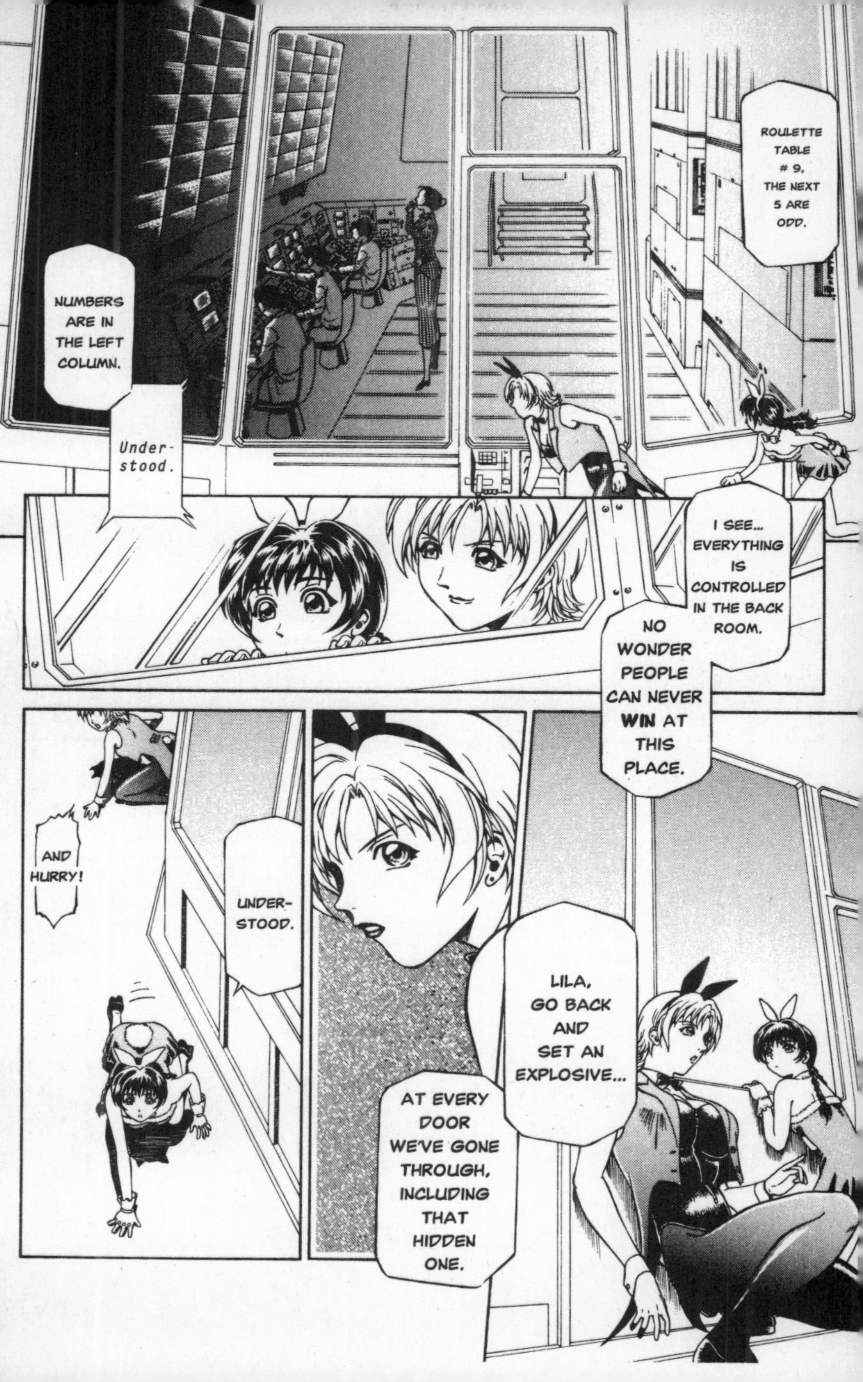
ROULETTE TABLE # 9, THE NEXT 5 ARE ODD.
NUMBERS ARE IN THE LEFT COLUMN.
Understood.
I SEE... EVERYTHING IS CONTROLLED IN THE BACK ROOM.
NO WONDER PEOPLE CAN NEVER WIN AT THIS PLACE.
LILA, GO BACK AND SET AN EXPLOSIVE...
AT EVERY DOOR WE'VE GONE THROUGH, INCLUDING THAT HIDDEN ONE.
UNDERSTOOD.
AND HURRY!

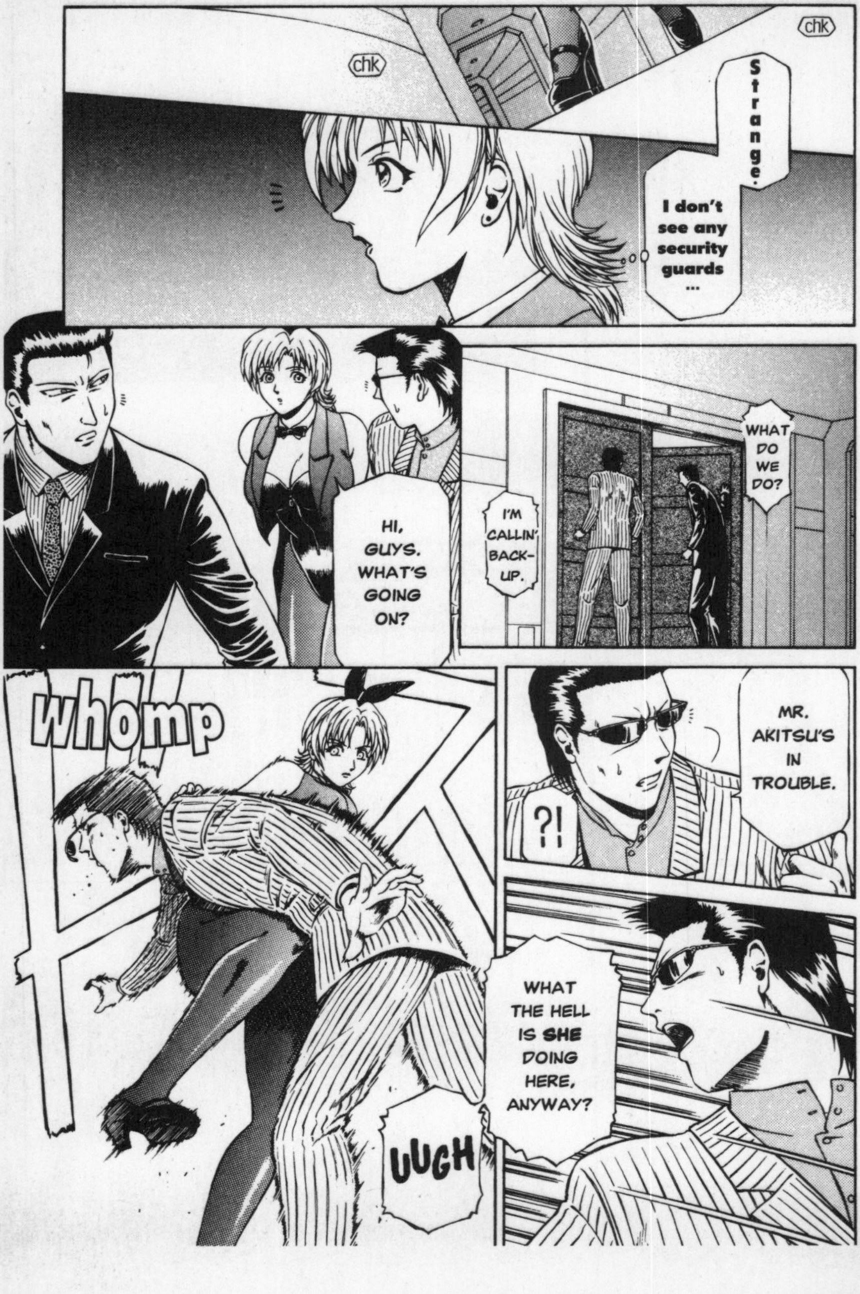
chk
chk
Strange.
I don't see any security guards ...
WHAT DO WE DO?
I'M CALLIN' BACK-UP.
HI, GUYS. WHAT'S GOING ON?
MR. AKITSU'S IN TROUBLE.
?!
WHAT THE HELL IS SHE DOING HERE, ANYWAY?
whomp
UUGH

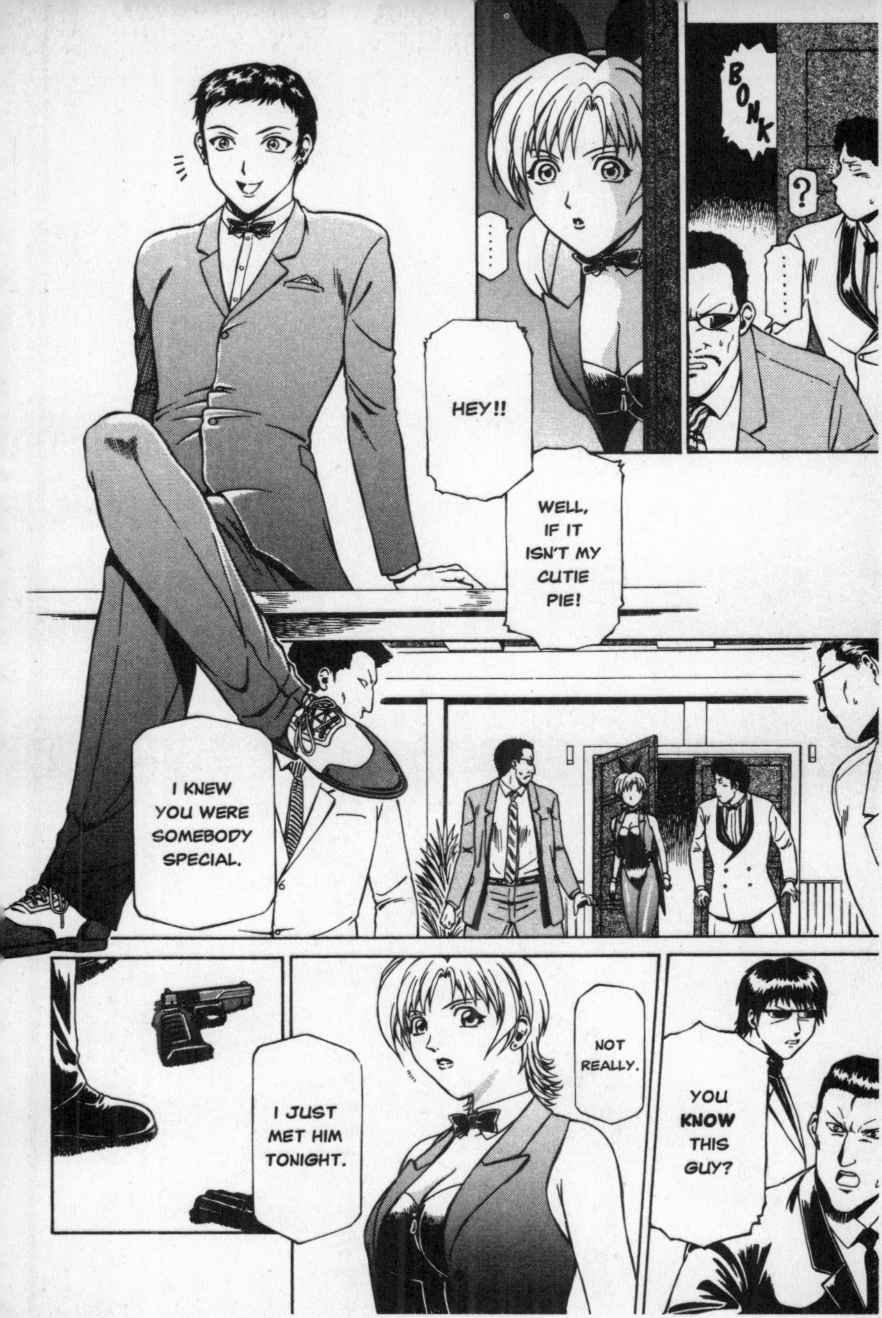
BONK
?
....
....
HEY!!
WELL, IF IT ISN'T MY CUTIE PIE!
I KNEW YOU WERE SOMEBODY SPECIAL.
YOU KNOW THIS GUY?
NOT REALLY.
I JUST MET HIM TONIGHT.

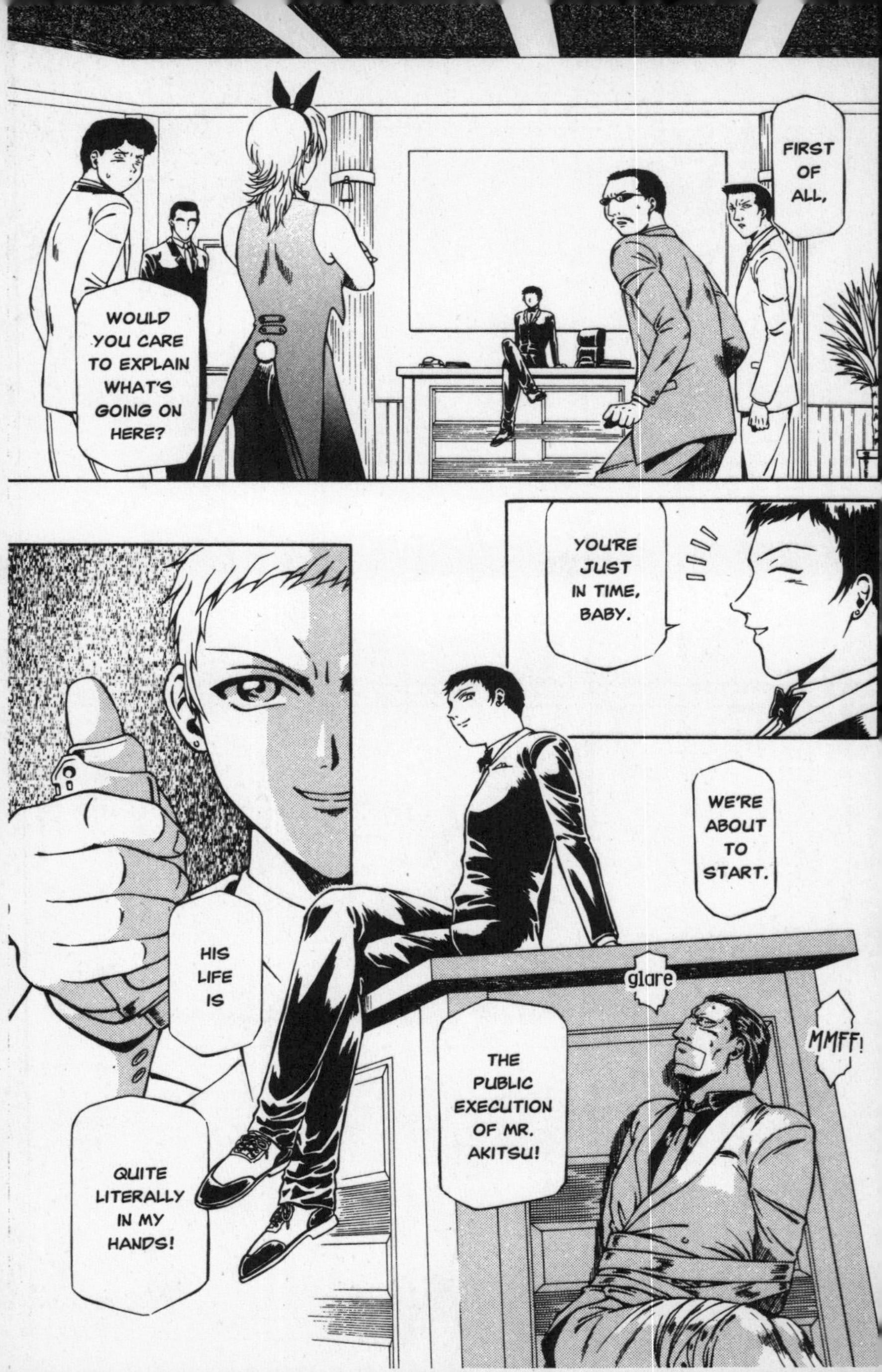
FIRST OF ALL,
WOULD YOU CARE TO EXPLAIN WHAT'S GOING ON HERE?
YOU'RE JUST IN TIME, BABY.
WE'RE ABOUT TO START.
glare
MMFF!
THE PUBLIC EXECUTION OF MR. AKITSU!
HIS LIFE IS
QUITE LITERALLY IN MY HANDS!

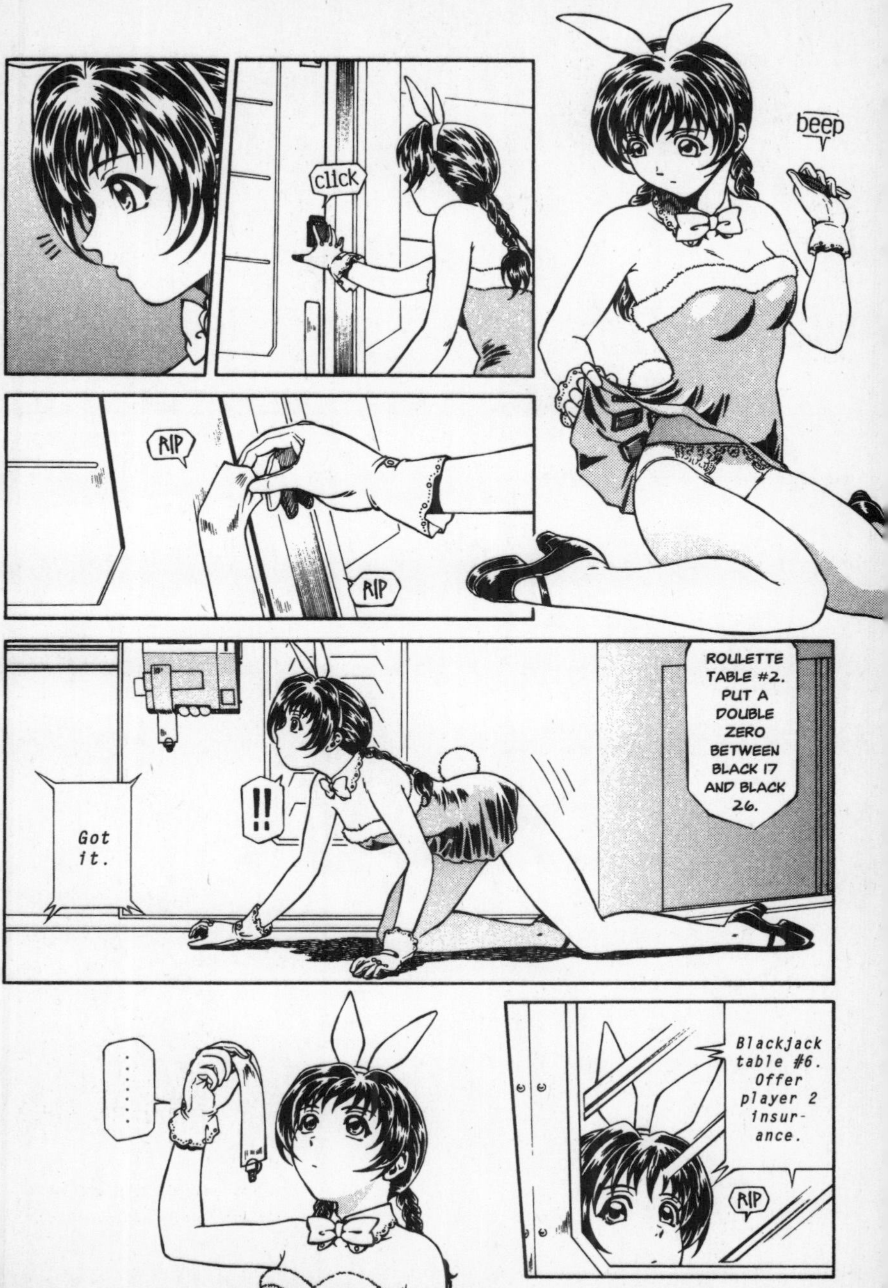
beep
click
RIP
RIP
ROULETTE TABLE #2. PUT A DOUBLE ZERO BETWEEN BLACK 17 AND BLACK 26.
!!
Got it.
Blackjack table #6. Offer player 2 insur-ance.
RIP
......

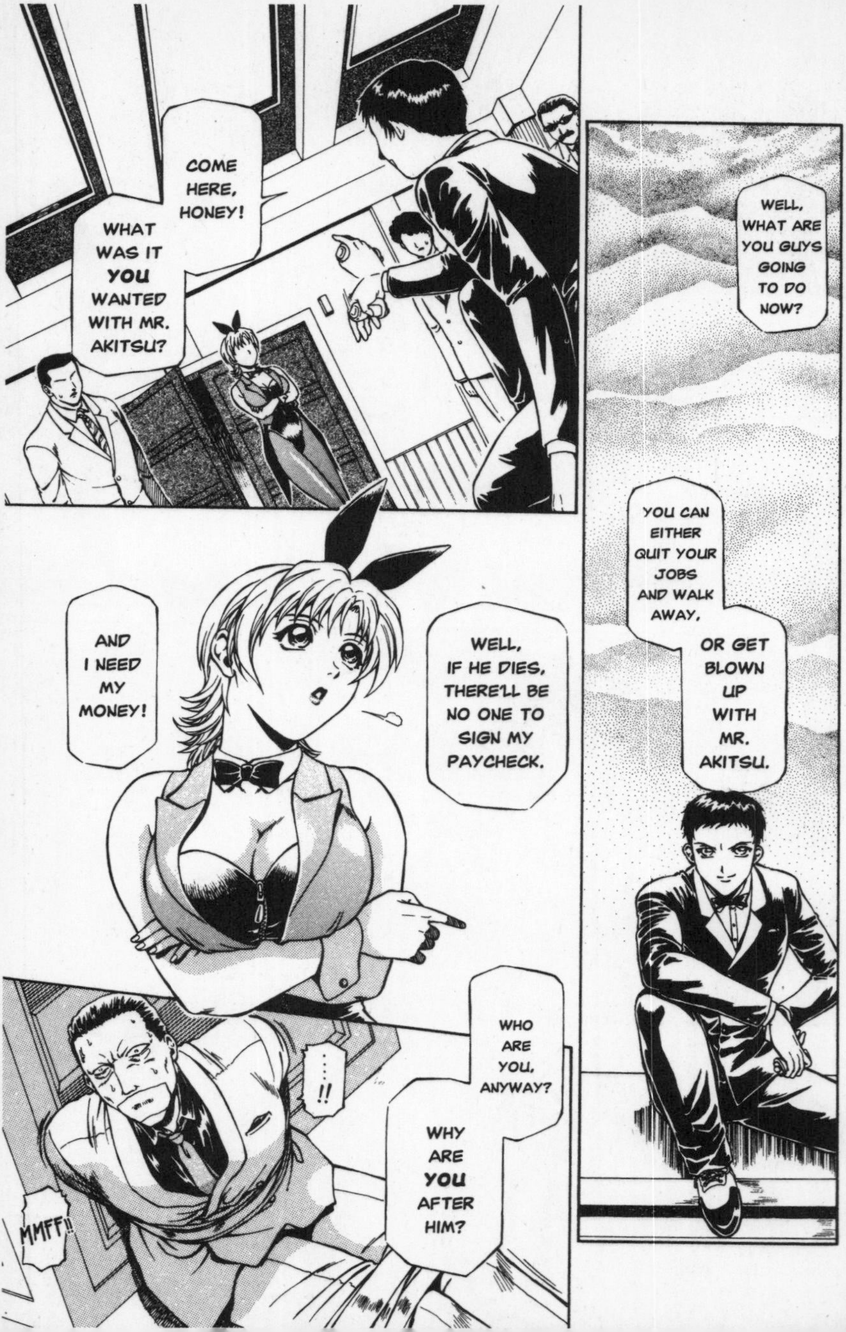
WELL, WHAT ARE YOU GUYS GOING TO DO NOW?
YOU CAN EITHER QUIT YOUR JOBS AND WALK AWAY,
OR GET BLOWN UP WITH MR. AKITSU.
COME HERE, HONEY!
WHAT WAS IT YOU WANTED WITH MR. AKITSU?
WELL, IF HE DIES, THERE'LL BE NO ONE TO SIGN MY PAYCHECK.
AND I NEED MY MONEY!
WHO ARE YOU, ANYWAY?
WHY ARE YOU AFTER HIM?
...!!
MMFF!!

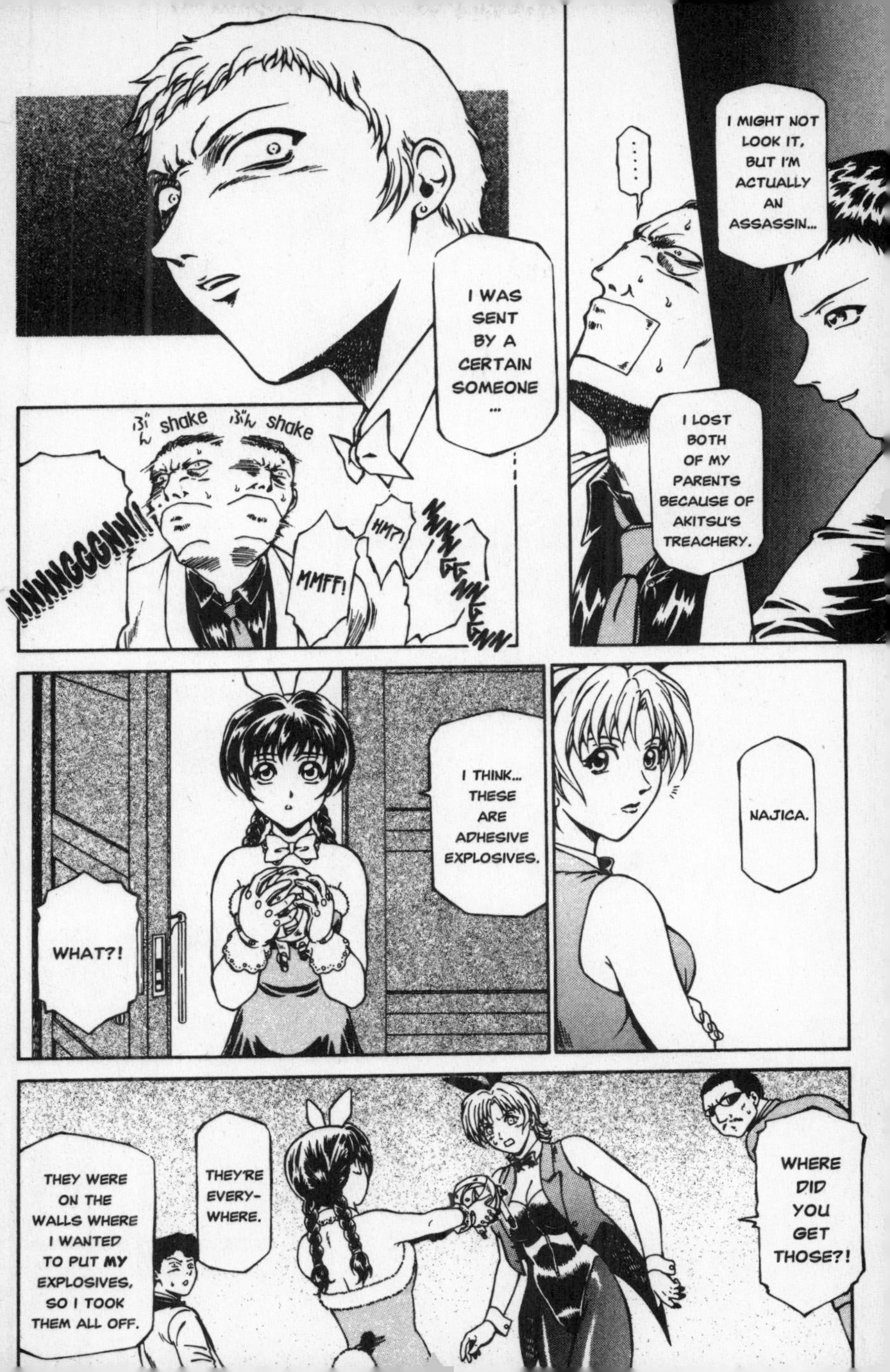
I MIGHT NOT LOOK IT, BUT I'M ACTUALLY AN ASSASSIN...
......
I LOST BOTH OF MY PARENTS BECAUSE OF AKITSU'S TREACHERY.
I WAS SENT BY A CERTAIN SOMEONE ...
ぶん shake ぶん shake
NNNNGGGNN!!
HM?!
MMFF!
NAJICA.
I THINK... THESE ARE ADHESIVE EXPLOSIVES.
WHAT?!
WHERE DID YOU GET THOSE?!
THEY'RE EVERY-WHERE.
THEY WERE ON THE WALLS WHERE I WANTED TO PUT MY EXPLOSIVES, SO I TOOK THEM ALL OFF.

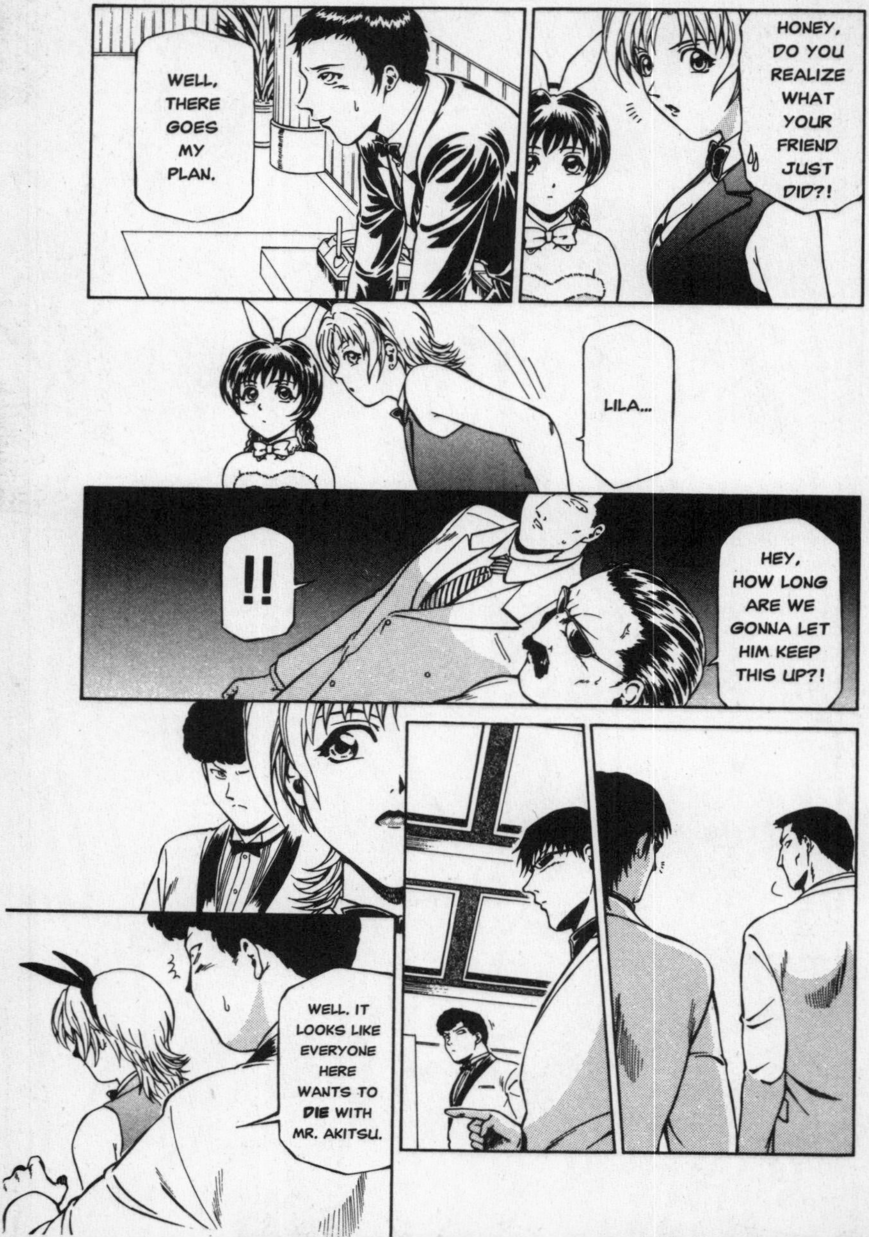
HONEY, DO YOU REALIZE WHAT YOUR FRIEND JUST DID?!
WELL, THERE GOES MY PLAN.
LILA...
HEY, HOW LONG ARE WE GONNA LET HIM KEEP THIS UP?!
!!
WELL, IT LOOKS LIKE EVERYONE HERE WANTS TO DIE WITH MR. AKITSU.

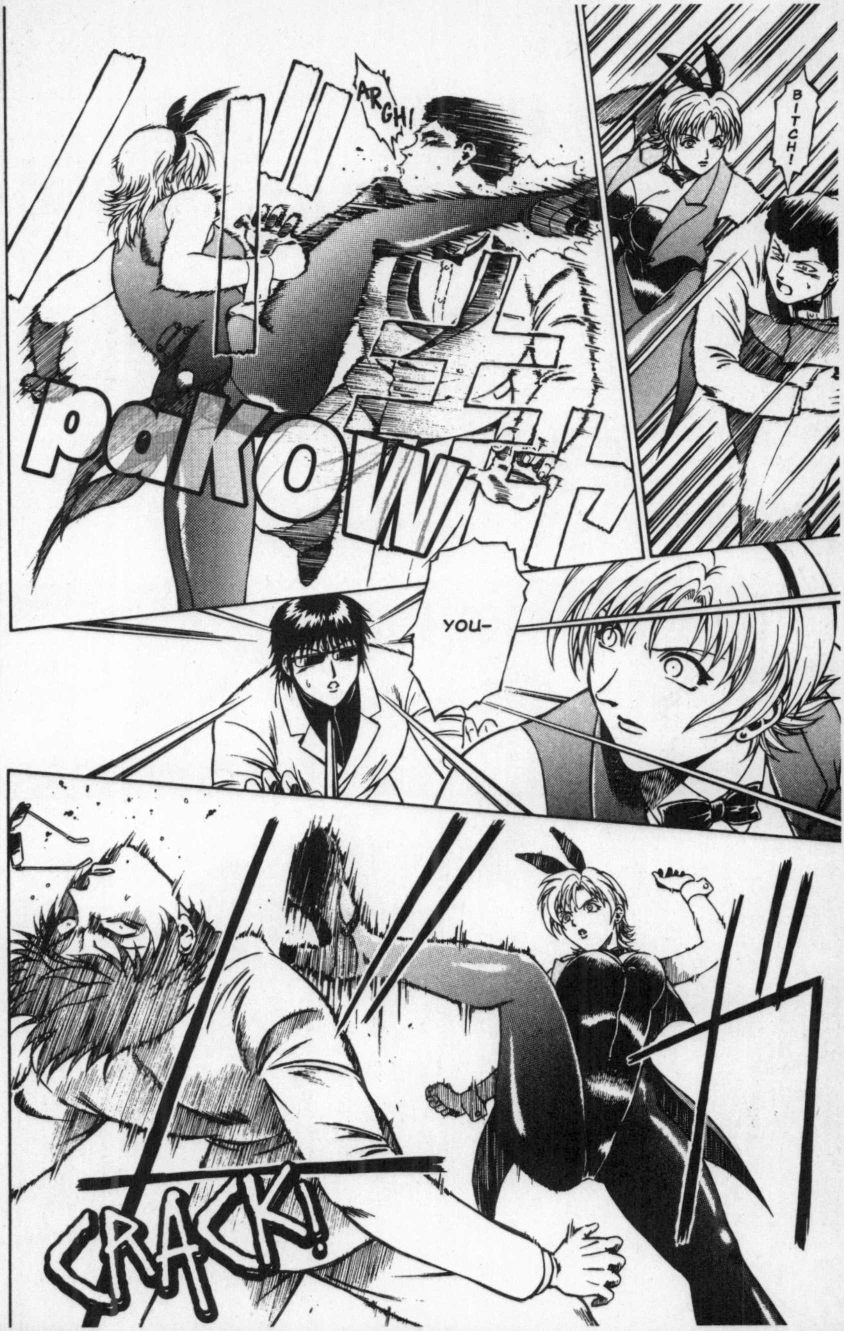

BITCH!
ARGH!
paKOW
YOU-
CRACK!

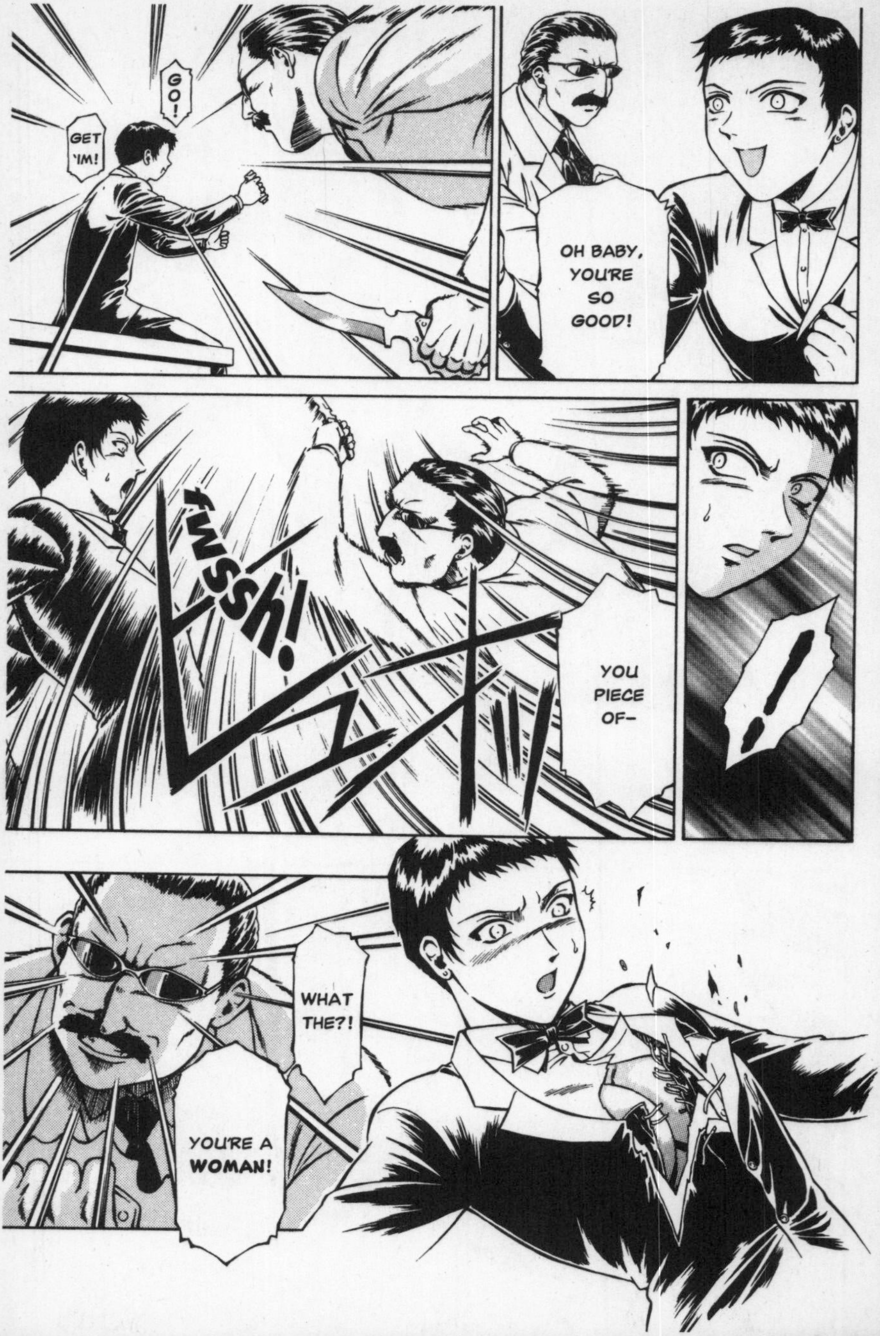
OH BABY, YOU'RE SO GOOD!
GO!
GET 'IM!
!
YOU PIECE OF–
fwssh!
WHAT THE?!
YOU'RE A WOMAN!

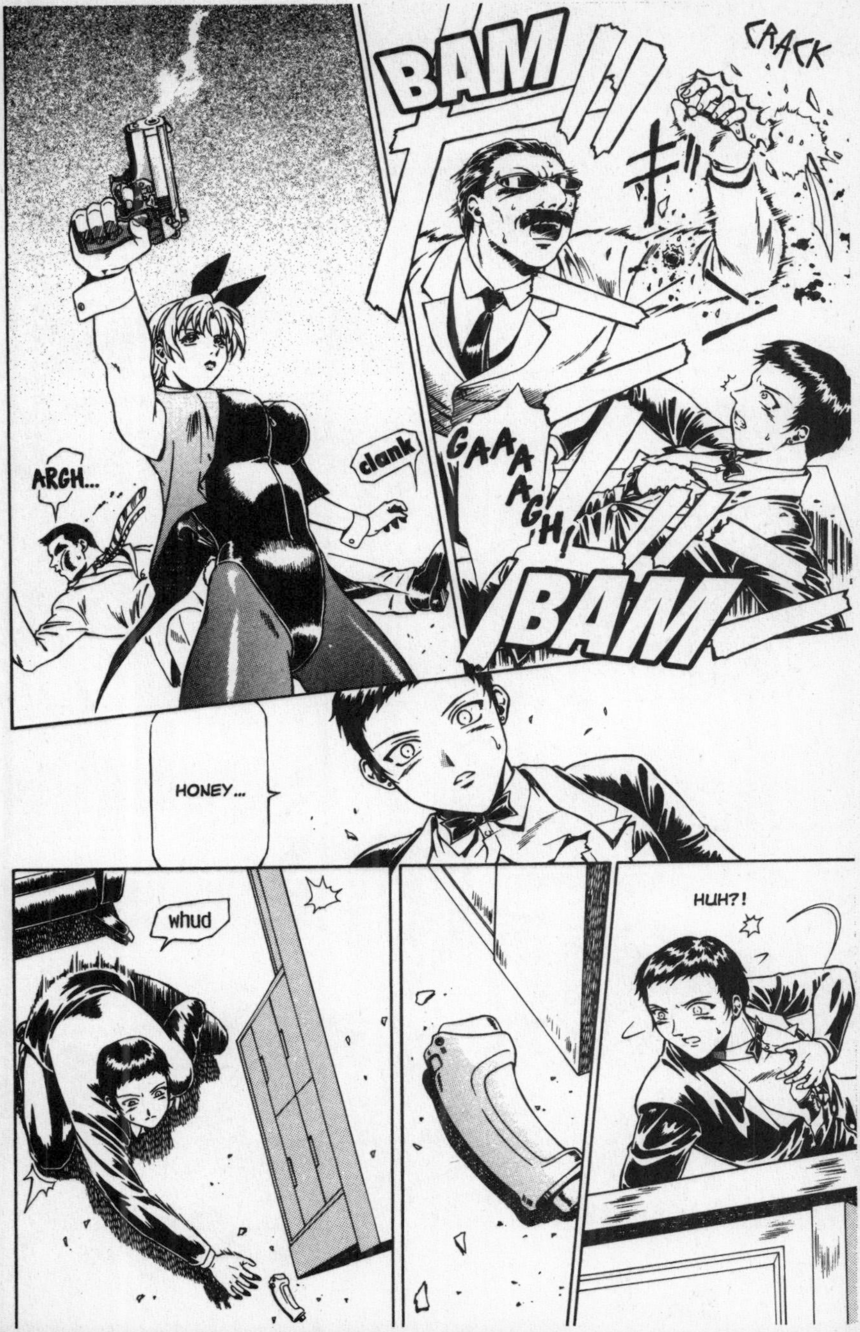
BAM
CRACK
GAAAAGH!
BAM
clank
ARGH...
HONEY...
HUH?!
whud

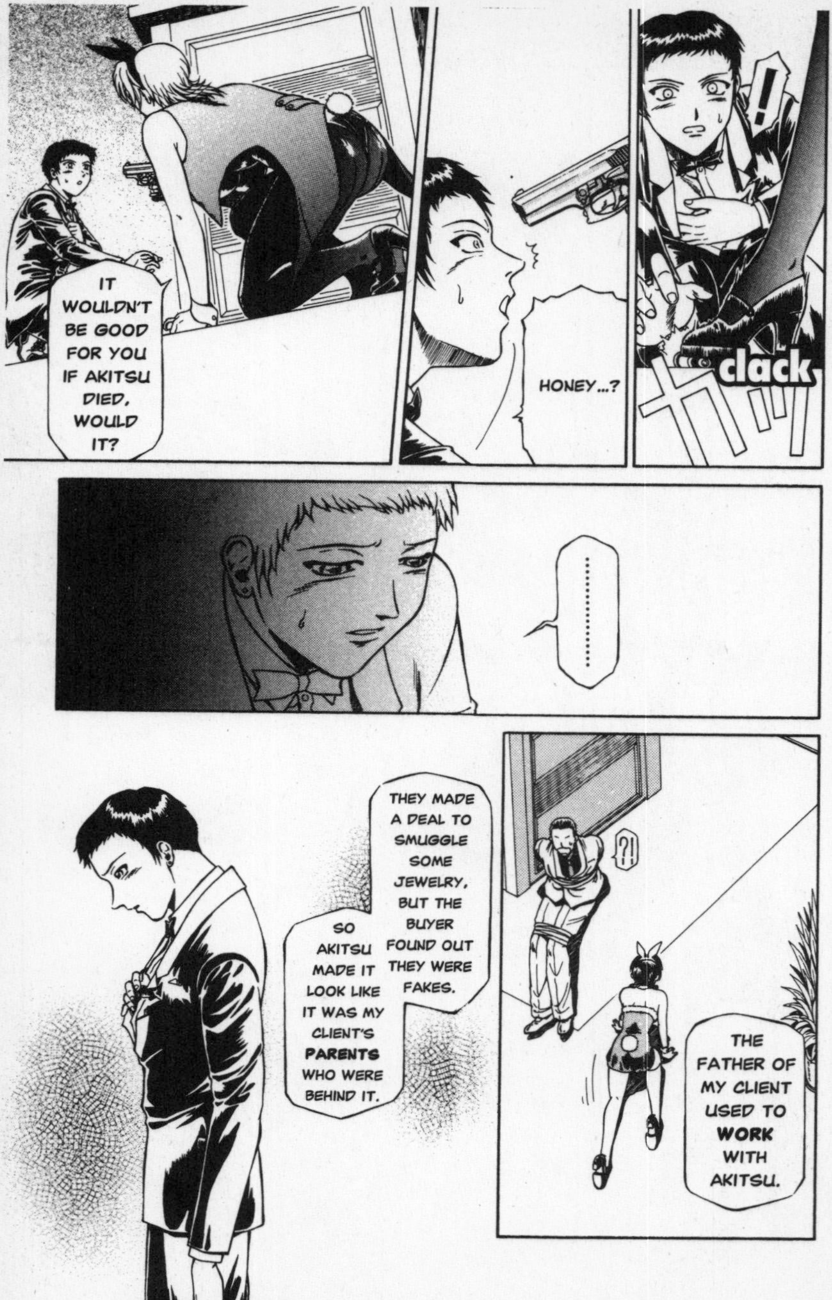
!
clack
HONEY...?
IT WOULDN'T BE GOOD FOR YOU IF AKITSU DIED, WOULD IT?
....
THE FATHER OF MY CLIENT USED TO **WORK** WITH AKITSU.
?!
THEY MADE A DEAL TO SMUGGLE SOME JEWELRY, BUT THE BUYER FOUND OUT THEY WERE FAKES.
SO AKITSU MADE IT LOOK LIKE IT WAS MY CLIENT'S **PARENTS** WHO WERE BEHIND IT.

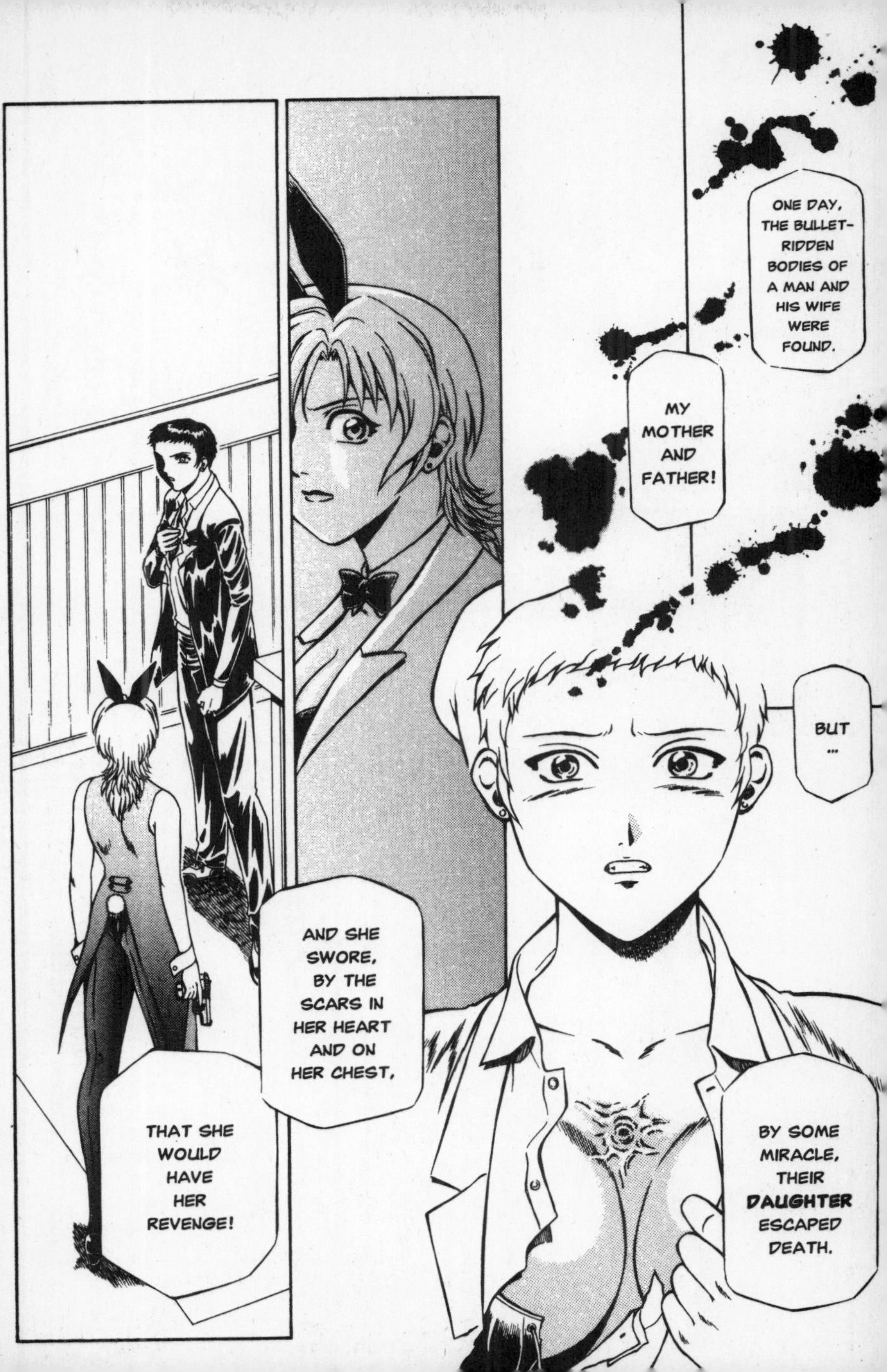
ONE DAY, THE BULLET-RIDDEN BODIES OF A MAN AND HIS WIFE WERE FOUND.
MY MOTHER AND FATHER!
BUT ...
BY SOME MIRACLE, THEIR **DAUGHTER** ESCAPED DEATH.
AND SHE SWORE, BY THE SCARS IN HER HEART AND ON HER CHEST,
THAT SHE WOULD HAVE HER REVENGE!

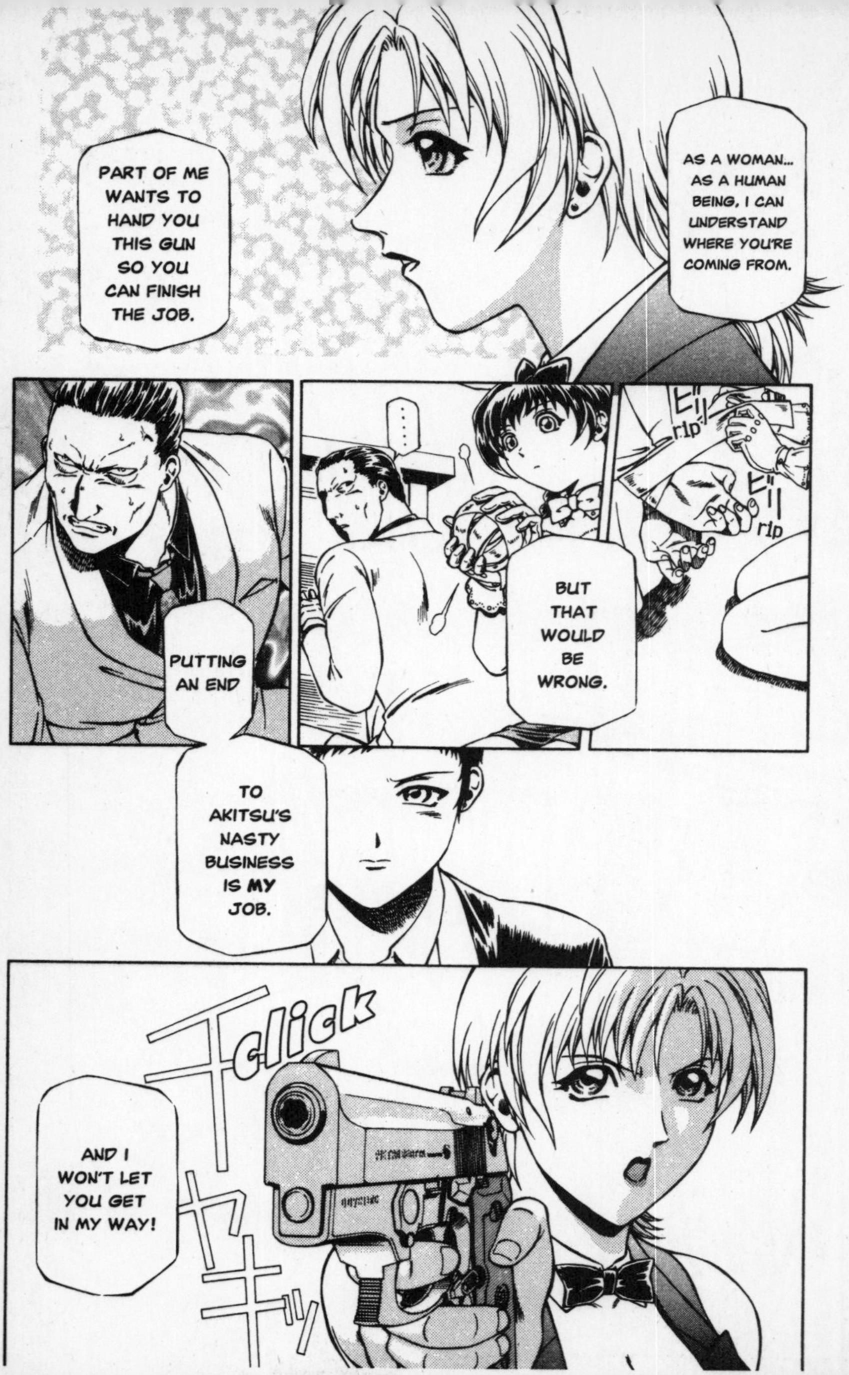
AS A WOMAN... AS A HUMAN BEING, I CAN UNDERSTAND WHERE YOU'RE COMING FROM.
PART OF ME WANTS TO HAND YOU THIS GUN SO YOU CAN FINISH THE JOB.
ビリ rip
ビリ rip
.....
BUT THAT WOULD BE WRONG.
PUTTING AN END
TO AKITSU'S NASTY BUSINESS IS MY JOB.
click
AND I WON'T LET YOU GET IN MY WAY!

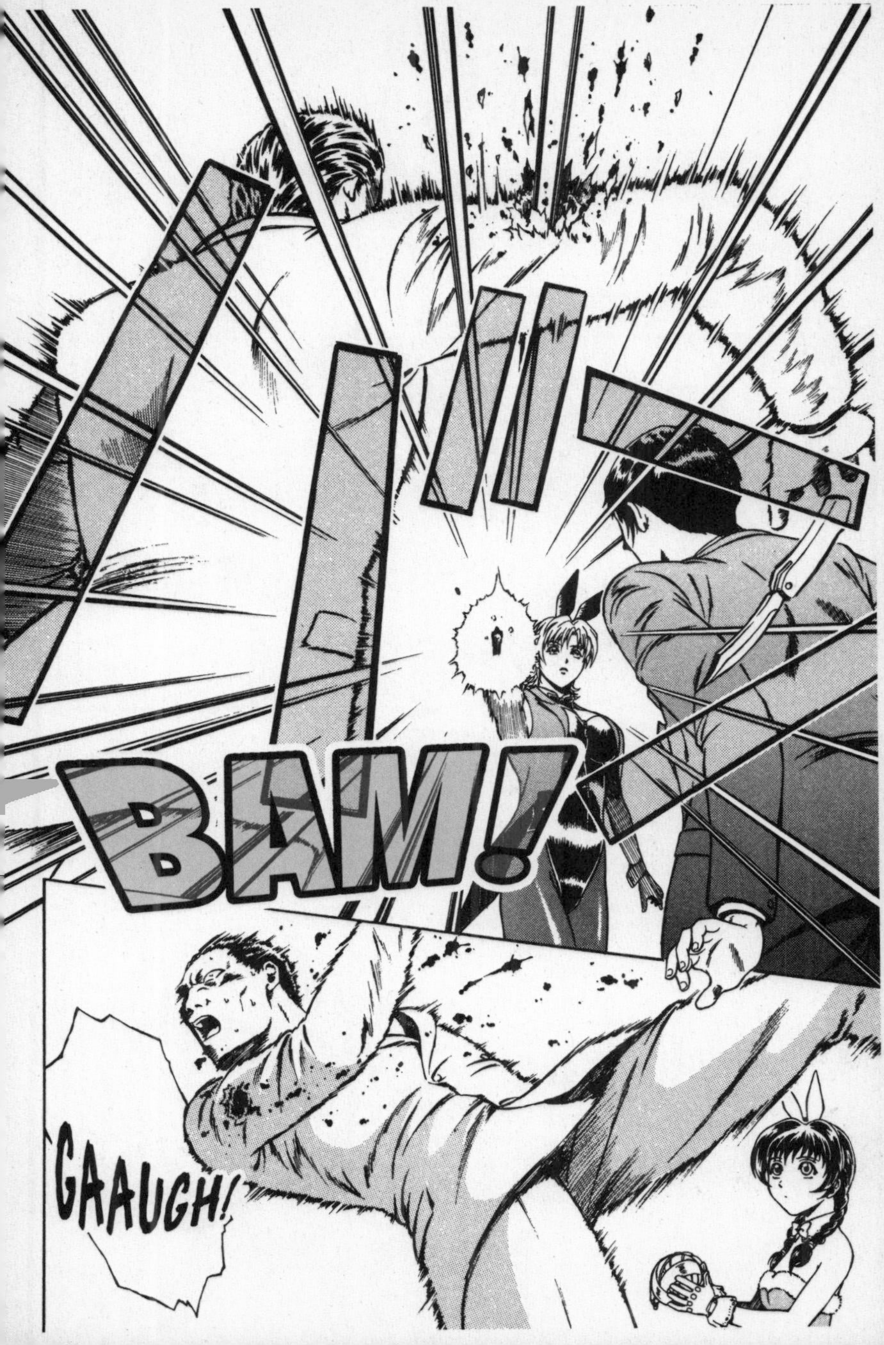
BAM!
GRAUGH!

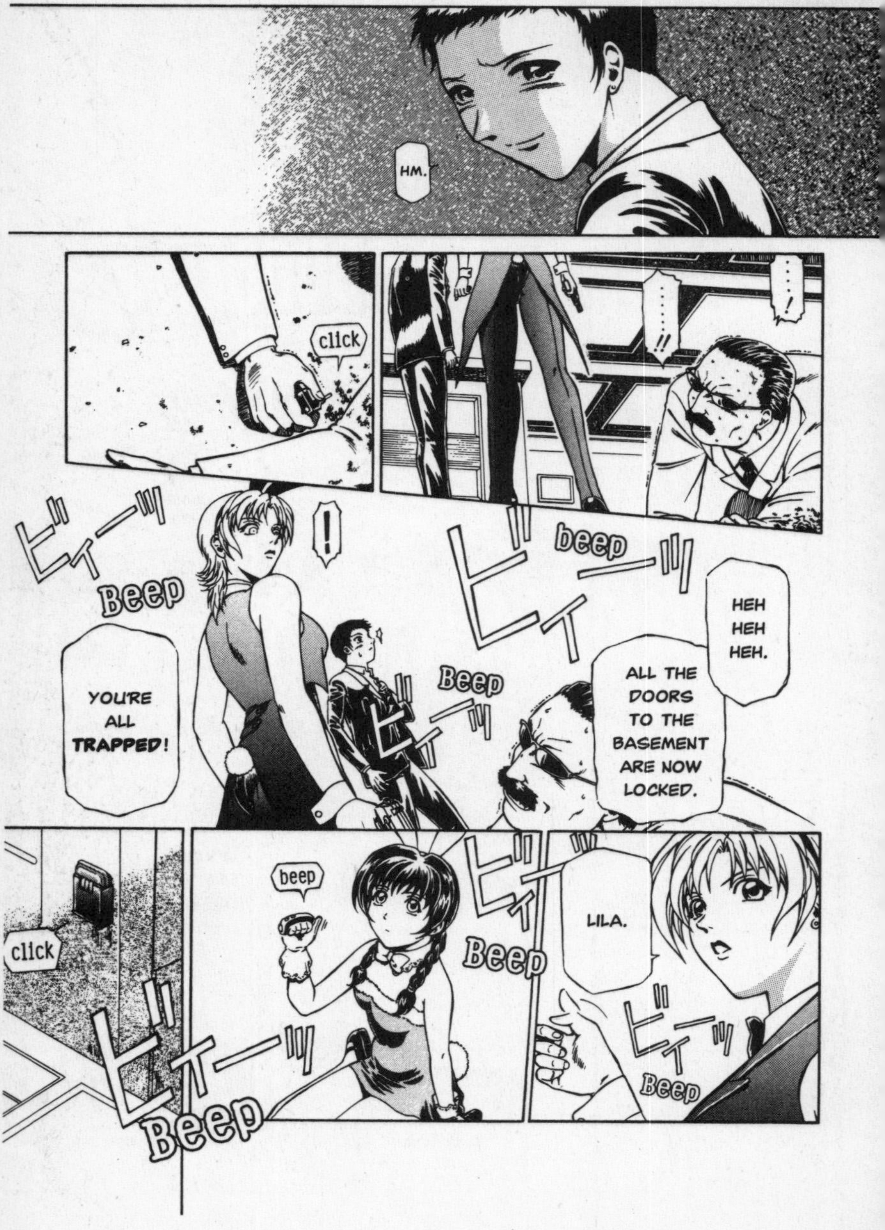

HM.
......!
......!!
click
beep
ビィーッ
HEH HEH HEH.
ALL THE DOORS TO THE BASEMENT ARE NOW LOCKED.
Beep
ビィーッ
YOU'RE ALL TRAPPED!
!
ビィーッ
Beep
LILA.
ビィーッ
Beep
ビィーッ
Beep
beep
click
ビィーッ
Beep

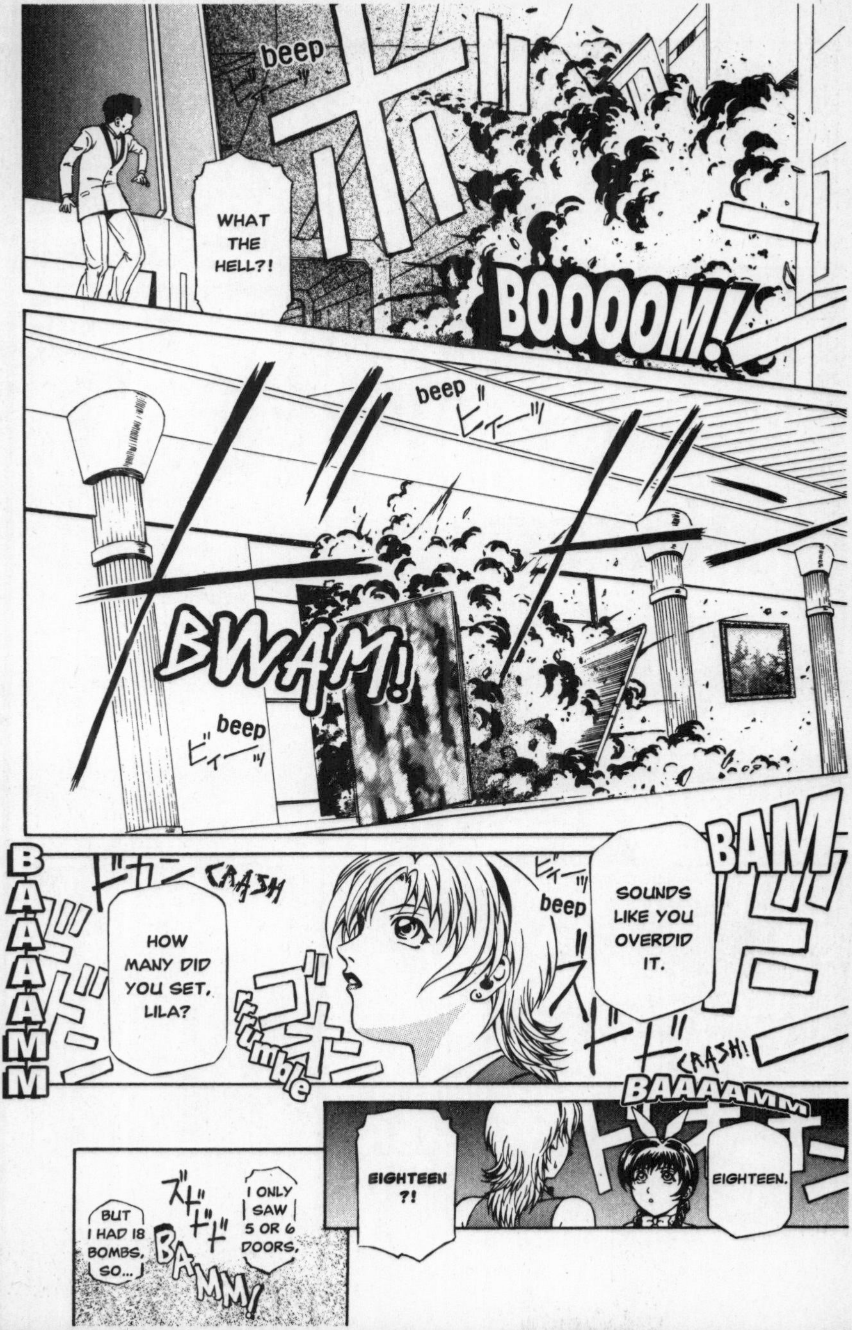

beep
ビィーッ
WHAT THE HELL?!
BOOOOM!
beep
ビィーッ
BWAM!
beep
ビィーッ
BAM
SOUNDS LIKE YOU OVERDID IT.
beep
ビィーッ
CRASH!
rrumble
HOW MANY DID YOU SET, LILA?
CRASH
BAAAAAMM
BAAAAMM
EIGHTEEN.
EIGHTEEN ?!
I ONLY SAW 5 OR 6 DOORS,
BUT I HAD 18 BOMBS, SO...
BAMM!

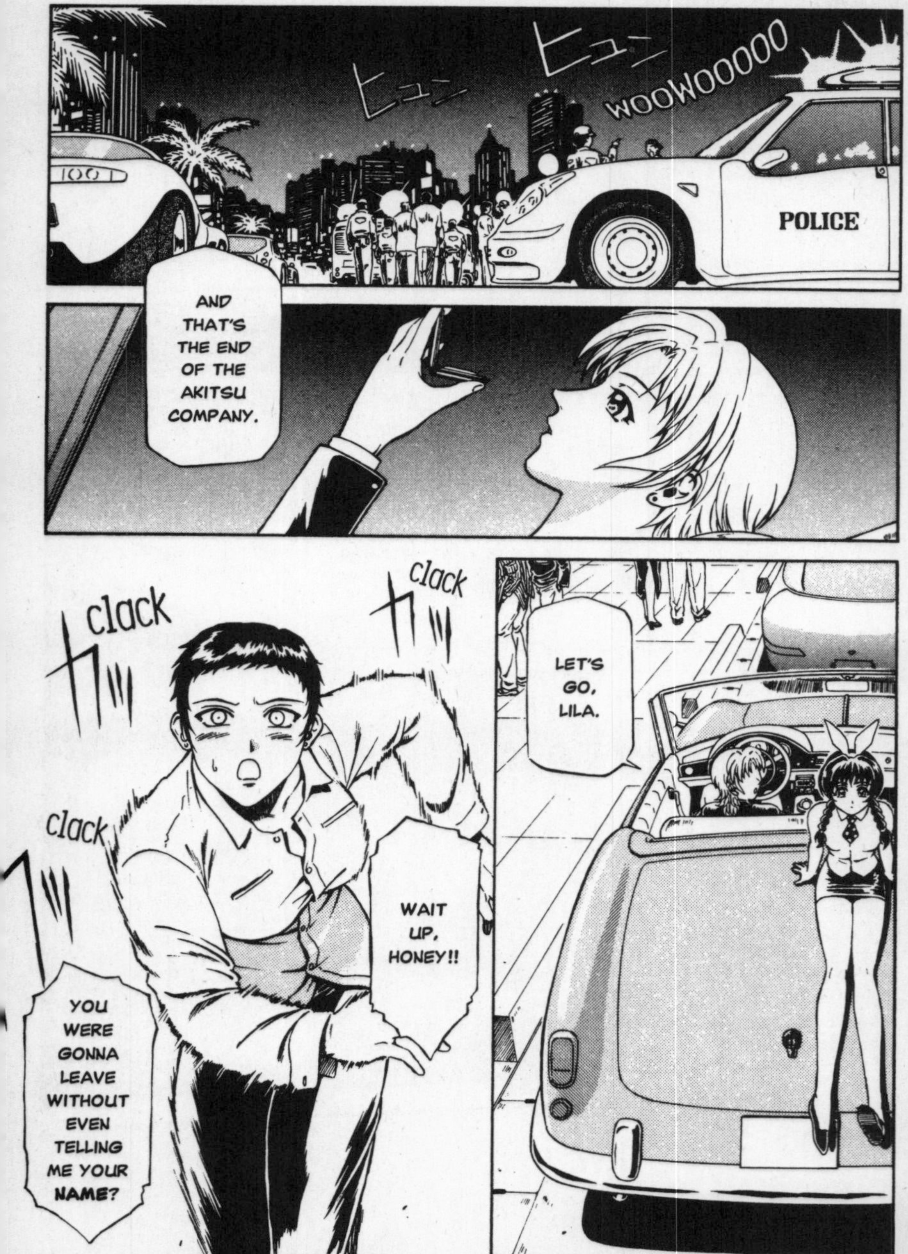

WOOWOOOOOO
POLICE
AND THAT'S THE END OF THE AKITSU COMPANY.
LET'S GO, LILA.
clack
clack
clack
WAIT UP, HONEY!!
YOU WERE GONNA LEAVE WITHOUT EVEN TELLING ME YOUR NAME?

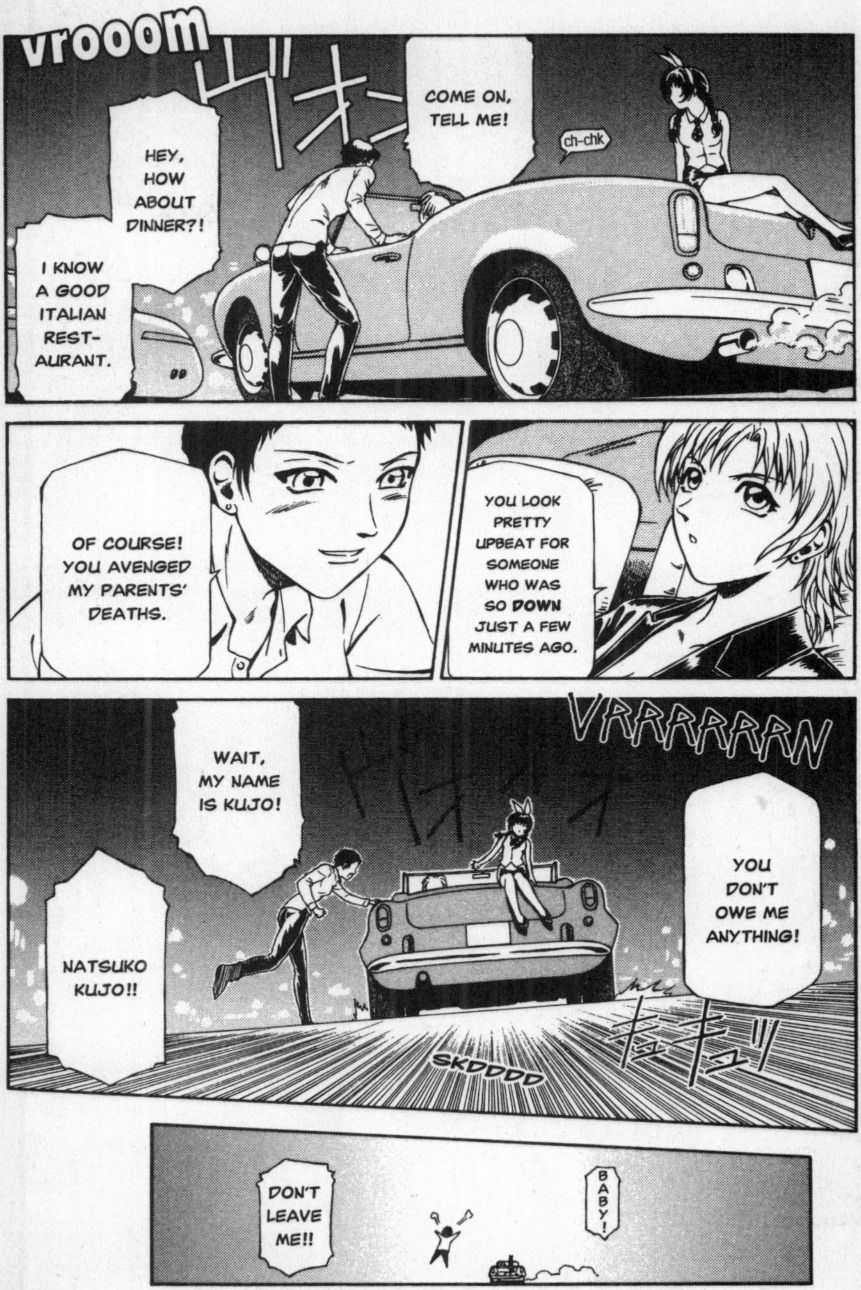
ch-chk
COME ON, TELL ME!
vrooom
HEY, HOW ABOUT DINNER?!
I KNOW A GOOD ITALIAN REST-AURANT.
YOU LOOK PRETTY UPBEAT FOR SOMEONE WHO WAS SO **DOWN** JUST A FEW MINUTES AGO.
OF COURSE! YOU AVENGED MY PARENTS' DEATHS.
VRRRRRRRN
YOU DON'T OWE ME ANYTHING!
WAIT, MY NAME IS KUJO!
NATSUKO KUJO!!
SKDDDDD
BABY!
DON'T LEAVE ME!!

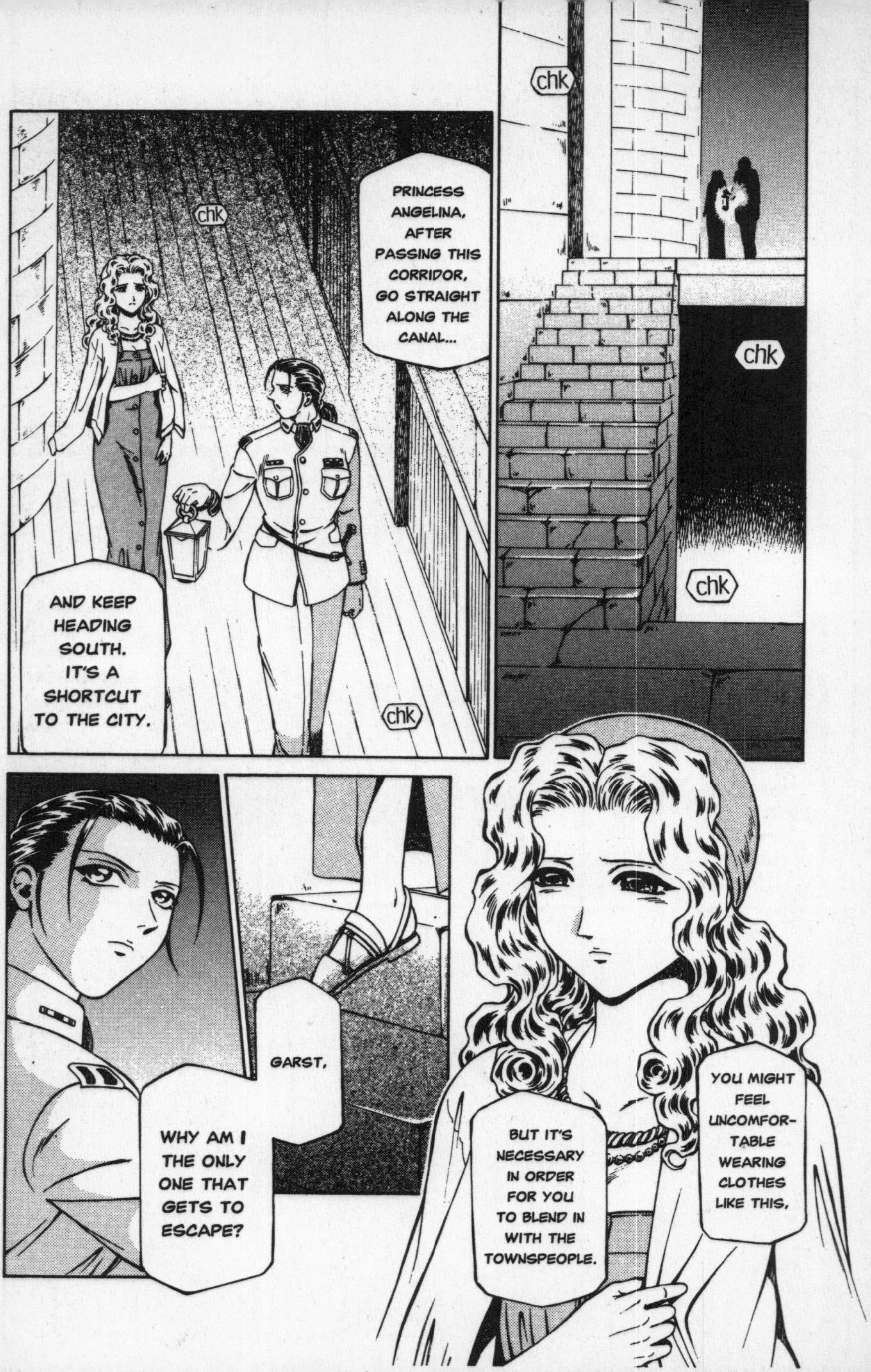
chk
chk
chk
PRINCESS ANGELINA, AFTER PASSING THIS CORRIDOR, GO STRAIGHT ALONG THE CANAL...
chk
AND KEEP HEADING SOUTH. IT'S A SHORTCUT TO THE CITY.
chk
YOU MIGHT FEEL UNCOMFOR-TABLE WEARING CLOTHES LIKE THIS,
BUT IT'S NECESSARY IN ORDER FOR YOU TO BLEND IN WITH THE TOWNSPEOPLE.
GARST,
WHY AM I THE ONLY ONE THAT GETS TO ESCAPE?

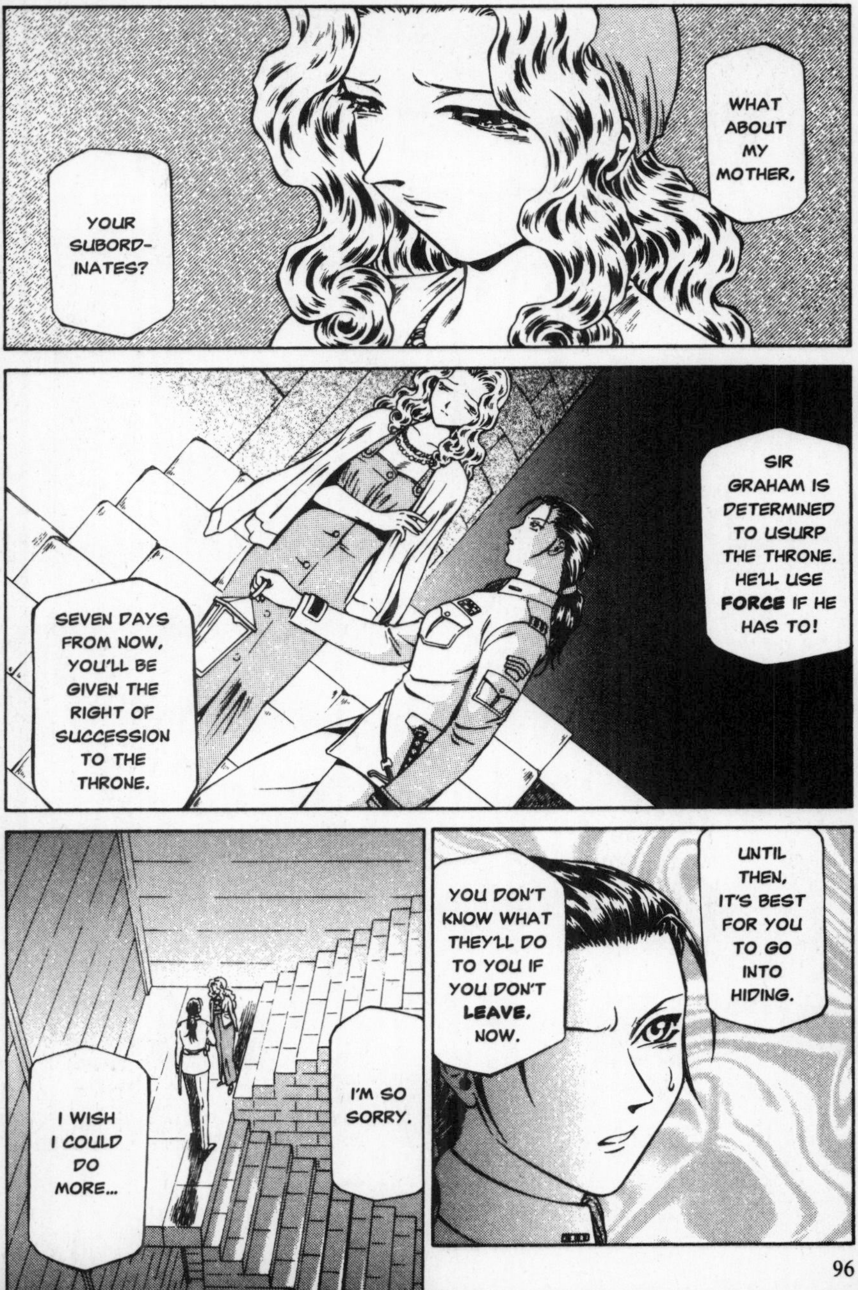
WHAT ABOUT MY MOTHER,
YOUR SUBORD-INATES?
SIR GRAHAM IS DETERMINED TO USURP THE THRONE. HE'LL USE **FORCE** IF HE HAS TO!
SEVEN DAYS FROM NOW, YOU'LL BE GIVEN THE RIGHT OF SUCCESSION TO THE THRONE.
UNTIL THEN, IT'S BEST FOR YOU TO GO INTO HIDING.
YOU DON'T KNOW WHAT THEY'LL DO TO YOU IF YOU DON'T **LEAVE**, NOW.
I'M SO SORRY.
I WISH I COULD DO MORE...

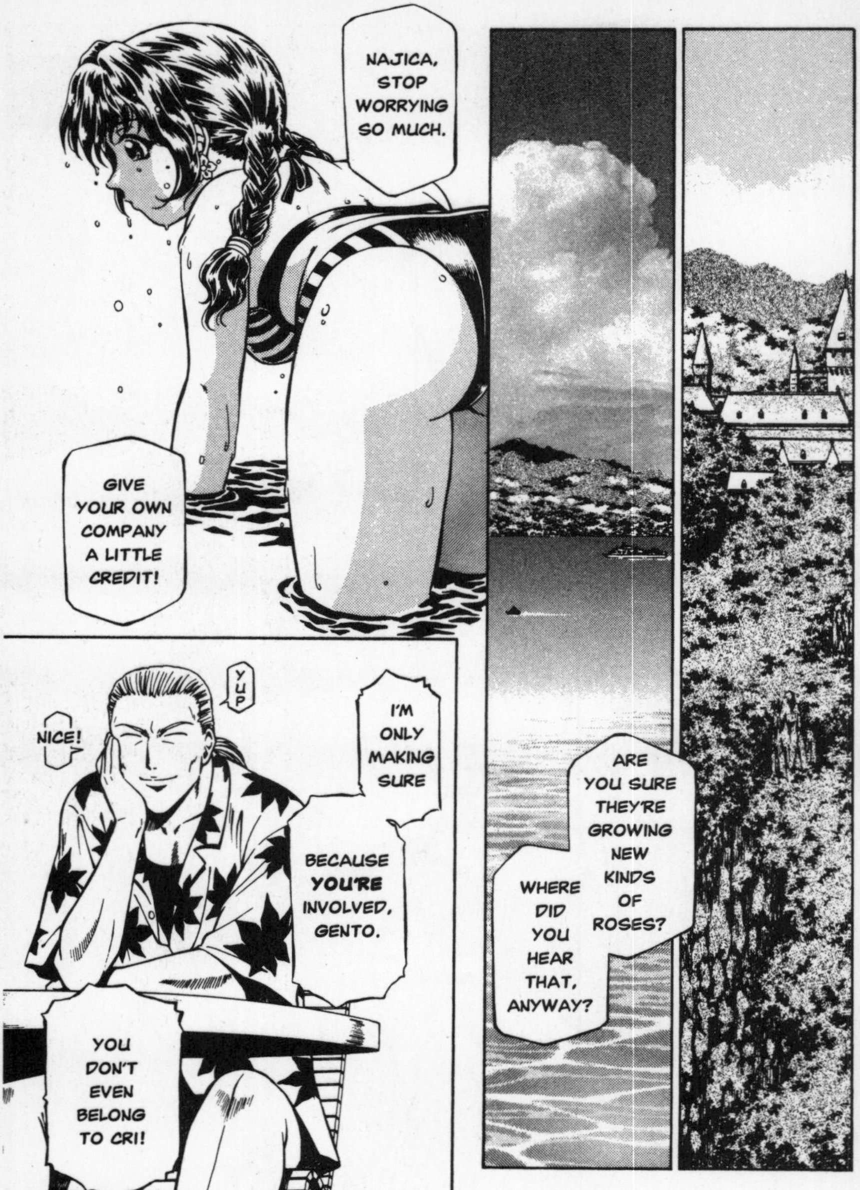
ARE YOU SURE THEY'RE GROWING NEW KINDS OF ROSES?
WHERE DID YOU HEAR THAT, ANYWAY?
NAJICA, STOP WORRYING SO MUCH.
GIVE YOUR OWN COMPANY A LITTLE CREDIT!
I'M ONLY MAKING SURE
BECAUSE YOU'RE INVOLVED, GENTO.
YUP
NICE!
YOU DON'T EVEN BELONG TO CRI!

Operation.4
THE LAND OF ROSES

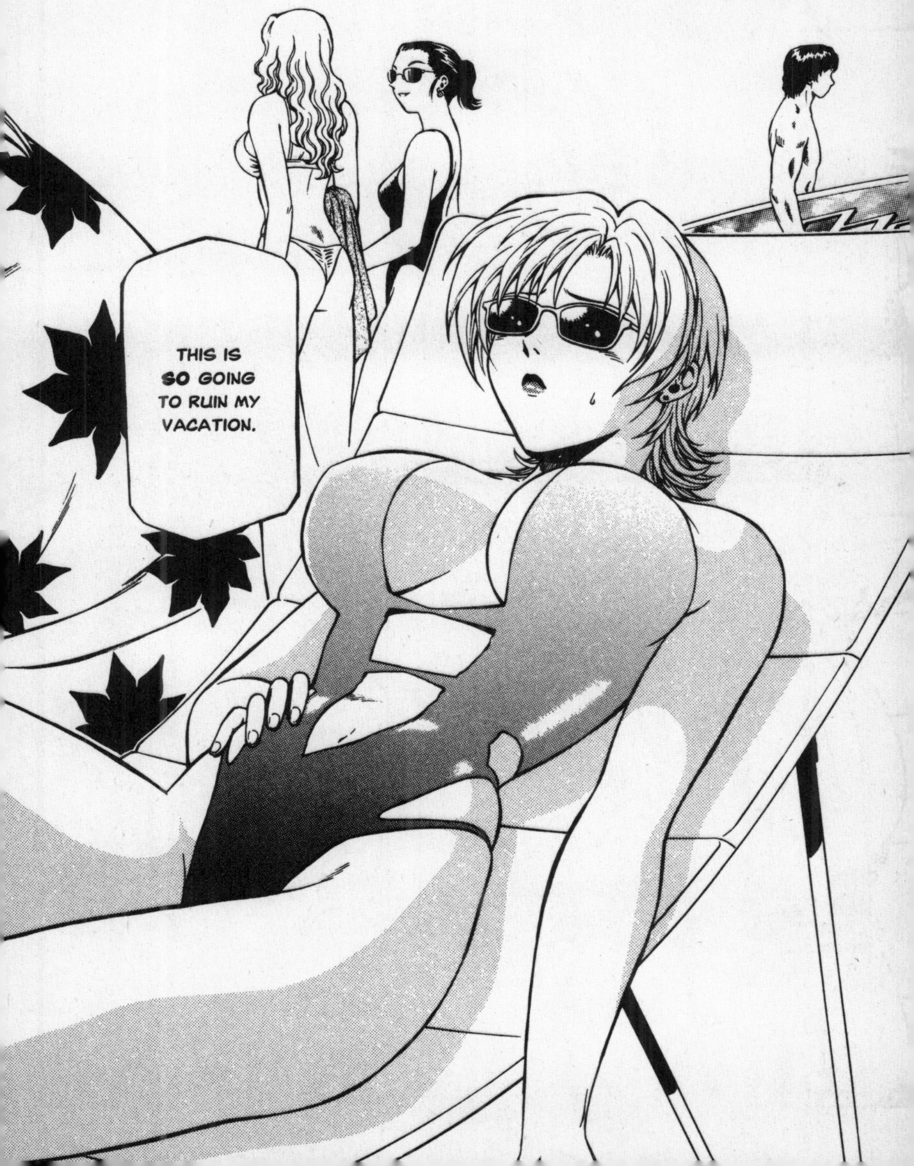
THIS IS SO GOING TO RUIN MY VACATION.

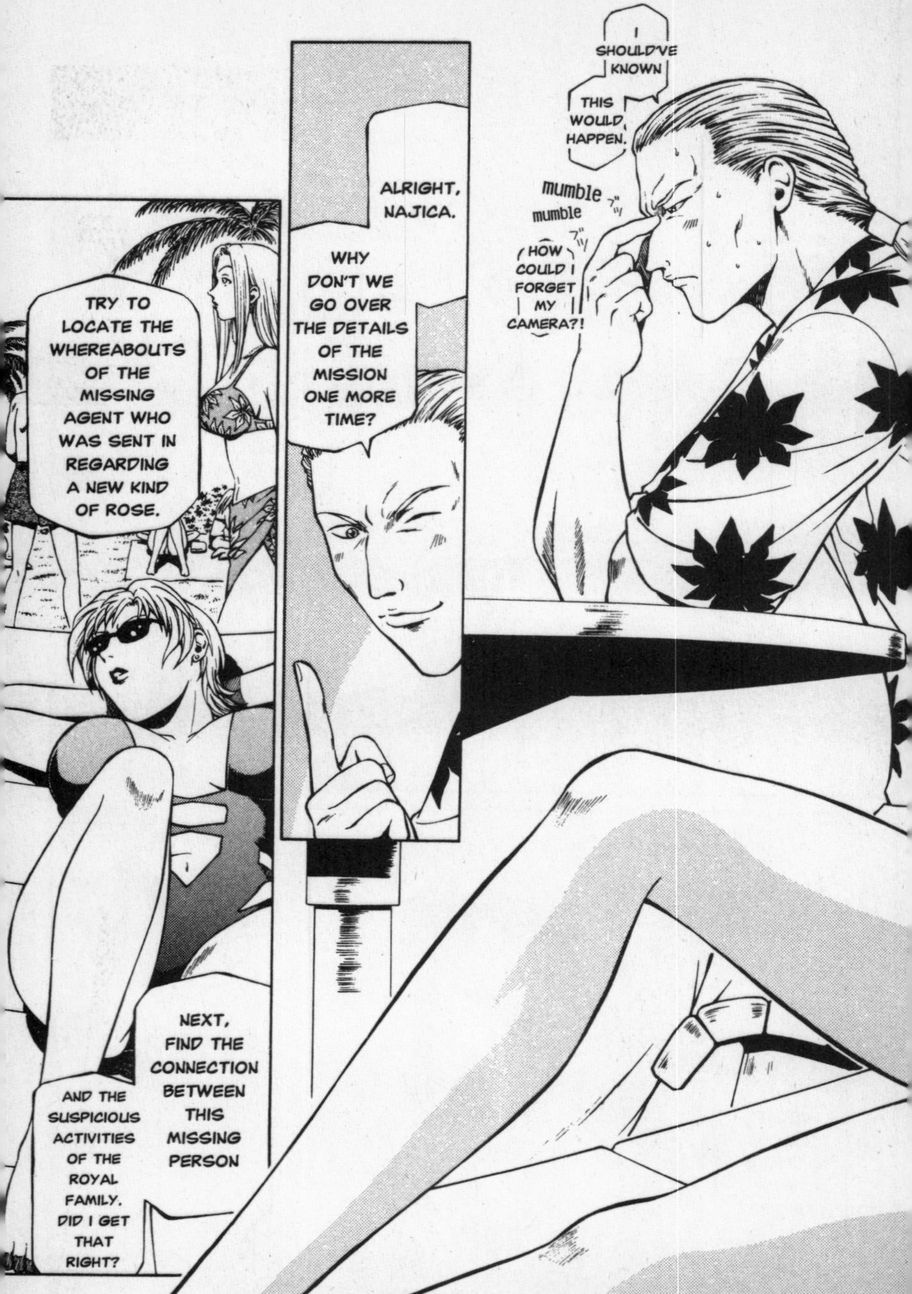
I SHOULD'VE KNOWN
THIS WOULD HAPPEN.
mumble
mumble
HOW COULD I FORGET MY CAMERA?!
ALRIGHT, NAJICA.
WHY DON'T WE GO OVER THE DETAILS OF THE MISSION ONE MORE TIME?
TRY TO LOCATE THE WHEREABOUTS OF THE MISSING AGENT WHO WAS SENT IN REGARDING A NEW KIND OF ROSE.
NEXT, FIND THE CONNECTION BETWEEN THIS MISSING PERSON
AND THE SUSPICIOUS ACTIVITIES OF THE ROYAL FAMILY. DID I GET THAT RIGHT?

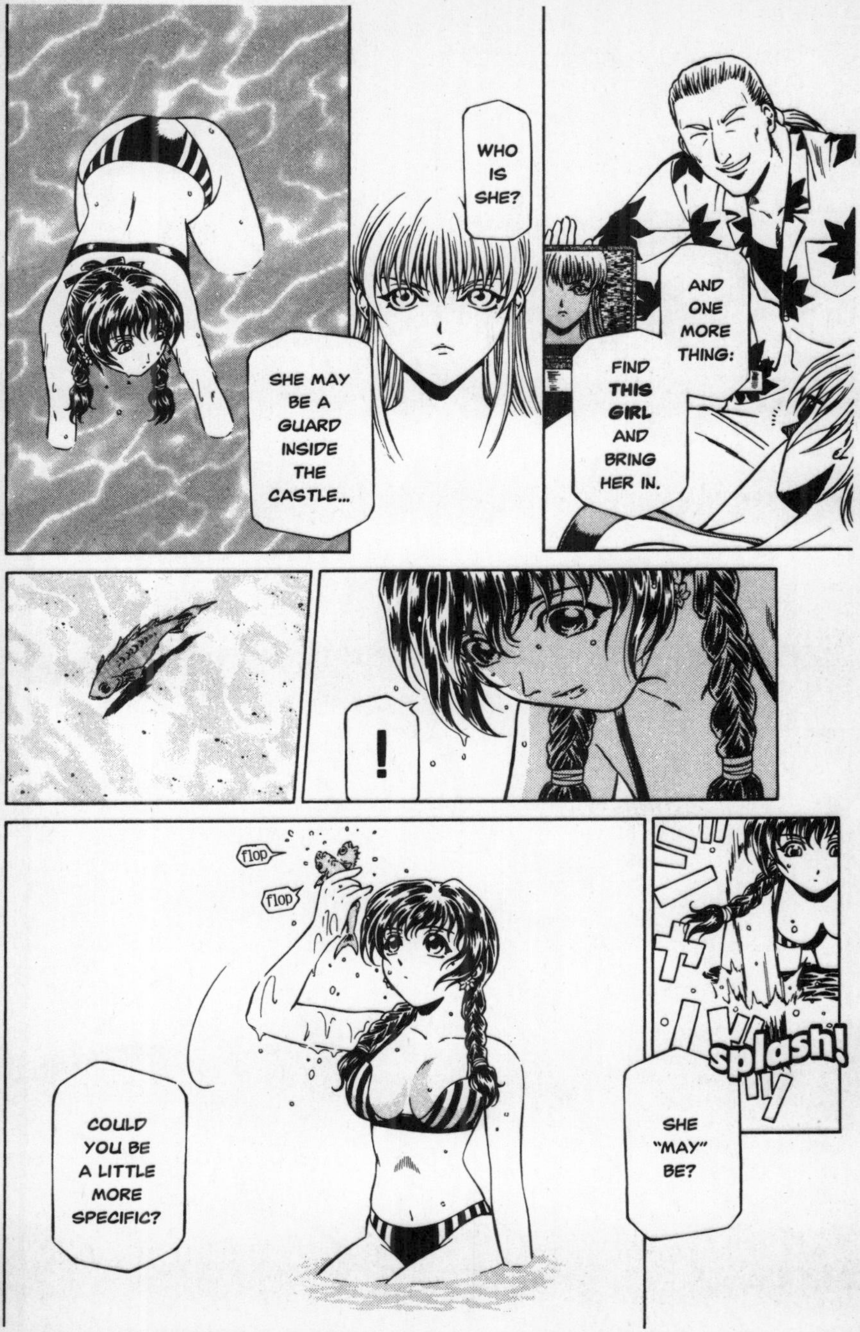
AND ONE MORE THING:
FIND THIS GIRL AND BRING HER IN.
WHO IS SHE?
SHE MAY BE A GUARD INSIDE THE CASTLE...
!
splash!
SHE "MAY" BE?
flop
flop
COULD YOU BE A LITTLE MORE SPECIFIC?

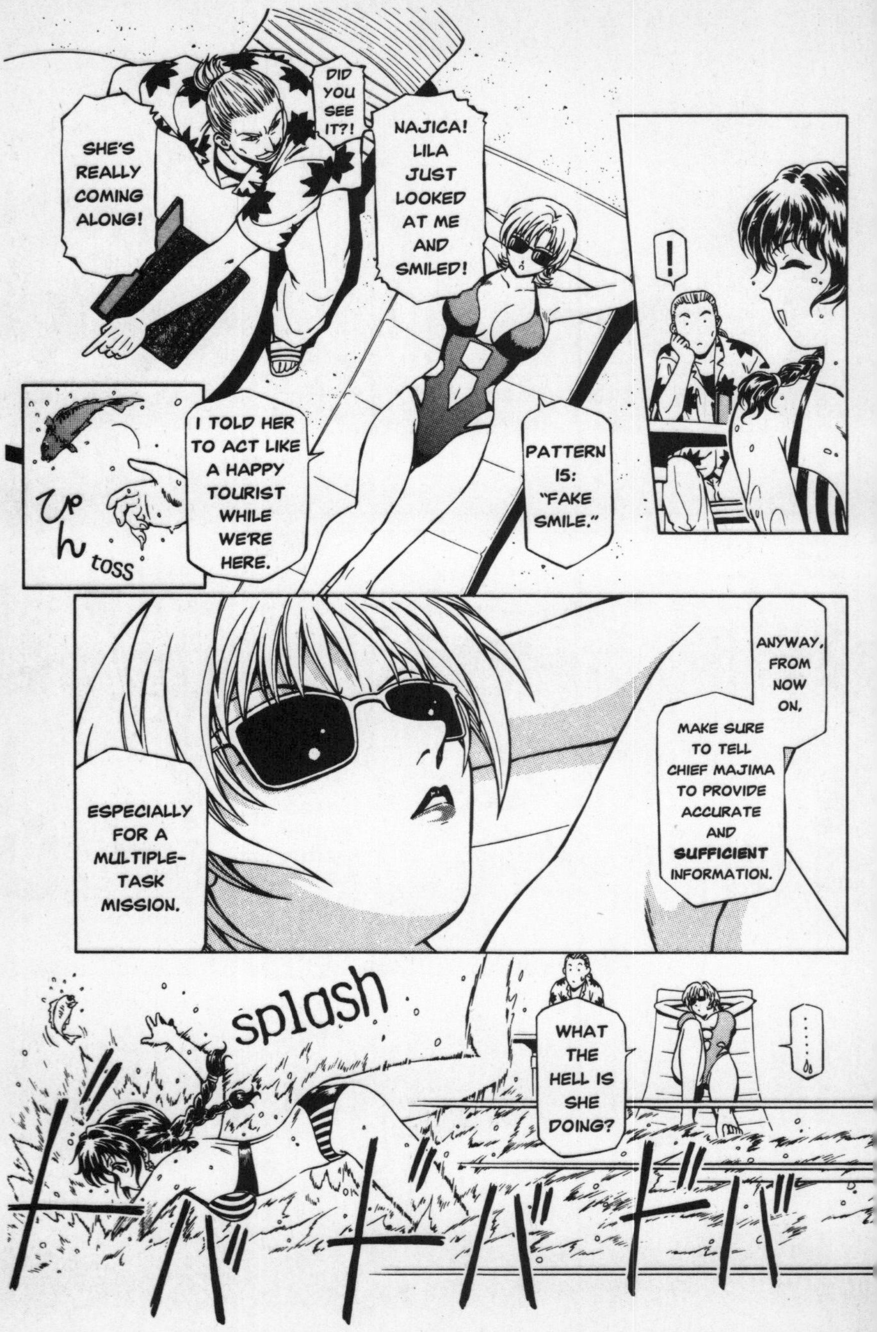
!
NAJICA! LILA JUST LOOKED AT ME AND SMILED!
DID YOU SEE IT?!
SHE'S REALLY COMING ALONG!
PATTERN IS: "FAKE SMILE."
I TOLD HER TO ACT LIKE A HAPPY TOURIST WHILE WE'RE HERE.
toss
ANYWAY, FROM NOW ON,
MAKE SURE TO TELL CHIEF MAJIMA TO PROVIDE ACCURATE AND SUFFICIENT INFORMATION.
ESPECIALLY FOR A MULTIPLE-TASK MISSION.
......
WHAT THE HELL IS SHE DOING?
splash

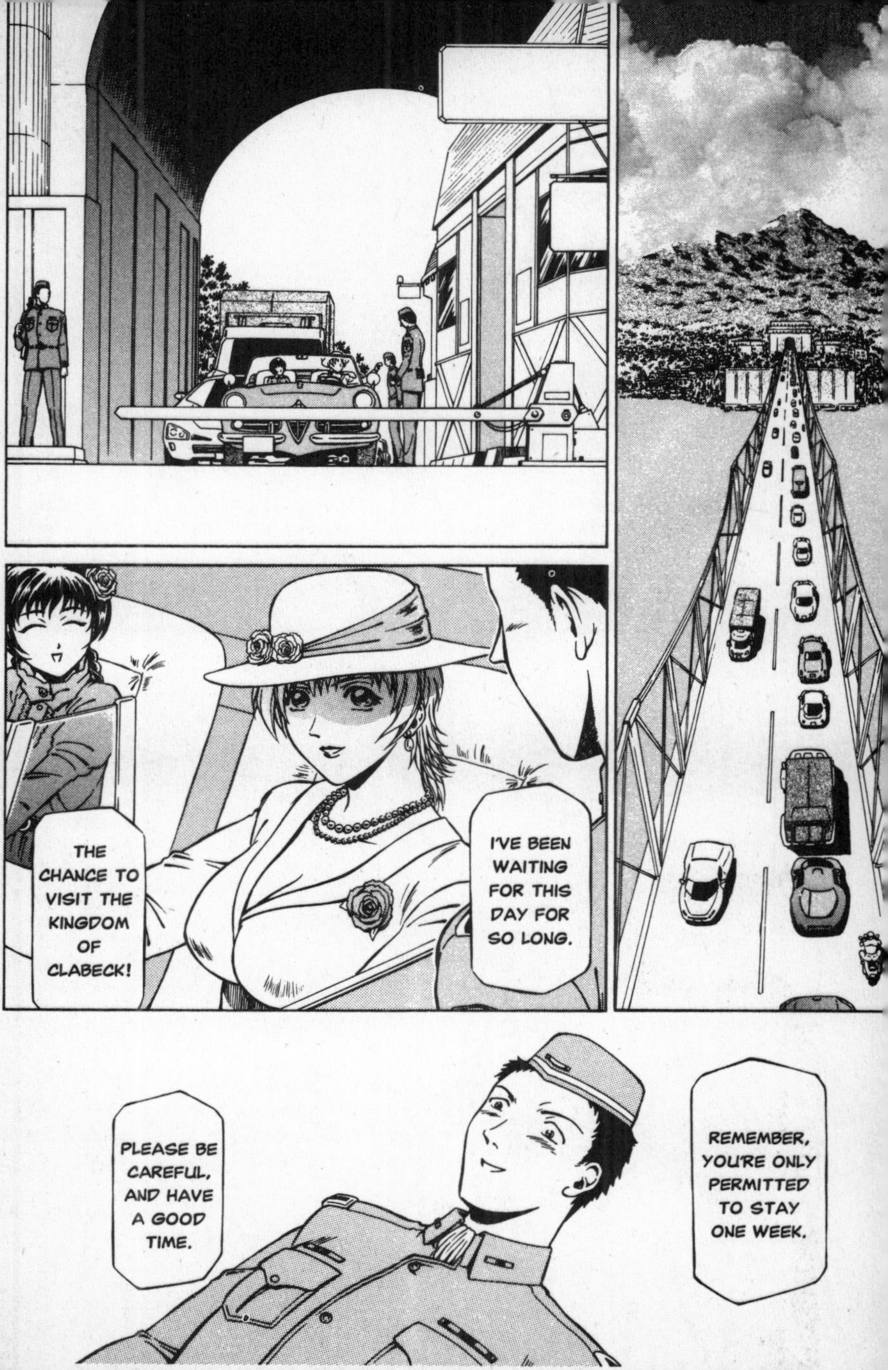
I'VE BEEN WAITING FOR THIS DAY FOR SO LONG.
THE CHANCE TO VISIT THE KINGDOM OF CLABECK!
REMEMBER, YOU'RE ONLY PERMITTED TO STAY ONE WEEK.
PLEASE BE CAREFUL, AND HAVE A GOOD TIME.

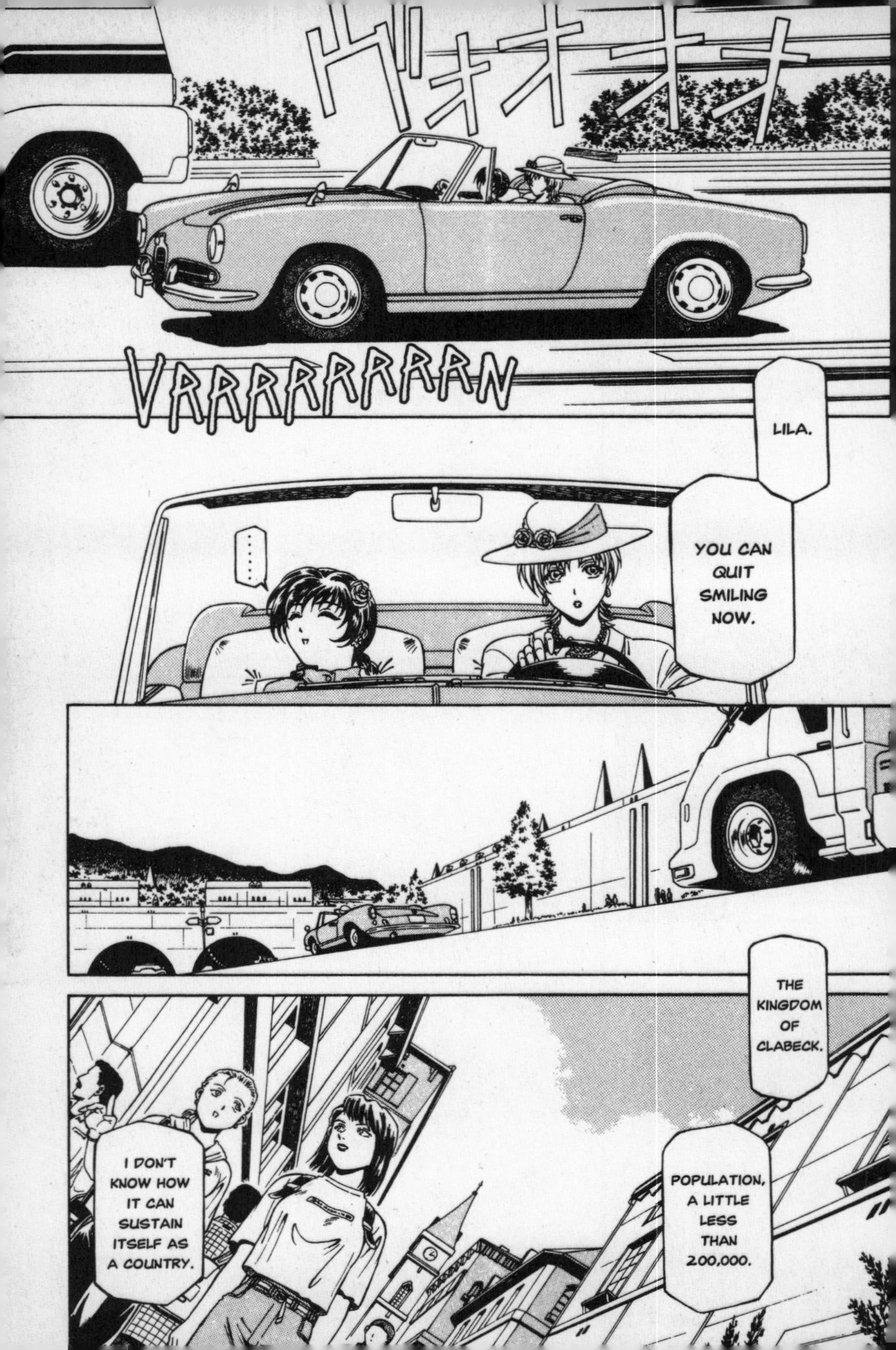
VRRRRRRRRN
LILA.
YOU CAN QUIT SMILING NOW.
......
THE KINGDOM OF CLABECK.
POPULATION, A LITTLE LESS THAN 200,000.
I DON'T KNOW HOW IT CAN SUSTAIN ITSELF AS A COUNTRY.

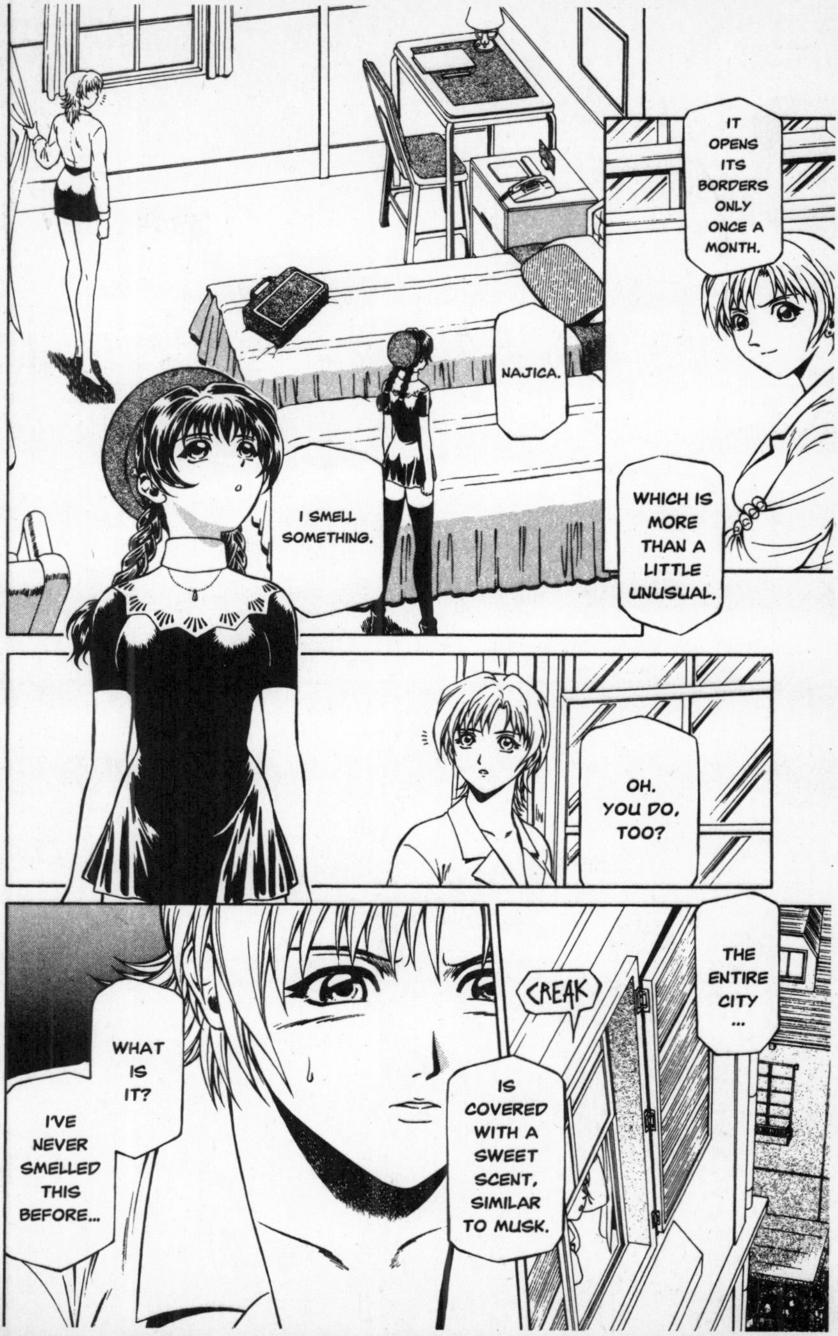
IT OPENS ITS BORDERS ONLY ONCE A MONTH.
WHICH IS MORE THAN A LITTLE UNUSUAL.
NAJICA.
I SMELL SOMETHING.
OH. YOU DO, TOO?
THE ENTIRE CITY ...
CREAK
IS COVERED WITH A SWEET SCENT, SIMILAR TO MUSK.
WHAT IS IT?
I'VE NEVER SMELLED THIS BEFORE...

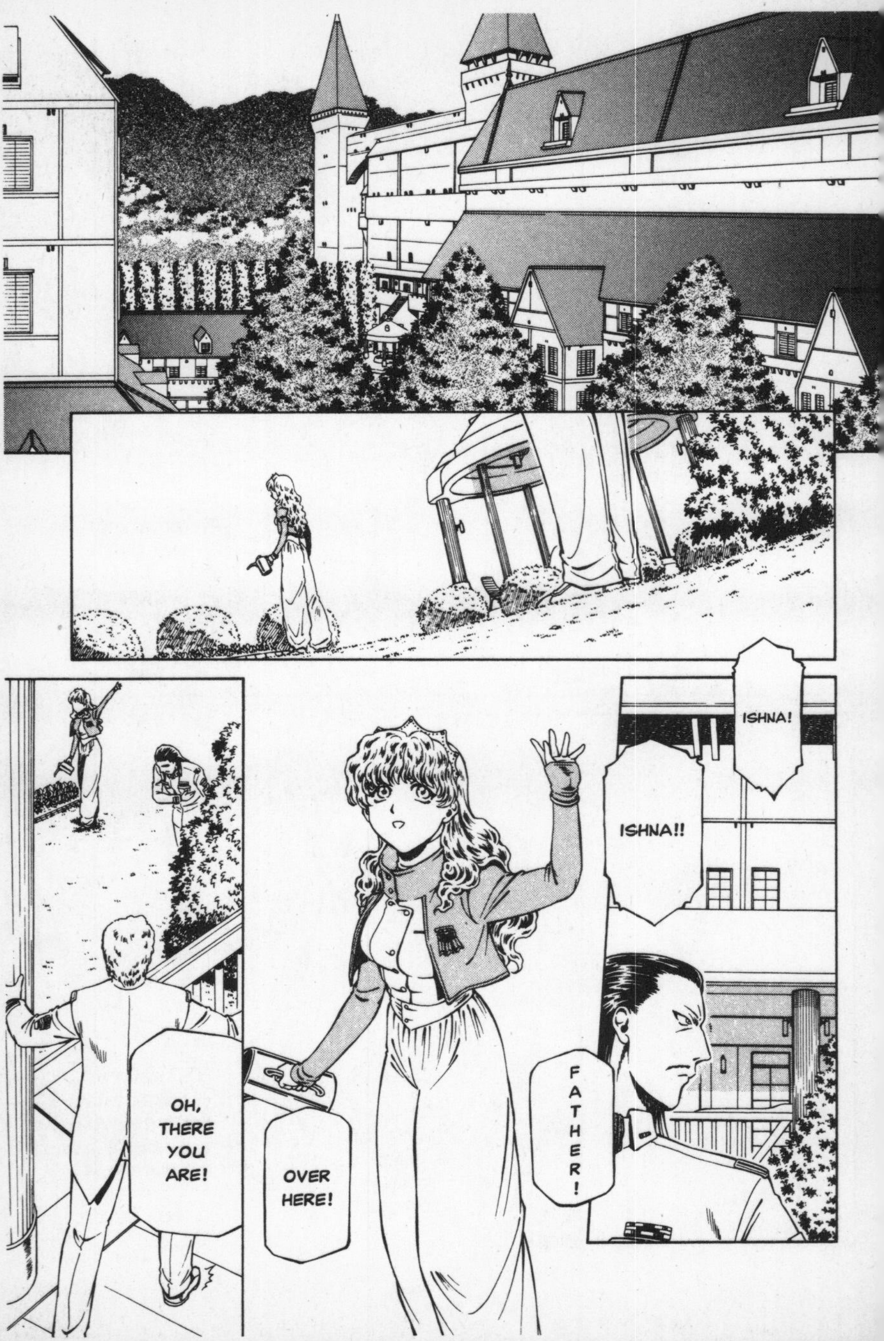
ISHNA!
ISHNA!!
FATHER!
OVER HERE!
OH, THERE YOU ARE!

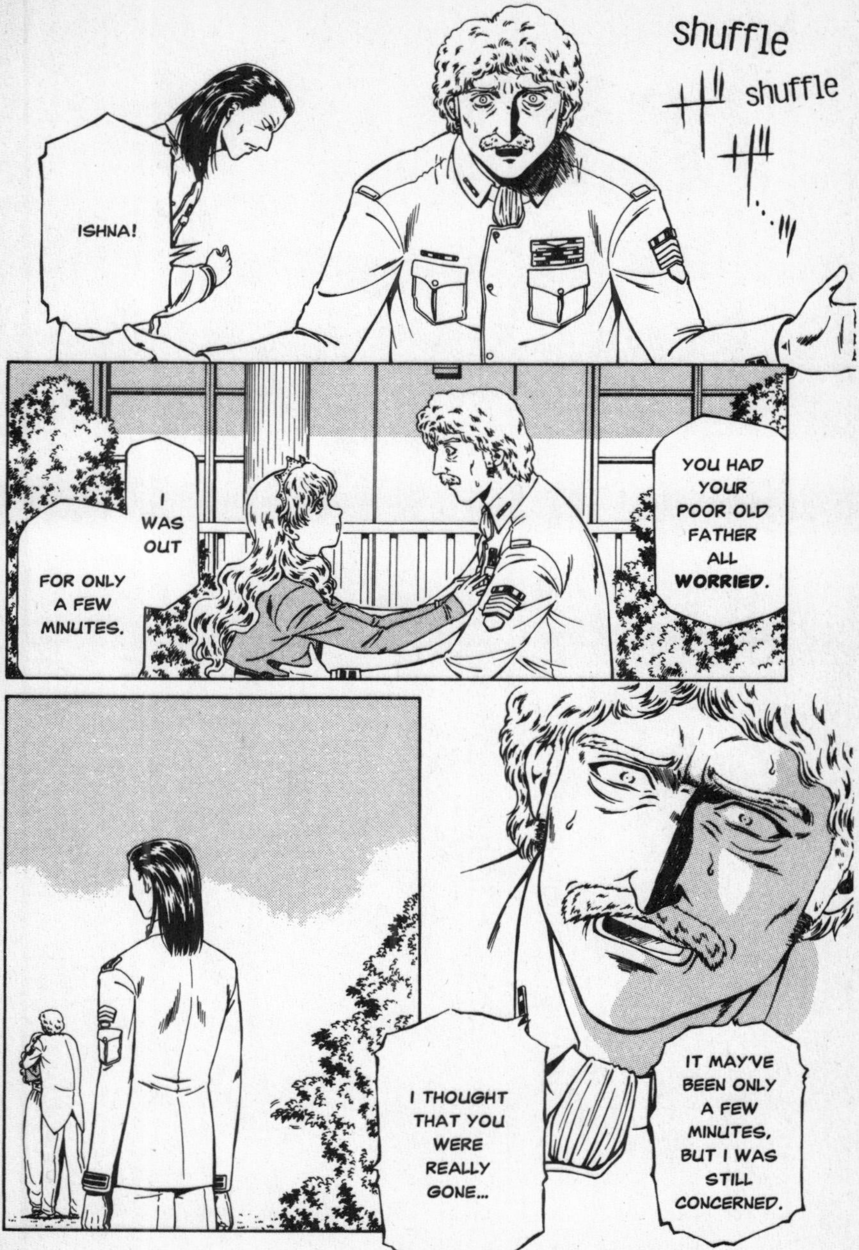
shuffle
shuffle
ISHNA!
YOU HAD YOUR POOR OLD FATHER ALL **WORRIED**.
I WAS OUT FOR ONLY A FEW MINUTES.
IT MAY'VE BEEN ONLY A FEW MINUTES, BUT I WAS STILL CONCERNED.
I THOUGHT THAT YOU WERE REALLY GONE...

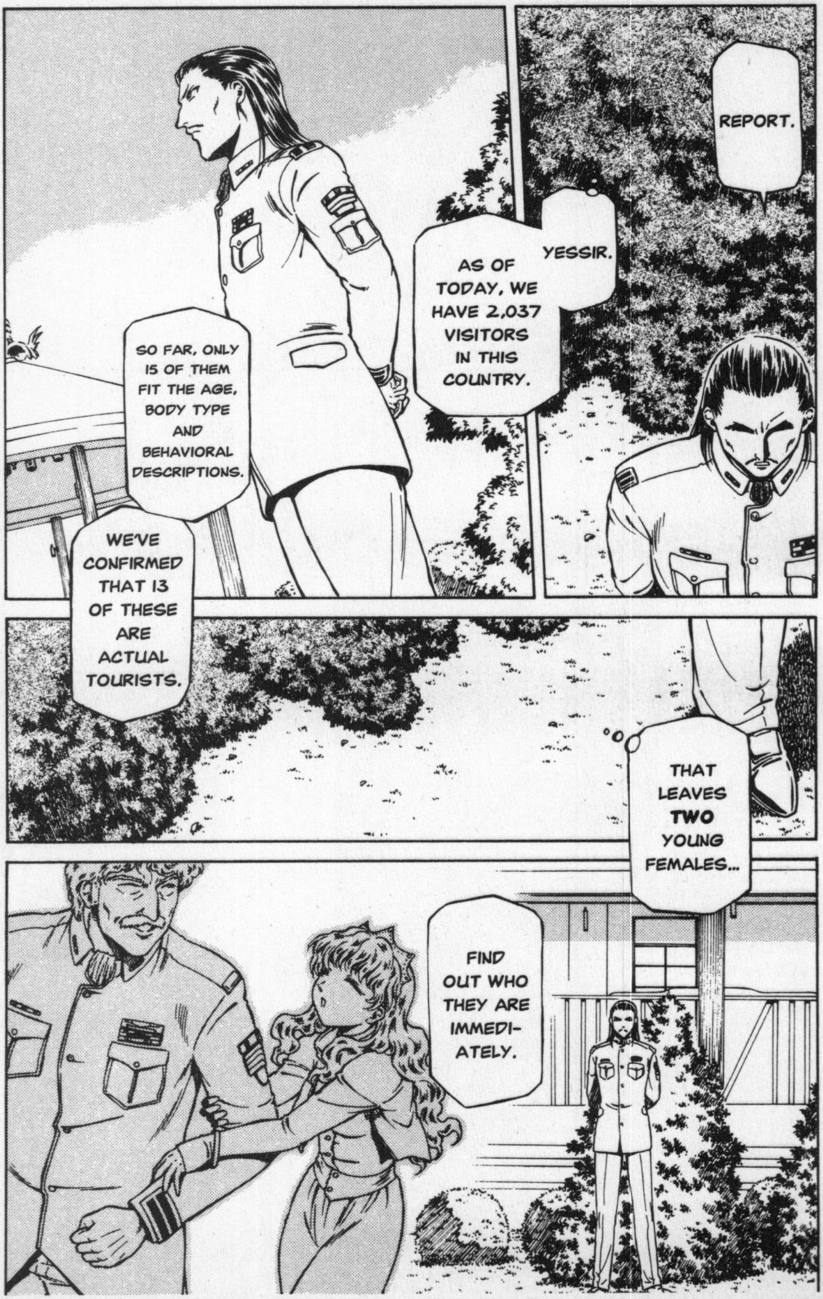
REPORT.
YESSIR.
AS OF TODAY, WE HAVE 2,037 VISITORS IN THIS COUNTRY.
SO FAR, ONLY 15 OF THEM FIT THE AGE, BODY TYPE AND BEHAVIORAL DESCRIPTIONS.
WE'VE CONFIRMED THAT 13 OF THESE ARE ACTUAL TOURISTS.
THAT LEAVES **TWO** YOUNG FEMALES...
FIND OUT WHO THEY ARE IMMEDIATELY.

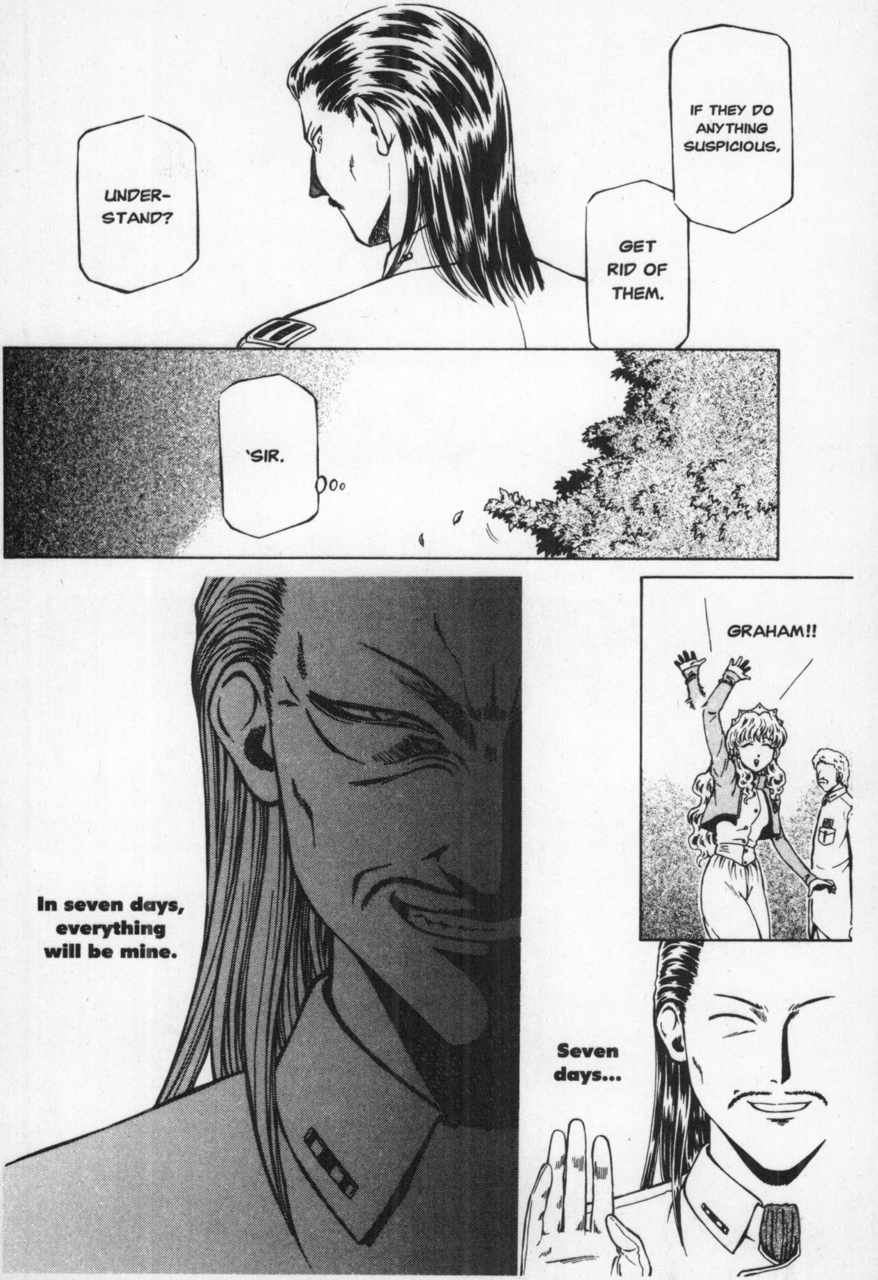
IF THEY DO ANYTHING SUSPICIOUS,
GET RID OF THEM.
UNDER-STAND?
'SIR.
GRAHAM!!
Seven days...
In seven days, everything will be mine.

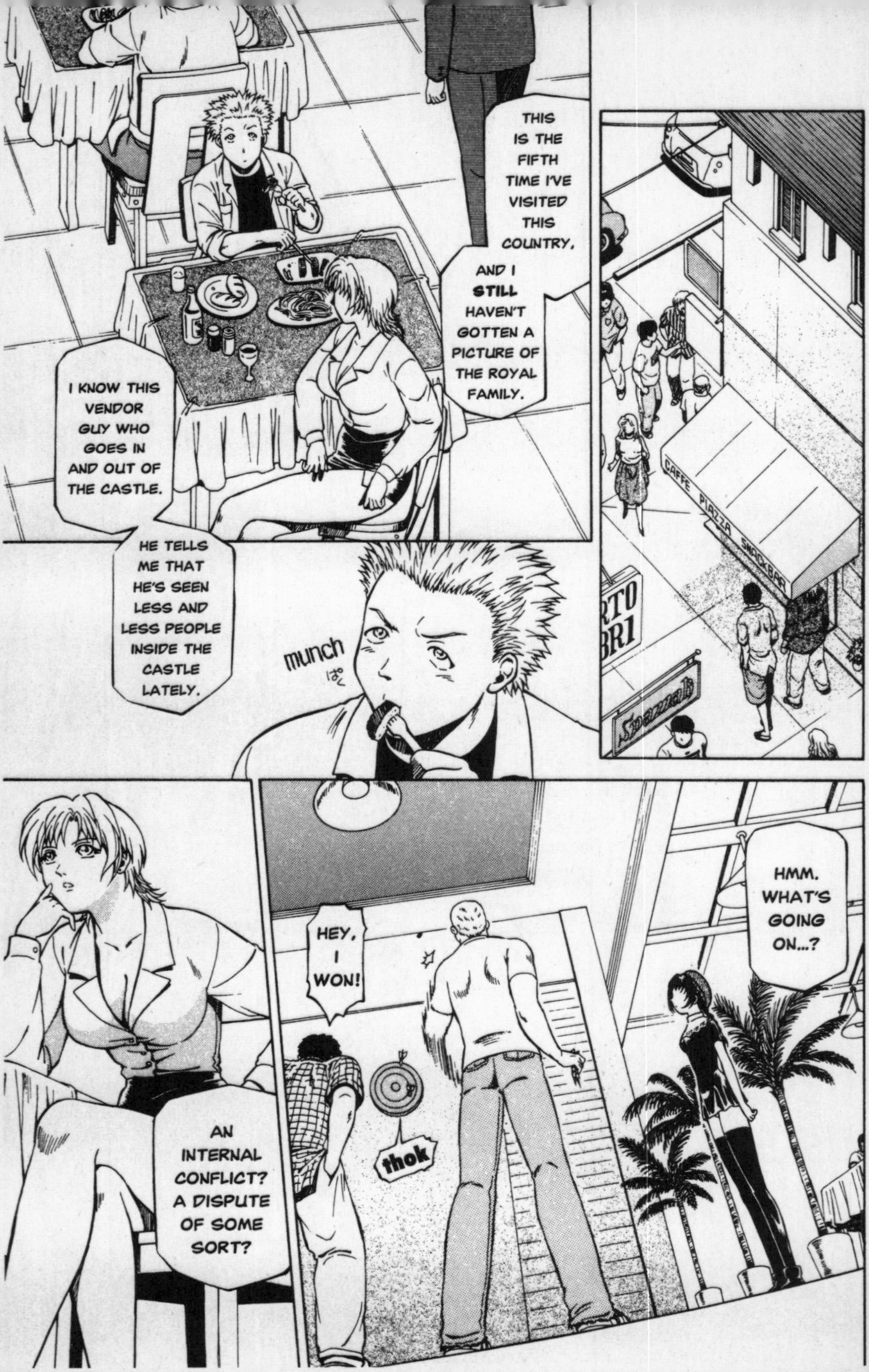
CAFFE PIAZZA SNACKBAR
THIS IS THE FIFTH TIME I'VE VISITED THIS COUNTRY,
AND I **STILL** HAVEN'T GOTTEN A PICTURE OF THE ROYAL FAMILY.
I KNOW THIS VENDOR GUY WHO GOES IN AND OUT OF THE CASTLE.
HE TELLS ME THAT HE'S SEEN LESS AND LESS PEOPLE INSIDE THE CASTLE LATELY.
munch
ぱく
HMM. WHAT'S GOING ON...?
HEY, I WON!
thok
AN INTERNAL CONFLICT? A DISPUTE OF SOME SORT?

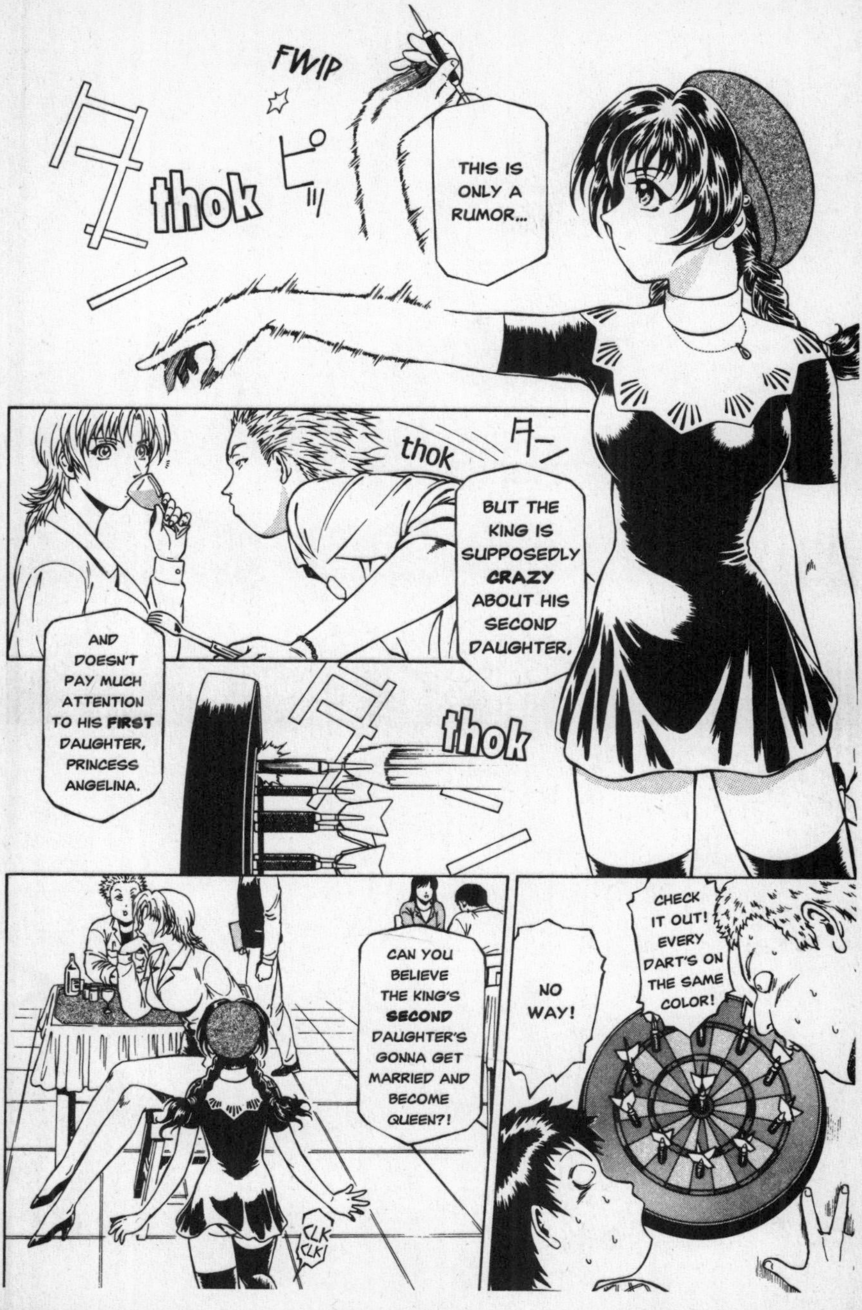
FWIP
タ
thok
ピッ
THIS IS ONLY A RUMOR...
thok
ターン
BUT THE KING IS SUPPOSEDLY CRAZY ABOUT HIS SECOND DAUGHTER,
AND DOESN'T PAY MUCH ATTENTION TO HIS FIRST DAUGHTER, PRINCESS ANGELINA.
タ
thok
CHECK IT OUT! EVERY DART'S ON THE SAME COLOR!
NO WAY!
CAN YOU BELIEVE THE KING'S SECOND DAUGHTER'S GONNA GET MARRIED AND BECOME QUEEN?!
CLK CLK

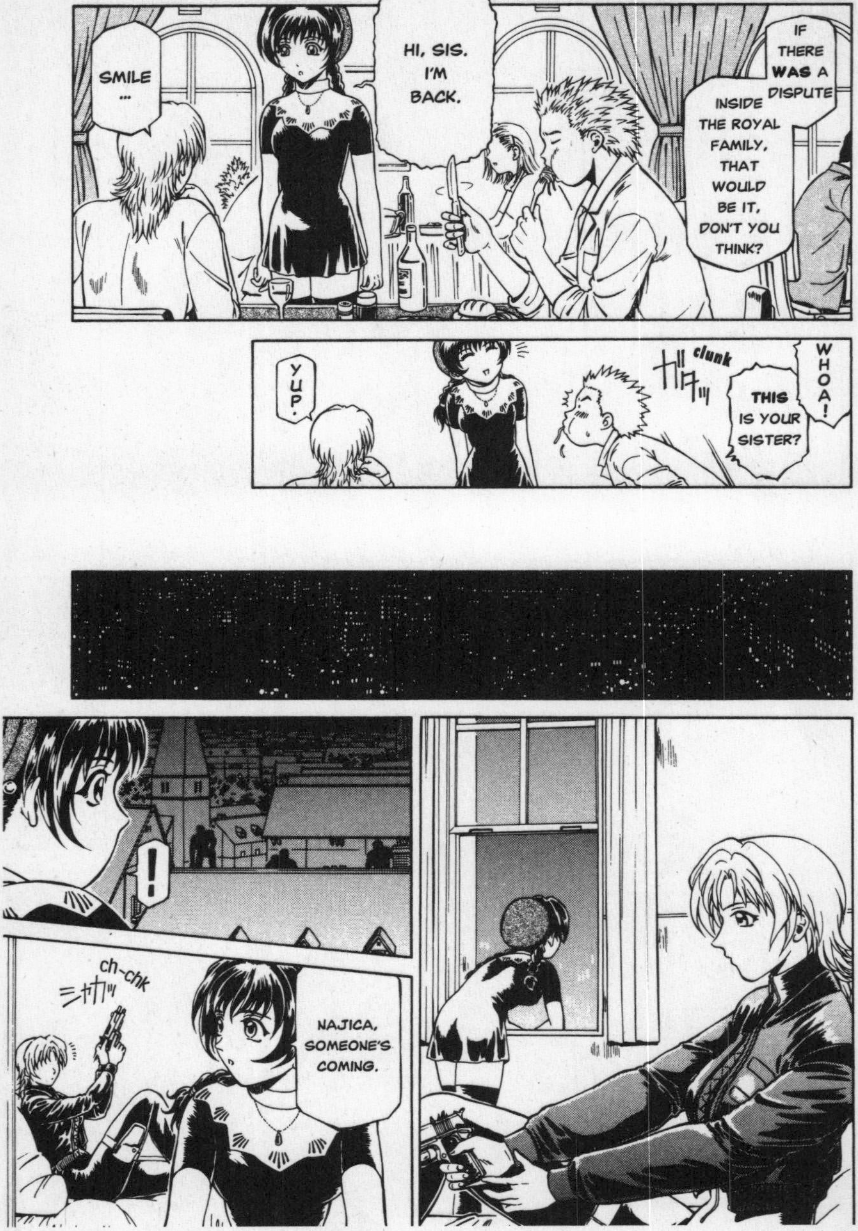
IF THERE WAS A DISPUTE
INSIDE THE ROYAL FAMILY, THAT WOULD BE IT, DON'T YOU THINK?
HI, SIS. I'M BACK.
SMILE ...
WHOA!
THIS IS YOUR SISTER?
ガタッ
clunk
YUP.
!
NAJICA, SOMEONE'S COMING.
シャカッ
ch-chk

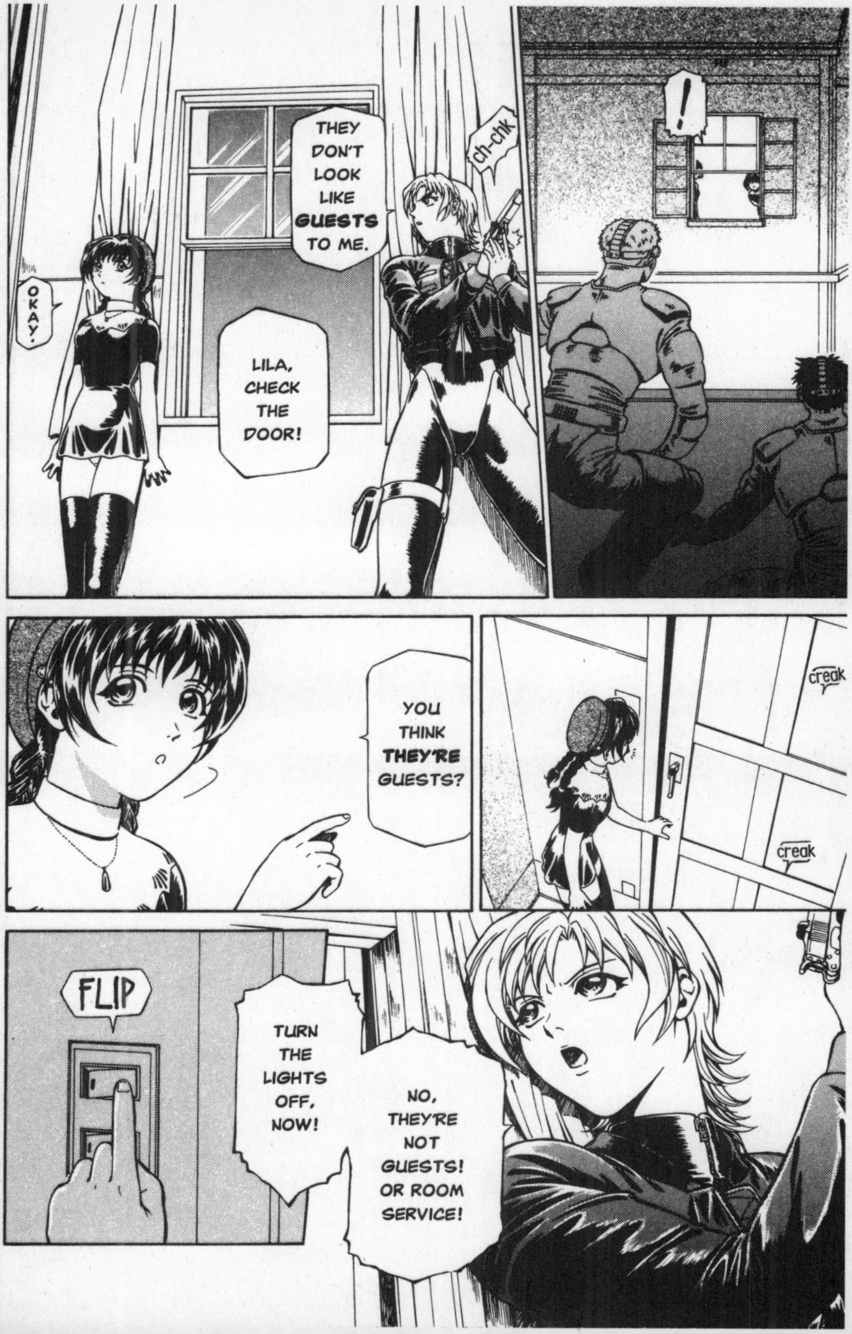
!
ch-chk
THEY DON'T LOOK LIKE GUESTS TO ME.
LILA, CHECK THE DOOR!
OKAY.
creak
creak
YOU THINK THEY'RE GUESTS?
NO, THEY'RE NOT GUESTS! OR ROOM SERVICE!
TURN THE LIGHTS OFF, NOW!
FLIP

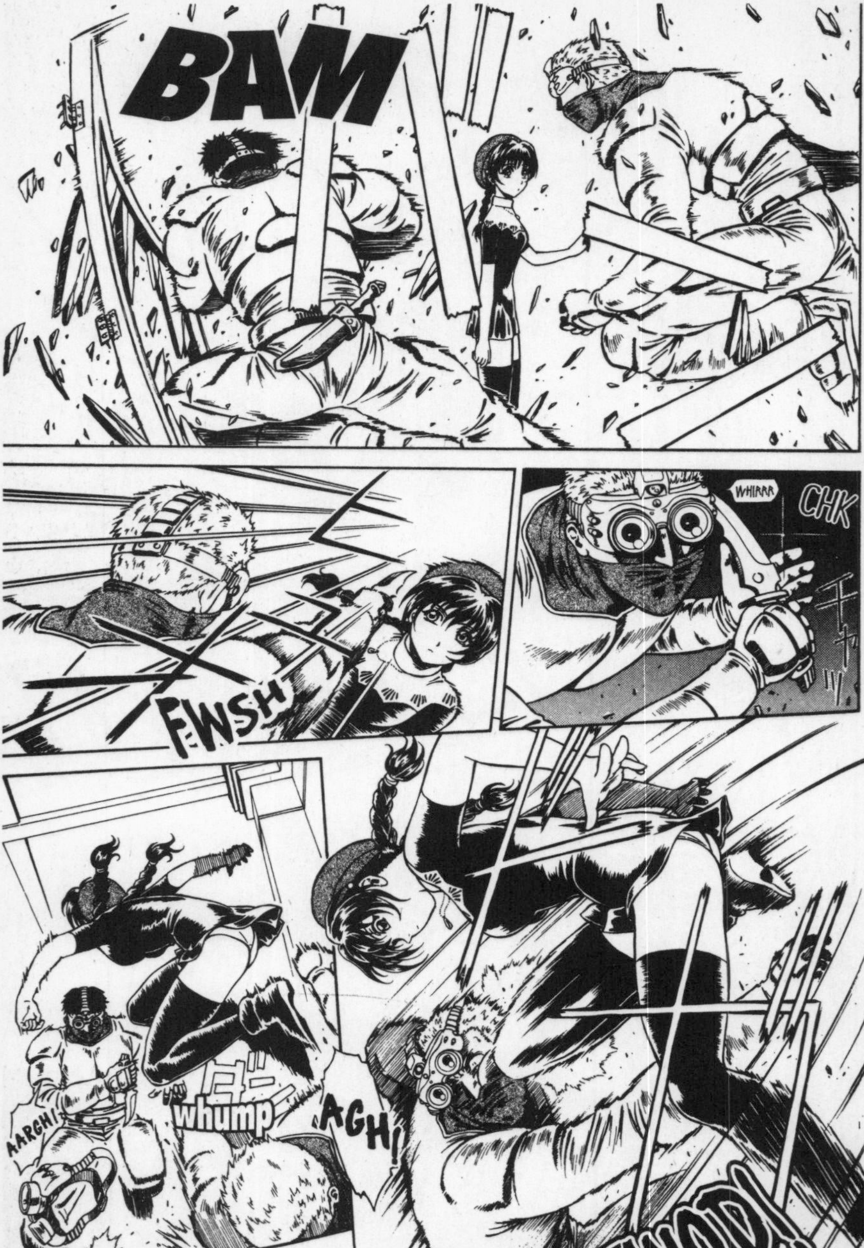
BAM
WHIRRR
CHK
FWSH
AGH!
TWOD!
whump
AARGH!

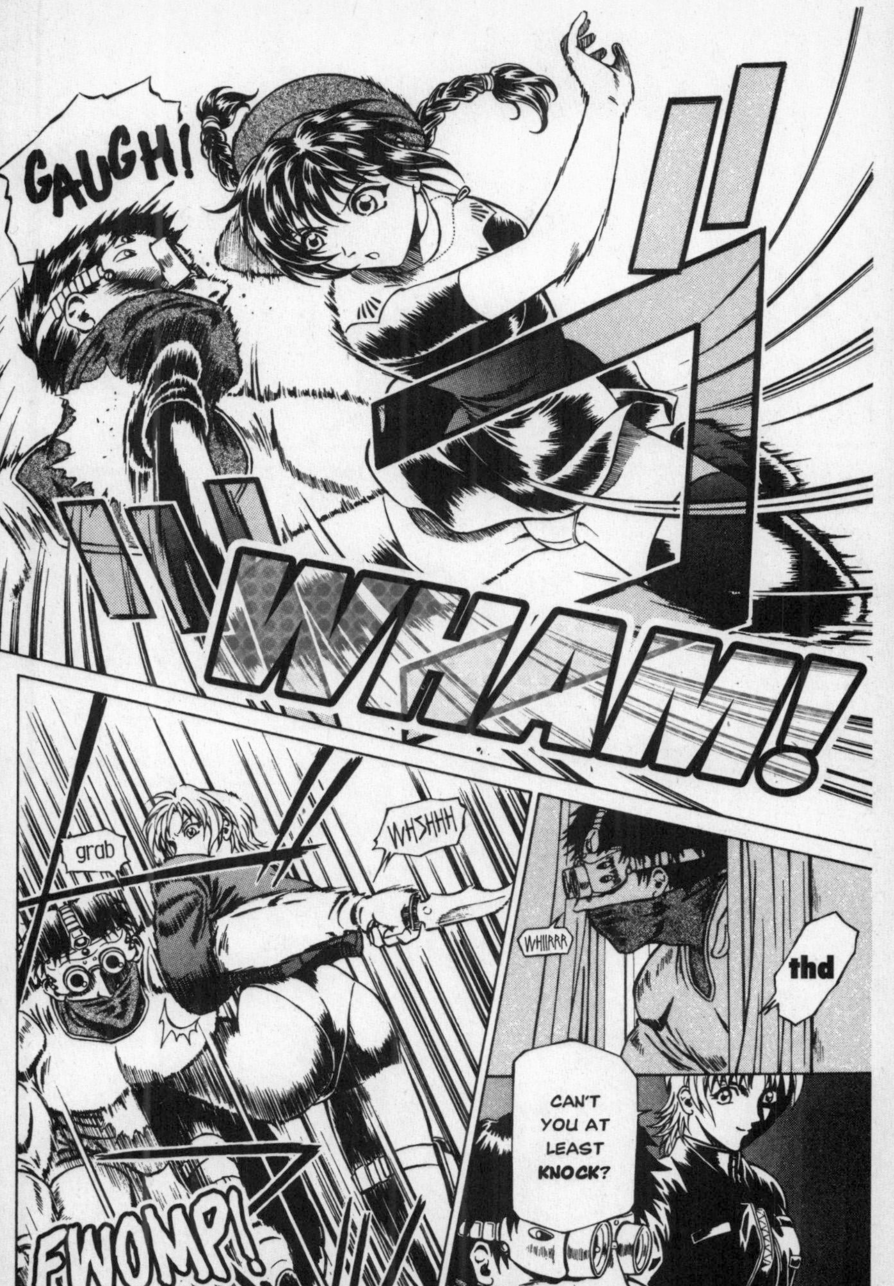
GAUGH!
WHAM!
WHIIRRR
thd
CAN'T YOU AT LEAST KNOCK?
WHSHHH
grab
FWOMP!

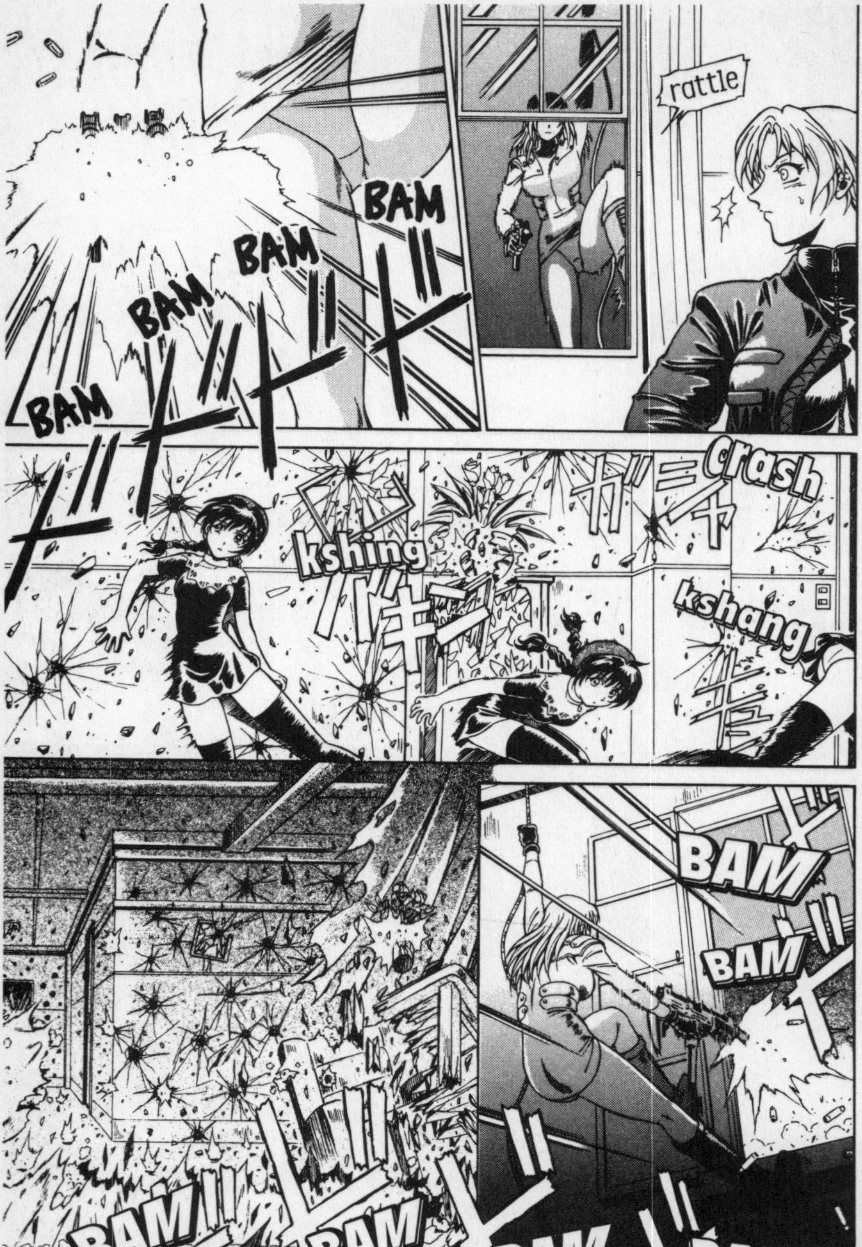
rattle
BAM
BAM
BAM
BAM
crash
kshang
kshing
BAM
BAM
BAM
BAM
BAM
BAM

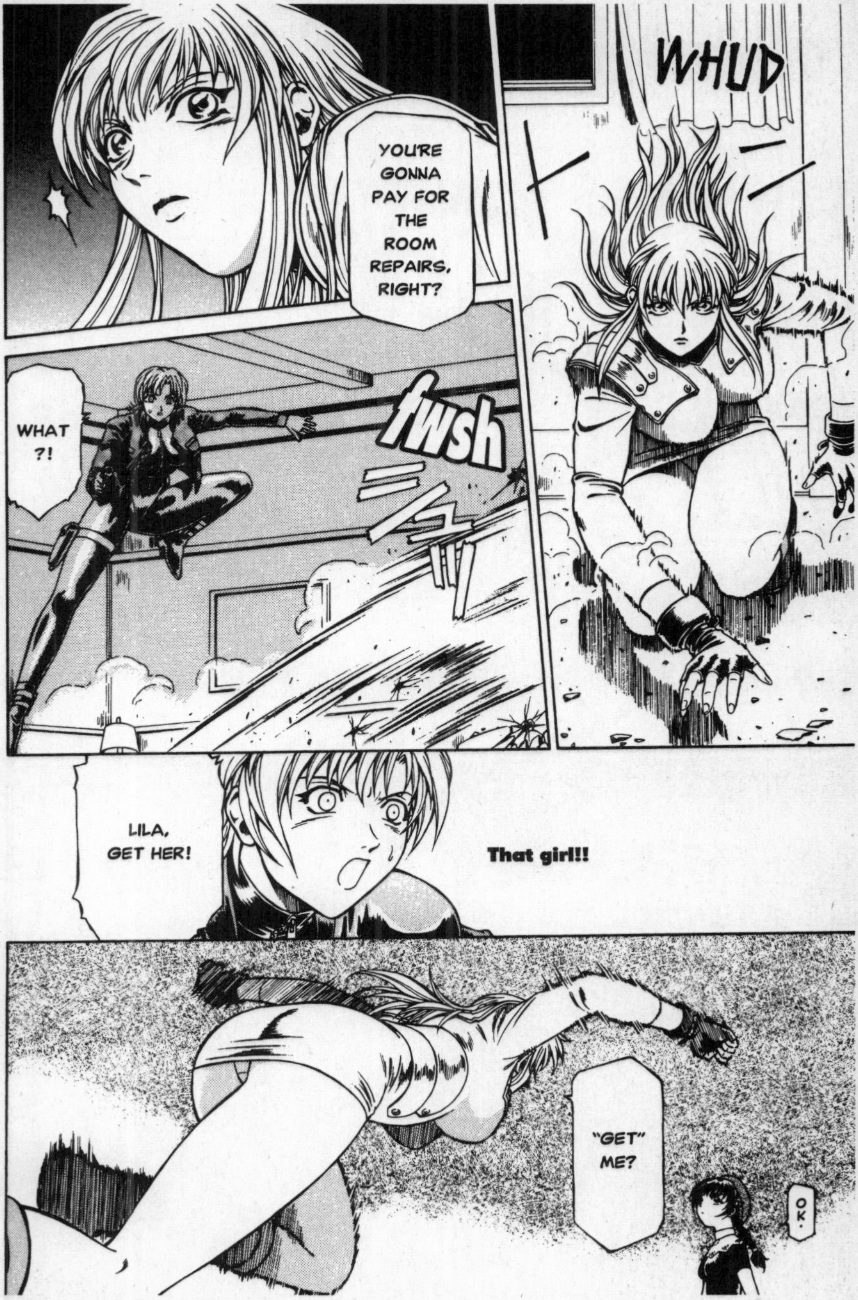
WHUD
YOU'RE GONNA PAY FOR THE ROOM REPAIRS, RIGHT?
fwsh
WHAT ?!
That girl!!
LILA, GET HER!
OK.
"GET" ME?

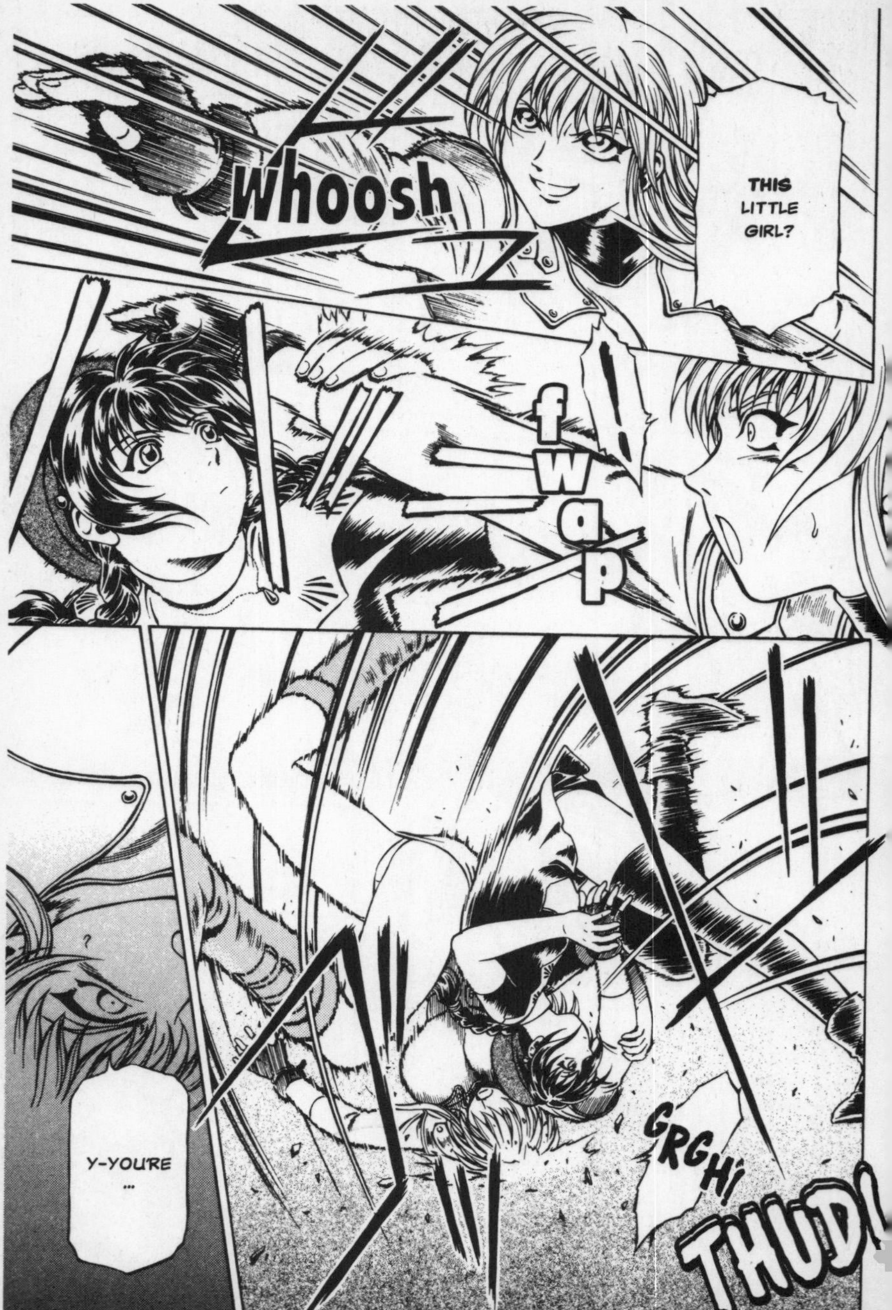

THIS LITTLE GIRL?
whoosh
fwap
THUD!
GRGH!
Y-YOU'RE ...

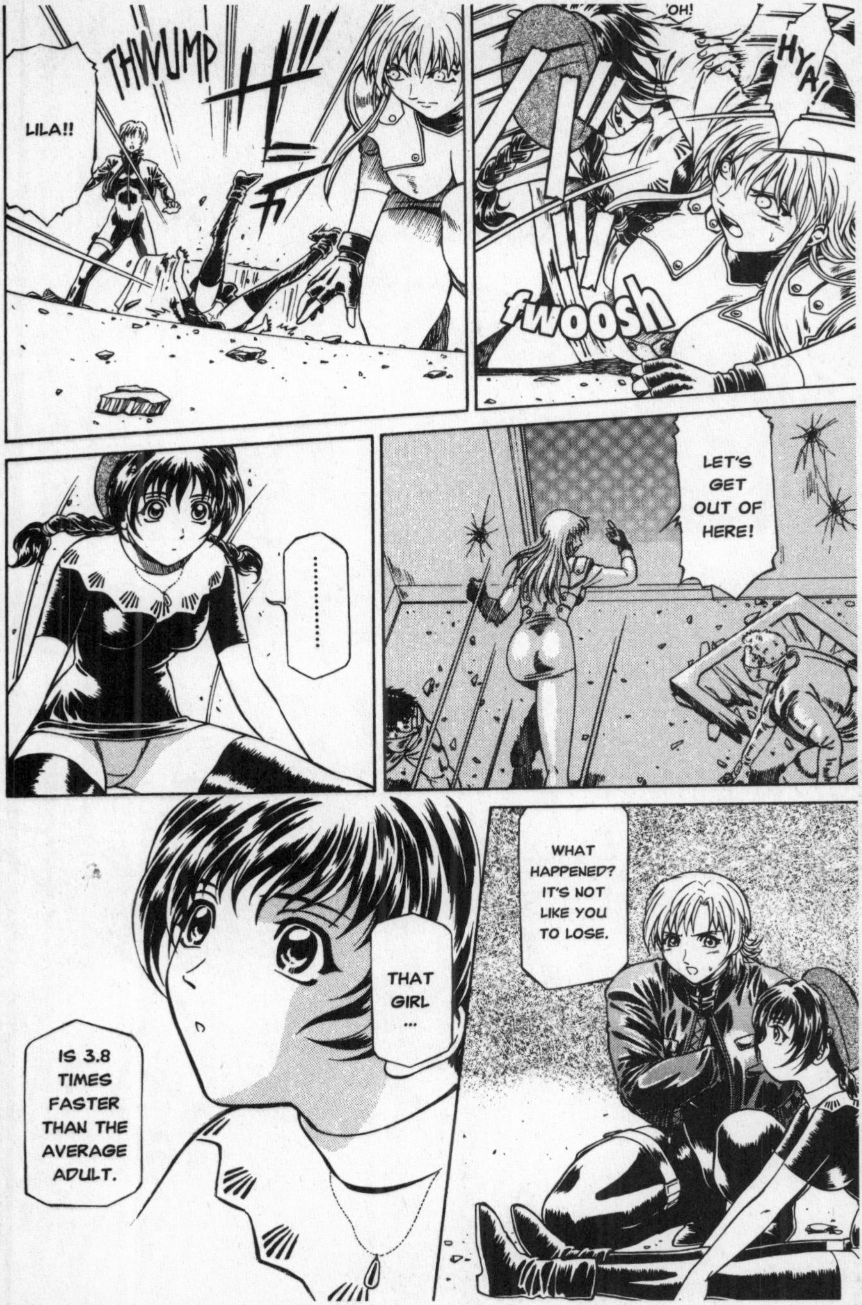
'OH!
HYA!
fwoosh
THWUMP
LILA!!
LET'S GET OUT OF HERE!
......
WHAT HAPPENED? IT'S NOT LIKE YOU TO LOSE.
THAT GIRL ...
IS 3.8 TIMES FASTER THAN THE AVERAGE ADULT.

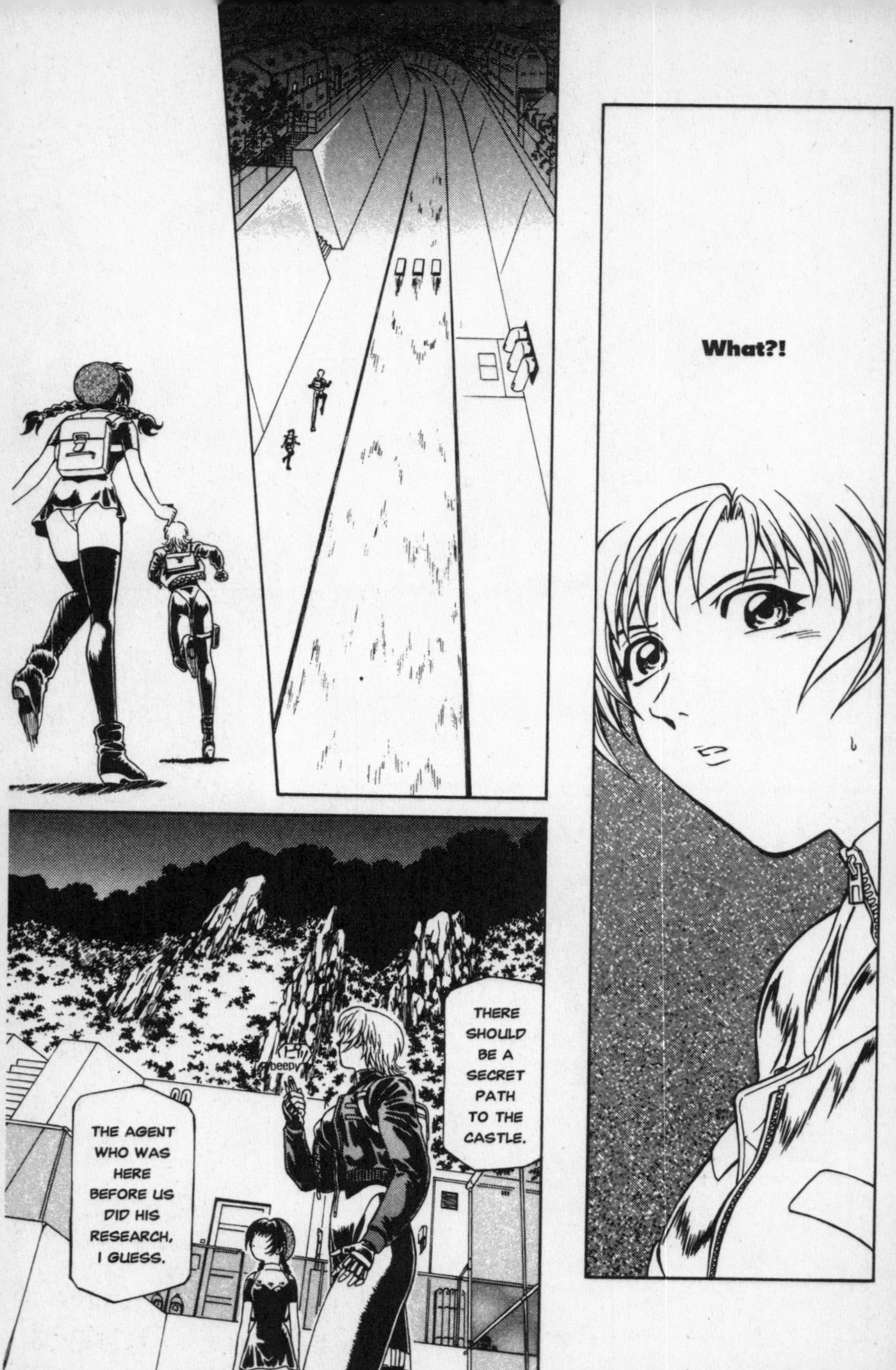
What?!
beepy
THERE SHOULD BE A SECRET PATH TO THE CASTLE.
THE AGENT WHO WAS HERE BEFORE US DID HIS RESEARCH, I GUESS.

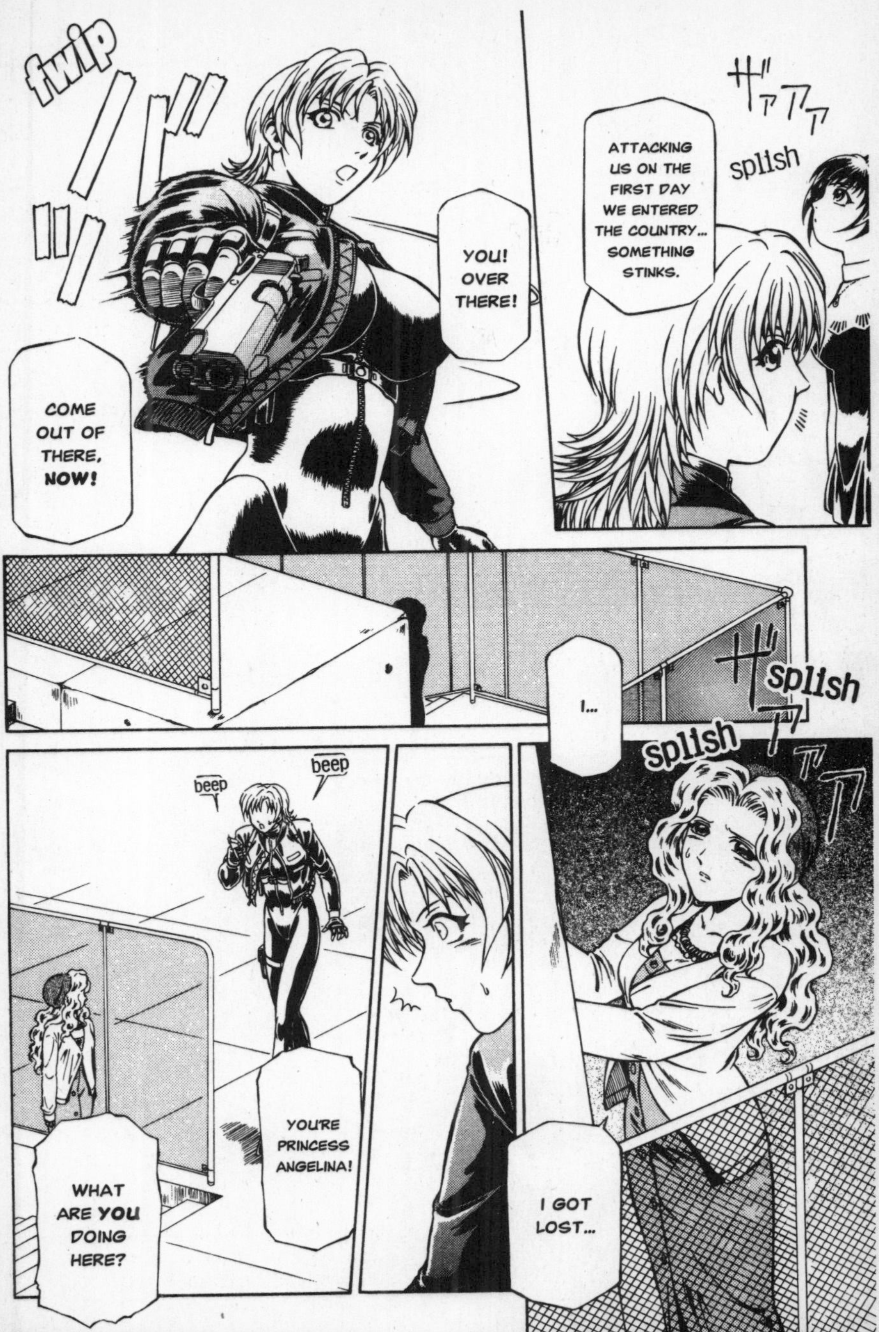
ザァァァ
splish
ATTACKING US ON THE FIRST DAY WE ENTERED THE COUNTRY... SOMETHING STINKS.
fwip
YOU! OVER THERE!
COME OUT OF THERE, NOW!
ザァ
splish
I...
splish
I GOT LOST...
beep
beep
YOU'RE PRINCESS ANGELINA!
WHAT ARE YOU DOING HERE?

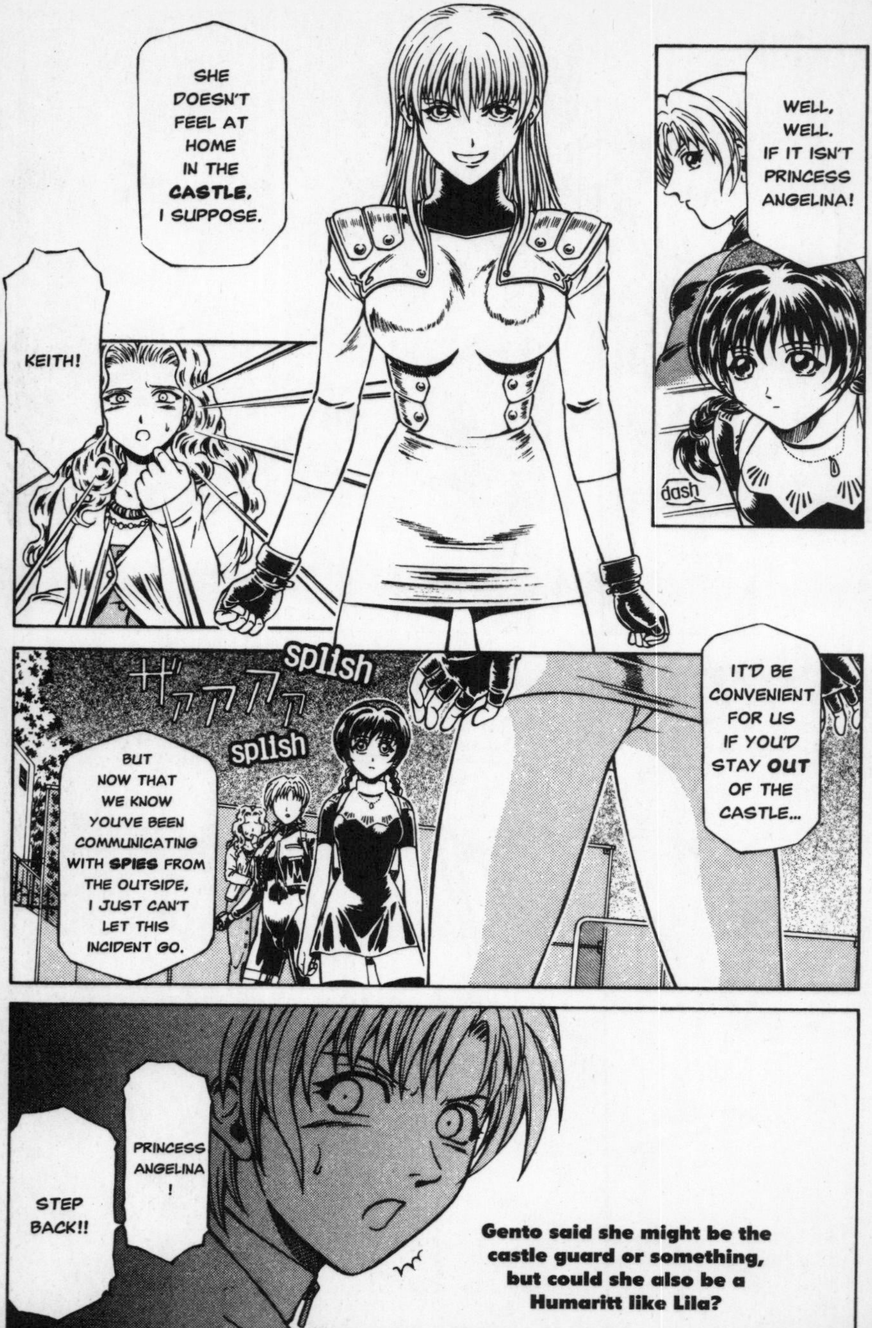

WELL, WELL. IF IT ISN'T PRINCESS ANGELINA!
dash
SHE DOESN'T FEEL AT HOME IN THE CASTLE, I SUPPOSE.
KEITH!
splish
splish
IT'D BE CONVENIENT FOR US IF YOU'D STAY OUT OF THE CASTLE...
BUT NOW THAT WE KNOW YOU'VE BEEN COMMUNICATING WITH SPIES FROM THE OUTSIDE, I JUST CAN'T LET THIS INCIDENT GO.
PRINCESS ANGELINA !
STEP BACK!!
Gento said she might be the castle guard or something, but could she also be a Humaritt like Lila?

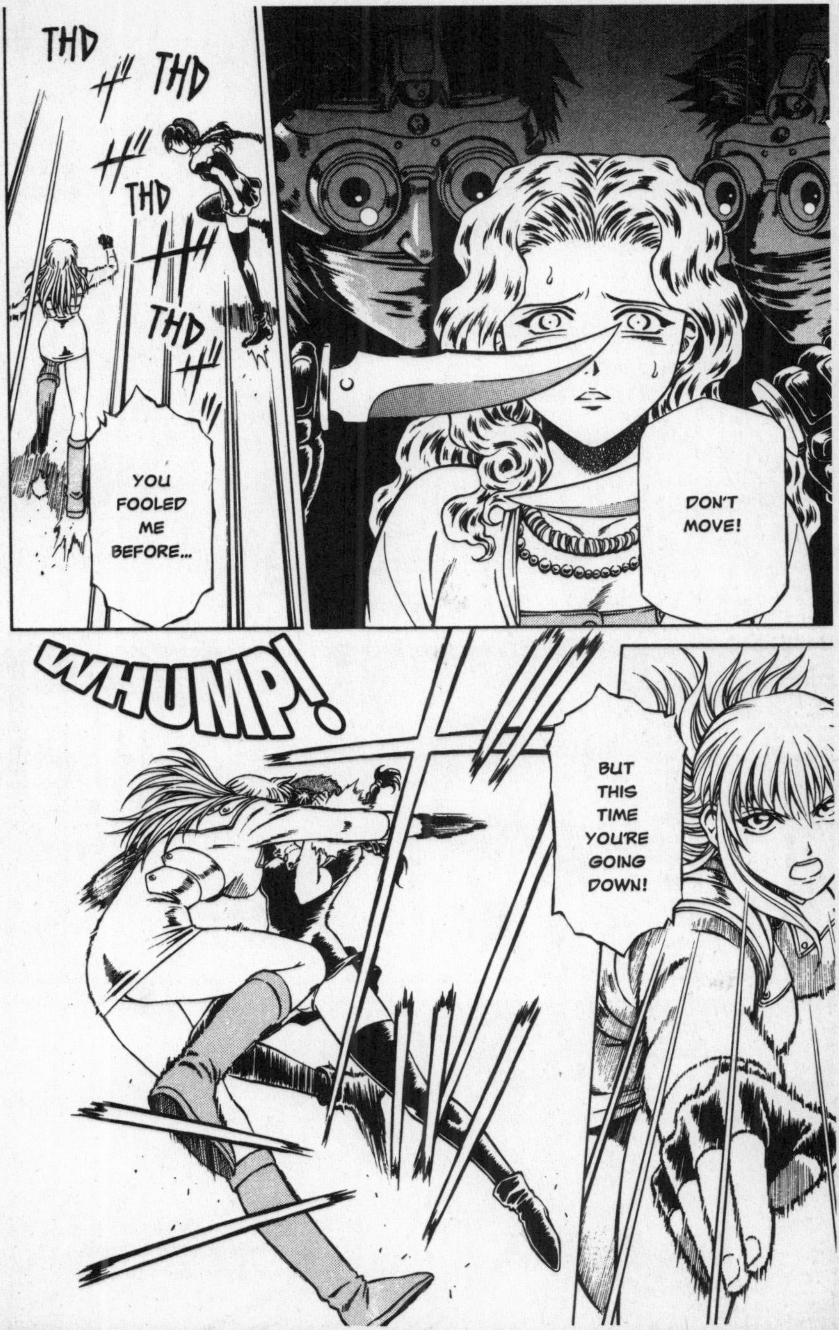
DON'T MOVE!
THD
THD
THD
THD
YOU FOOLED ME BEFORE...
BUT THIS TIME YOU'RE GOING DOWN!
WHUMP!

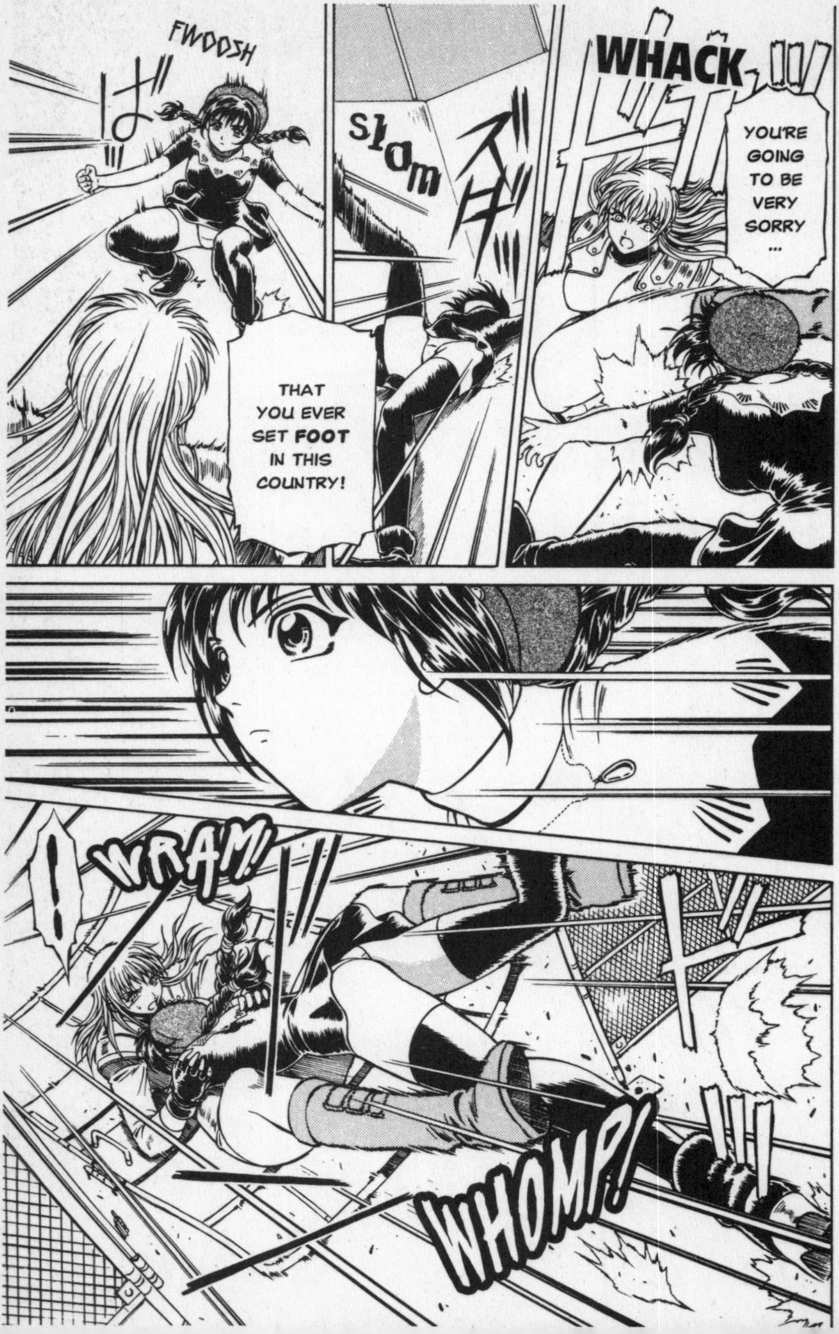
WHACK
YOU'RE GOING TO BE VERY SORRY ...
Slam
FWOOSH
THAT YOU EVER SET **FOOT** IN THIS COUNTRY!
WRAM!
WHOMP!

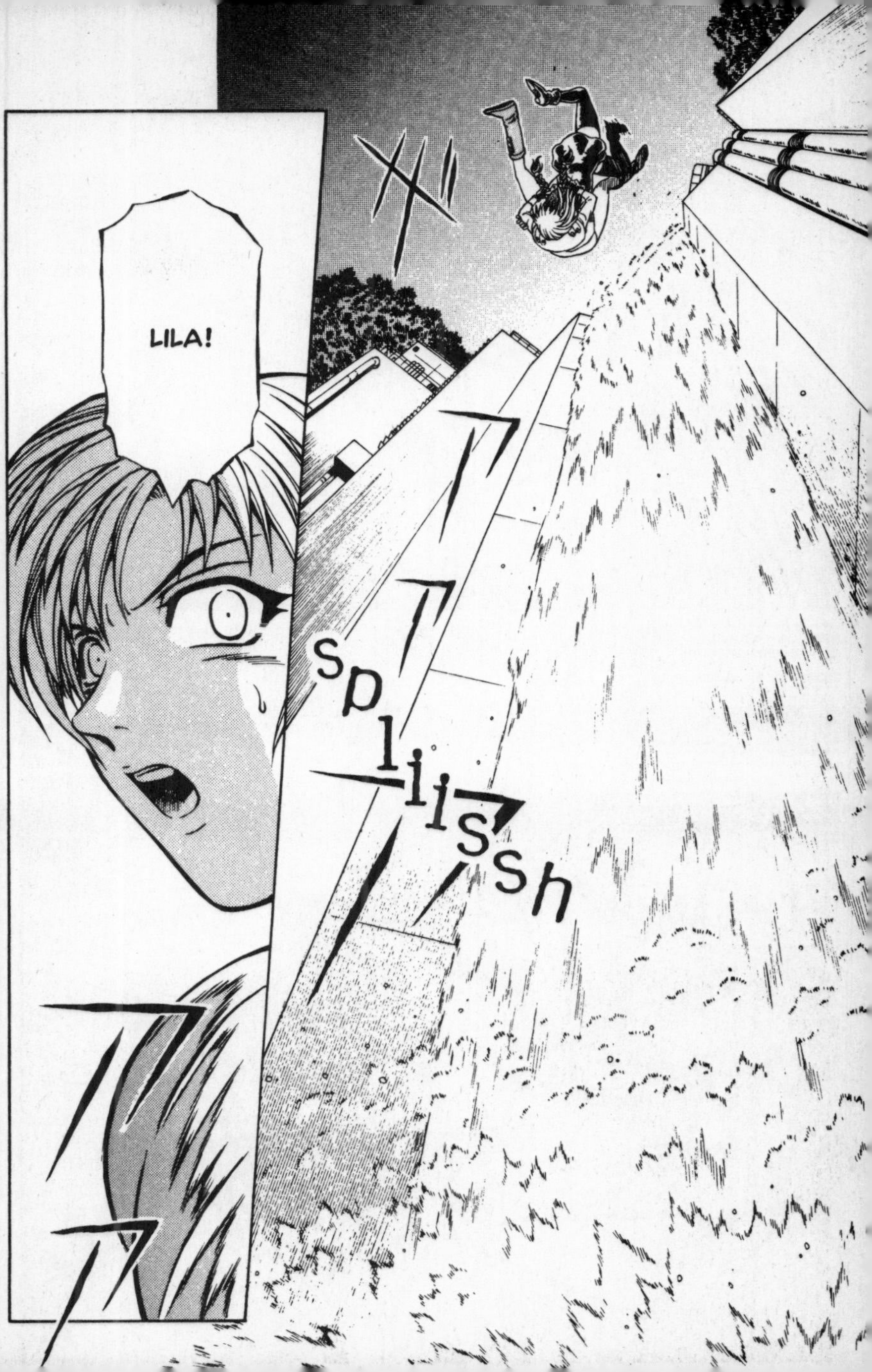
LILA!
splissh

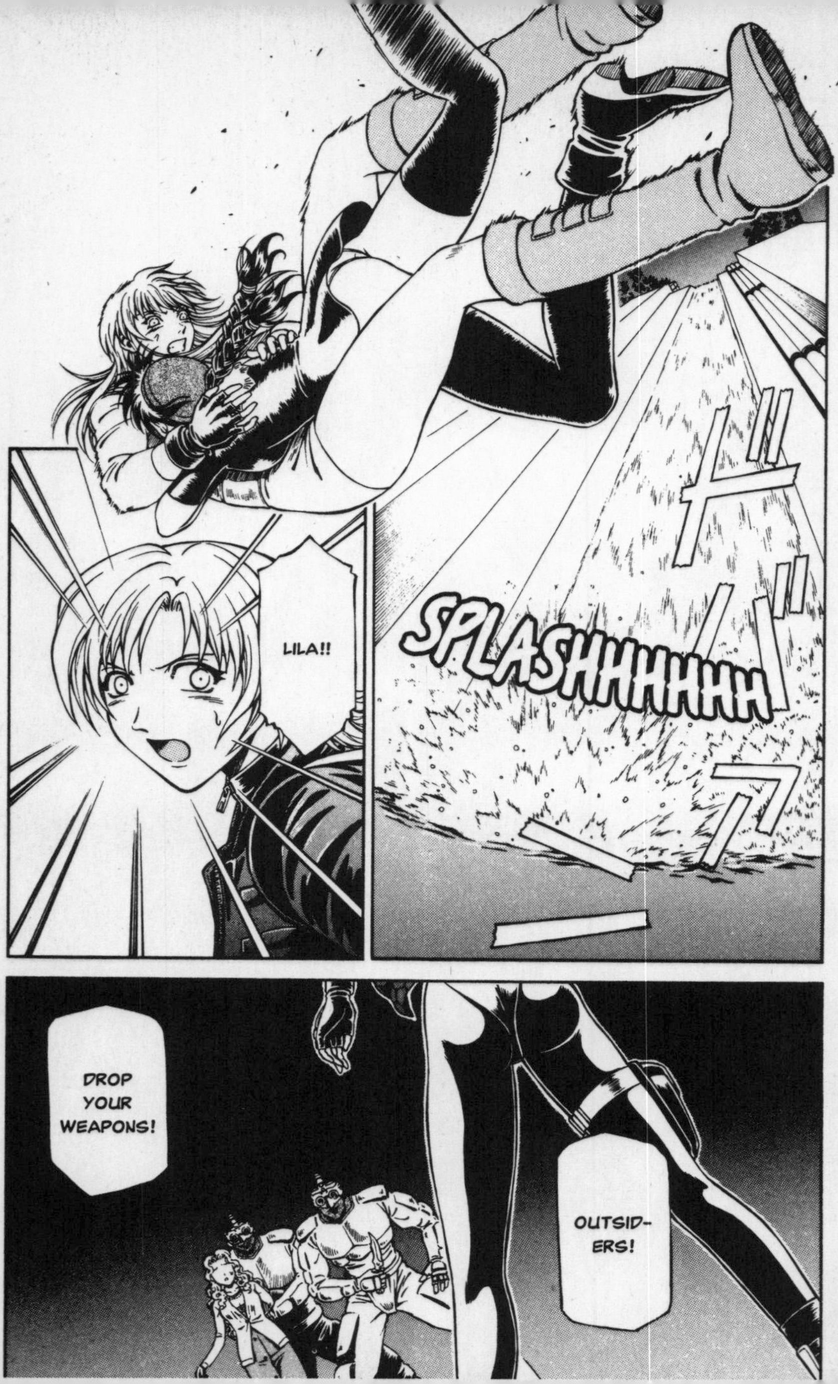
SPLASHHHHHHH
LILA!!
OUTSID-
ERS!
DROP
YOUR
WEAPONS!

Operation.5 THE LAND OF ROSES 2

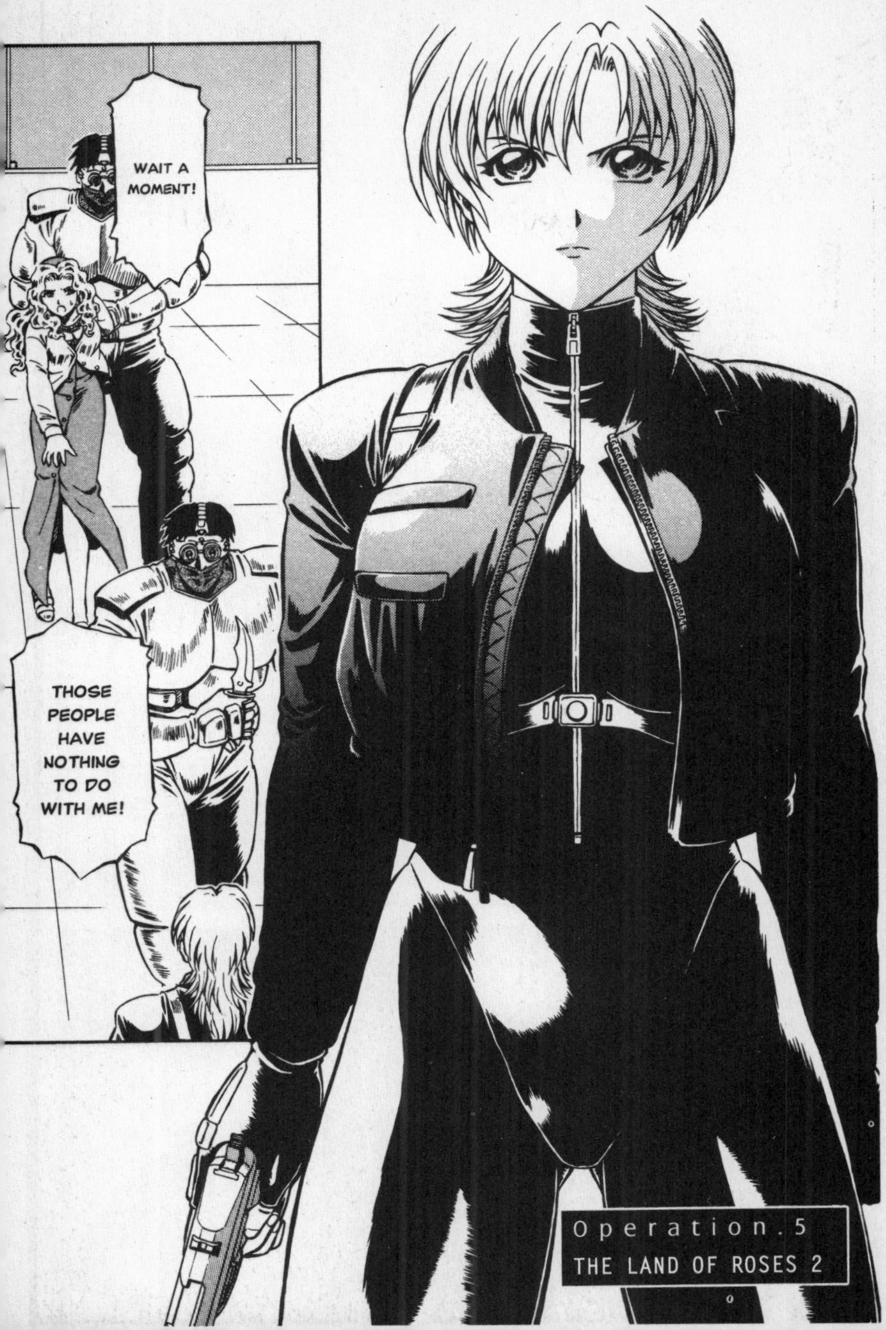
WAIT A MOMENT!
THOSE PEOPLE HAVE NOTHING TO DO WITH ME!

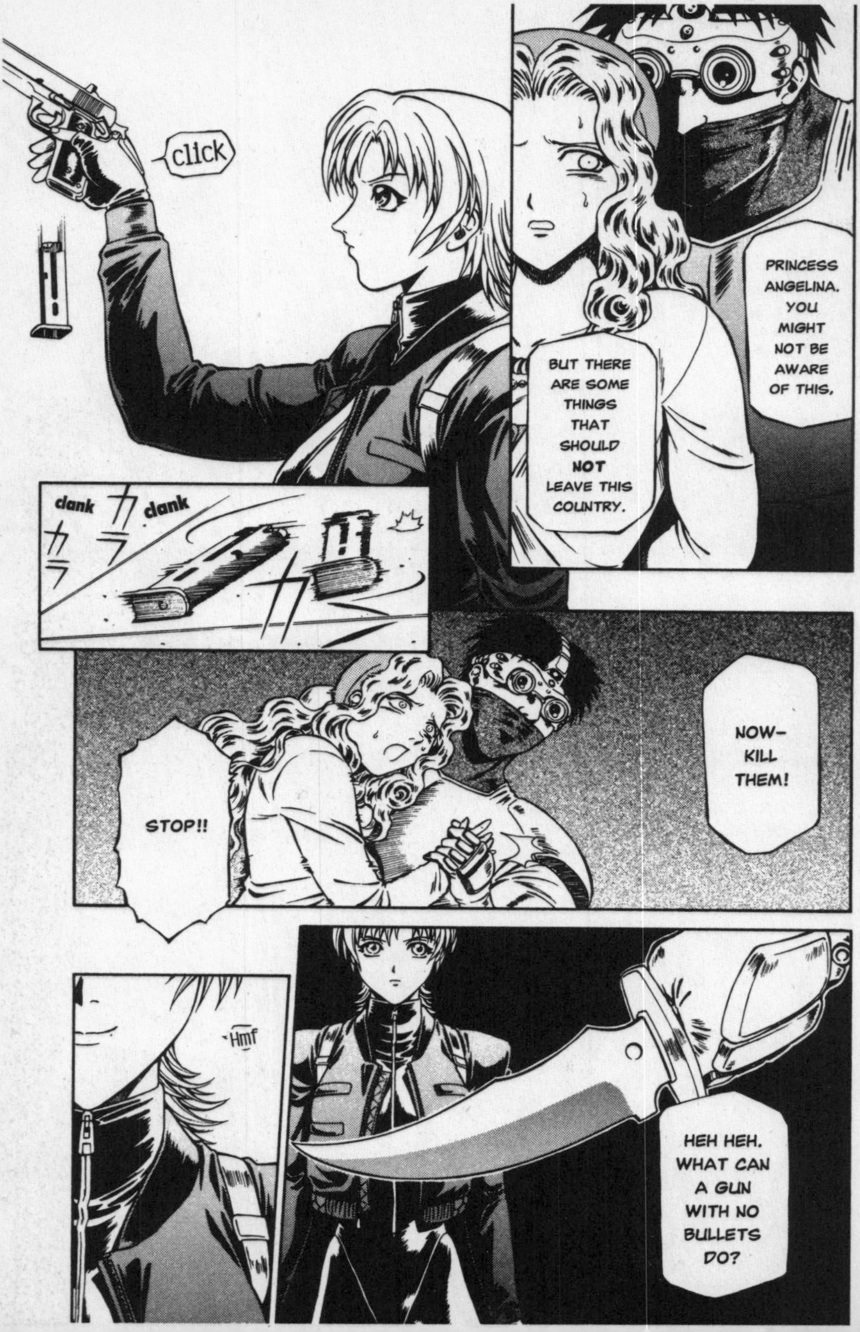
PRINCESS ANGELINA. YOU MIGHT NOT BE AWARE OF THIS,
BUT THERE ARE SOME THINGS THAT SHOULD **NOT** LEAVE THIS COUNTRY.
click
clank
カラ
clank
カラ
カラ
NOW-KILL THEM!
STOP!!
HEH HEH. WHAT CAN A GUN WITH NO BULLETS DO?
Hmf

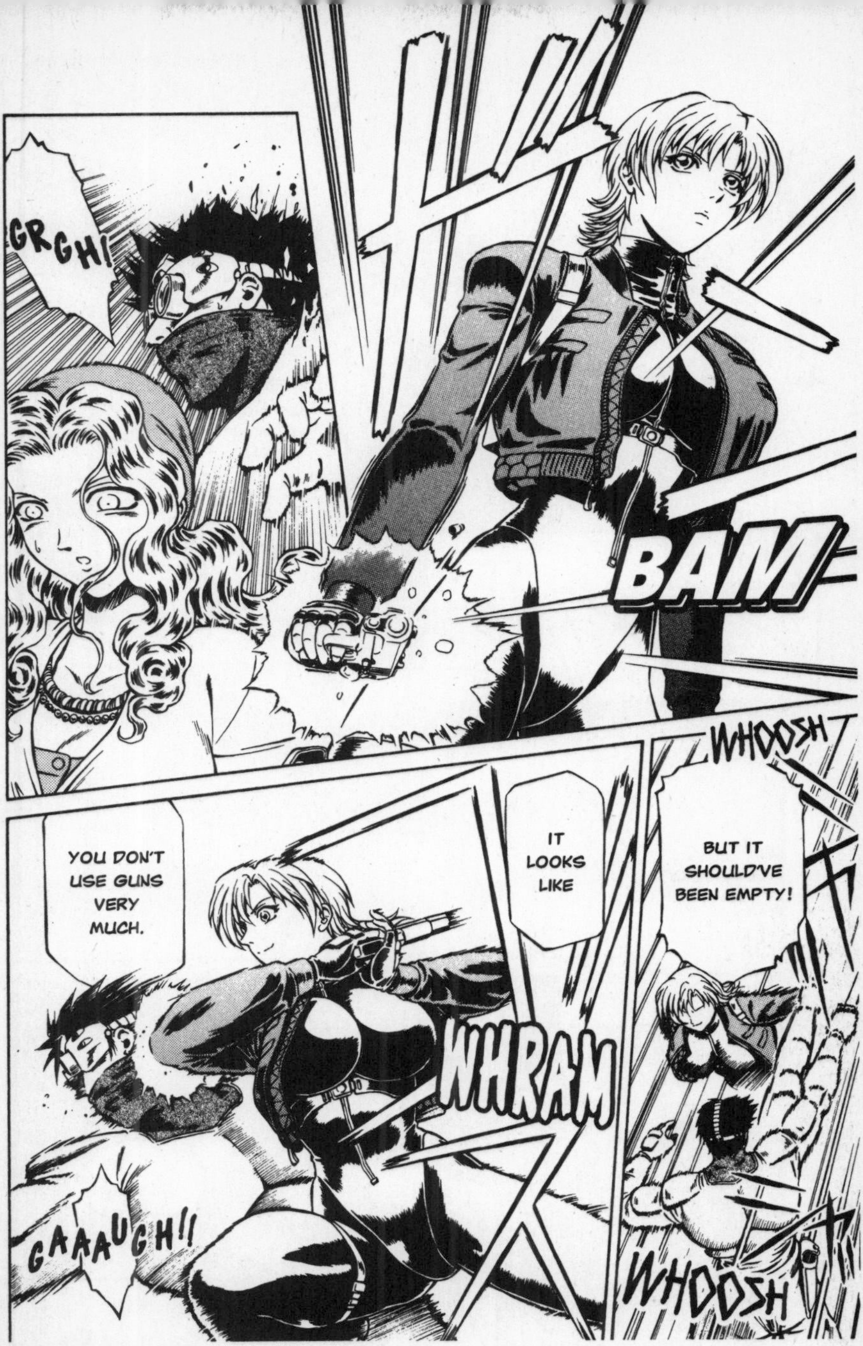
BAM
GRGH!
WHOOSH
BUT IT SHOULD'VE BEEN EMPTY!
WHOOSH
IT LOOKS LIKE
YOU DON'T USE GUNS VERY MUCH.
WHRAM
GAAAUGH!!

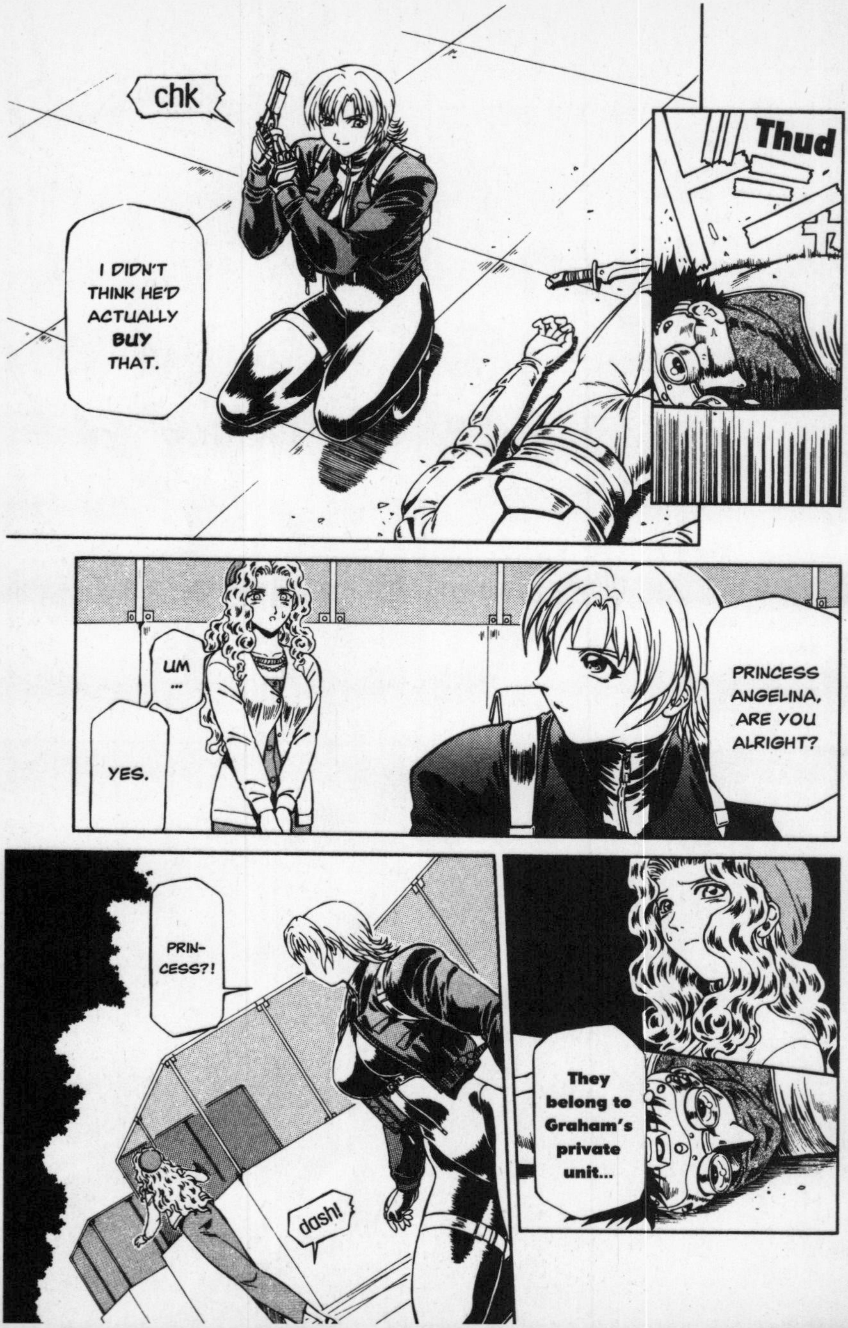
Thud
chk
I DIDN'T THINK HE'D ACTUALLY BUY THAT.
PRINCESS ANGELINA, ARE YOU ALRIGHT?
UM ...
YES.
They belong to Graham's private unit...
PRIN-CESS?!
dash!

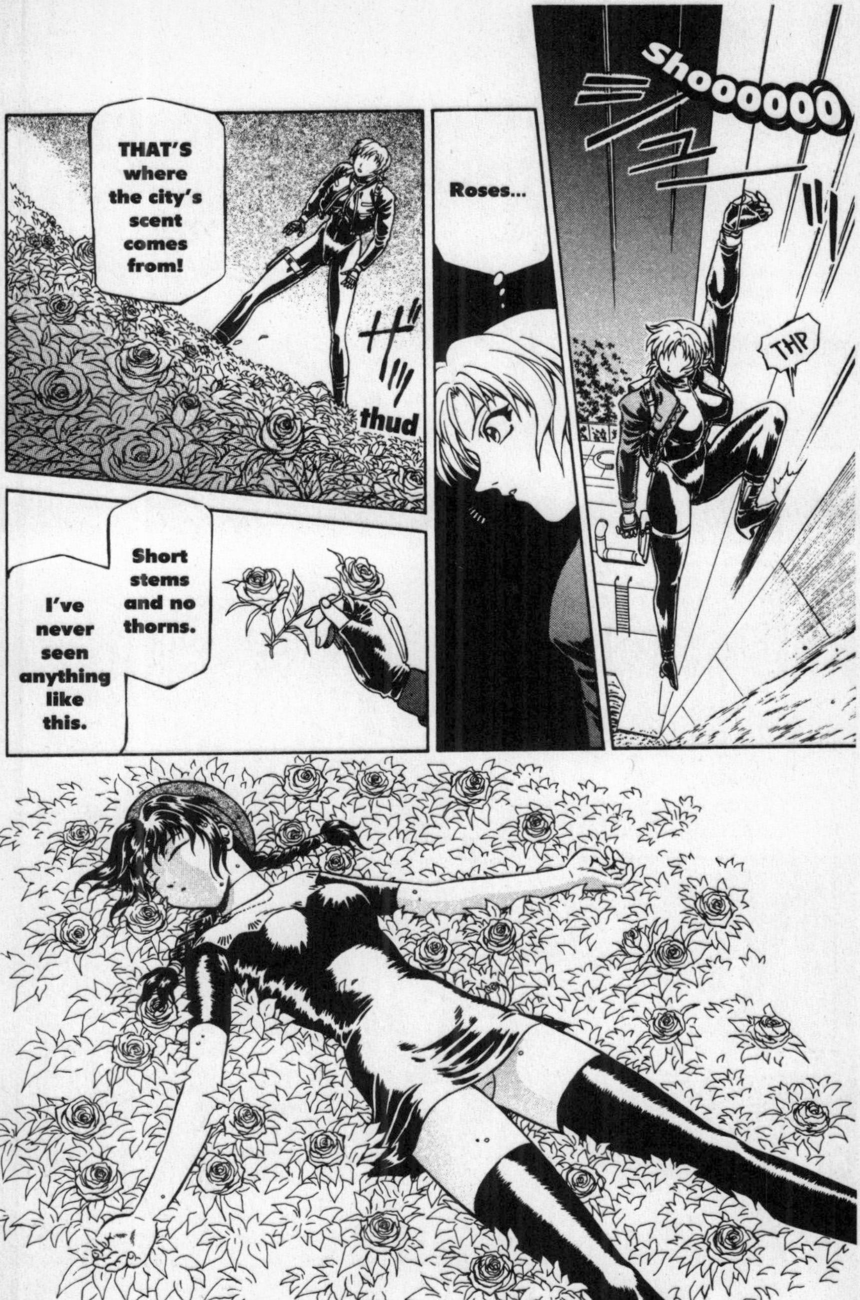
Shoooooo
THP
Roses...
THAT'S where the city's scent comes from!
thud
Short stems and no thorns.
I've never seen anything like this.

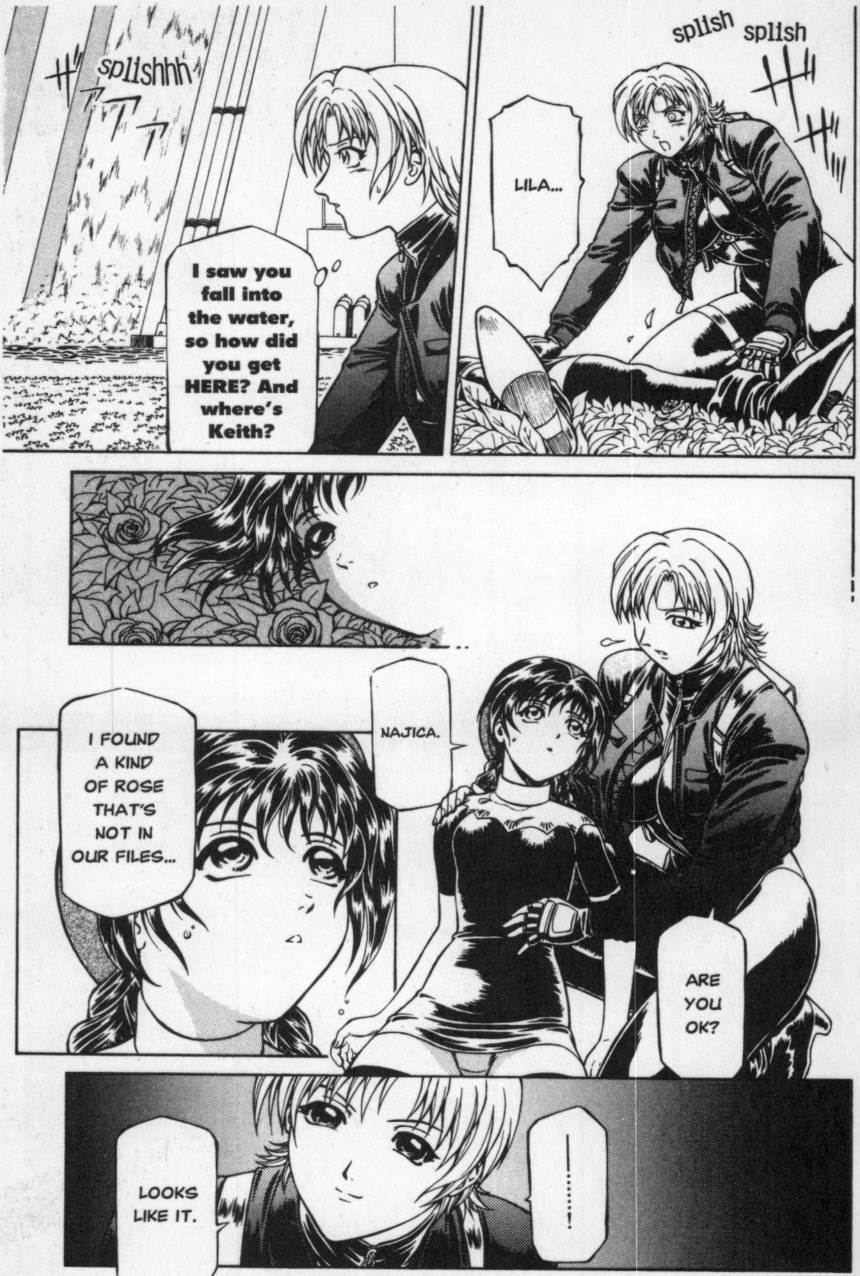
splish splish
LILA...
splishhh
I saw you fall into the water, so how did you get HERE? And where's Keith?
NAJICA.
ARE YOU OK?
I FOUND A KIND OF ROSE THAT'S NOT IN OUR FILES...
......!
LOOKS LIKE IT.

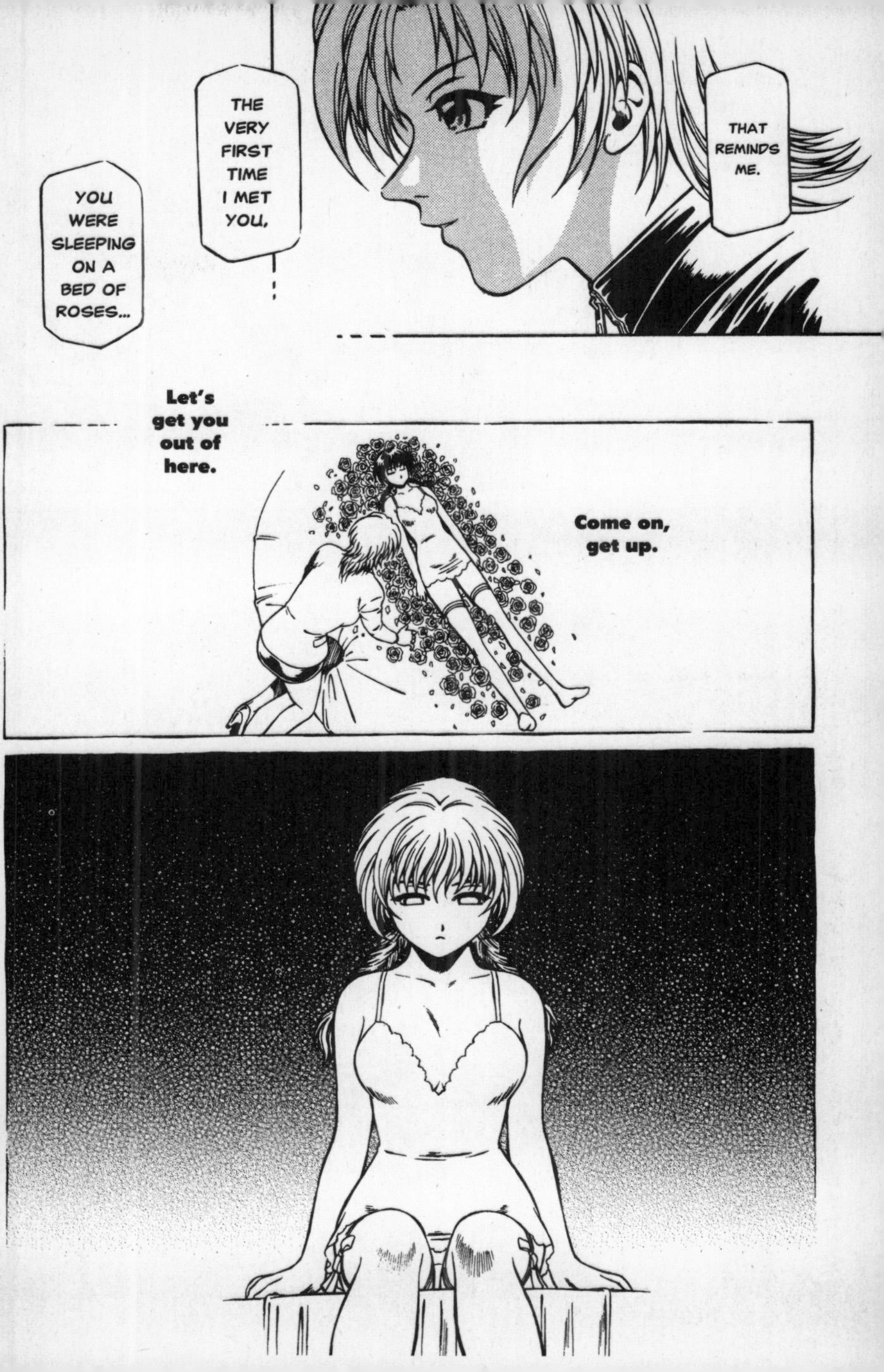
THAT REMINDS ME.
THE VERY FIRST TIME I MET YOU,
YOU WERE SLEEPING ON A BED OF ROSES...
Come on, get up.
Let's get you out of here.

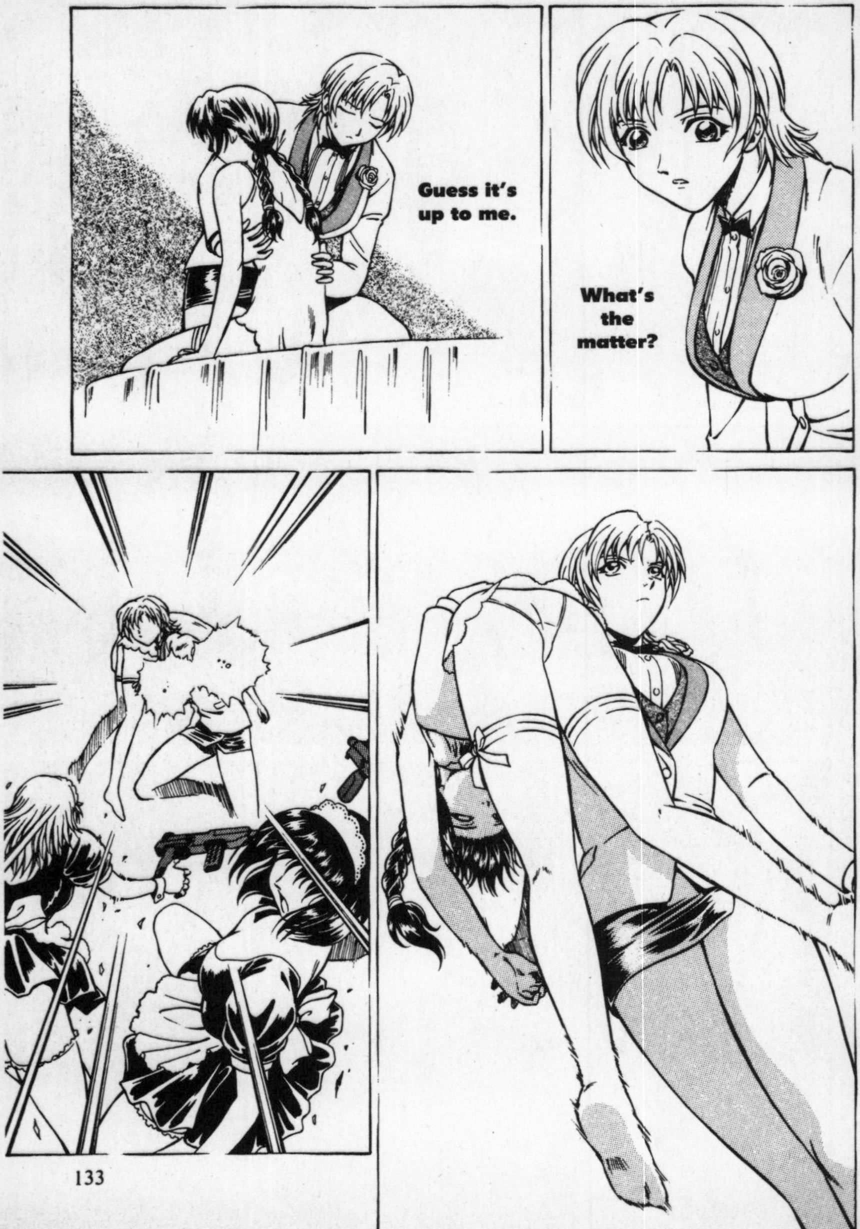
What's the matter?
Guess it's up to me.

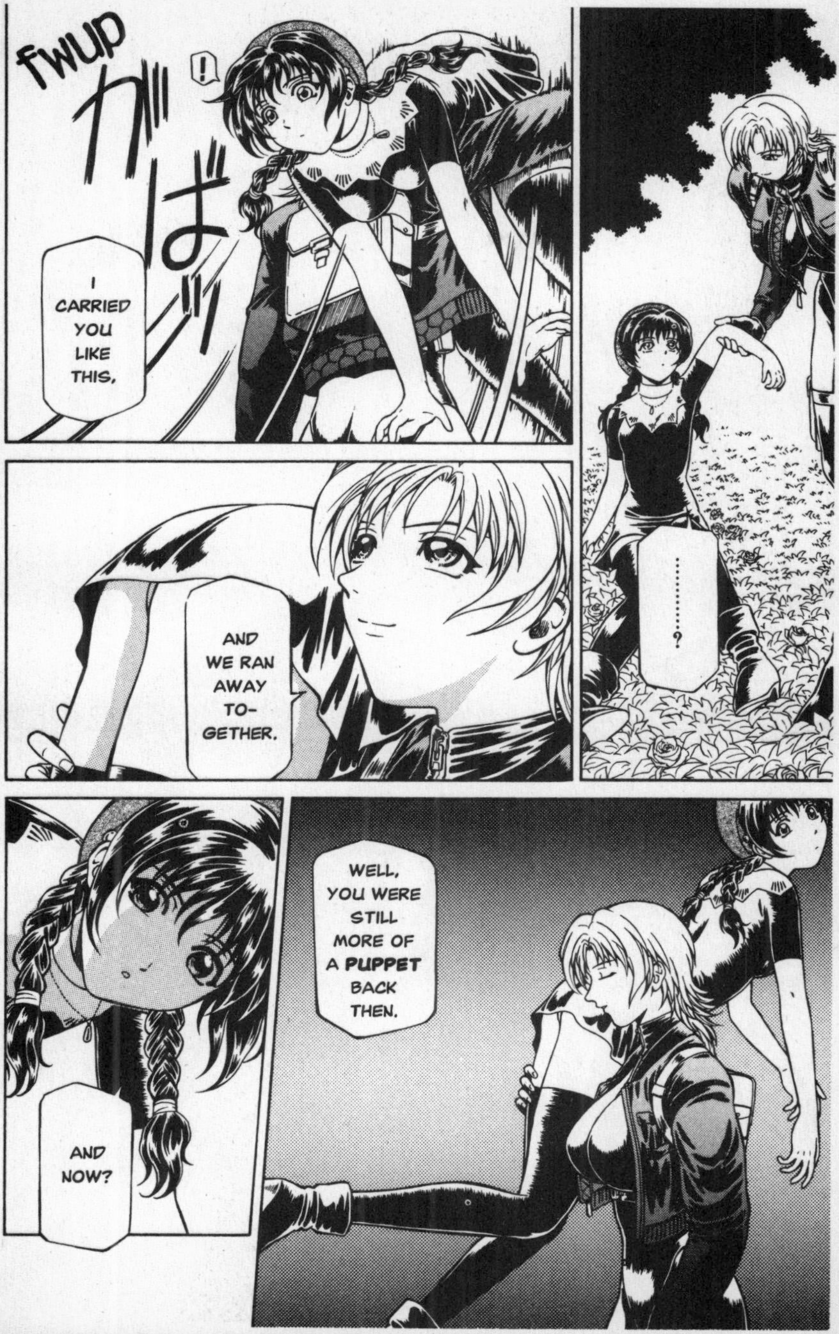

……?
FWUP
かば
!
I CARRIED YOU LIKE THIS,
AND WE RAN AWAY TO-GETHER.
WELL, YOU WERE STILL MORE OF A **PUPPET** BACK THEN.
AND NOW?

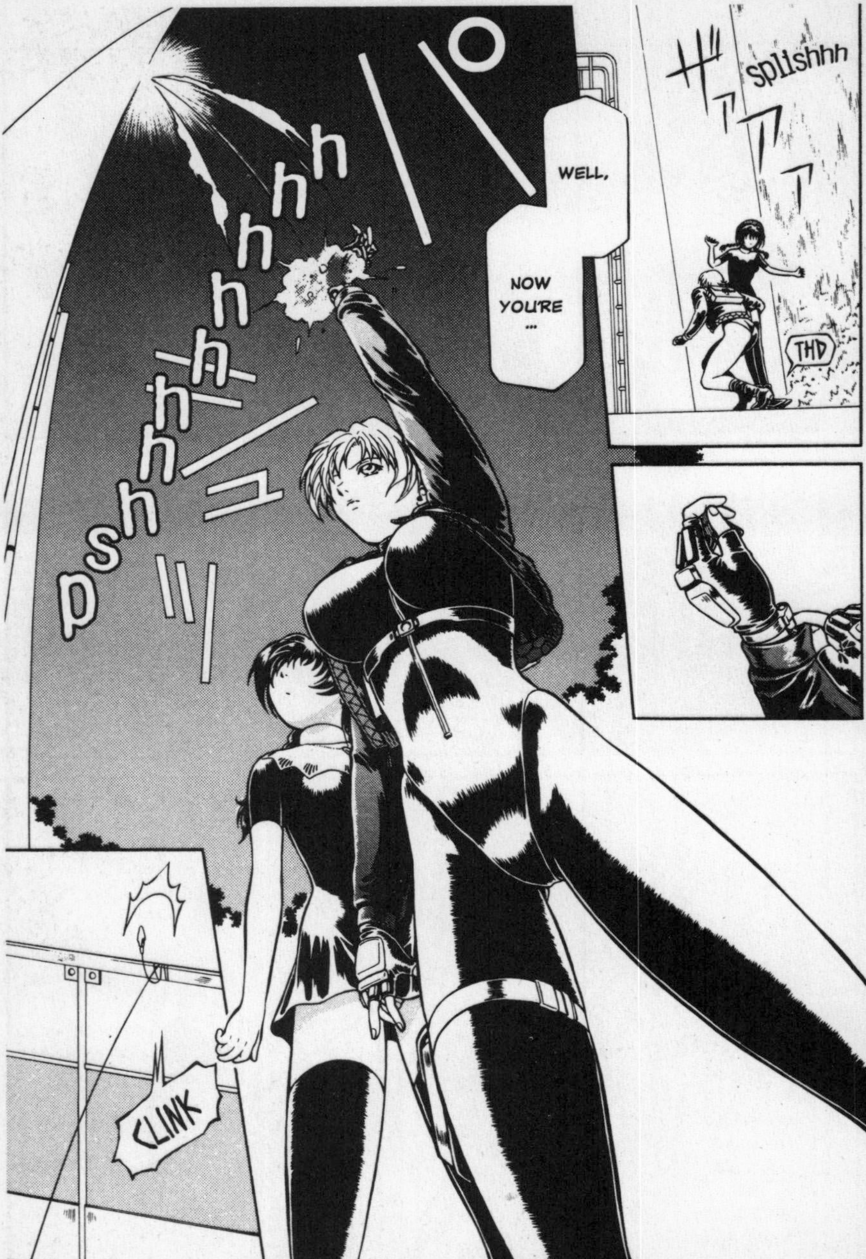

ザァァァ
splishhh
THD
パーシュッー
pshhhhhhhhh
WELL,
NOW YOU'RE ...
CLINK

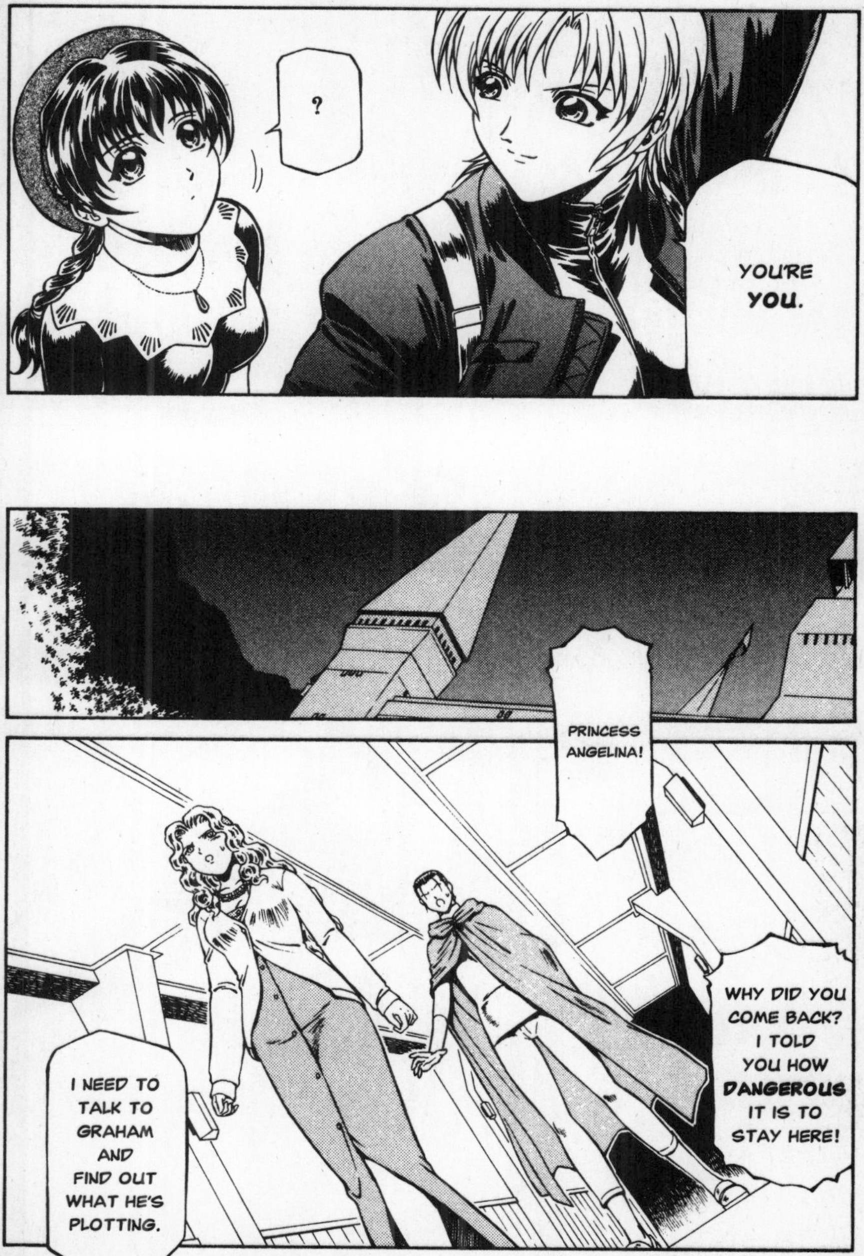
?
YOU'RE YOU.
PRINCESS ANGELINA!
WHY DID YOU COME BACK? I TOLD YOU HOW DANGEROUS IT IS TO STAY HERE!
I NEED TO TALK TO GRAHAM AND FIND OUT WHAT HE'S PLOTTING.

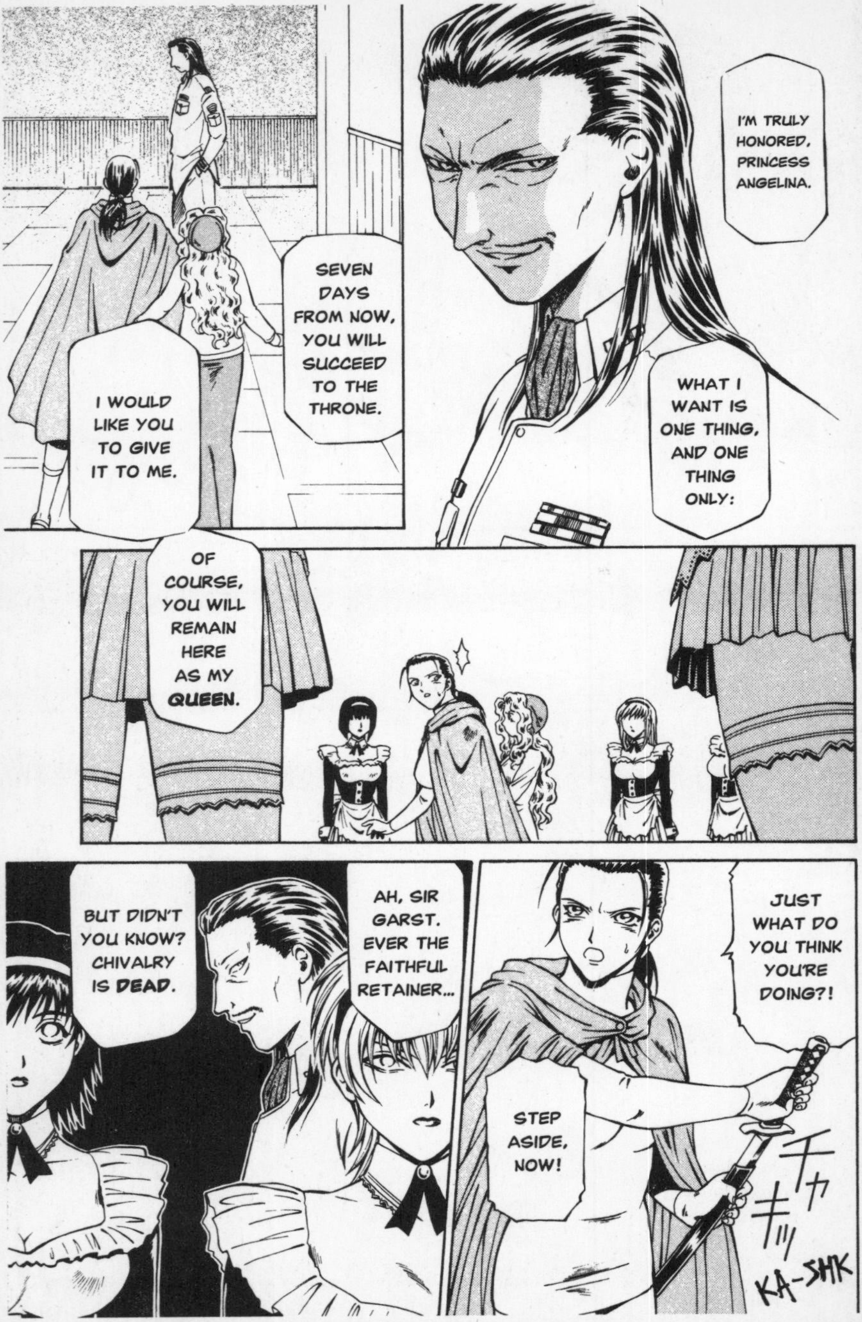
I'M TRULY HONORED, PRINCESS ANGELINA.
WHAT I WANT IS ONE THING, AND ONE THING ONLY:
SEVEN DAYS FROM NOW, YOU WILL SUCCEED TO THE THRONE.
I WOULD LIKE YOU TO GIVE IT TO ME.
OF COURSE, YOU WILL REMAIN HERE AS MY **QUEEN**.
JUST WHAT DO YOU THINK YOU'RE DOING?!
STEP ASIDE, NOW!
チャキッ
KA-SHK
AH, SIR GARST. EVER THE FAITHFUL RETAINER...
BUT DIDN'T YOU KNOW? CHIVALRY IS **DEAD**.

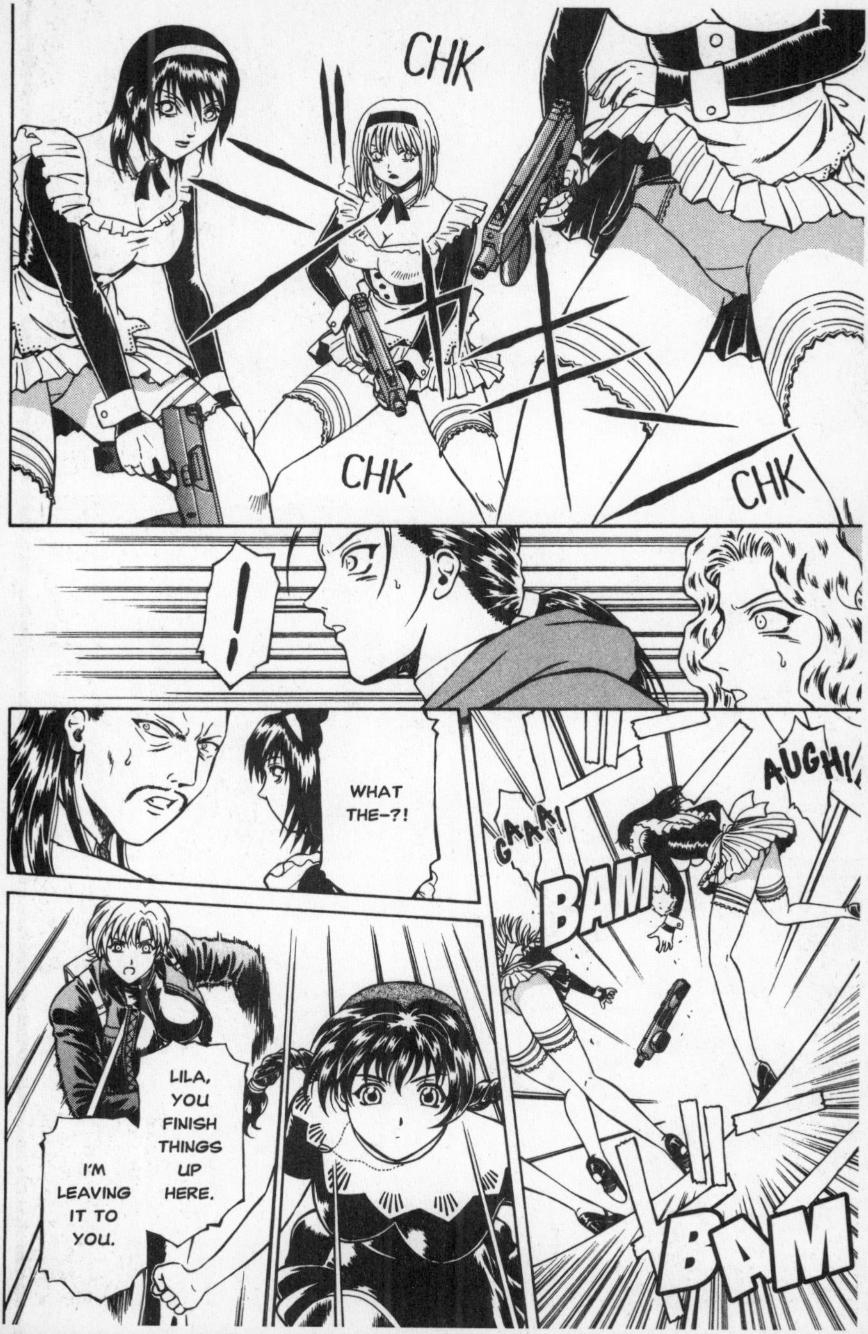
CHK
CHK
CHK
!
AUGH!
GAAA!
BAM
BAM
WHAT THE-?!
LILA, YOU FINISH THINGS UP HERE.
I'M LEAVING IT TO YOU.

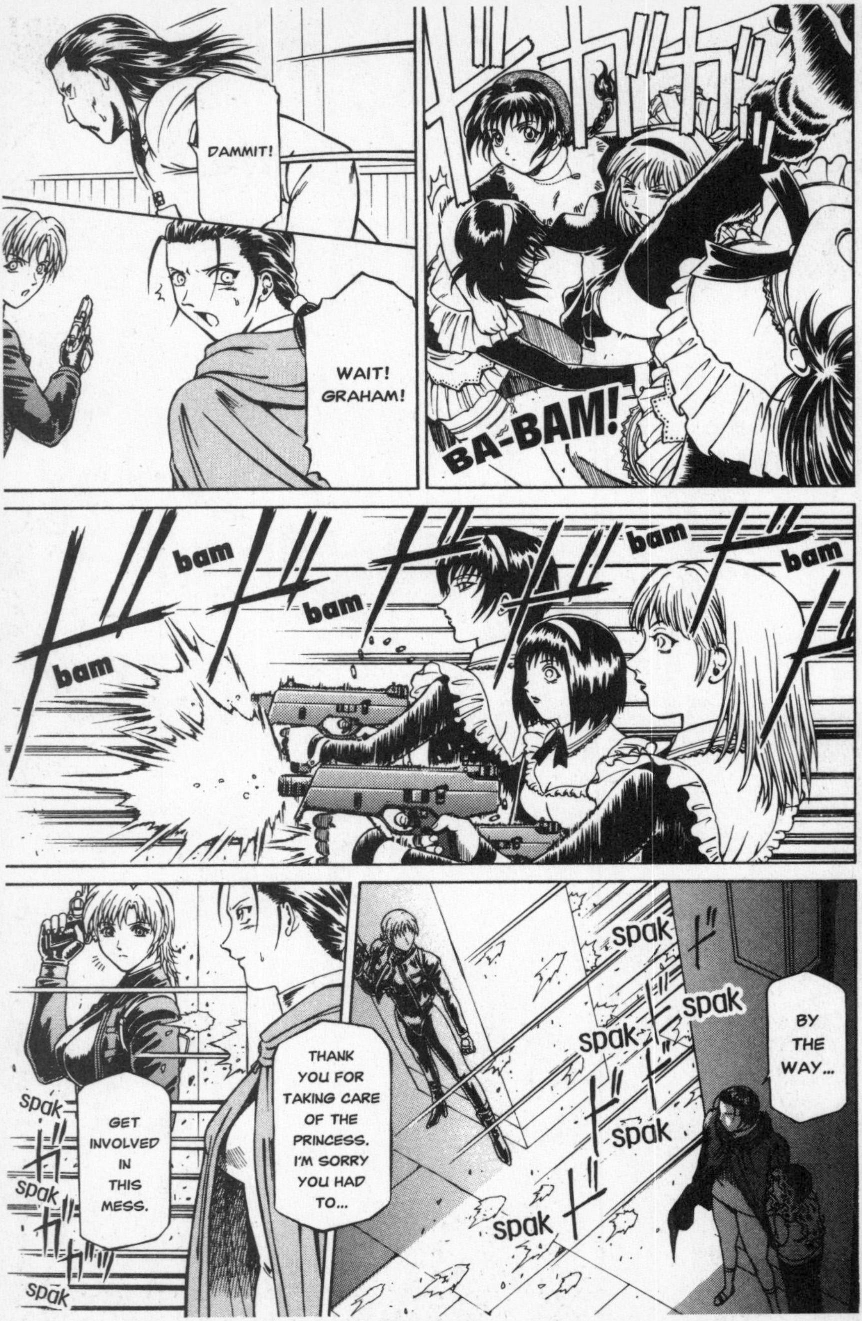
BA-BAM!
DAMMIT!
WAIT! GRAHAM!
bam
bam
bam
bam
bam
spak
spak
spak
spak
spak
BY THE WAY...
THANK YOU FOR TAKING CARE OF THE PRINCESS. I'M SORRY YOU HAD TO...
GET INVOLVED IN THIS MESS.
spak
spak
spak

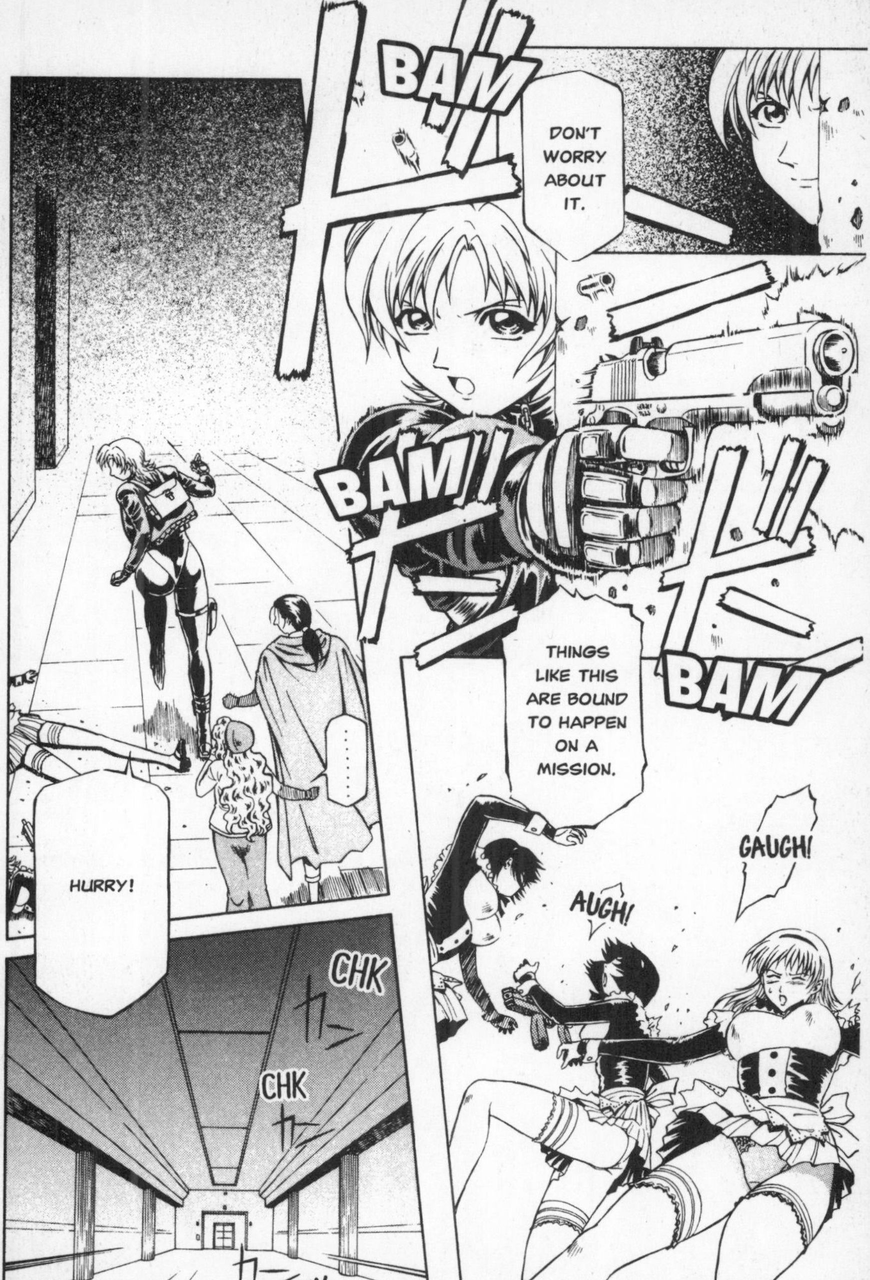

BAM
DON'T WORRY ABOUT IT.
BAM!
BAM
THINGS LIKE THIS ARE BOUND TO HAPPEN ON A MISSION.
GAUGH!
AUGH!
......
HURRY!
CHK
CHK
CHK

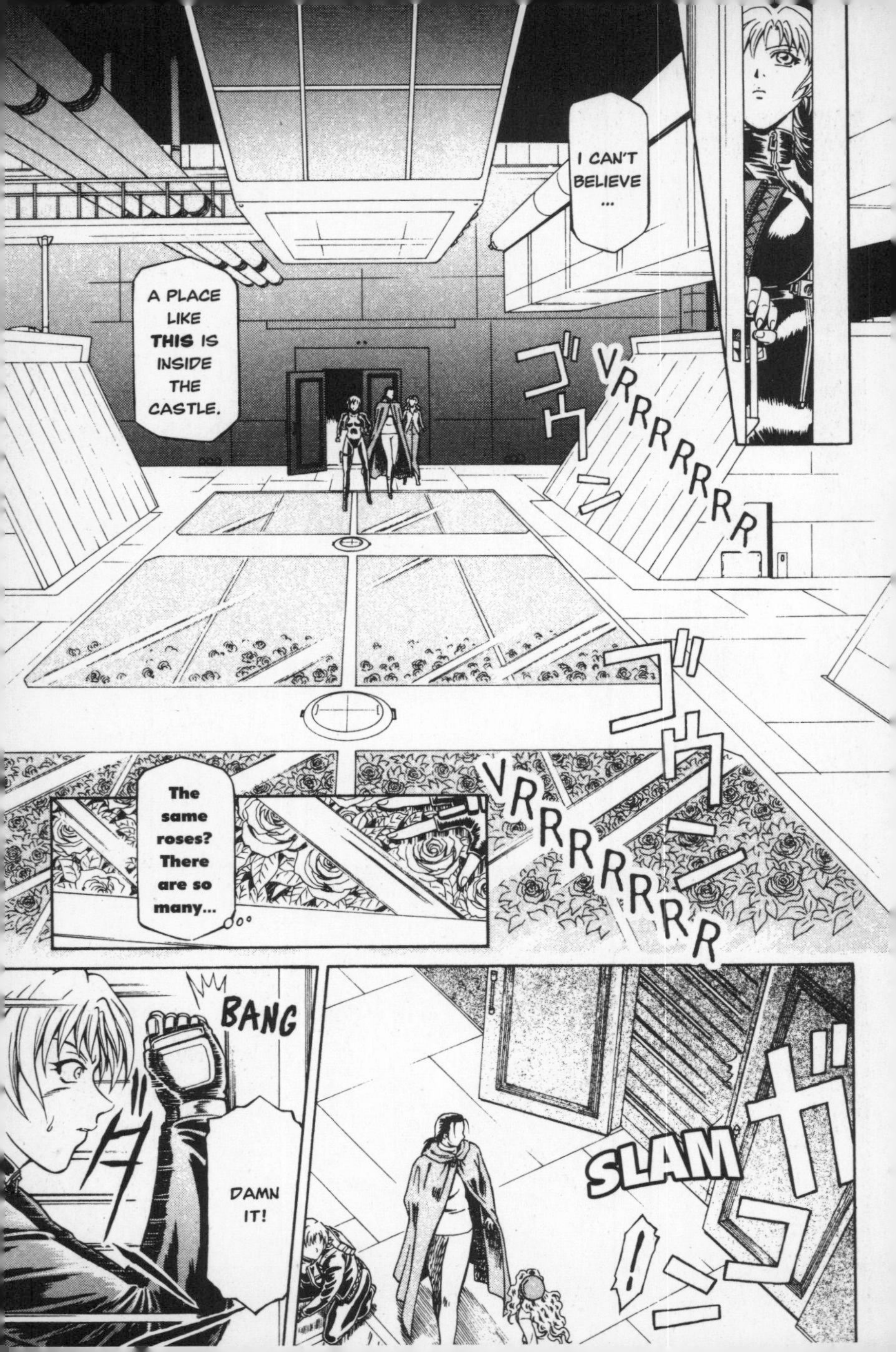
I CAN'T BELIEVE ...
A PLACE LIKE THIS IS INSIDE THE CASTLE.
VRRRRRRR
VRRRRRRRR
The same roses? There are so many...
SLAM
BANG
DAMN IT!

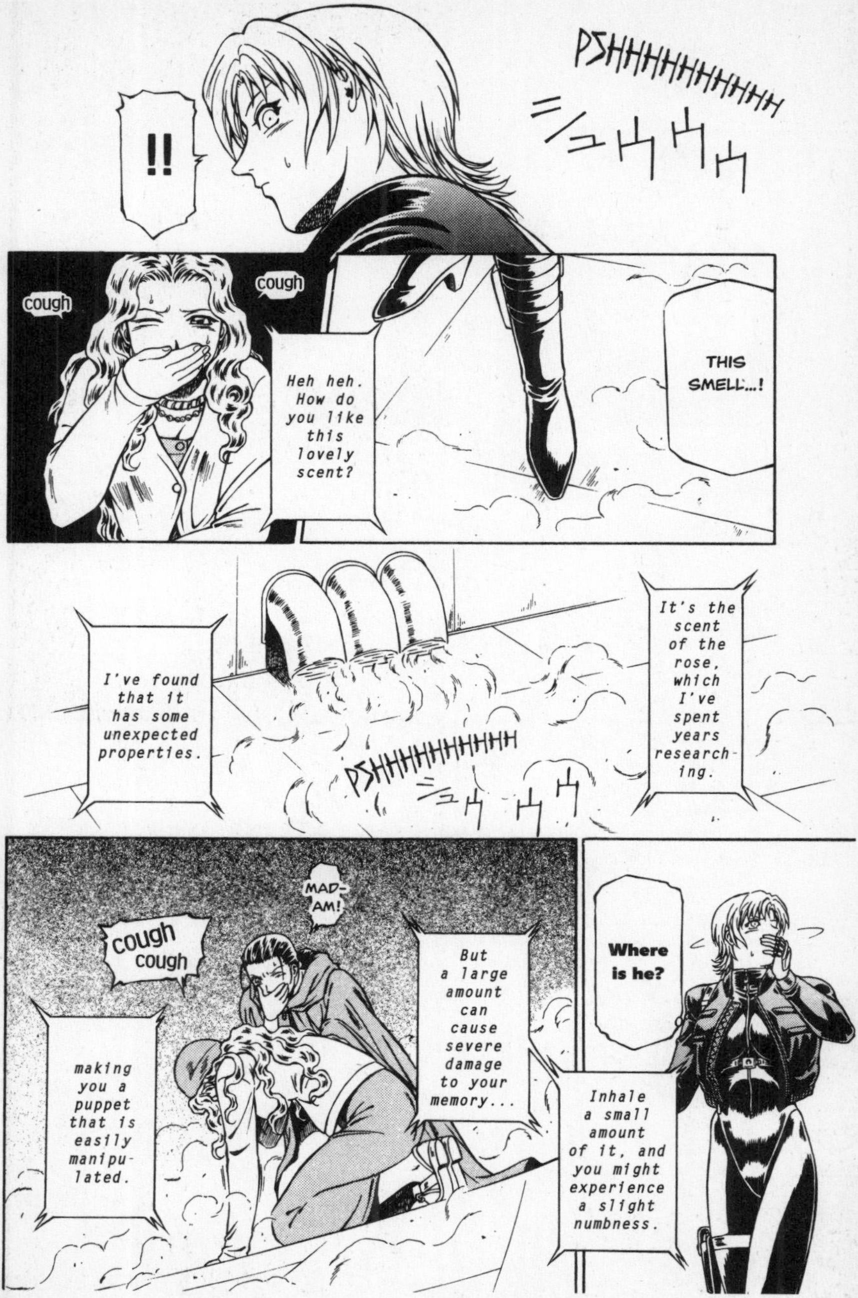
PSHHHHHHHHHHH
シュウウウ
!!
THIS SMELL...!
cough
cough
Heh heh. How do you like this lovely scent?
It's the scent of the rose, which I've spent years research-ing.
PSHHHHHHHHHH
シュウウウ
I've found that it has some unexpected properties.
Where is he?
Inhale a small amount of it, and you might experience a slight numbness.
MAD-AM!
But a large amount can cause severe damage to your memory...
cough cough
making you a puppet that is easily manipu-lated.

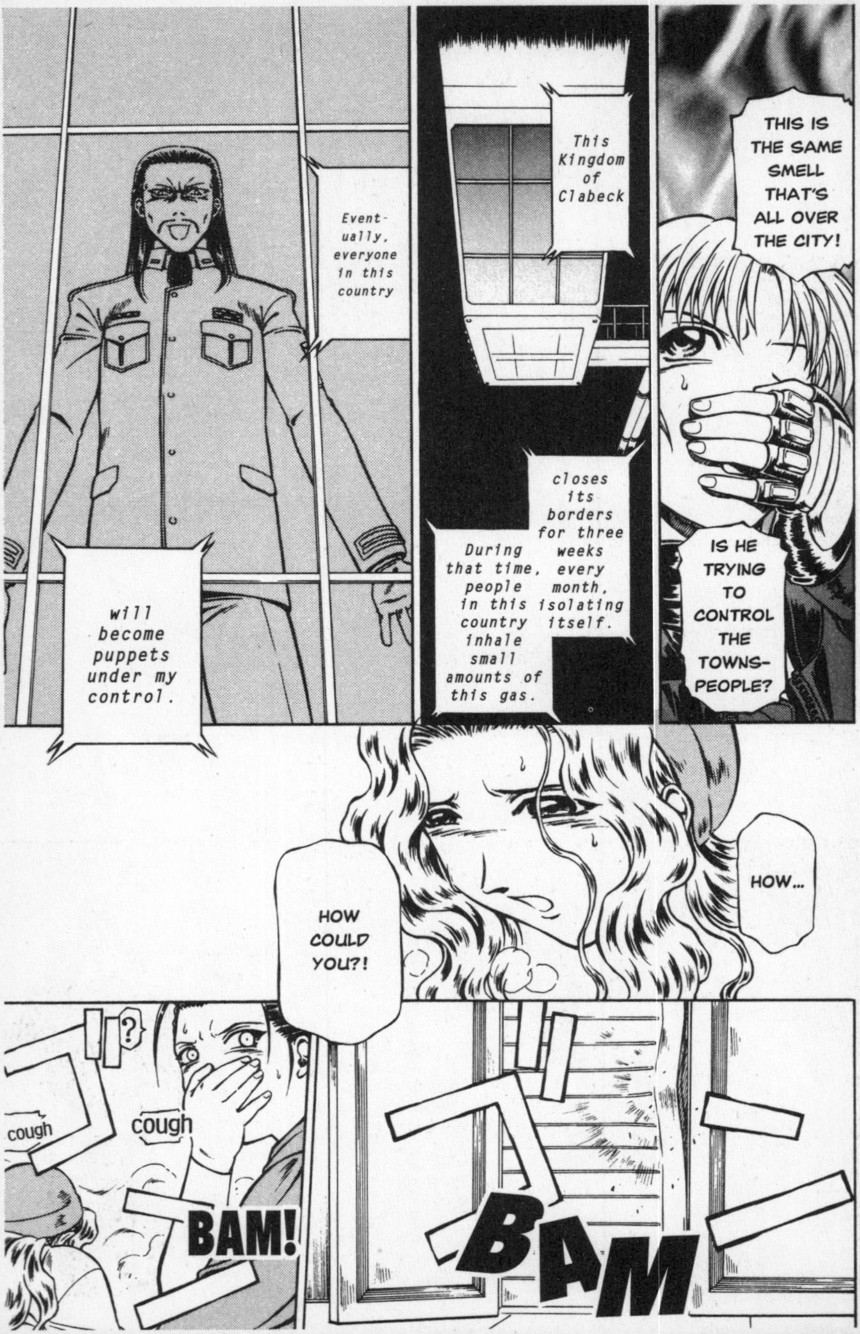
THIS IS THE SAME SMELL THAT'S ALL OVER THE CITY!
IS HE TRYING TO CONTROL THE TOWNS-PEOPLE?
This Kingdom of Clabeck
closes its borders for three weeks every month, isolating itself.
During that time, people in this country inhale small amounts of this gas.
Event-ually, everyone in this country
will become puppets under my control.
HOW...
HOW COULD YOU?!
BAM
?
cough
cough
BAM!

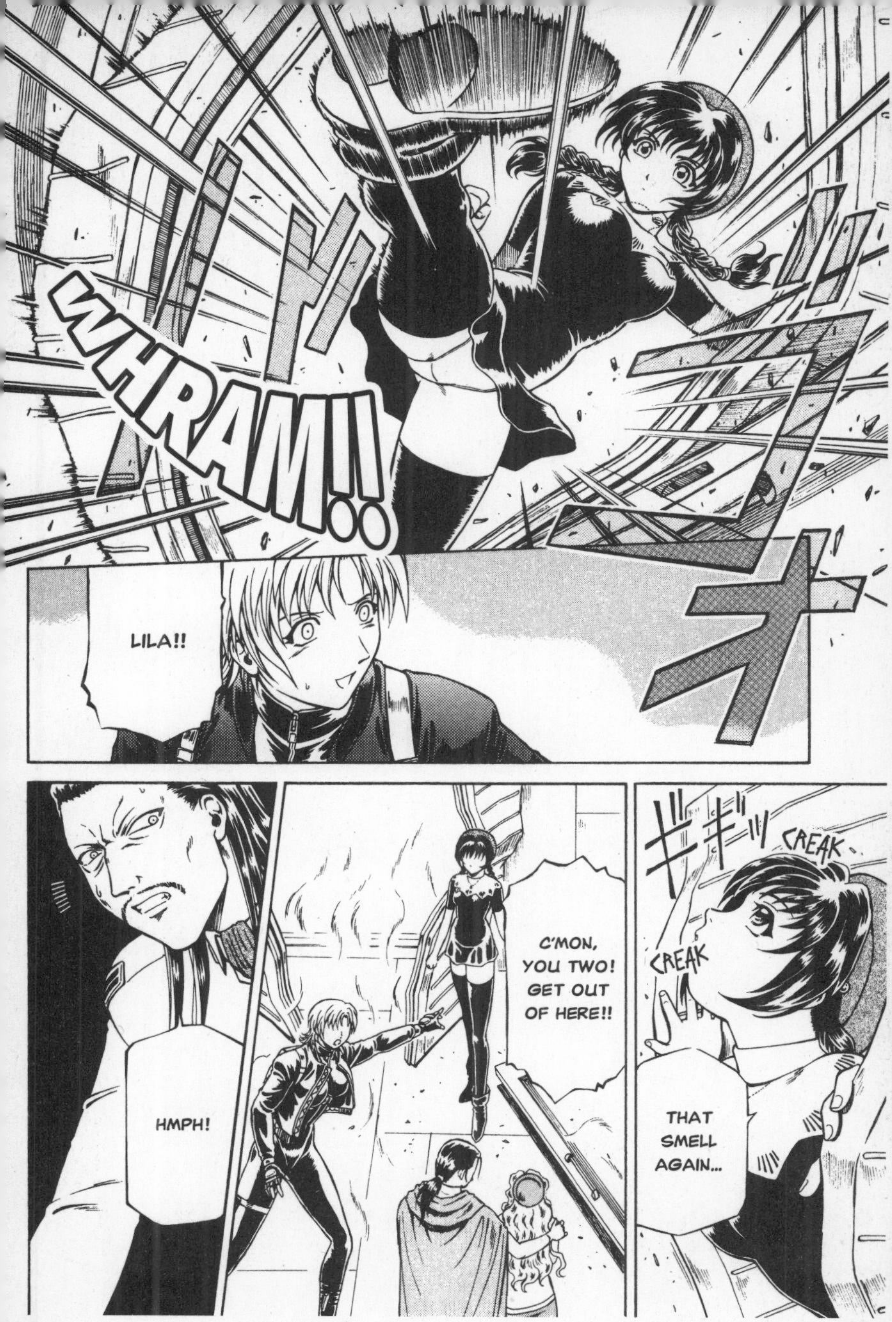
WHRAM!!
LILA!!
ギギッ
CREAK
CREAK
THAT SMELL AGAIN...
C'MON, YOU TWO! GET OUT OF HERE!!
HMPH!

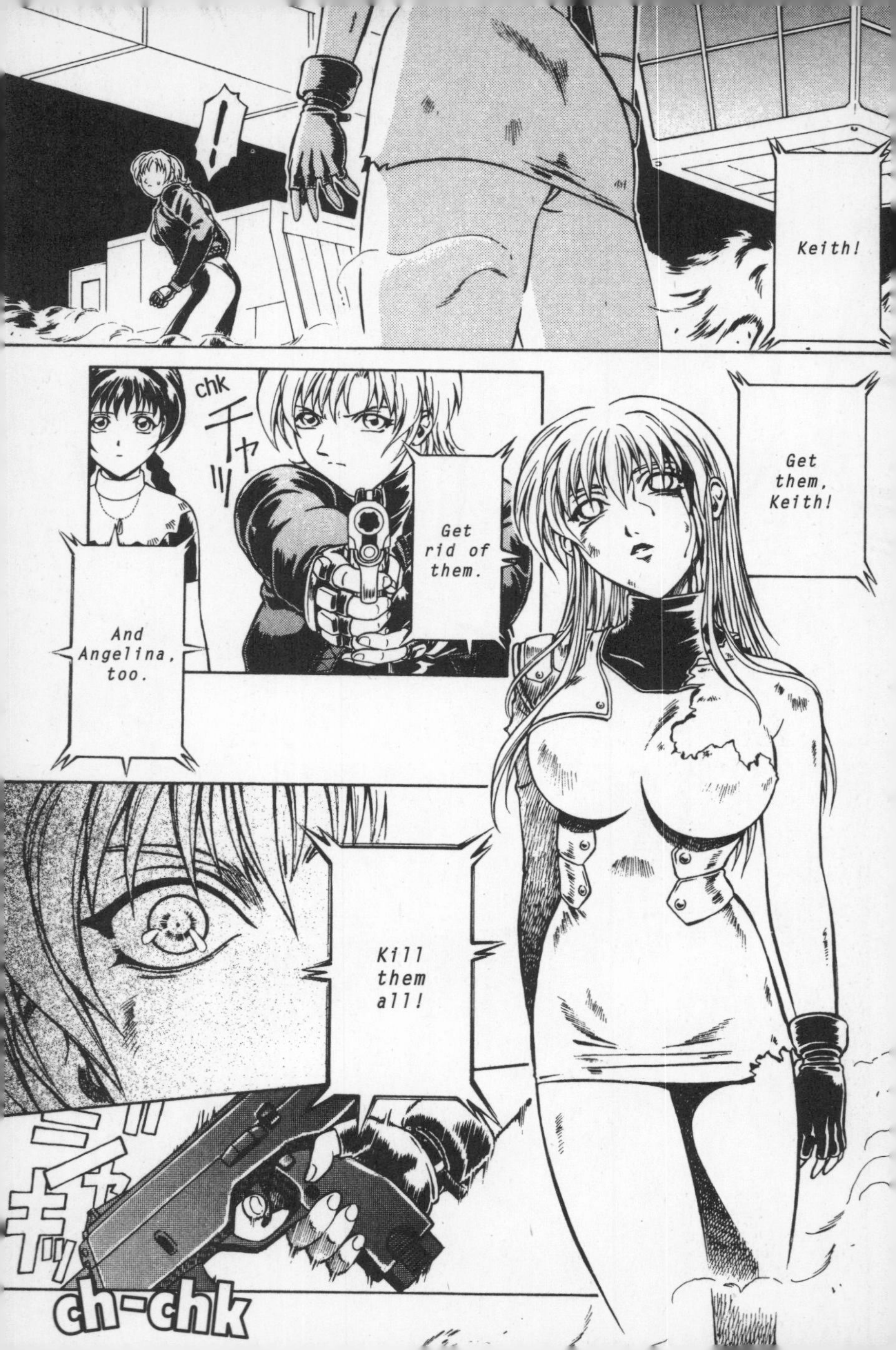
Keith!
!
Get them, Keith!
chk
チャッ
Get rid of them.
And Angelina, too.
Kill them all!
ジャキッ
ch-chk

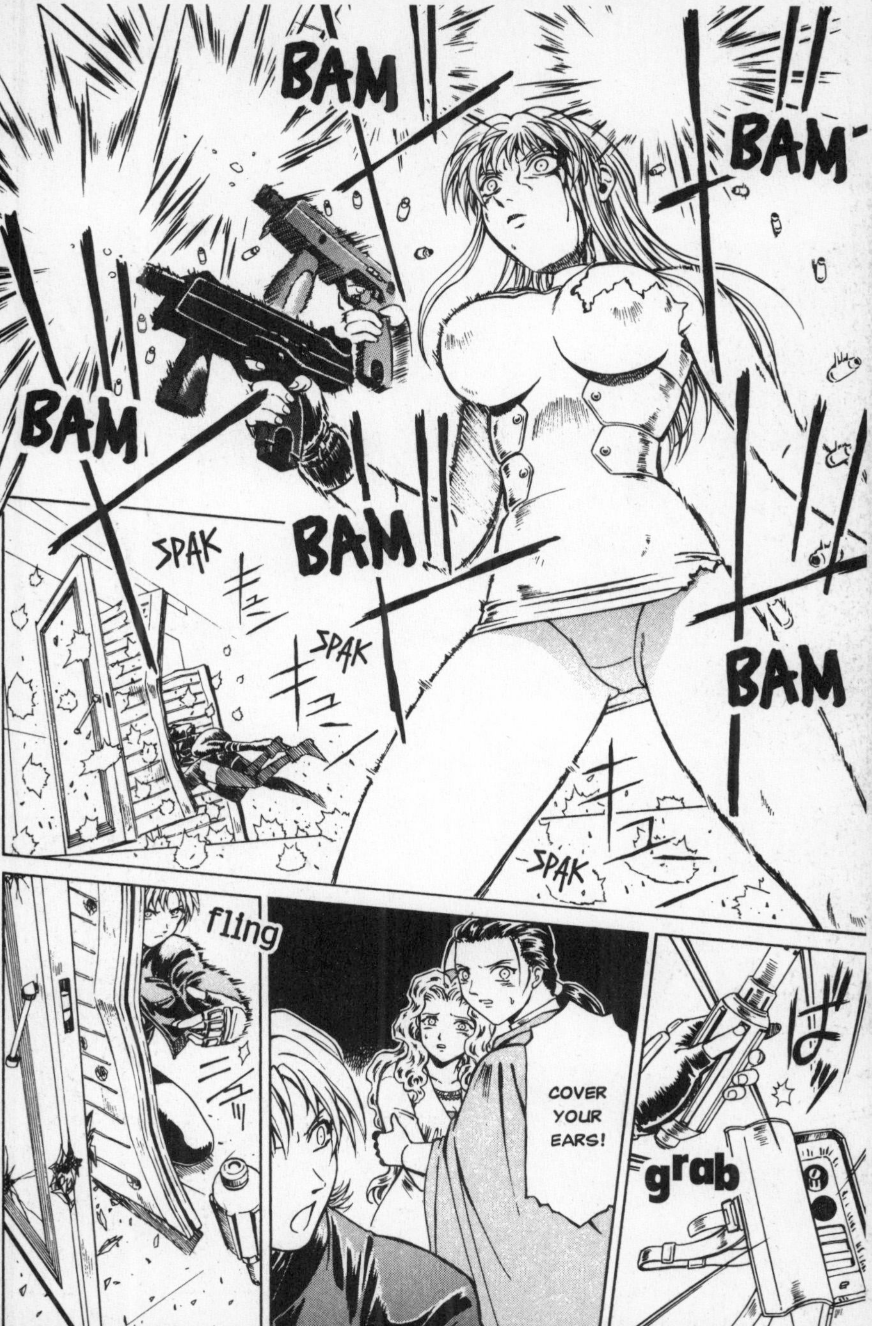

BAM
BAM
BAM
BAM!!
BAM
BAM
SPAK
キュ
SPAK
キュ
キュ
SPAK
ば
grab
COVER YOUR EARS!
fling

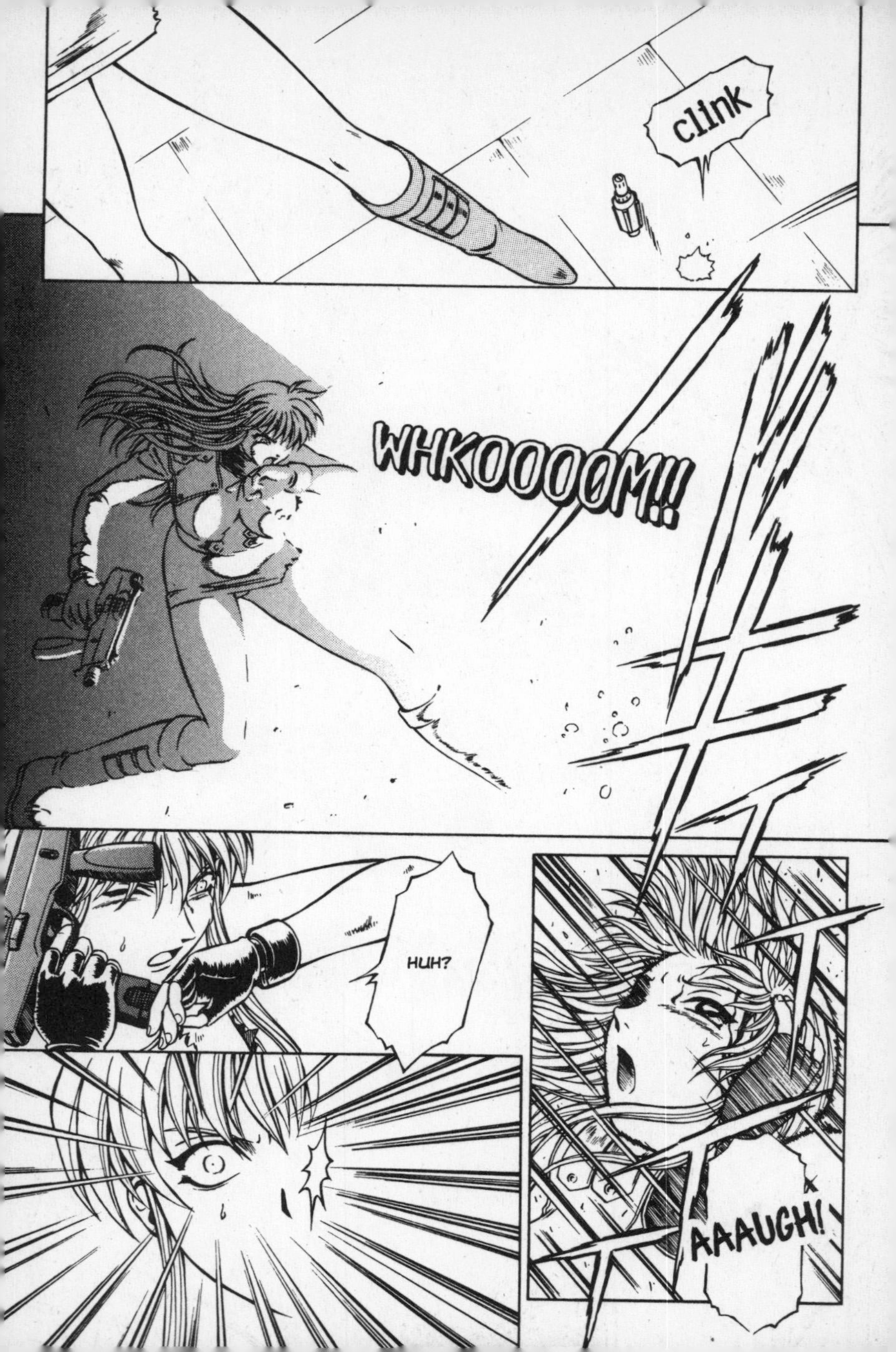
clink
WHKOOOOM!!
AAAUGH!
HUH?

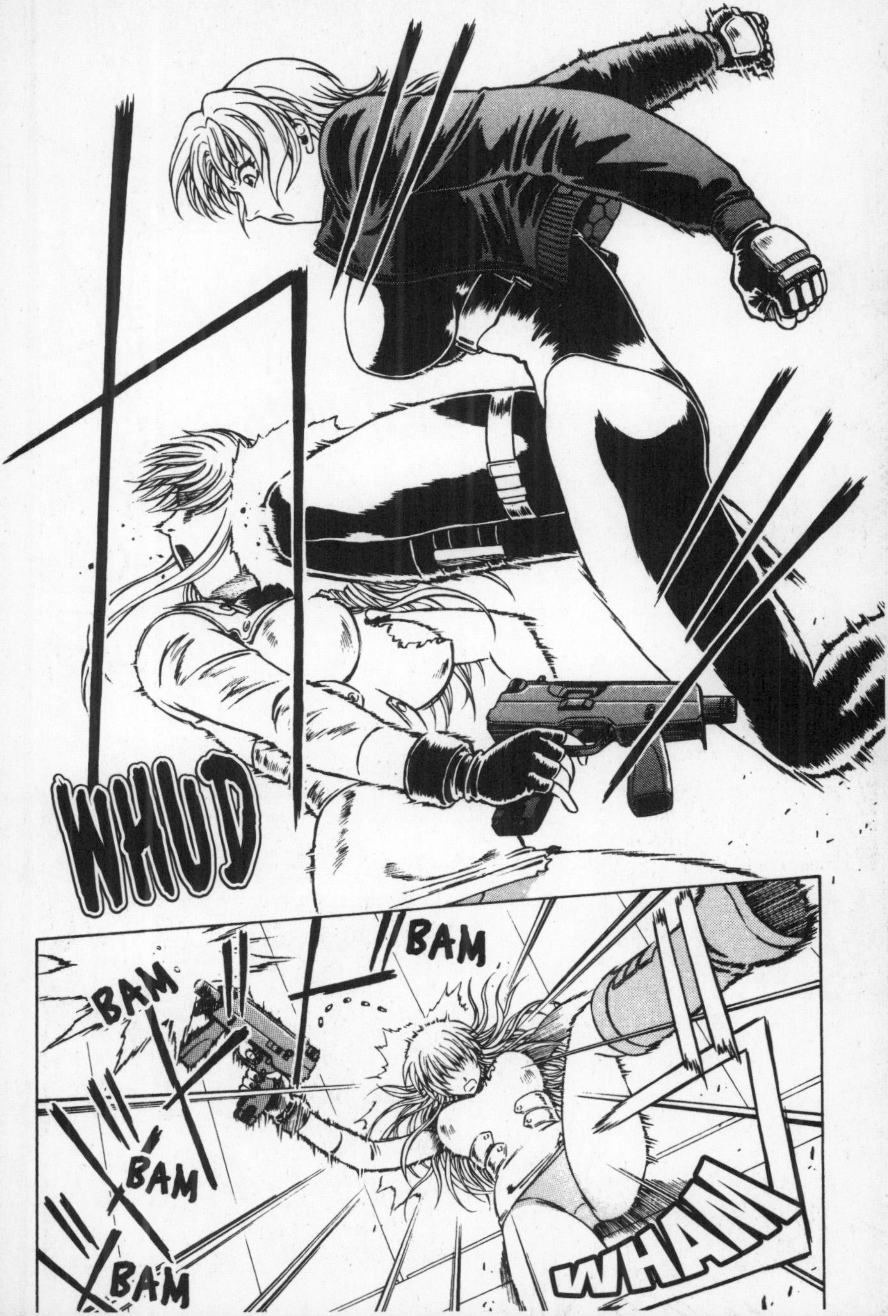
WHUD
BAM
BAM
BAM
BAM
WHAM

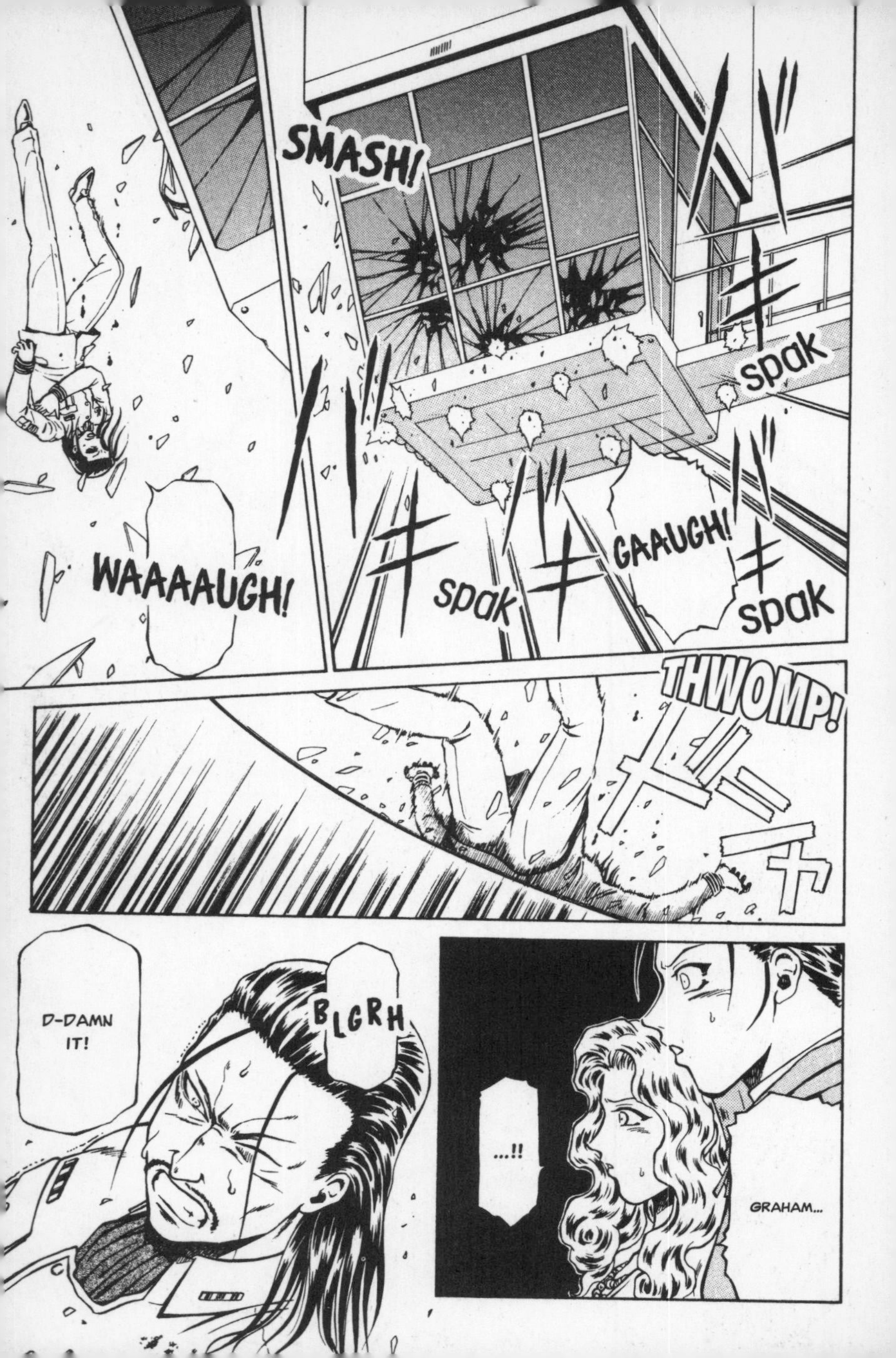

SMASH!
spak
GAAUGH!
spak
spak
WAAAAUGH!
THWOMP!
GRAHAM...
...!!
BLGRH
D-DAMN IT!

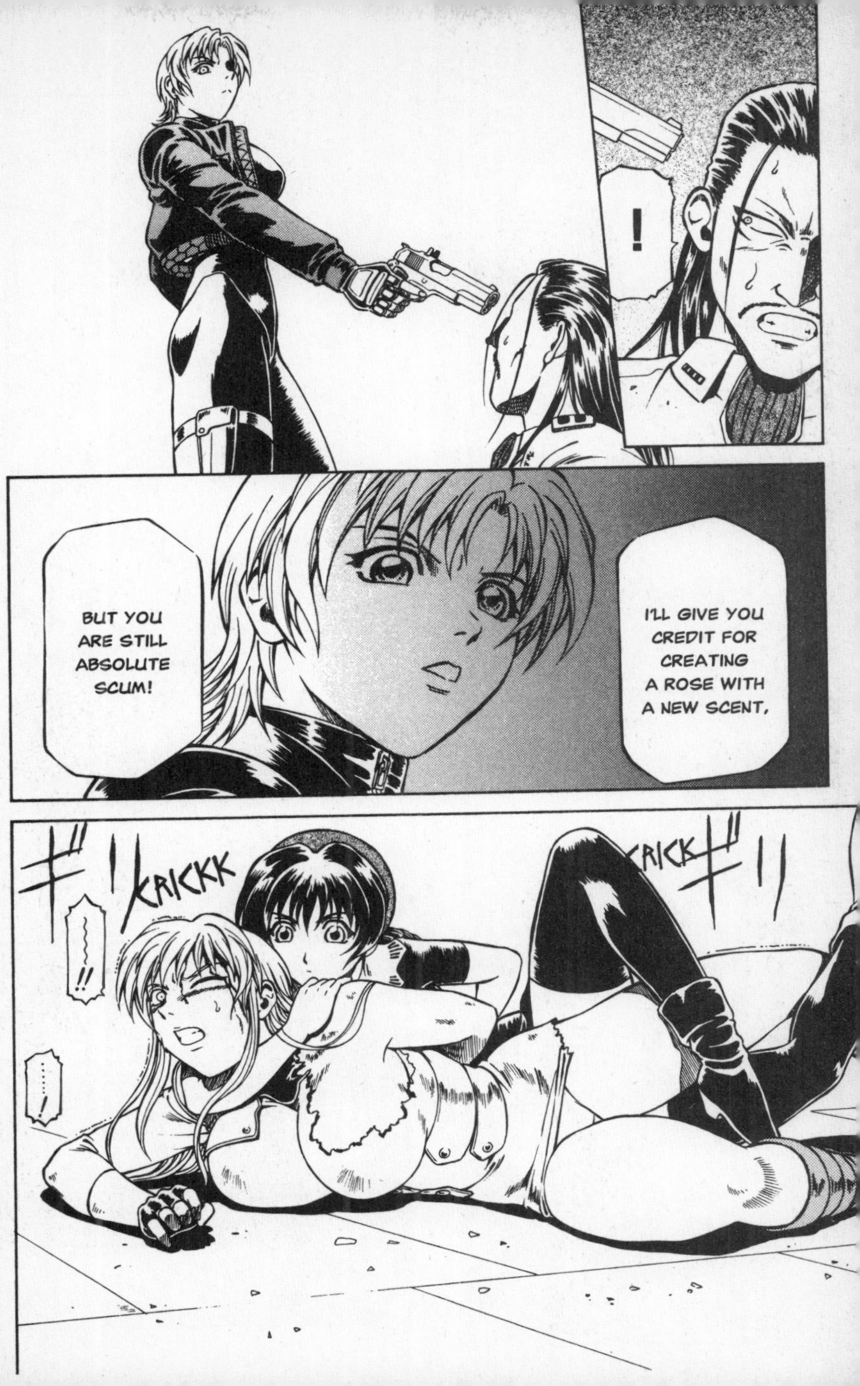
!
I'LL GIVE YOU CREDIT FOR CREATING A ROSE WITH A NEW SCENT,
BUT YOU ARE STILL ABSOLUTE SCUM!
KRICK
ギリ
KRICKK
ギリ
...!!
...!

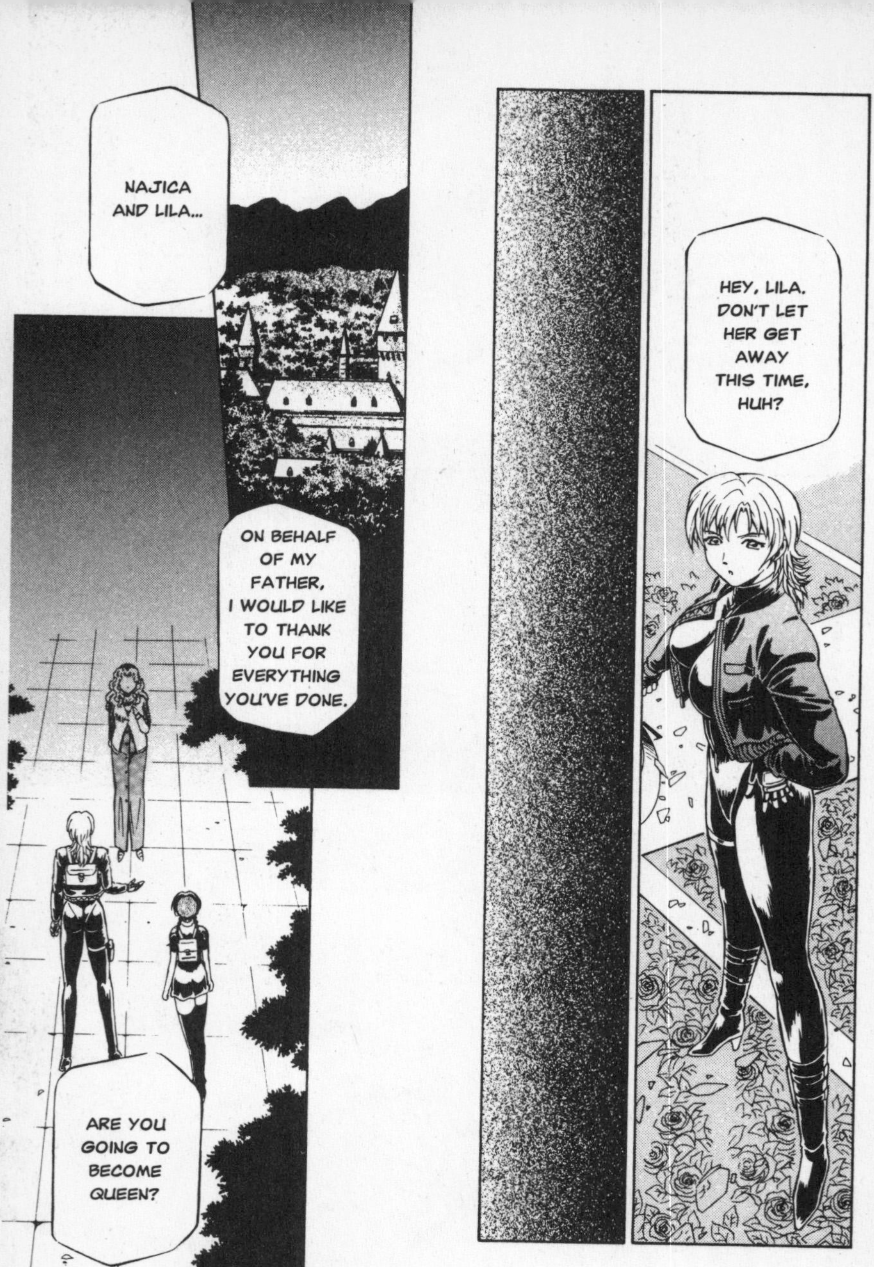
HEY, LILA. DON'T LET HER GET AWAY THIS TIME, HUH?
NAJICA AND LILA...
ON BEHALF OF MY FATHER, I WOULD LIKE TO THANK YOU FOR EVERYTHING YOU'VE DONE.
ARE YOU GOING TO BECOME QUEEN?

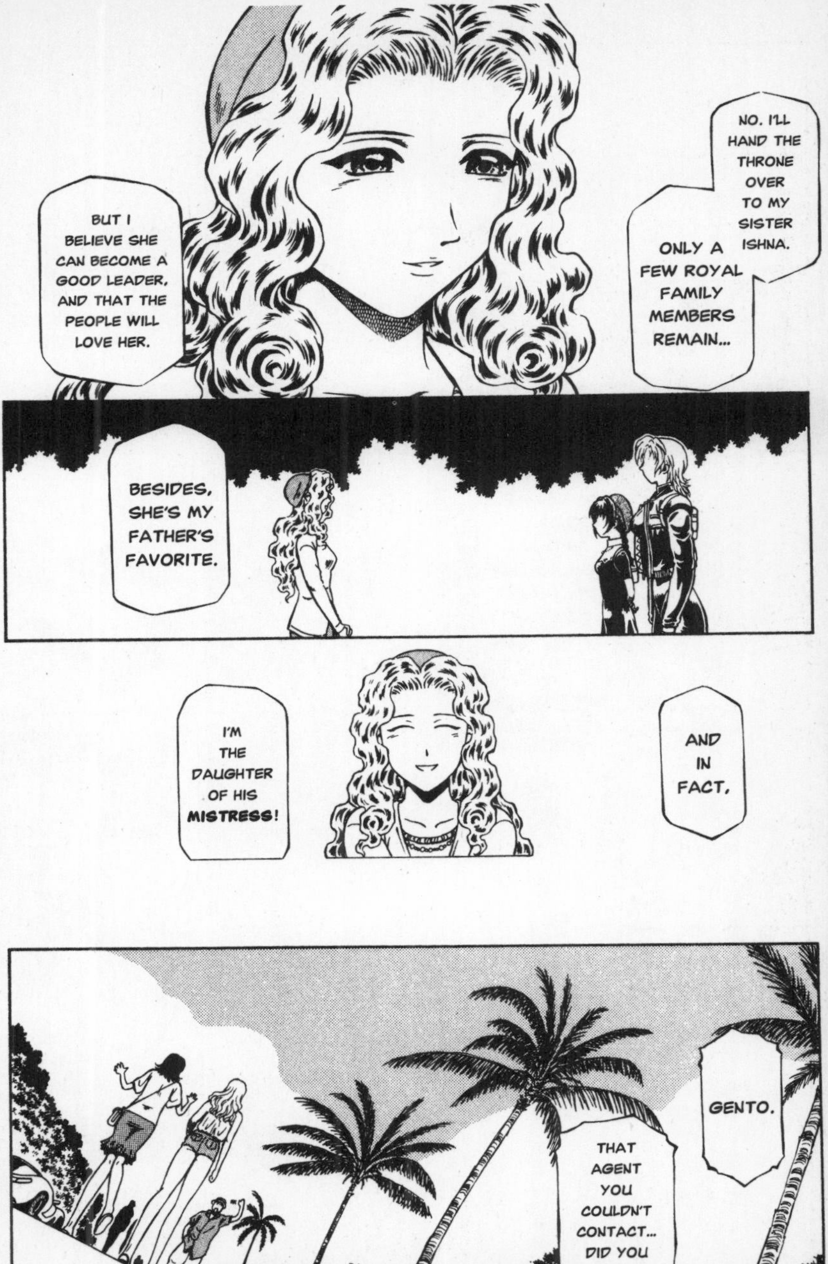
NO. I'LL HAND THE THRONE OVER TO MY SISTER ISHNA.
ONLY A FEW ROYAL FAMILY MEMBERS REMAIN...
BUT I BELIEVE SHE CAN BECOME A GOOD LEADER, AND THAT THE PEOPLE WILL LOVE HER.
BESIDES, SHE'S MY FATHER'S FAVORITE.
AND IN FACT,
I'M THE DAUGHTER OF HIS MISTRESS!
GENTO.
THAT AGENT YOU COULDN'T CONTACT... DID YOU MEAN KEITH?!

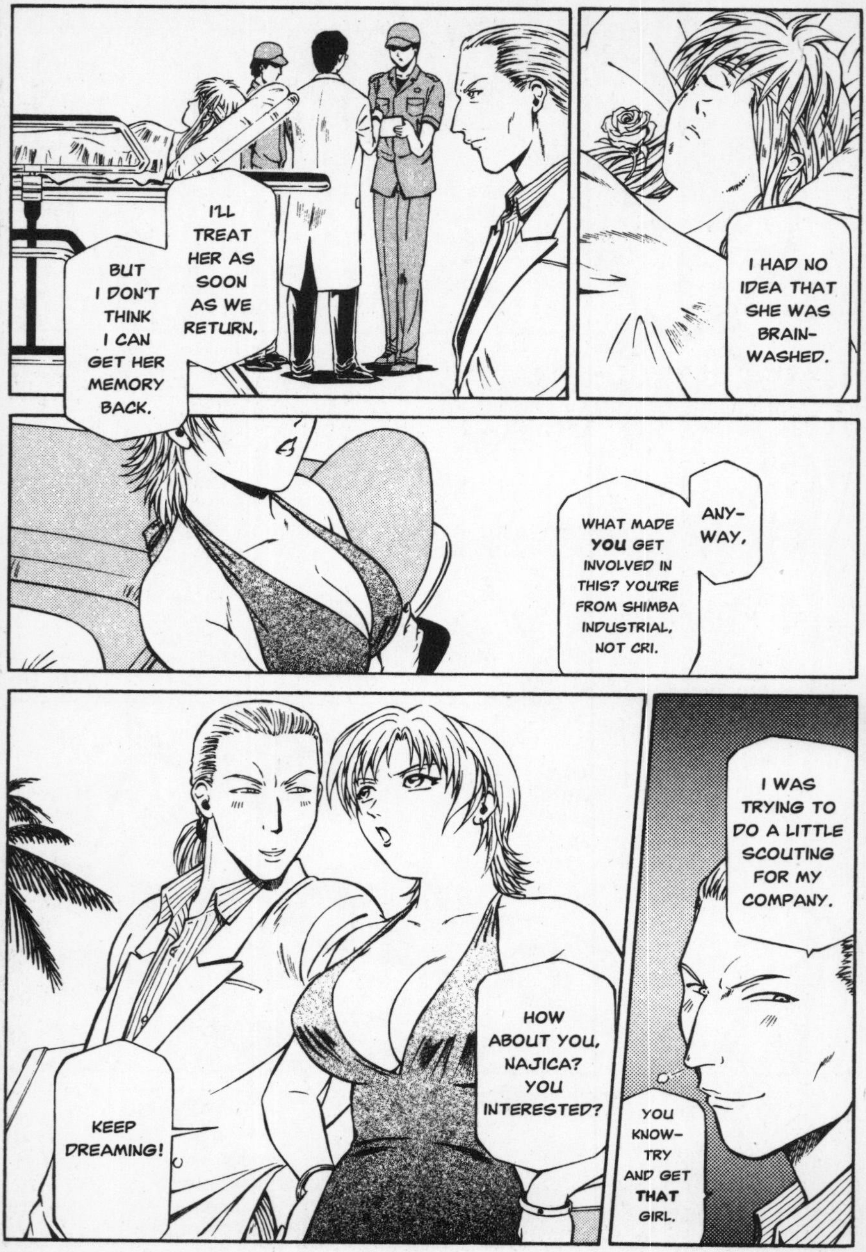
I HAD NO IDEA THAT SHE WAS BRAIN-WASHED.
I'LL TREAT HER AS SOON AS WE RETURN,
BUT I DON'T THINK I CAN GET HER MEMORY BACK.
ANY-WAY,
WHAT MADE YOU GET INVOLVED IN THIS? YOU'RE FROM SHIMBA INDUSTRIAL, NOT CRI.
I WAS TRYING TO DO A LITTLE SCOUTING FOR MY COMPANY.
YOU KNOW—TRY AND GET THAT GIRL.
HOW ABOUT YOU, NAJICA? YOU INTERESTED?
KEEP DREAMING!

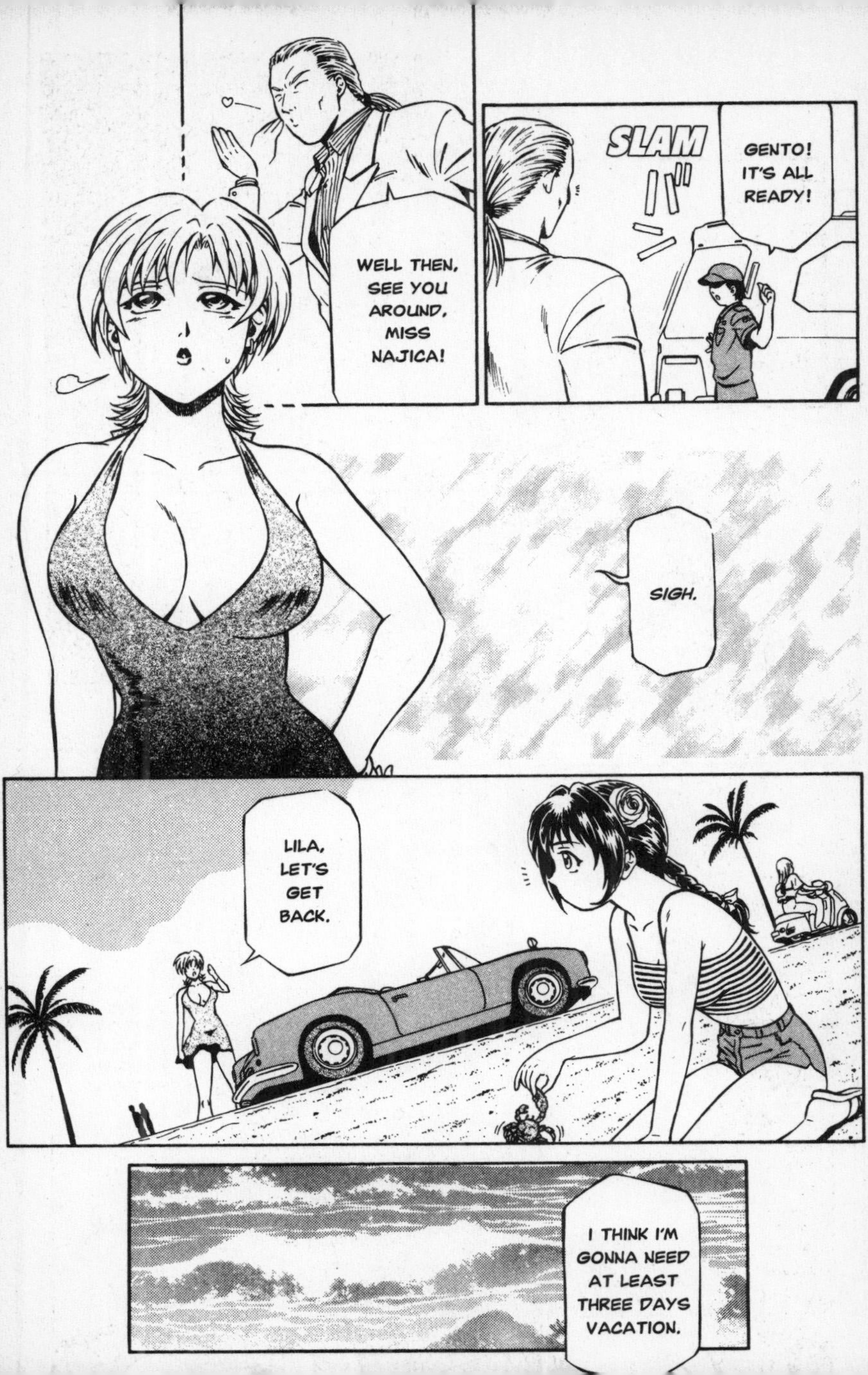
GENTO! IT'S ALL READY!
SLAM
WELL THEN, SEE YOU AROUND, MISS NAJICA!
SIGH.
LILA, LET'S GET BACK.
I THINK I'M GONNA NEED AT LEAST THREE DAYS VACATION.

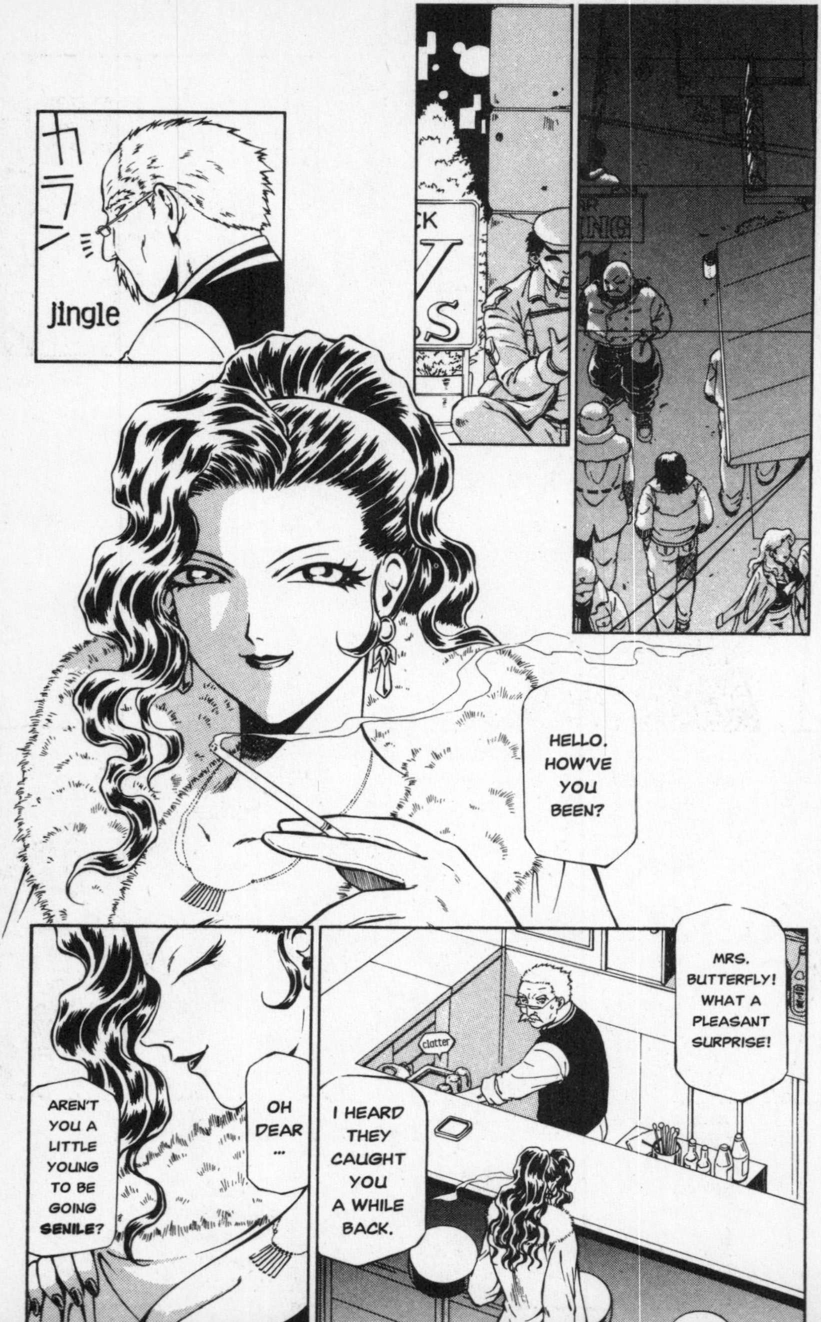
カラン
jingle
HELLO. HOW'VE YOU BEEN?
MRS. BUTTERFLY! WHAT A PLEASANT SURPRISE!
clatter
I HEARD THEY CAUGHT YOU A WHILE BACK.
OH DEAR ...
AREN'T YOU A LITTLE YOUNG TO BE GOING SENILE?

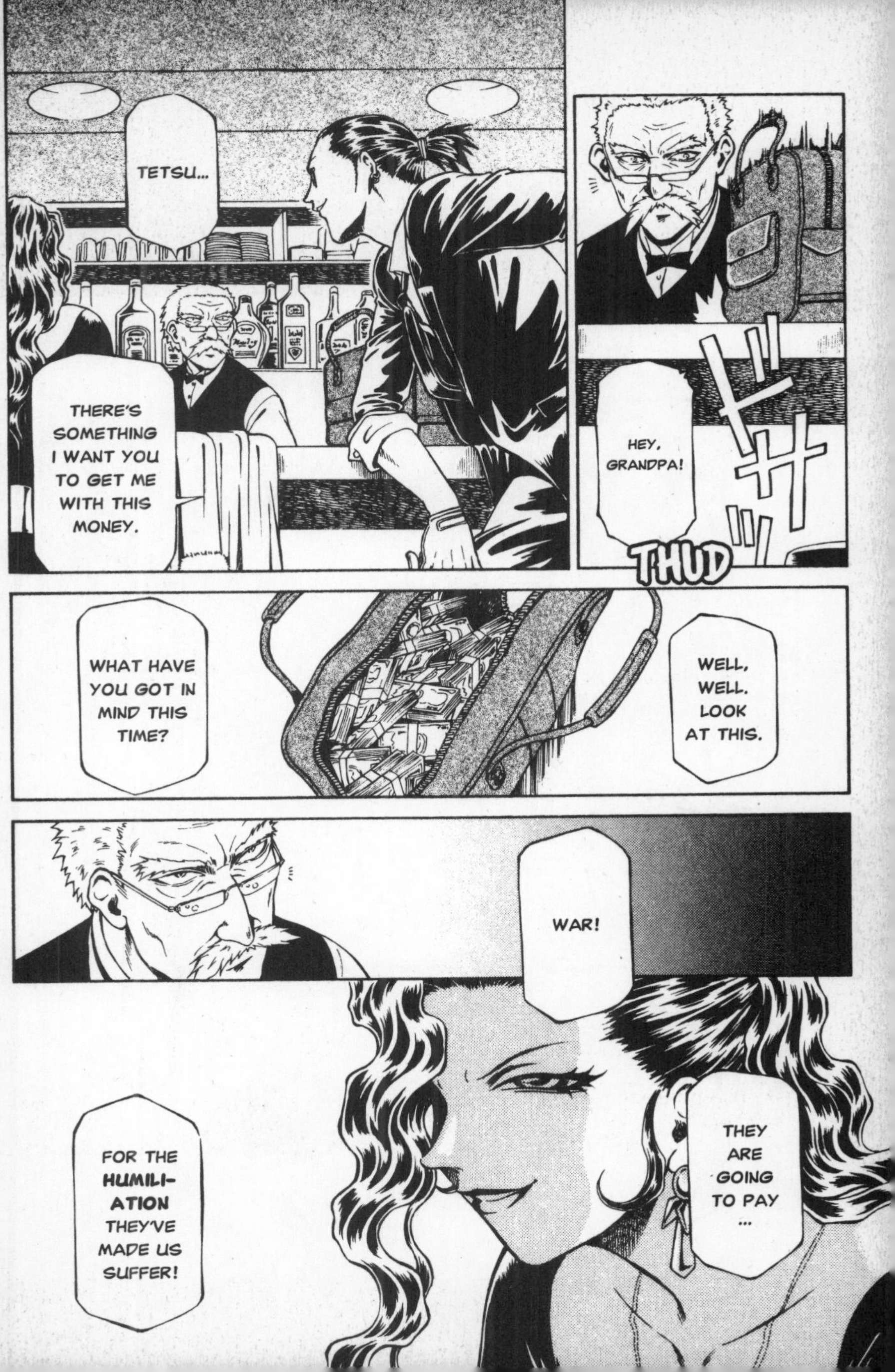
HEY, GRANDPA!
THUD
TETSU...
THERE'S SOMETHING I WANT YOU TO GET ME WITH THIS MONEY.
WELL, WELL. LOOK AT THIS.
WHAT HAVE YOU GOT IN MIND THIS TIME?
WAR!
THEY ARE GOING TO PAY ...
FOR THE **HUMILIATION** THEY'VE MADE US SUFFER!

Operation.6
HIGHWAY CHASE

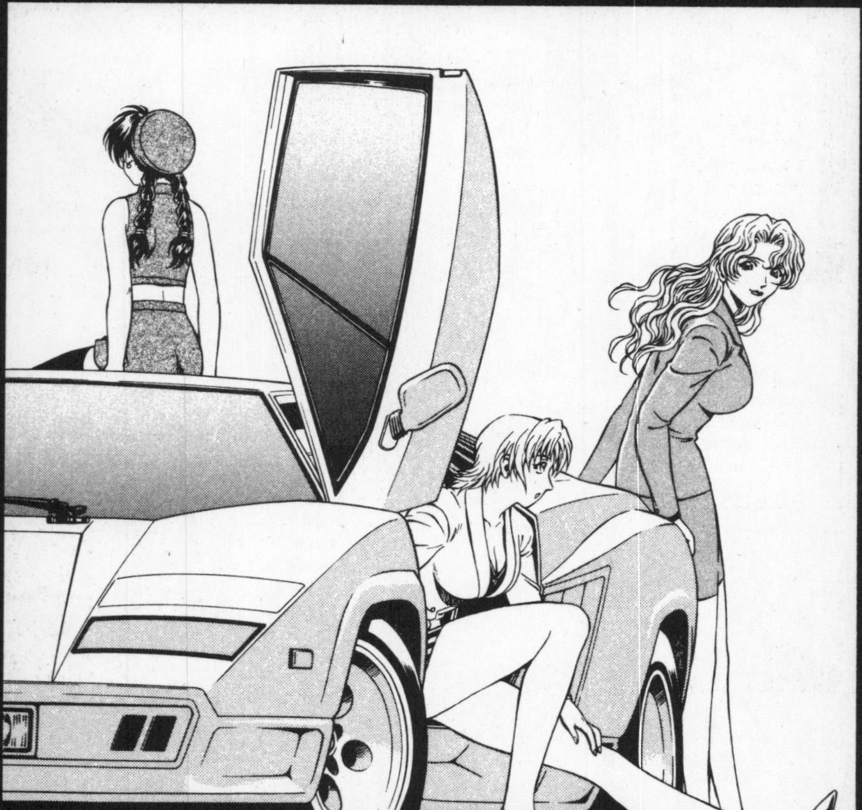

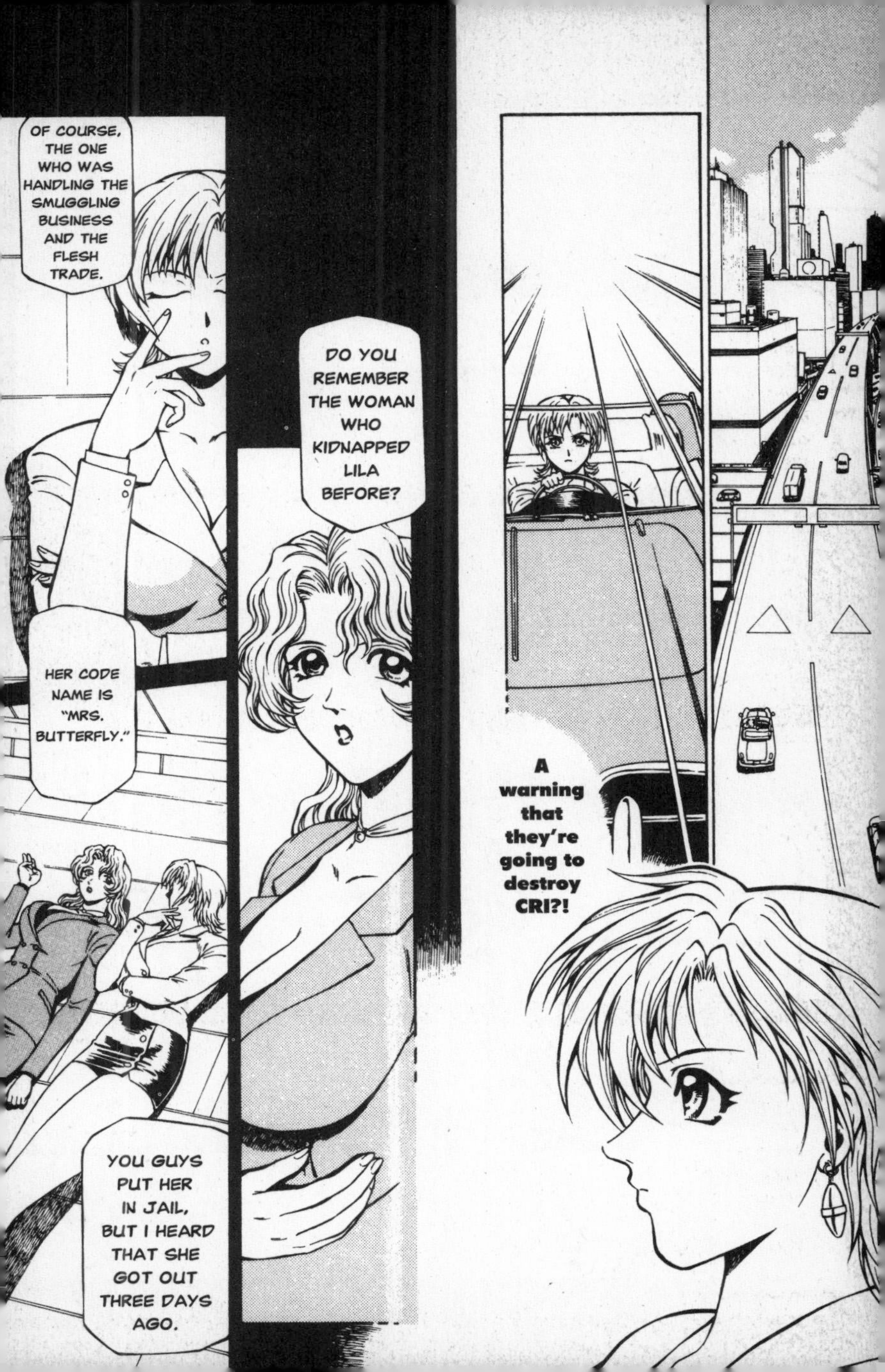
A warning that they're going to destroy CRI?!
DO YOU REMEMBER THE WOMAN WHO KIDNAPPED LILA BEFORE?
OF COURSE, THE ONE WHO WAS HANDLING THE SMUGGLING BUSINESS AND THE FLESH TRADE.
HER CODE NAME IS "MRS. BUTTERFLY."
YOU GUYS PUT HER IN JAIL, BUT I HEARD THAT SHE GOT OUT THREE DAYS AGO.

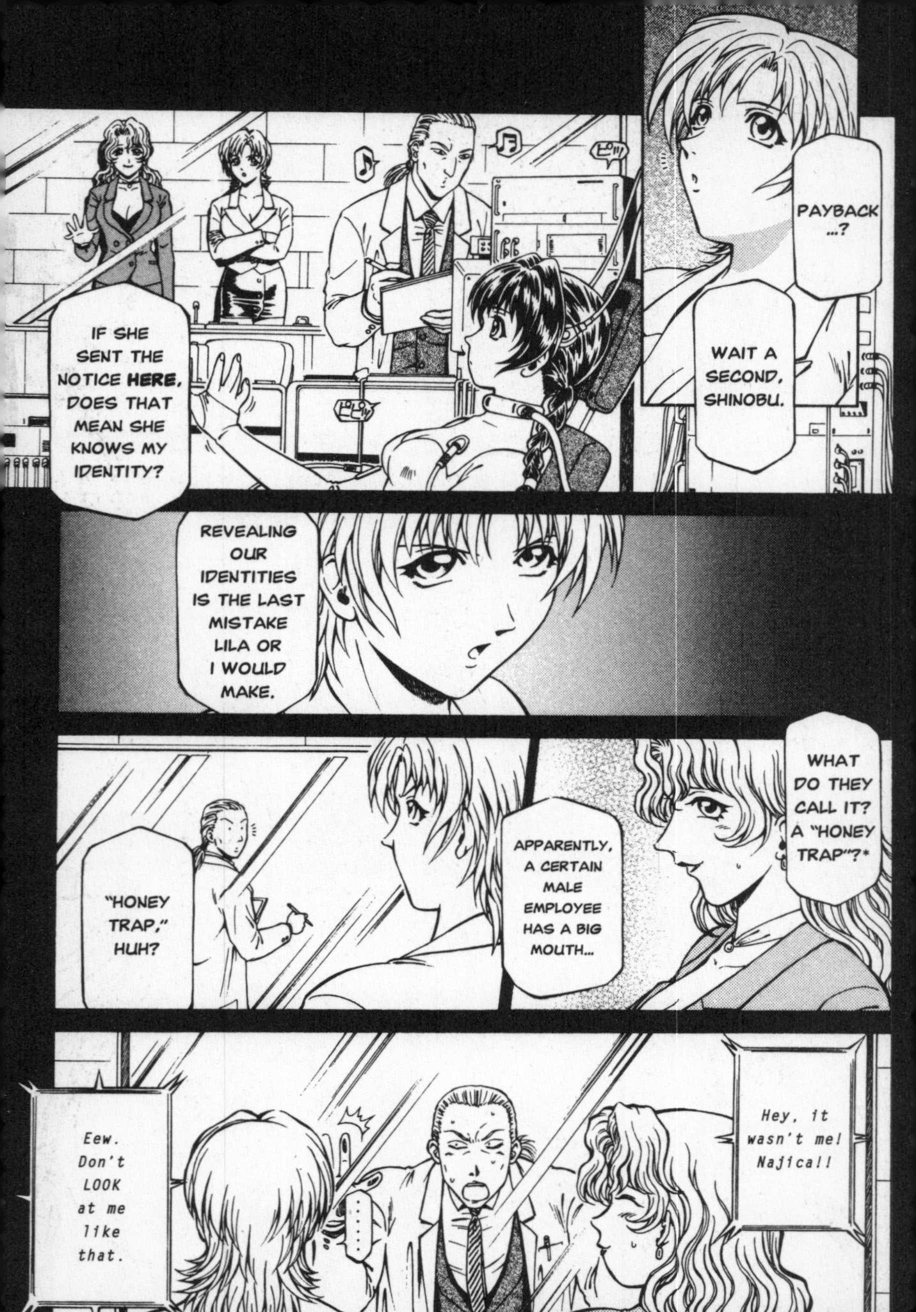
PAYBACK ...?
WAIT A SECOND, SHINOBU.
IF SHE SENT THE NOTICE **HERE**, DOES THAT MEAN SHE KNOWS MY IDENTITY?
REVEALING OUR IDENTITIES IS THE LAST MISTAKE LILA OR I WOULD MAKE.
WHAT DO THEY CALL IT? A "HONEY TRAP"?*
APPARENTLY, A CERTAIN MALE EMPLOYEE HAS A BIG MOUTH...
"HONEY TRAP," HUH?
Hey, it wasn't me! Najica!!
Eew. Don't LOOK at me like that.

* A "honey trap" is when a female operative uses seduction to get information.

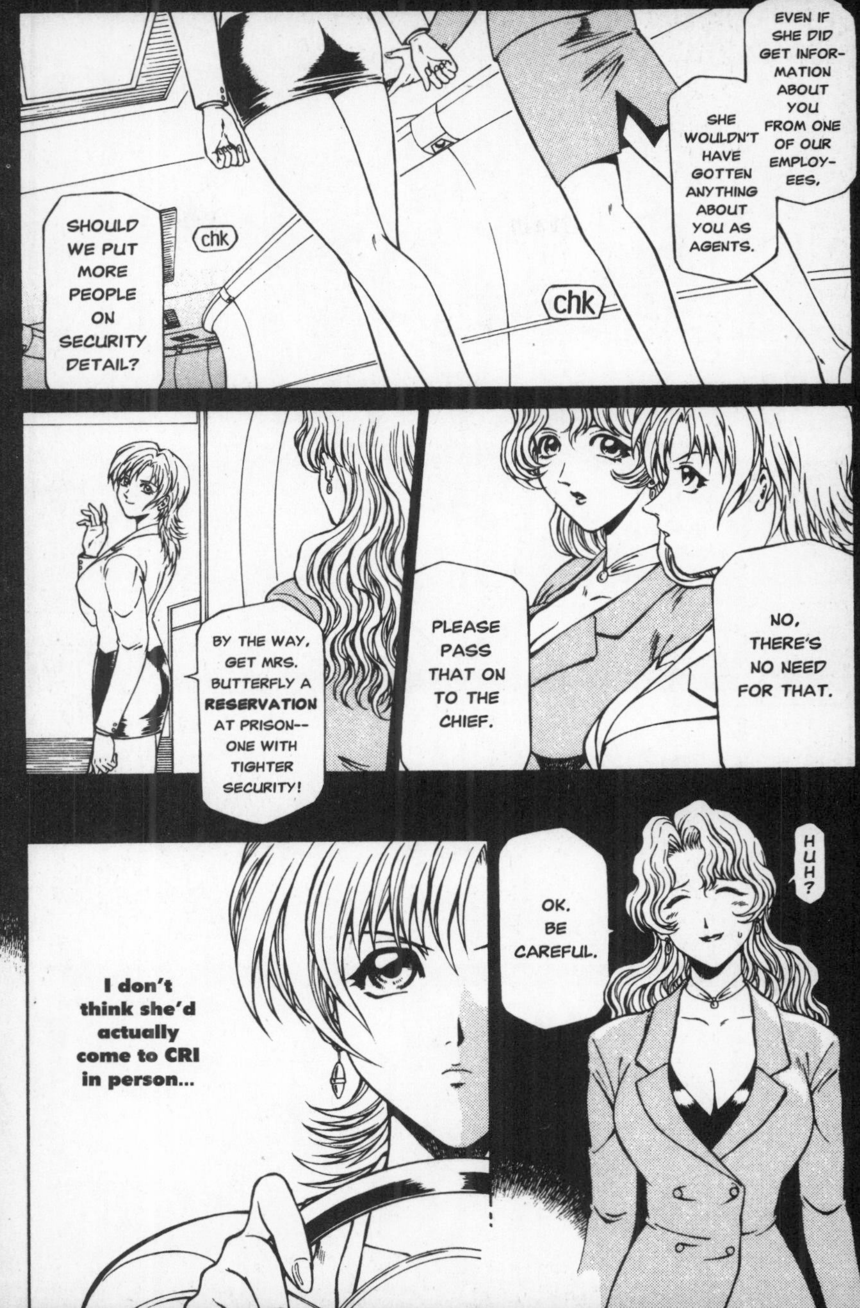
EVEN IF SHE DID GET INFORMATION ABOUT YOU FROM ONE OF OUR EMPLOYEES,
SHE WOULDN'T HAVE GOTTEN ANYTHING ABOUT YOU AS AGENTS.
chk
chk
SHOULD WE PUT MORE PEOPLE ON SECURITY DETAIL?
NO, THERE'S NO NEED FOR THAT.
PLEASE PASS THAT ON TO THE CHIEF.
BY THE WAY, GET MRS. BUTTERFLY A RESERVATION AT PRISON-- ONE WITH TIGHTER SECURITY!
HUH?
OK. BE CAREFUL.
I don't think she'd actually come to CRI in person...

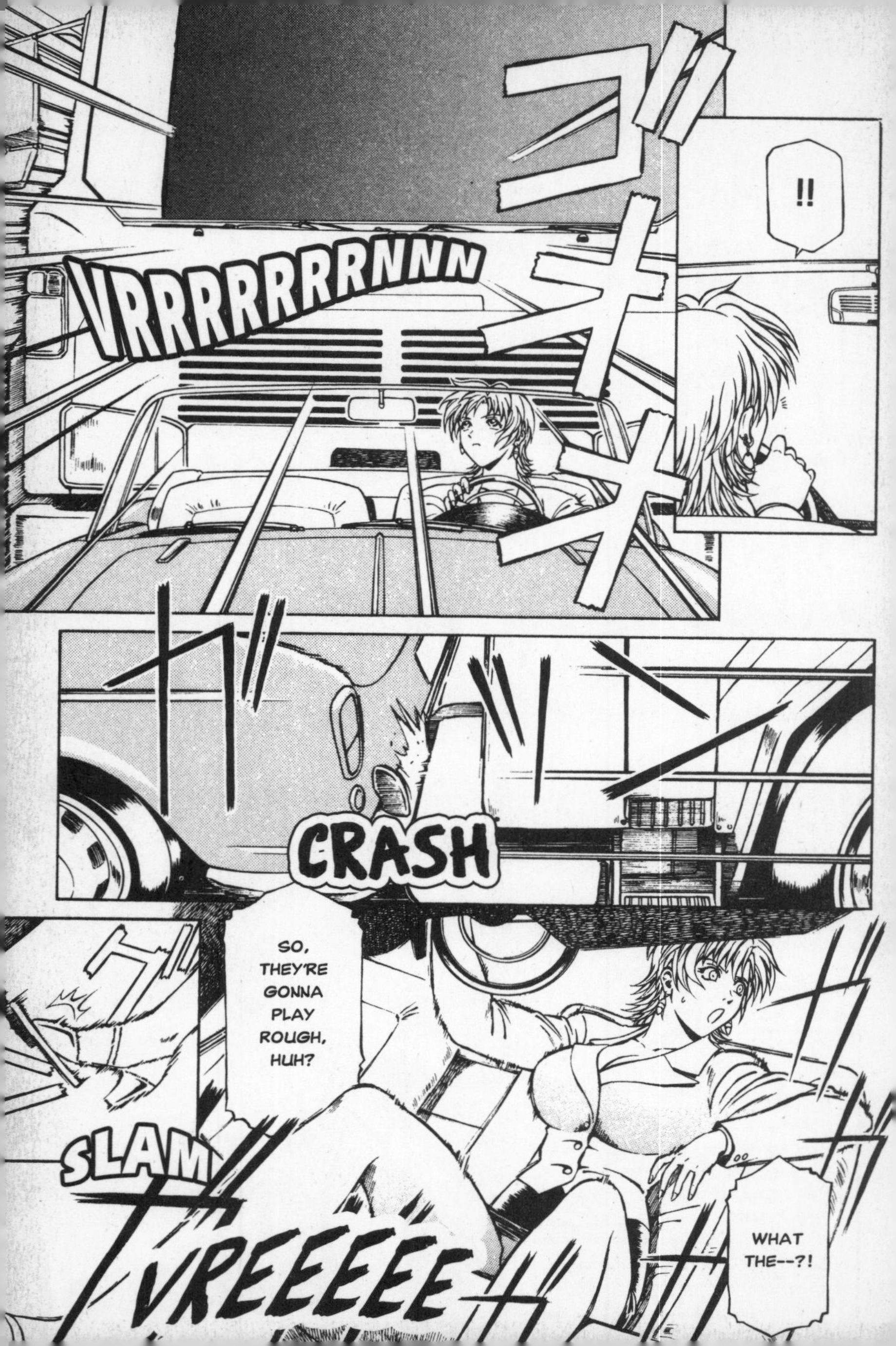
!!
VRRRRRRRNNN
CRASH
WHAT THE--?!
SO, THEY'RE GONNA PLAY ROUGH, HUH?
SLAM
VREEEEEE

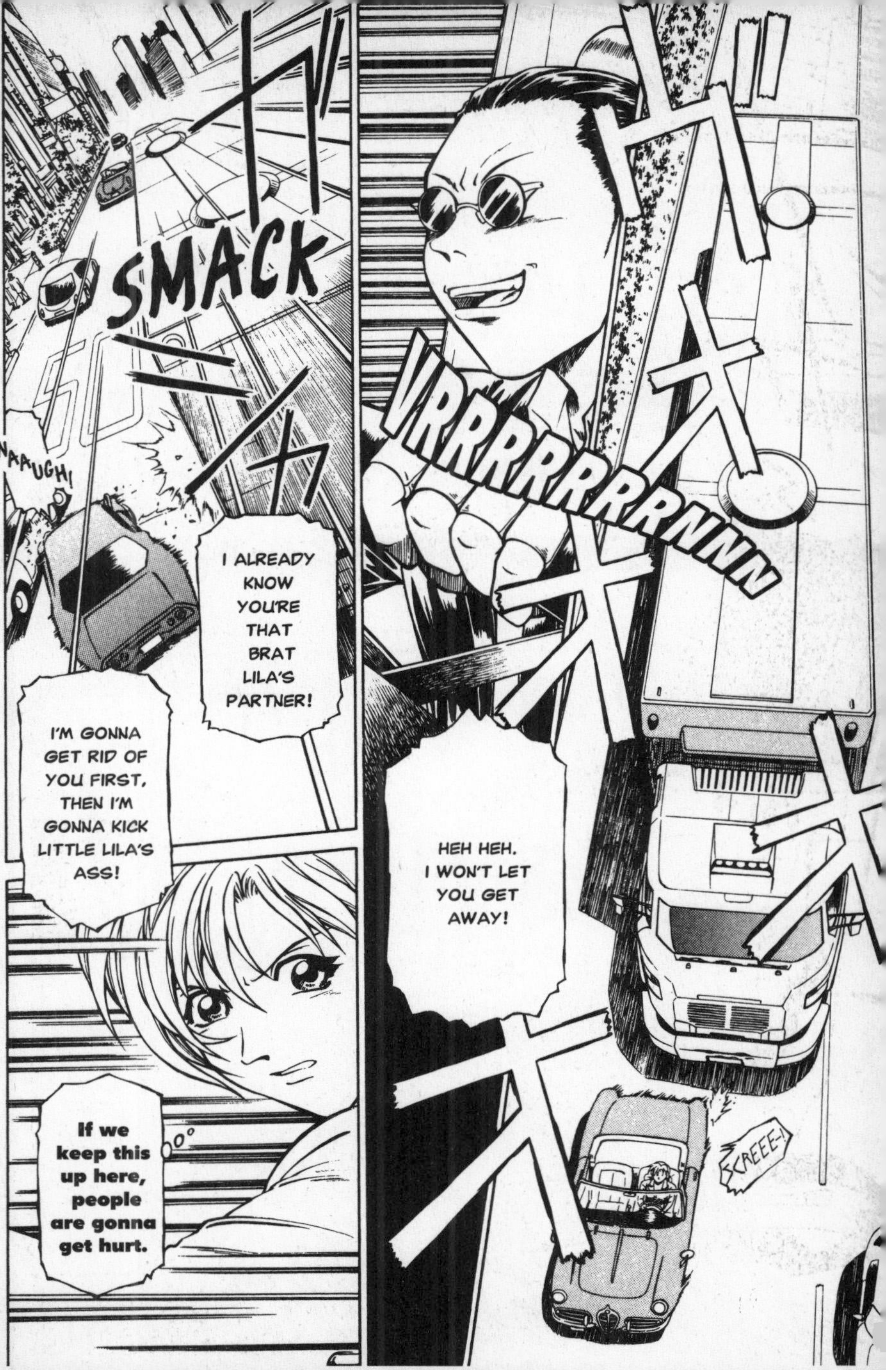
VRRRRRRRRNNNN
HEH HEH. I WON'T LET YOU GET AWAY!
SCREEE-!
SMACK
WAAUGH!
I ALREADY KNOW YOU'RE THAT BRAT LILA'S PARTNER!
I'M GONNA GET RID OF YOU FIRST, THEN I'M GONNA KICK LITTLE LILA'S ASS!
If we keep this up here, people are gonna get hurt.

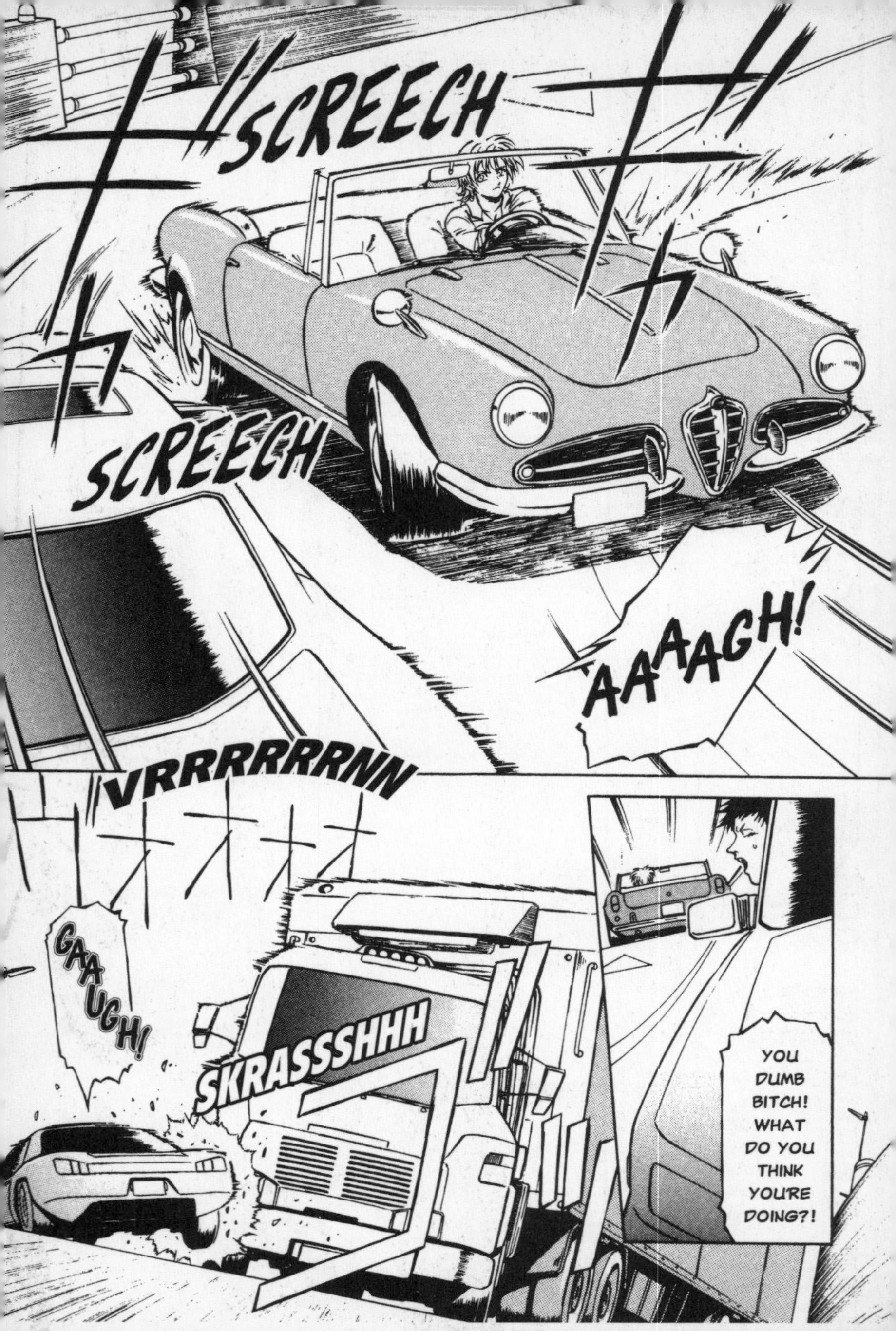
SCREECH
SCREECH
AAAAGH!
YOU DUMB BITCH! WHAT DO YOU THINK YOU'RE DOING?!
VRRRRRRNN
GAAUGH!
SKRASSSHHH

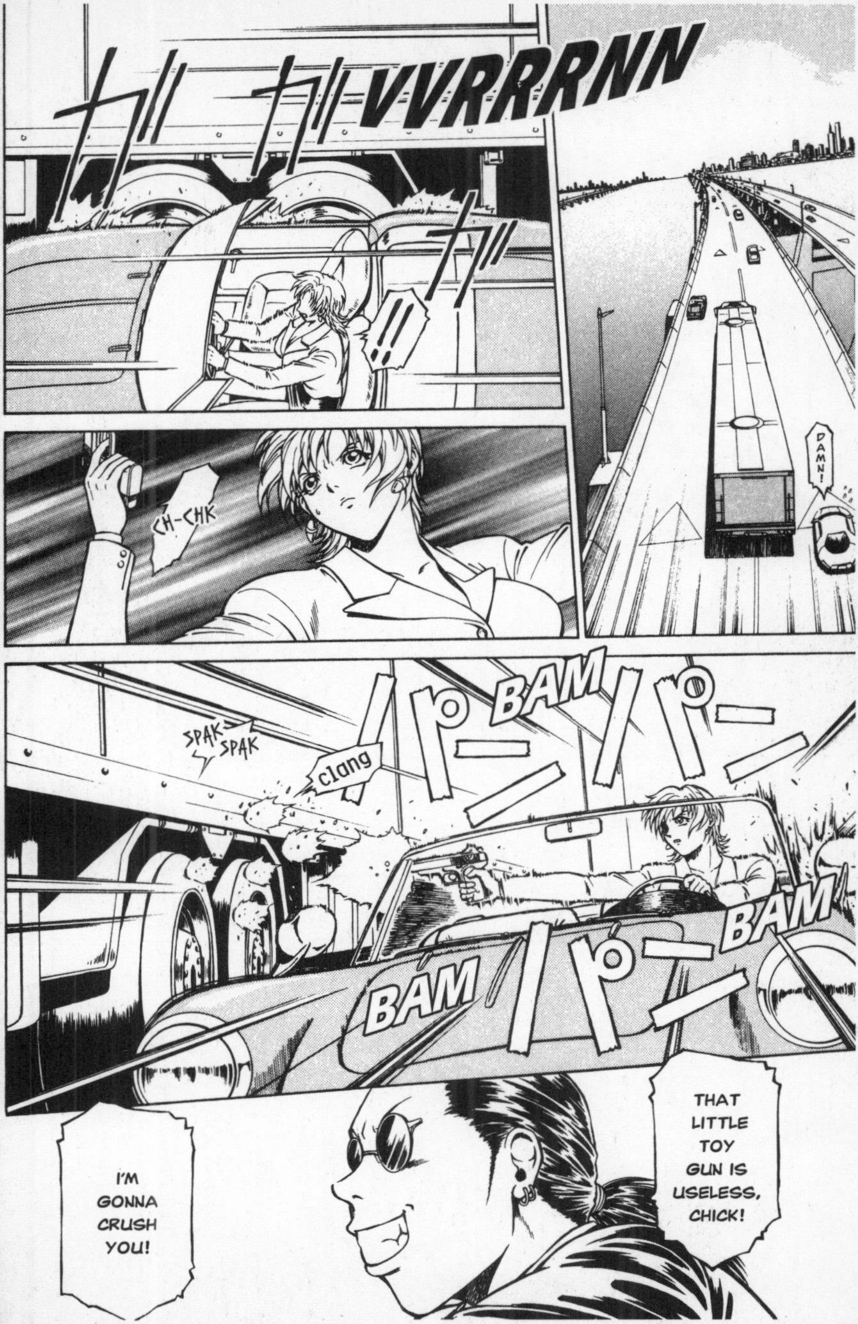
DAMN!
ガ ガ VVRRRNN
ガ
!!
CH-CHK
パー BAM パー
SPAK SPAK
clang
パー BAM
BAM
THAT LITTLE TOY GUN IS USELESS, CHICK!
I'M GONNA CRUSH YOU!

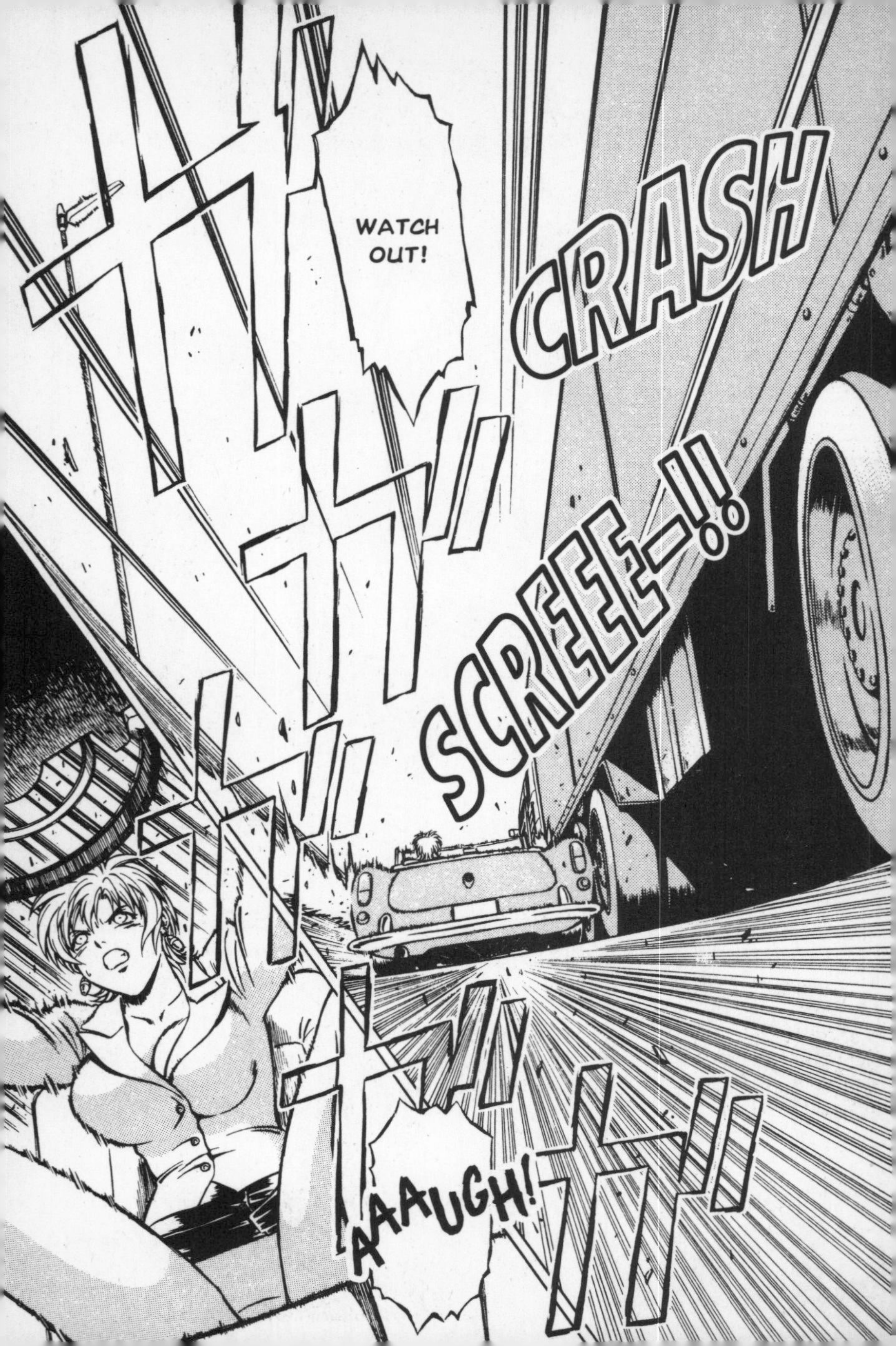
CRASH
WATCH OUT!
SCREEE-!!
AAAUGH!

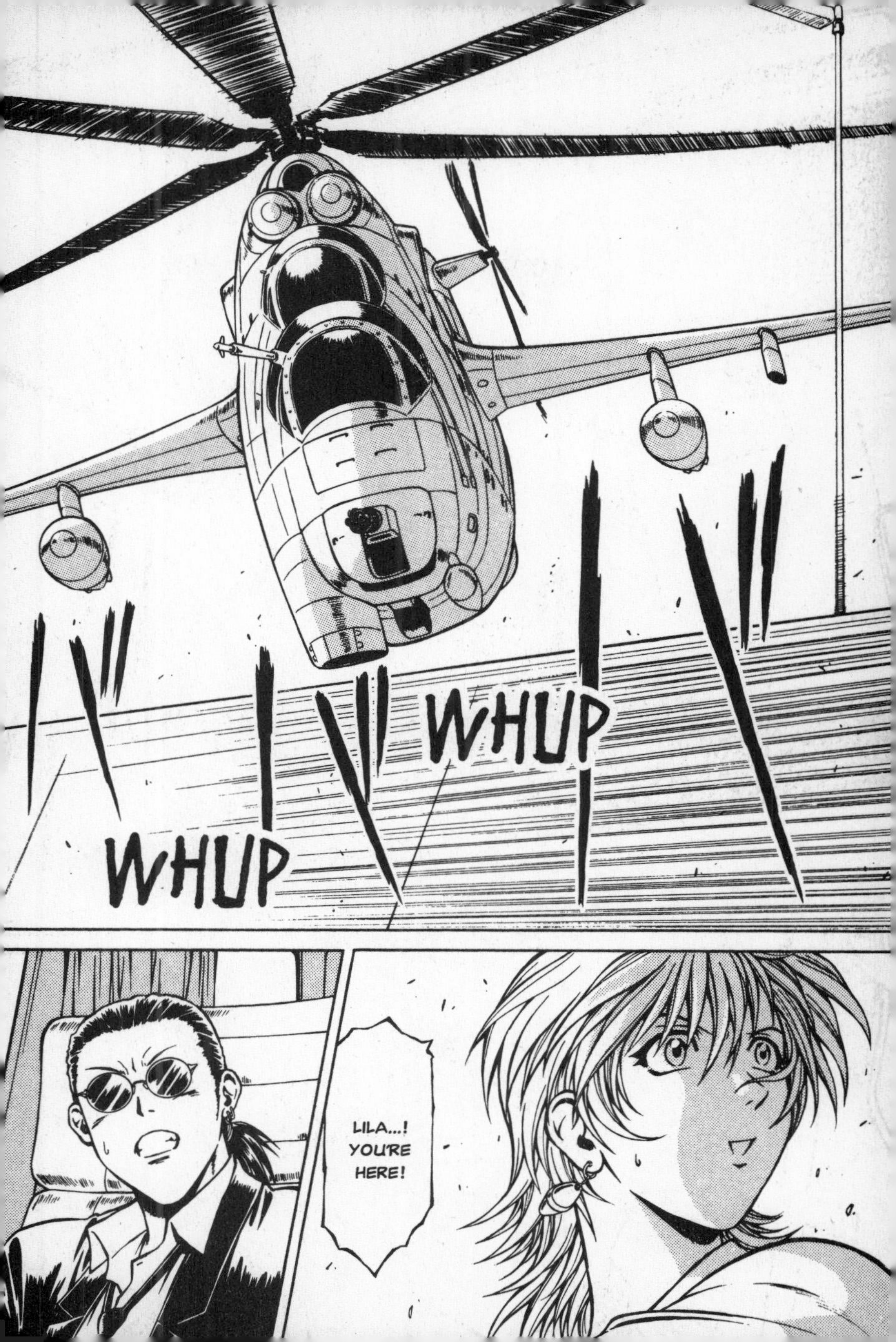
WHUP
WHUP
LILA...! YOU'RE HERE!

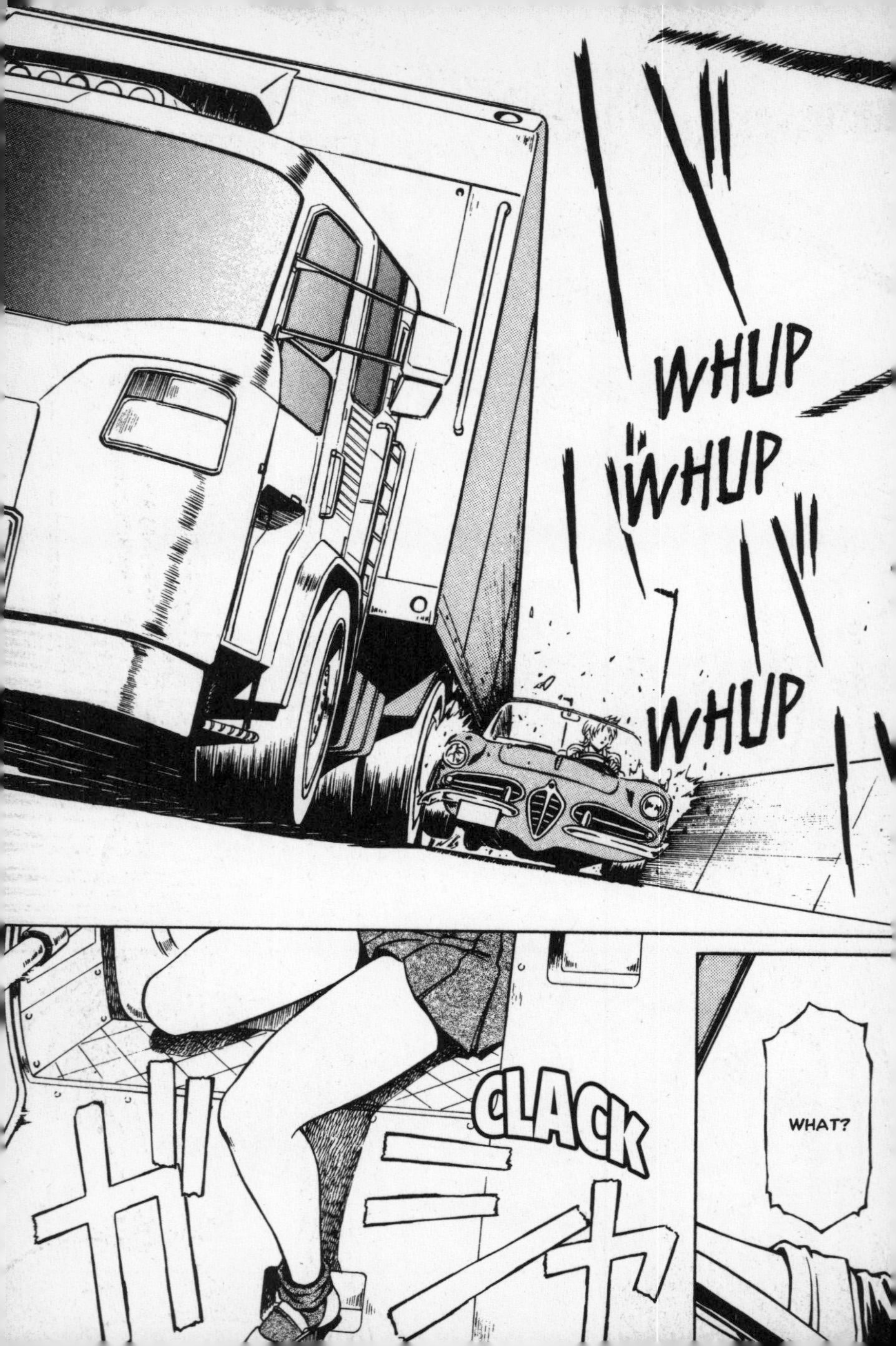
WHUP
WHUP
WHUP
WHAT?
CLACK

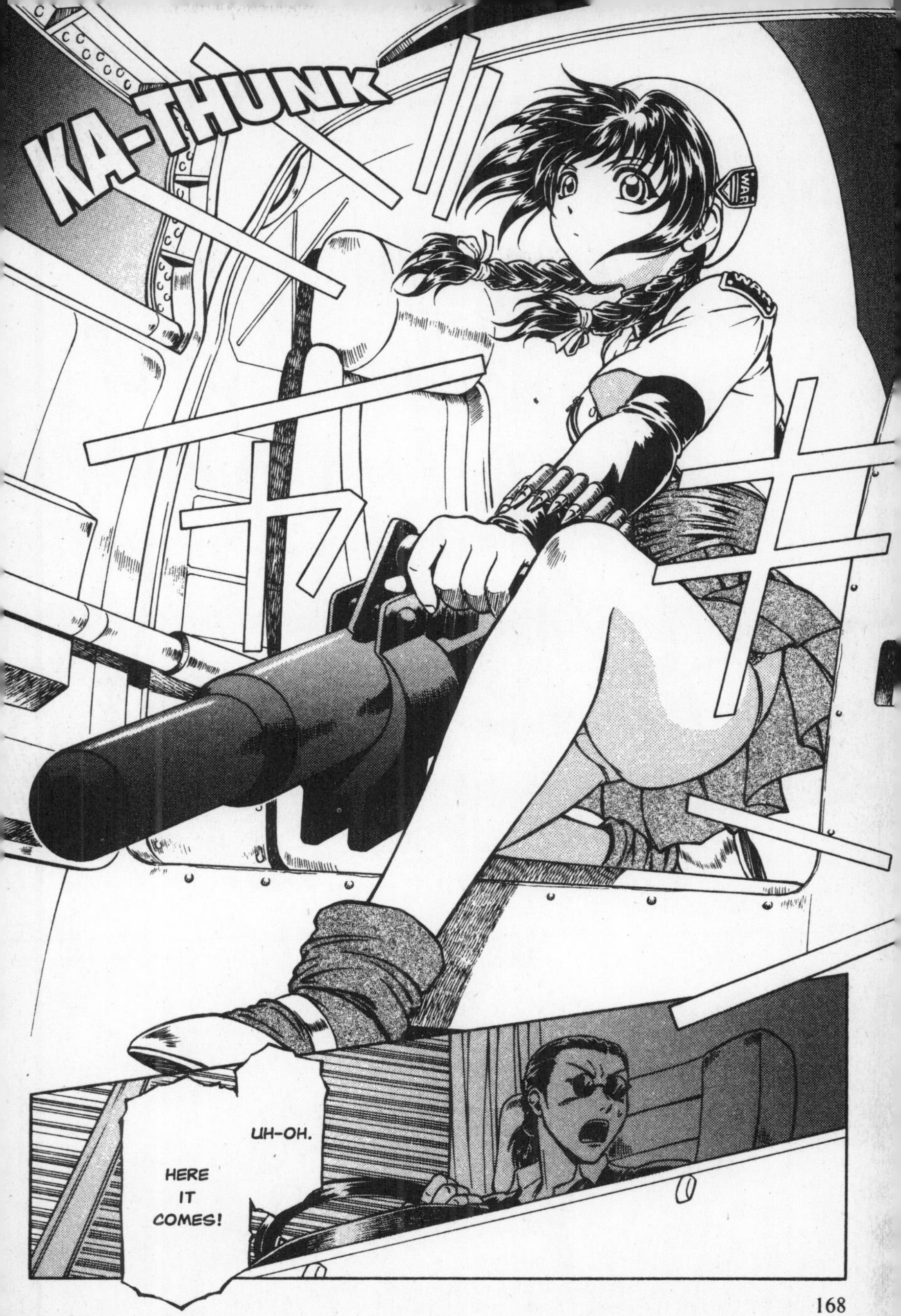
KA-THUNK
WAR
WAR
UH-OH.
HERE IT COMES!

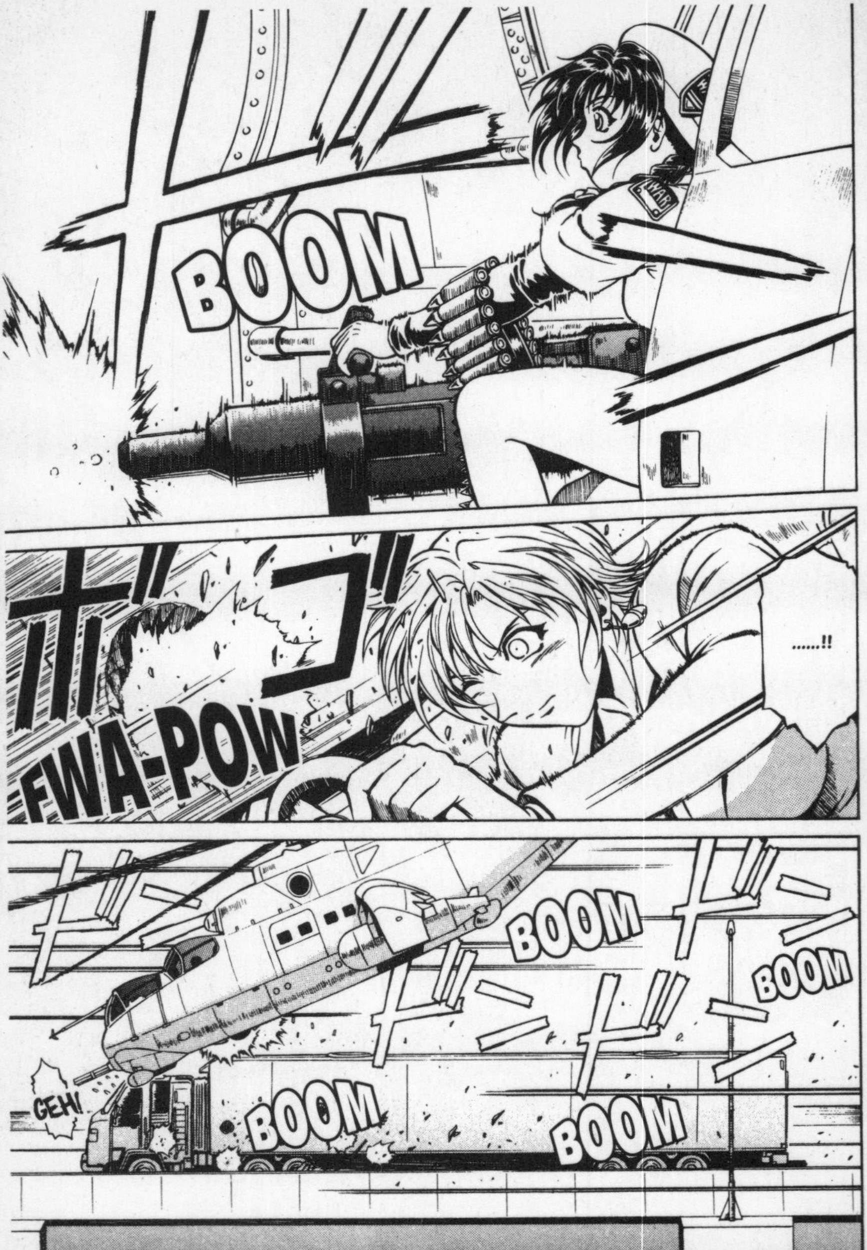
BOOM
......!!
ボゴ
FWA-POW
BOOM
BOOM
BOOM
BOOM
GEH!

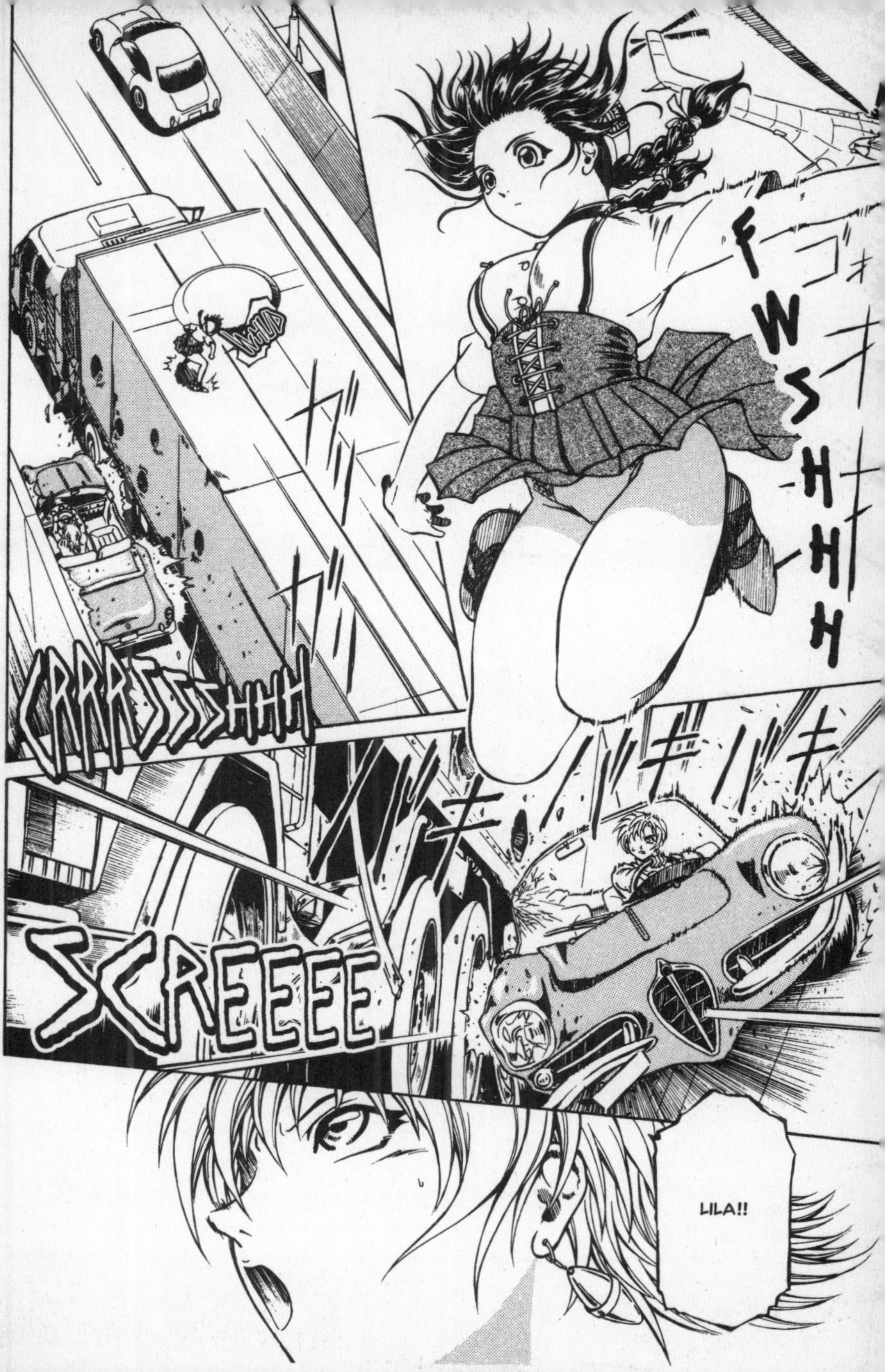
FWSHHHH
CRRRSSSHHH
SCREEEE
LILA!!

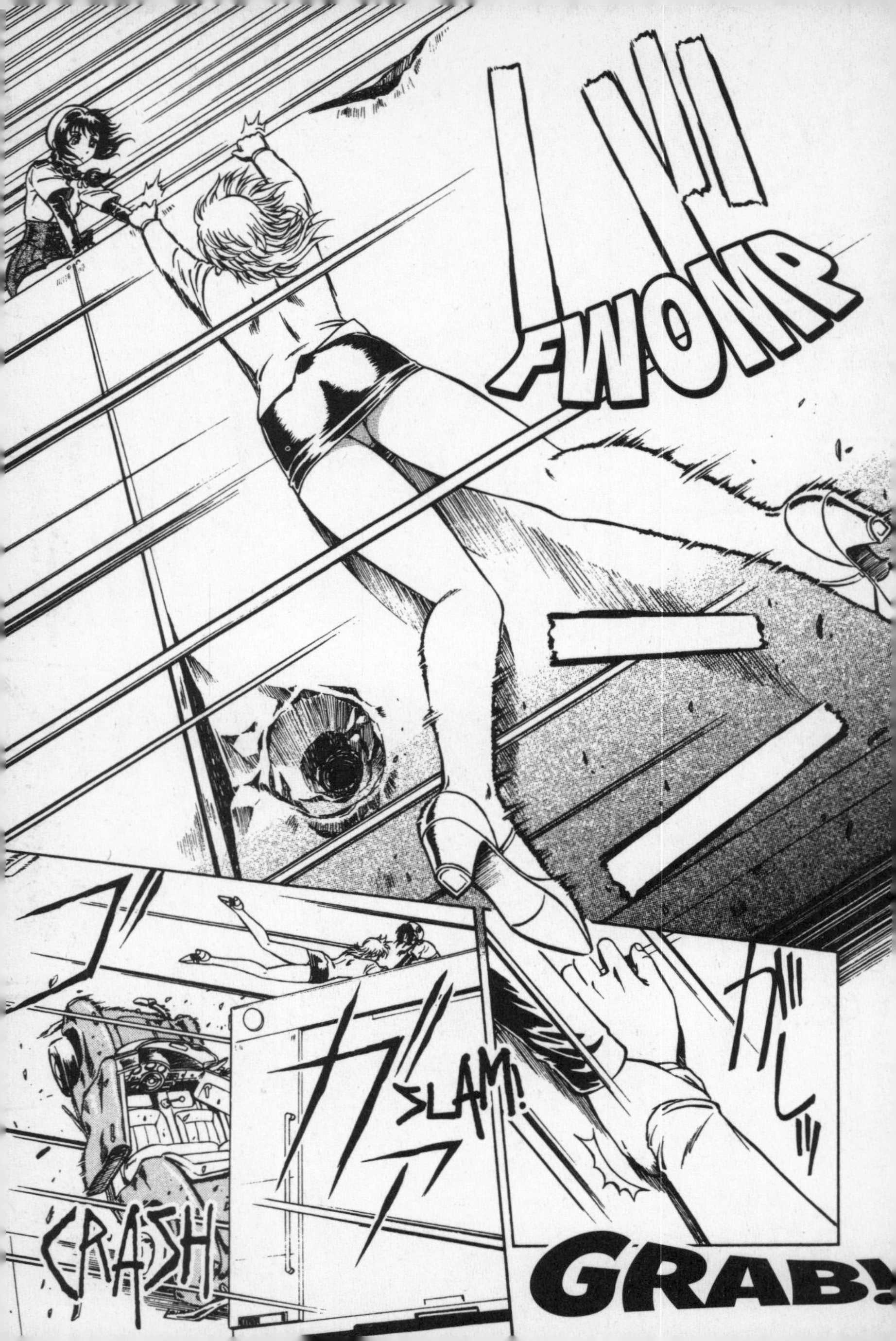
FWOMP
GRAB!
SLAM!
CRASH

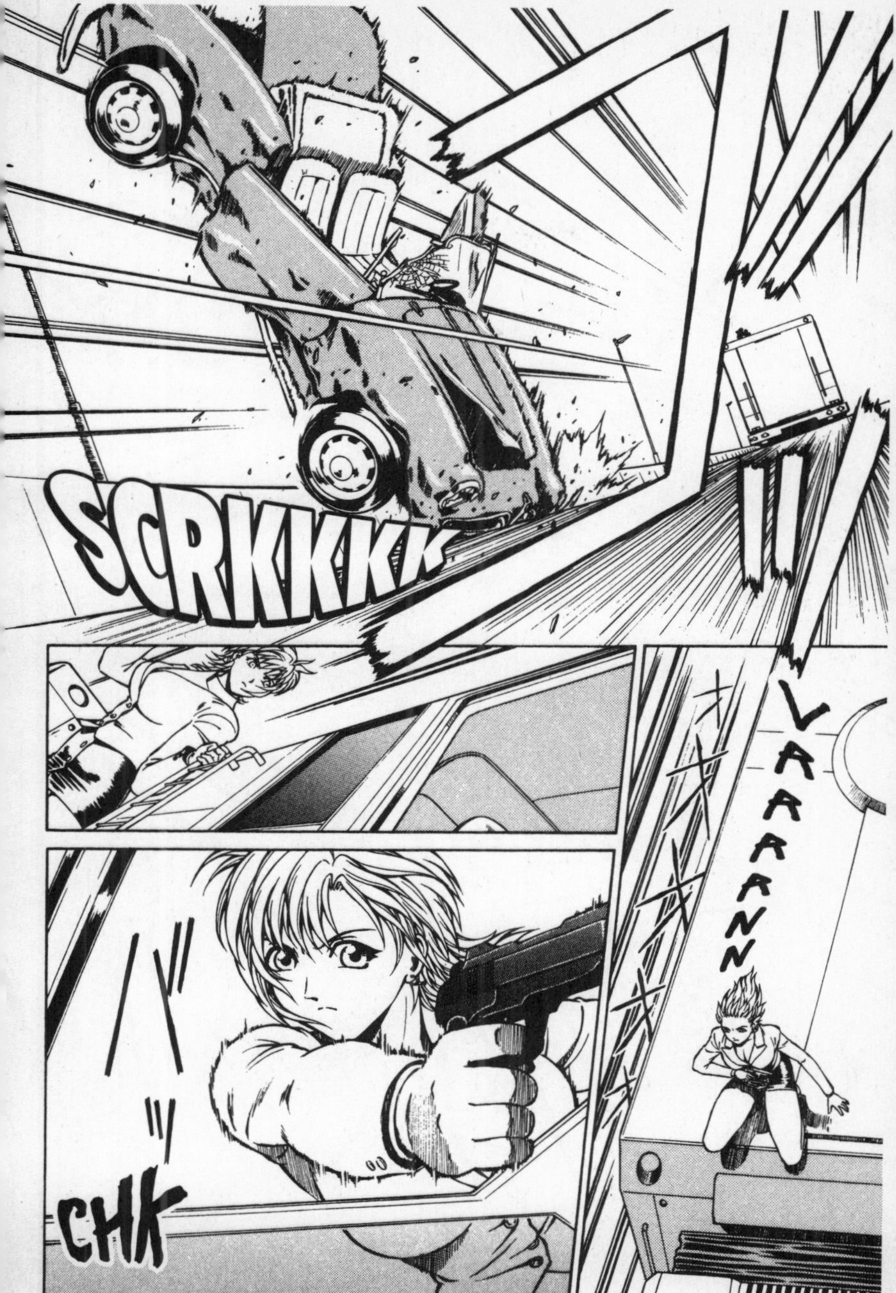
SCRKKKK
VRRRRNN
CHK

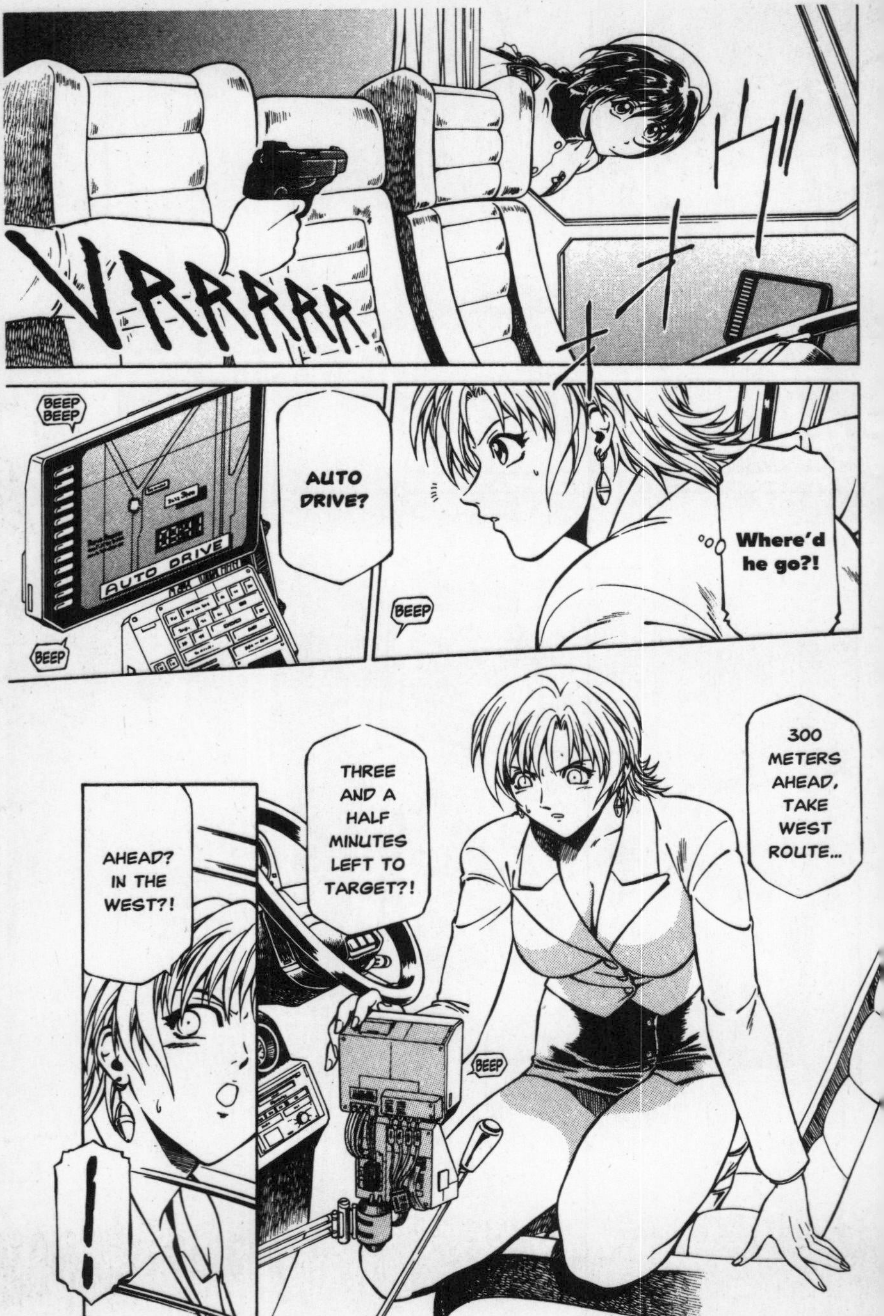
VRRRRR
Where'd he go?!
BEEP
BEEP BEEP
AUTO DRIVE?
AUTO DRIVE
BEEP
300 METERS AHEAD, TAKE WEST ROUTE...
THREE AND A HALF MINUTES LEFT TO TARGET?!
BEEP
AHEAD? IN THE WEST?!
!

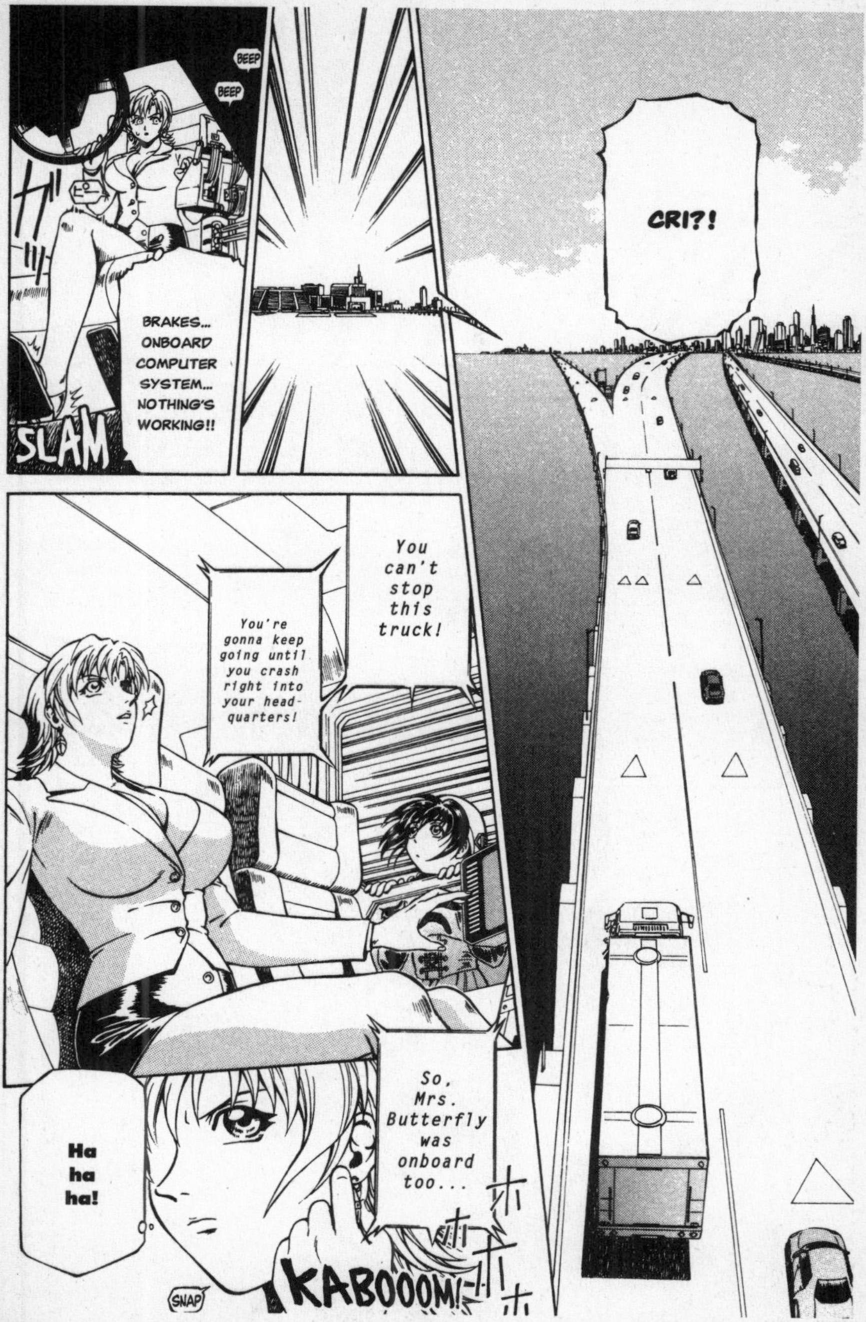
CRI?!
BEEP
BEEP
BRAKES... ONBOARD COMPUTER SYSTEM... NOTHING'S WORKING!!
SLAM
You can't stop this truck!
You're gonna keep going until you crash right into your headquarters!
So, Mrs. Butterfly was onboard too...
Ha ha ha!
KABOOOM!
SNAP

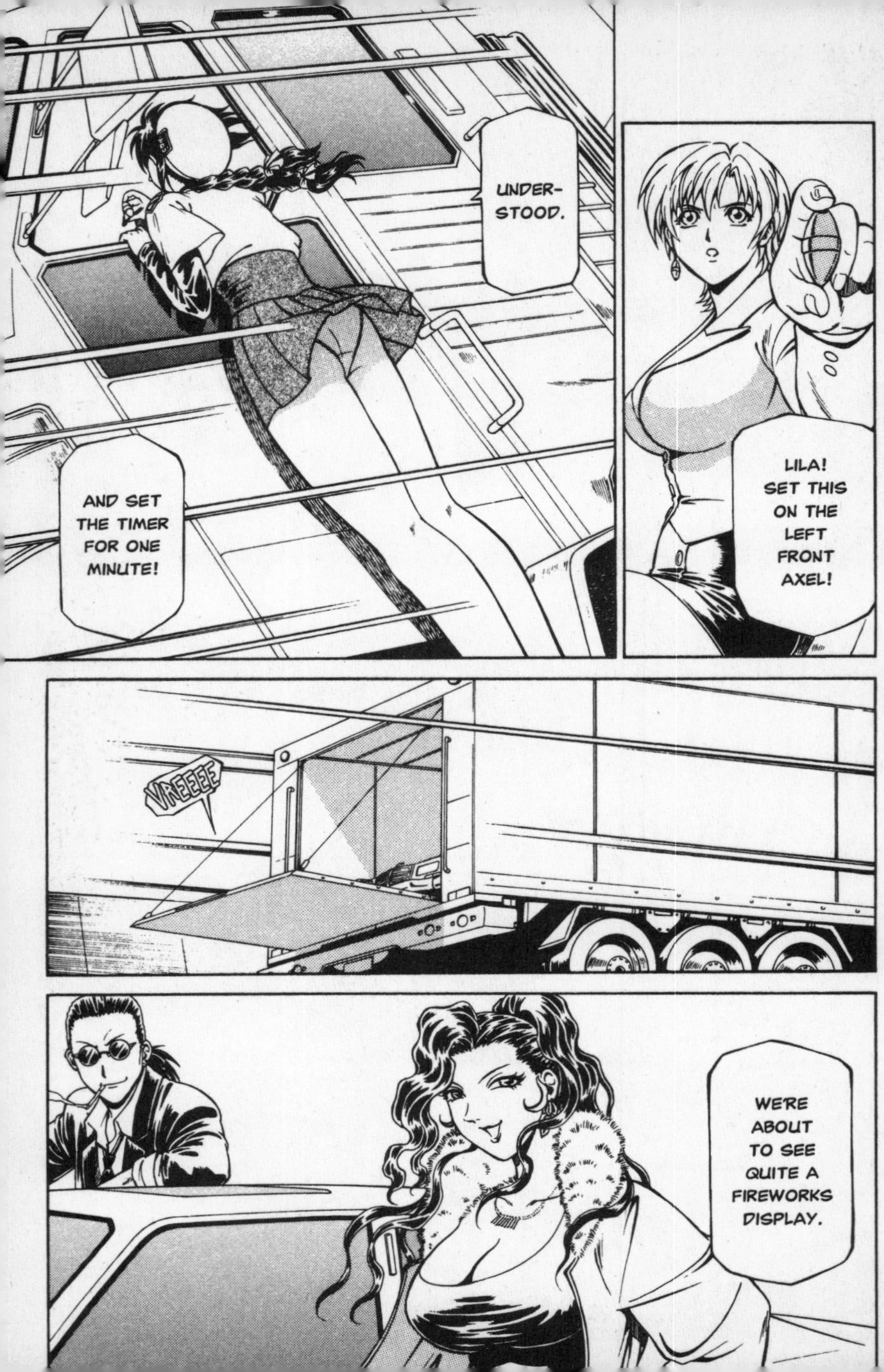
LILA! SET THIS ON THE LEFT FRONT AXEL!
UNDER-STOOD.
AND SET THE TIMER FOR ONE MINUTE!
VREEEE
WE'RE ABOUT TO SEE QUITE A FIREWORKS DISPLAY.

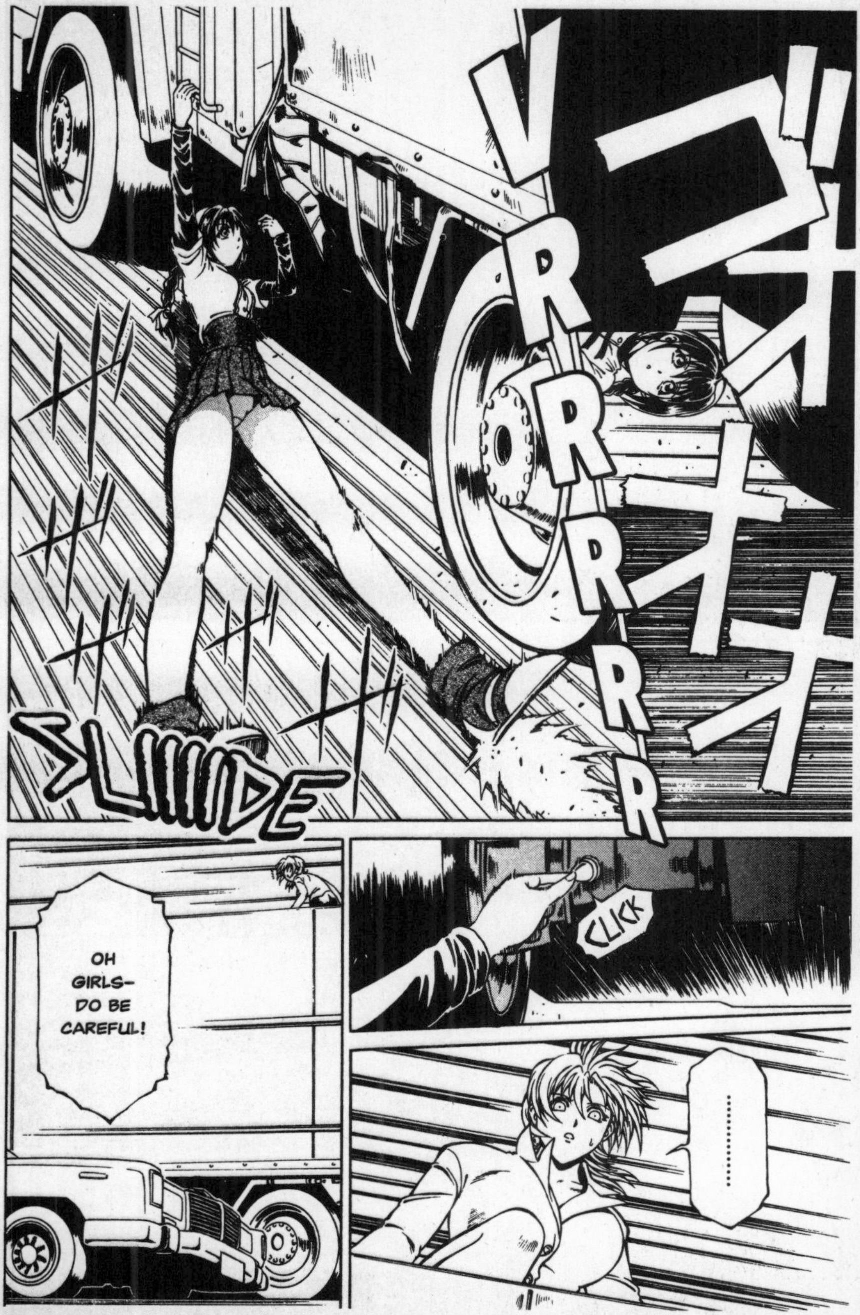
ゴオオオ
VRRRRR
SLIIIIDE
CLICK
......
OH GIRLS-
DO BE
CAREFUL!

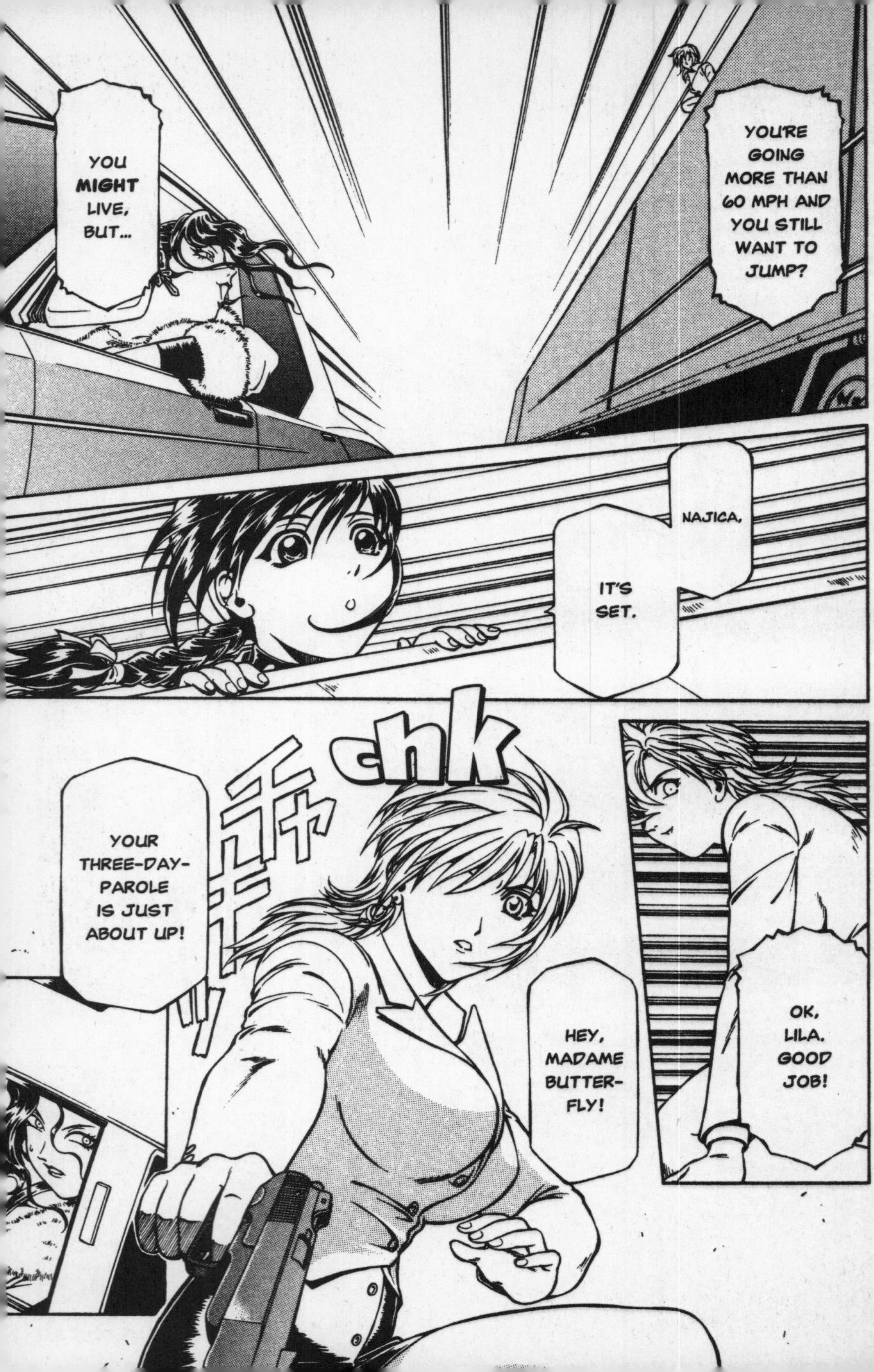
YOU'RE GOING MORE THAN 60 MPH AND YOU STILL WANT TO JUMP?
YOU **MIGHT** LIVE, BUT...
NAJICA,
IT'S SET.
OK, LILA. GOOD JOB!
chk
チャキ
HEY, MADAME BUTTER-FLY!
YOUR THREE-DAY-PAROLE IS JUST ABOUT UP!

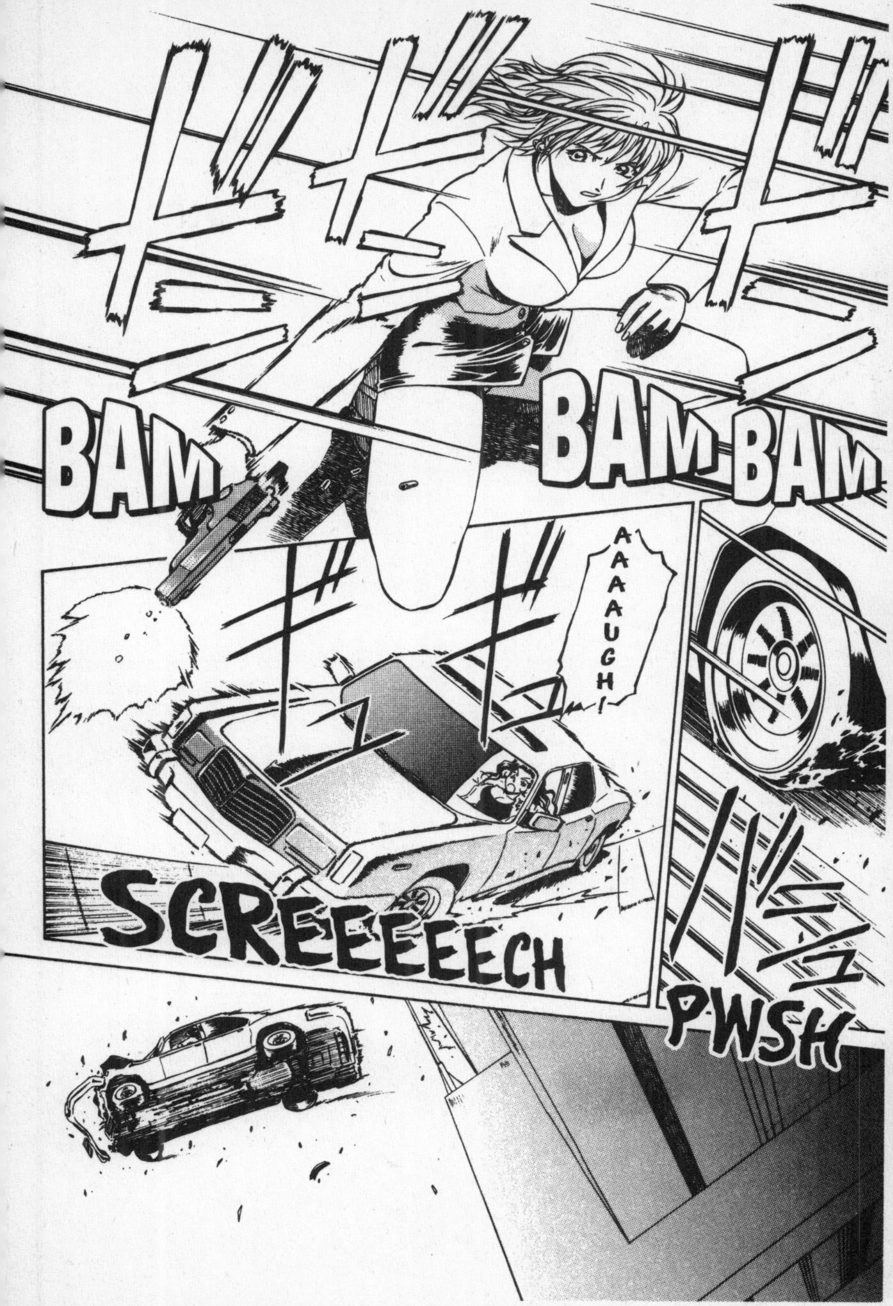
BAM BAM
BAM
PWSH
AAAAAUGH!
SCREEEEEECH

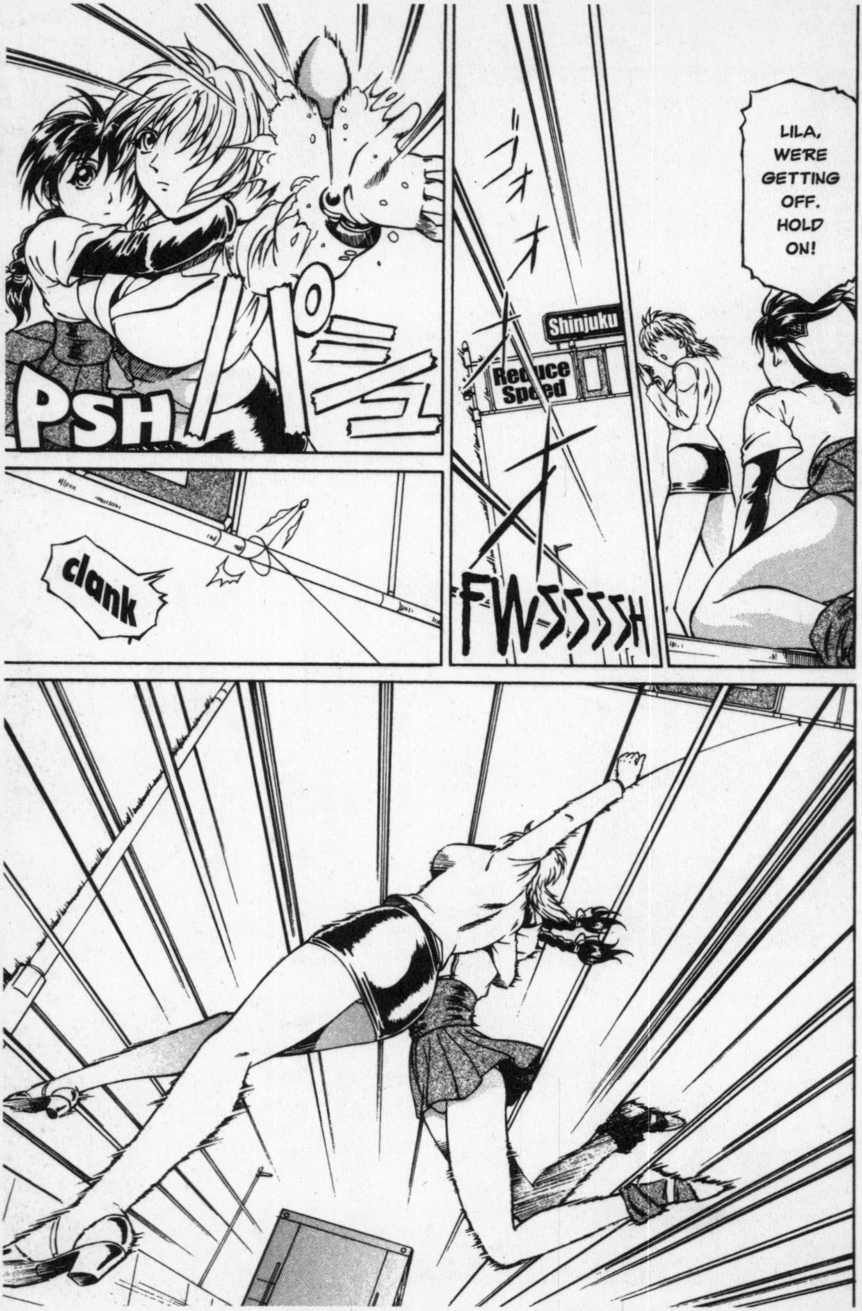
LILA, WE'RE GETTING OFF. HOLD ON!
Shinjuku
Reduce Speed
FWSSSSH
PSH
clank

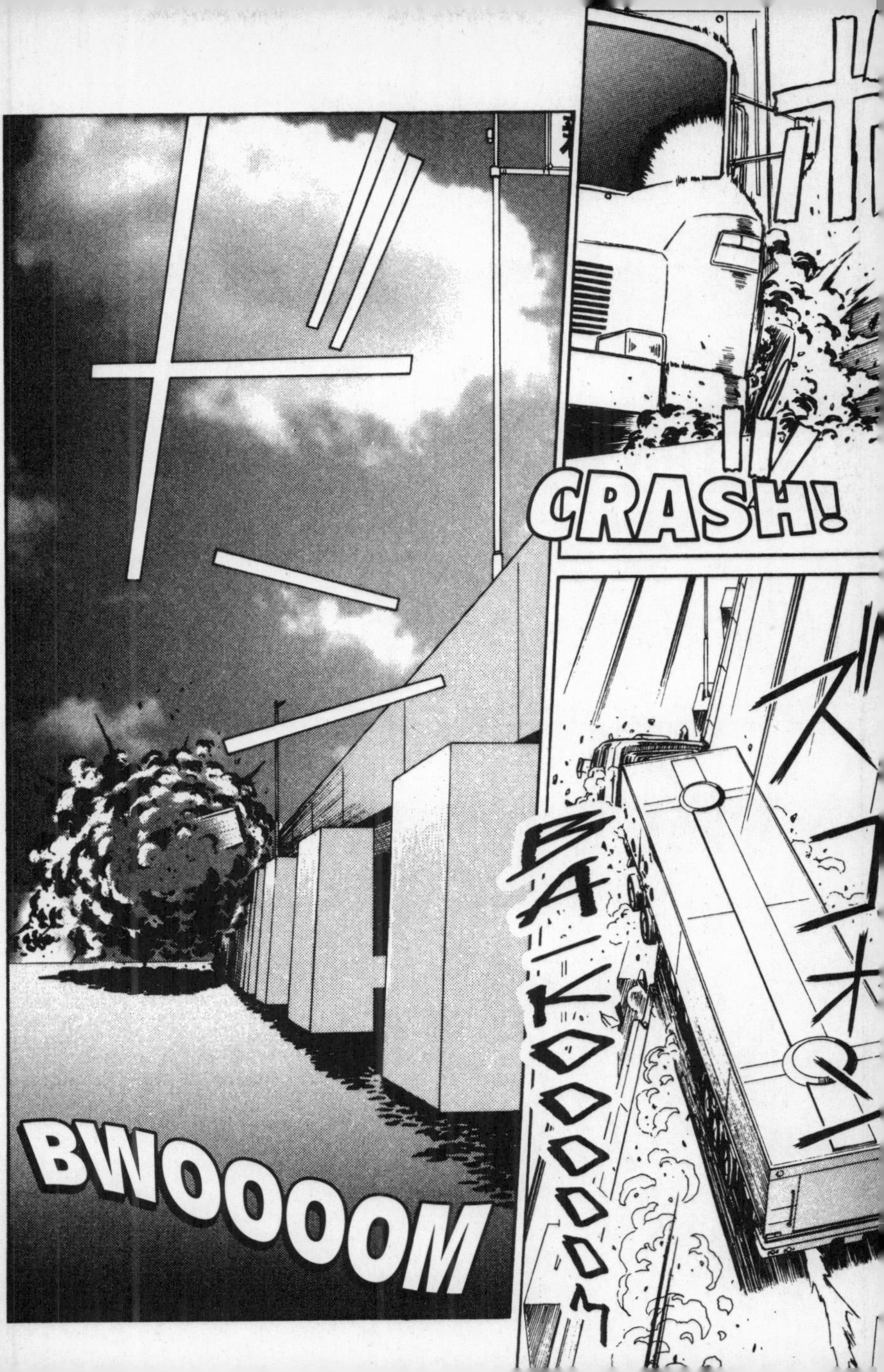
CRASH!
BA-KOOOOOM
BWOOOOM

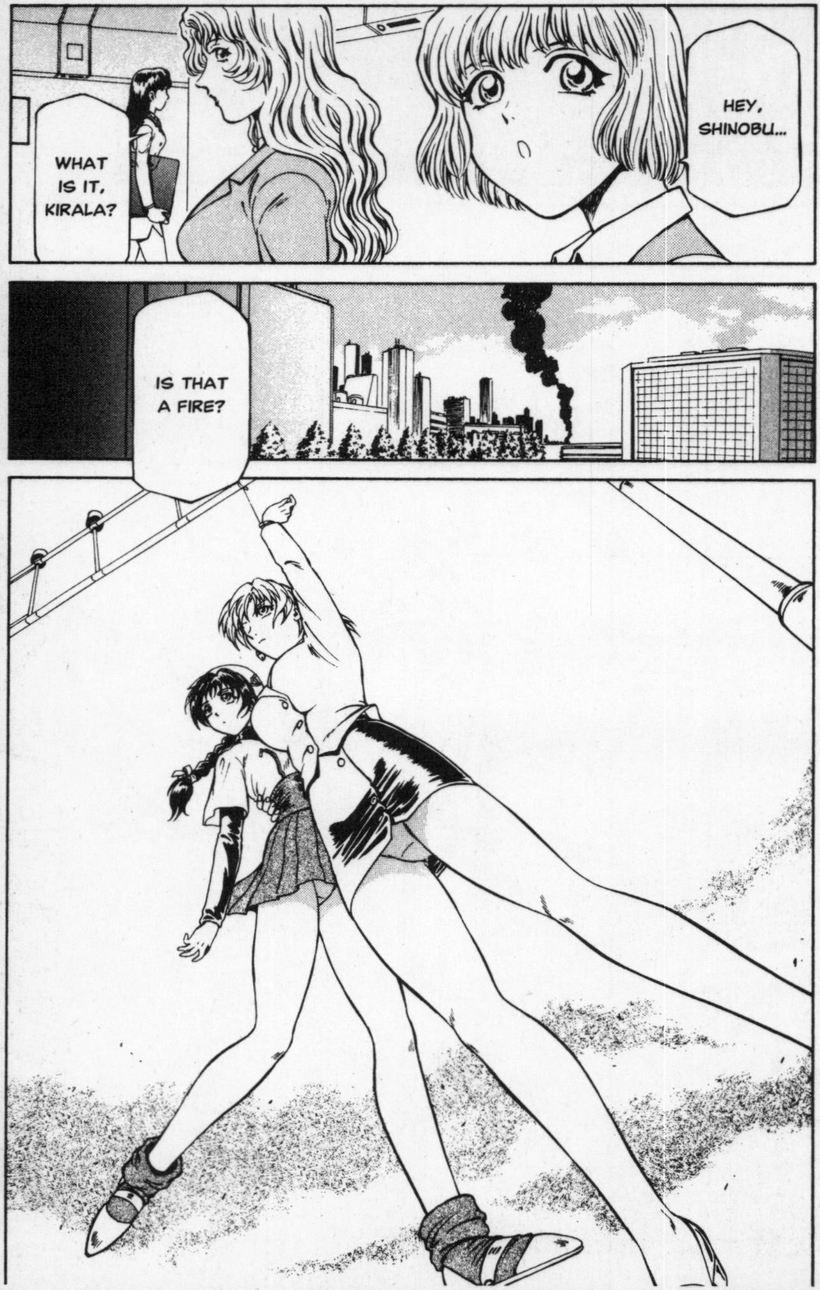
HEY, SHINOBU...
WHAT IS IT, KIRALA?
IS THAT A FIRE?

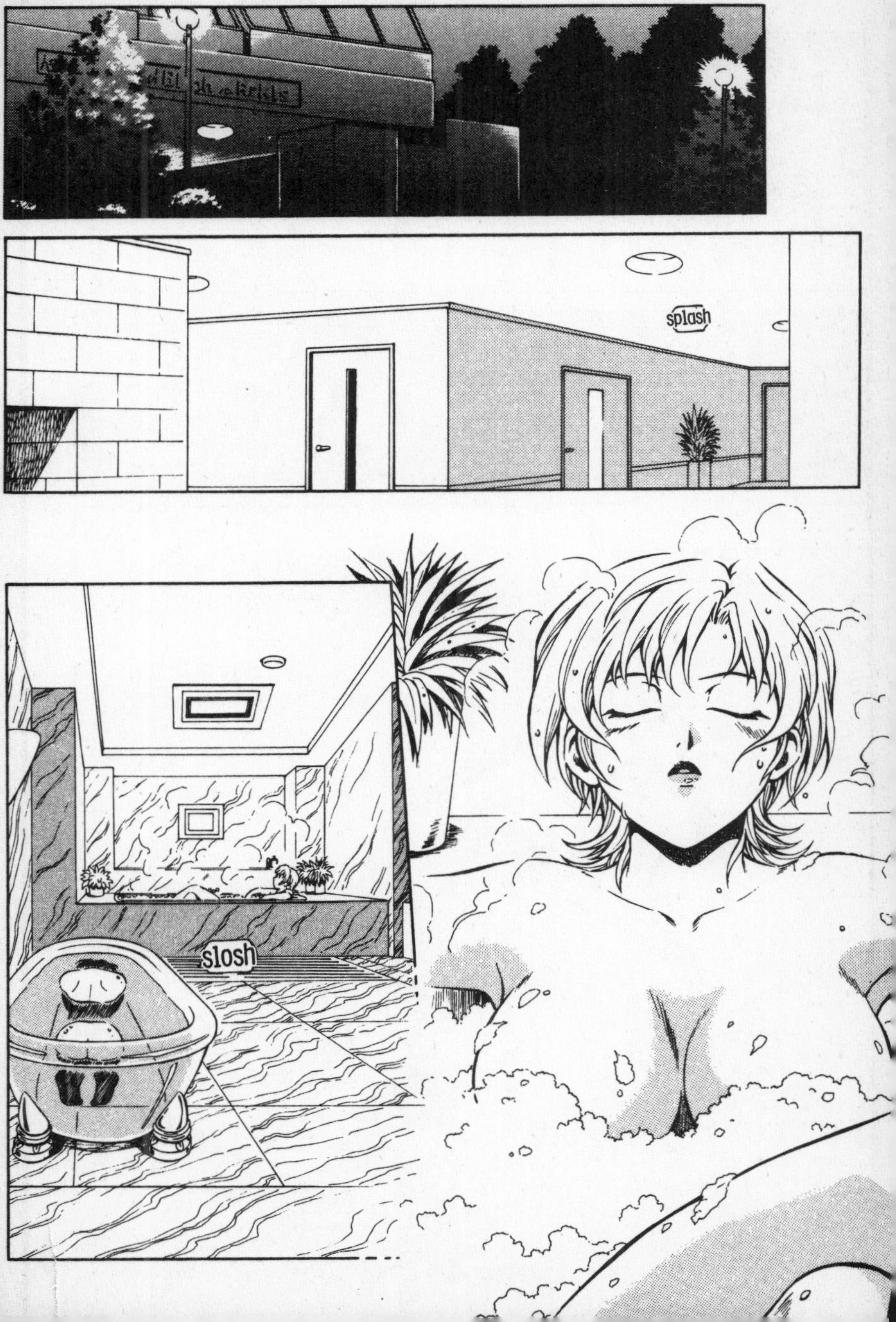
splash
slosh

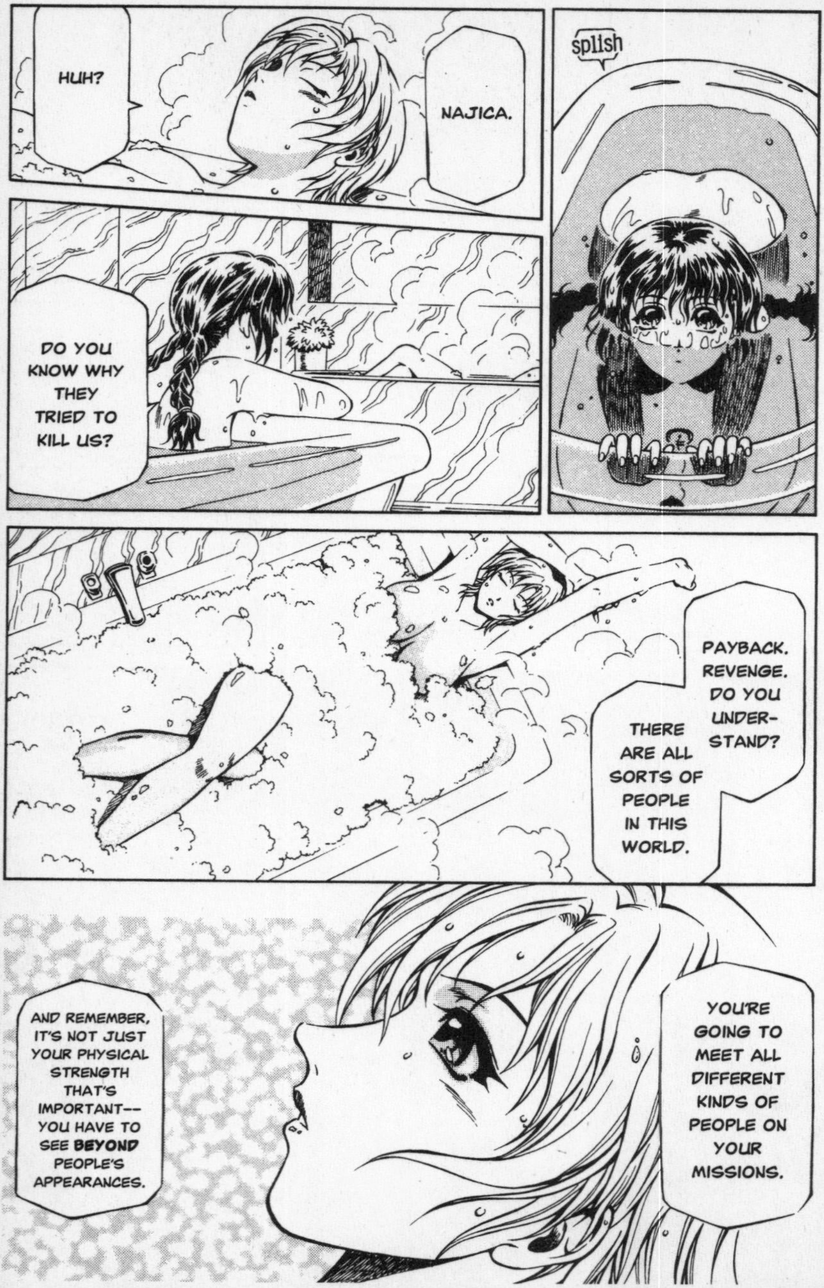
splish
NAJICA.
HUH?
DO YOU KNOW WHY THEY TRIED TO KILL US?
PAYBACK. REVENGE. DO YOU UNDER-STAND?
THERE ARE ALL SORTS OF PEOPLE IN THIS WORLD.
YOU'RE GOING TO MEET ALL DIFFERENT KINDS OF PEOPLE ON YOUR MISSIONS.
AND REMEMBER, IT'S NOT JUST YOUR PHYSICAL STRENGTH THAT'S IMPORTANT-- YOU HAVE TO SEE **BEYOND** PEOPLE'S APPEARANCES.

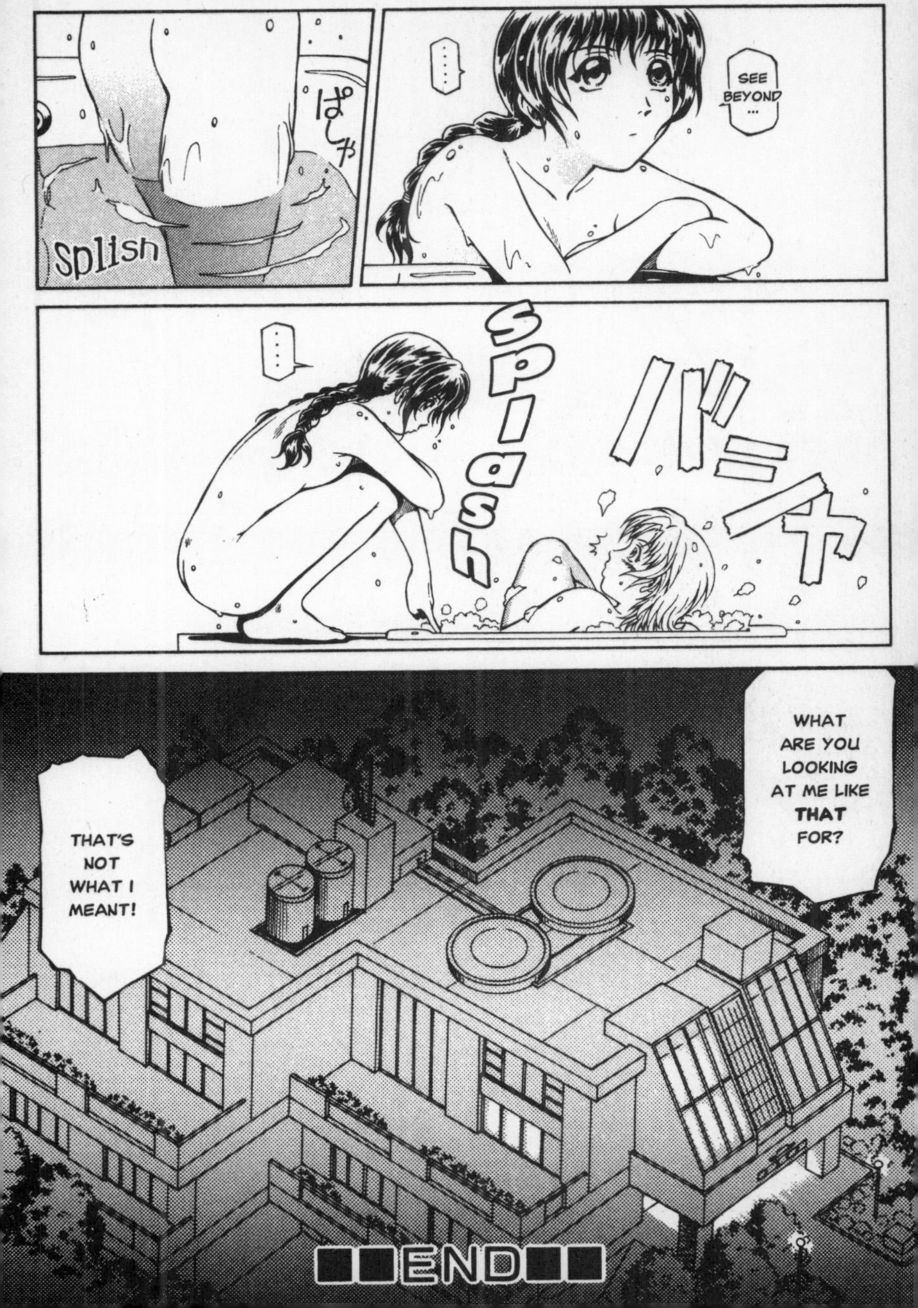
SEE BEYOND ...
......
ぱしゃ
Splish
バシャ
Splash
......
WHAT ARE YOU LOOKING AT ME LIKE THAT FOR?
THAT'S NOT WHAT I MEANT!
END

Guest Illustrations
from Nishijima (Director)
& Yamauchi (General Illustration Director)

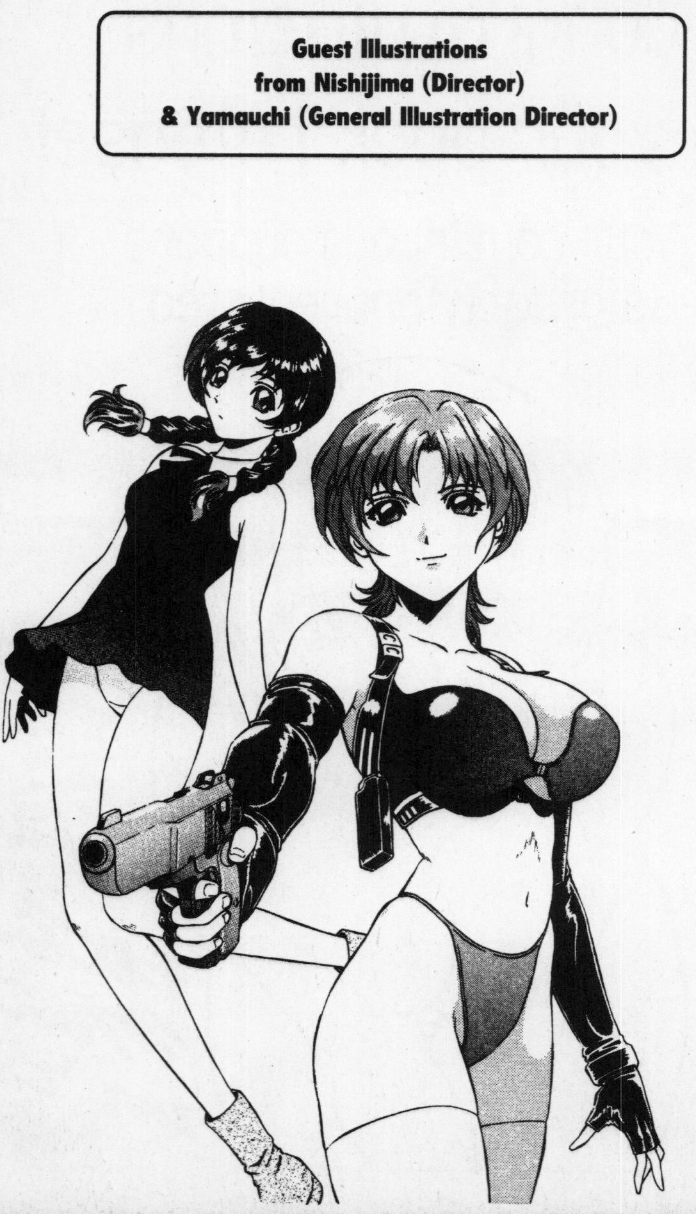
CIC

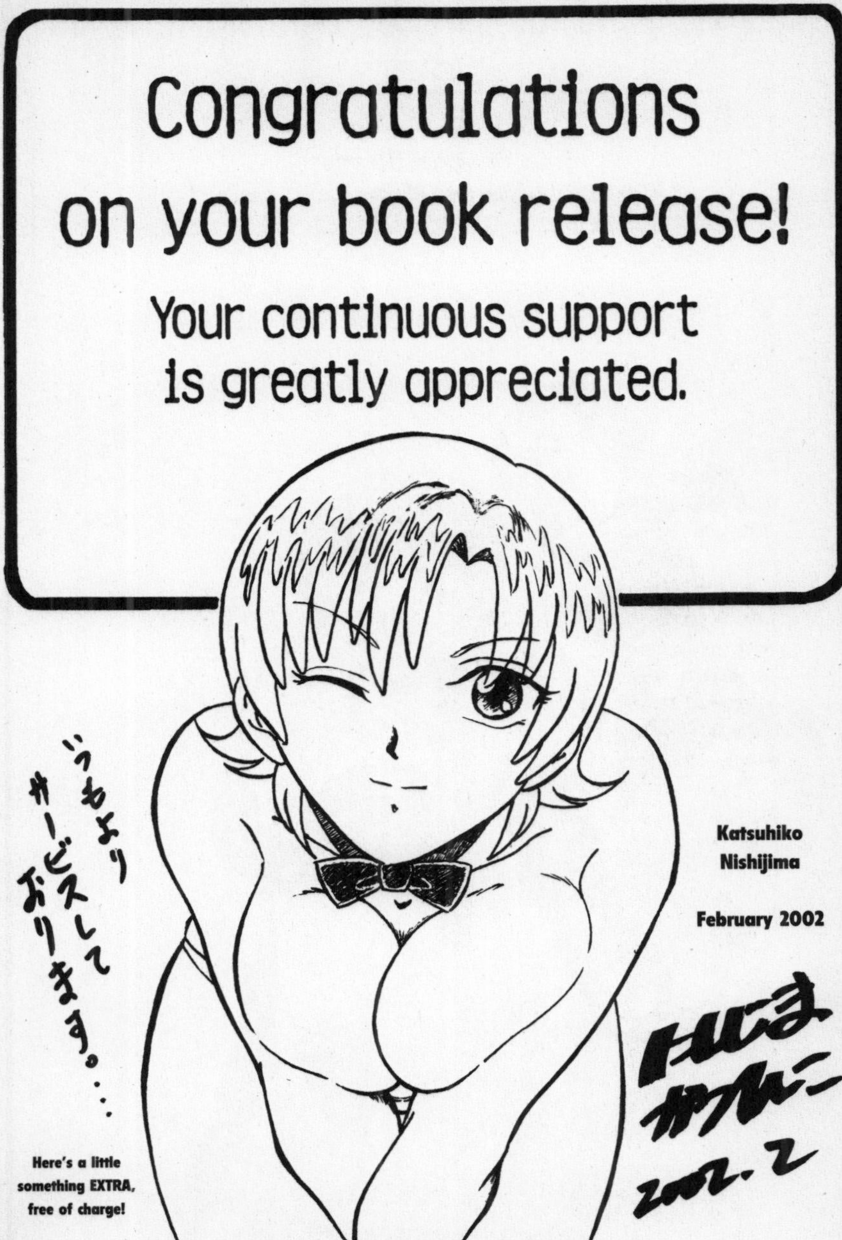
Congratulations on your book release!
Your continuous support is greatly appreciated.
いつもよりサービスしております。...
Here's a little something EXTRA, free of charge!
Katsuhiko Nishijima
February 2002
にしじま かつひこ 2002.2

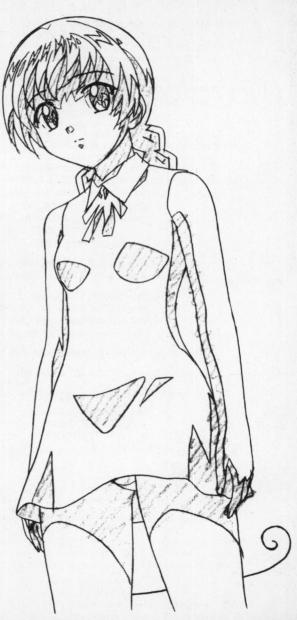

Fantastic job on your manga! There's nothing better than cute girls kicking butt. The TV version is over, but I'm looking forward to seeing more of these lovely girls in action in the future.

Noriyasu Yamauchi

Najica Blitz Tactics
Volume 1

© 2002 by Takuya Tashiro/STUDIO FANTASIA • AFW/NAJICA Project/MEDIA FACTORY
First published in Japan in 2002 by MEDIA FACTORY, Inc.
English Translation rights reserved by A.D.Vision, Inc.
Under the license from MEDIA FACTORY, Inc., Tokyo.

Translator	**KAY BERTRAND**
Lead Translator/Translation Supervisor	**JAVIER LOPEZ**
ADV Manga Translation Staff	**AMY FORSYTH, BRENDAN FRAYNE, HARUKA KANEKO-SMITH, MADOKA MOROE AND EIKO McGREGOR**
Print Production/ Art Studio Manager	**LISA PUCKETT**
Pre-press Manager	**KLYS REEDYK**
Art Production Manager	**RYAN MASON**
Sr. Designer/Creative Manager	**JORGE ALVARADO**
Graphic Designer/Group Leader	**SHANNON RASBERRY**
Graphic Designer	**KERRI KALINEC**
Graphic Artists	**HEATHER GARY, SHANNA JENSCHKE, WINDI MARTIN AND GEORGE REYNOLDS**
Graphic Intern	**MARK MEZA**
International Coordinator	**TORU IWAKAMI**
International Coordinator	**ATSUSHI KANBAYASHI**
Publishing Editor	**SUSAN ITIN**
Assistant Editor	**MARGARET SCHAROLD**
Editorial Assistant	**VARSHA BHUCHAR**
Proofreaders	**SHERIDAN JACOBS AND STEVEN REED**
Research/ Traffic Coordinator	**MARSHA ARNOLD**
Executive VP, CFO, COO	**KEVIN CORCORAN**
President, CEO & Publisher	**JOHN LEDFORD**

Email: editor@adv-manga.com
www.adv-manga.com
www.advfilms.com

For sales and distribution inquiries, please call 1.800.282.7202

ADV MANGA™ is a division of A.D. Vision, Inc.
10114 W. Sam Houston Parkway, Suite 200, Houston, Texas 77099

English text © 2004 published by A.D. Vision, Inc. under exclusive license.
ADV MANGA is a trademark of A.D. Vision, Inc.

ISBN: 1-4139-0018-6
First printing, August 2004
10 9 8 7 6 5 4 3 2 1
Printed in Canada

LETTER FROM THE ADV MANGA TRANSLATION STAFF

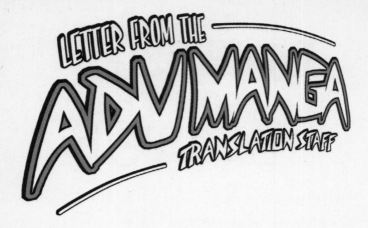

Dear Reader,

On behalf of the ADV Manga translation team, thank you for purchasing an ADV book. We are enthusiastic and committed to our work, and strive to carry our enthusiasm over into the book you hold in your hands.

Our goal is to retain the spirit of the original Japanese book. While great care has been taken to render a true and accurate translation, some cultural or readability issues may require a line to be adapted for greater accessibility to our readers. At times, manga titles that include culturally-specific concepts will feature a "Translator's Notes" section, which explains noteworthy references to the original text.

We hope our commitment to a faithful translation is evident in every ADV book you purchase.

Sincerely,

Madoka Moroe

Haruka Kaneko-Smith

Javier Lopez
Lead Translator

Eiko McGregor

Kay Bertrand

ADV Manga™

Brendan Frayne

Amy Forsyth

LETTER
FROM THE
EDITOR

Dear Reader,

Thank you for purchasing an ADV Manga book. We hope you enjoyed the sexy and suspenseful espionage of *Najica* Volume One.

It is our sincere commitment in reproducing Asian comics and graphic novels to retain as much of the character of the original book as possible. From the right-to-left format of the Japanese books to the meaning of the story in the original language, the ADV Manga team is working hard to publish a quality book for our fans and readers. Write to us with your questions or comments, and tell us how you liked this and other ADV books. Be sure to visit our website at www.adv-manga.com and view the list of upcoming titles, sign up for special announcements, and fill out our survey.

The ADV Manga team of translators, designers, graphic artists, production managers, traffic managers, and editors hope you will buy more ADV books—there's a lot more in store from ADV Manga!

www.adv-manga.com

Publishing Editor	Assistant Editor	Editorial Assistant
Susan B. Itin	Margaret Scharold	Varsha Bhuchar

Najica and Lila are back to recover more Humaritts from their eccentric and downright frightful captors, but their missions will take them far beyond the airtight walls of CRI Cosmetics. Onboard a luxury liner,

Najica Blitz Tactics
Volume 2

on a small island nestled in the Pacific, this is looking less like secret agent work and more like an all-expenses-paid getaway, but Najica and her right-arm gal will see some serious action before they have any fun in the sun!

The skirts are shorter, the guns are louder and the action is nonstop in *Najica Blitz Tactics* Volume 2!

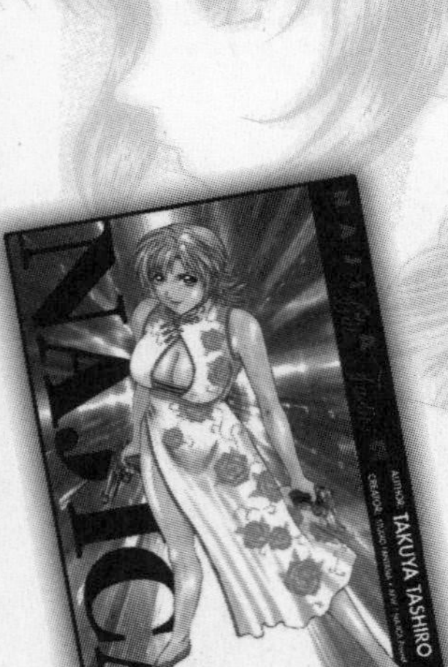

Available October 2004

EDITOR'S
PICKS

If you liked Najica Blitz Tactics Volume 1,
then you'll love these!

PICK 1

JINKI: EXTEND

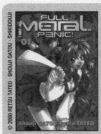

A mysterious explosion rocks La Gran Sabana, Venezuela, marking the beginning of the "Lost Life Phenomenon," a series of strange occurrences ranging from random murders to sudden disappearances of entire populations of villages.Three years later, heroine Akao Hiiragi suddenly finds herself piloting a jinki, a gigantic battle robot. But even as this young girl seeks to use her newfound power for good, a group of mysterious masked villains is after her, determined to take her captive. As she stands against these enemies, Akao will only face newer, tougher jinkis, but as long as young pilots like herself crave vengeance, the struggle will continue.

PICK 2

FULL METAL PANIC!

Kaname Chidori appears to be leading a normal life as a popular high school student, but unbeknownst to her, a group of terrorists believes she possesses the special powers of "The Whispered." When the terrorists' plan to kidnap Kaname reaches the ears of MITHRIL, a secret military organization, they send one of their own to pose as a student while acting as protector to the teenaged social butterfly. This MITHRIL member, Sosuke Sagara, is gung-ho, war-crazed and completely out-of-control, finding his mission as a high school student to be sheer torture. Kaname, on the other hand, finds herself thinking more and more about her undercover classmate, but refuses to own up to it. Her chances are running out! With attempted murders and kidnappings, will these two ever have a moment of truth? It's an exciting blend of fully-loaded action and teenage romance in the thrilling tale of **Full Metal Panic!**

PICK 3

CHRONO CRUSADE

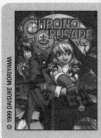

Villains and demonic creatures are flocking to America and infesting the cities. One woman is fighting the invasion of these damned beings, and she shows little mercy. Flanked by her partner Chrono, Sister Rosette is the one nun who can flatten demonic enemies and save the souls of their prey. Together they are pulling out their tommy-guns to protect the entire population, but with a combination of hellfire and holy water, this nun's rampage might lead to the destruction of more than demons!

CHECK 'EM OUT TODAY!

www.adv-manga.com

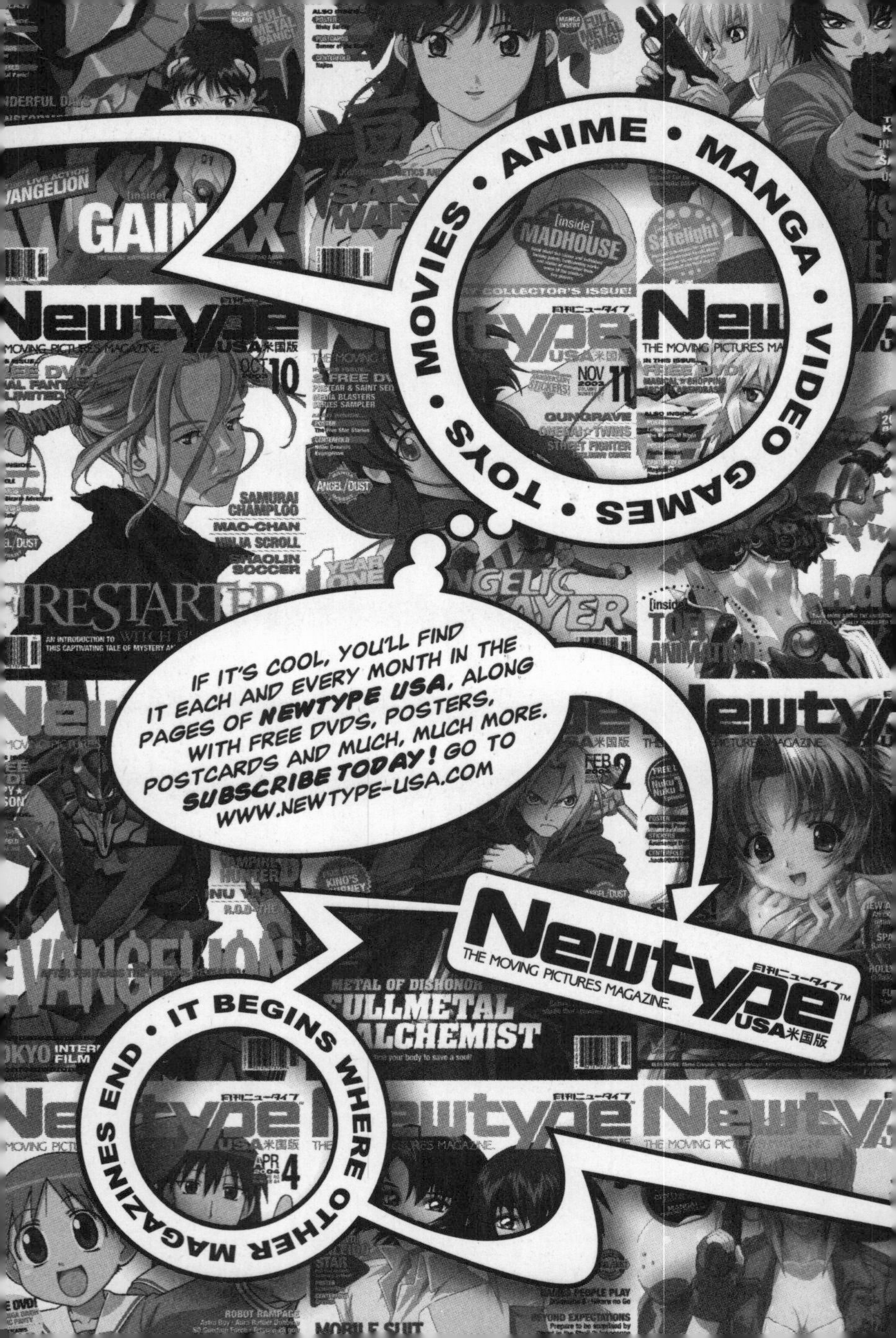
ANIME • MANGA • VIDEO GAMES • TOYS • MOVIES •
IF IT'S COOL, YOU'LL FIND IT EACH AND EVERY MONTH IN THE PAGES OF **NEWTYPE USA**, ALONG WITH FREE DVDS, POSTERS, POSTCARDS AND MUCH, MUCH MORE. **SUBSCRIBE TODAY!** GO TO WWW.NEWTYPE-USA.COM
Newtype™ THE MOVING PICTURES MAGAZINE. 月刊ニュータイプ USA 米国版
IT BEGINS WHERE OTHER MAGAZINES END •

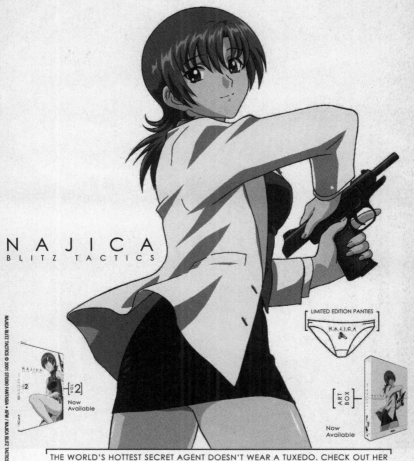
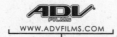

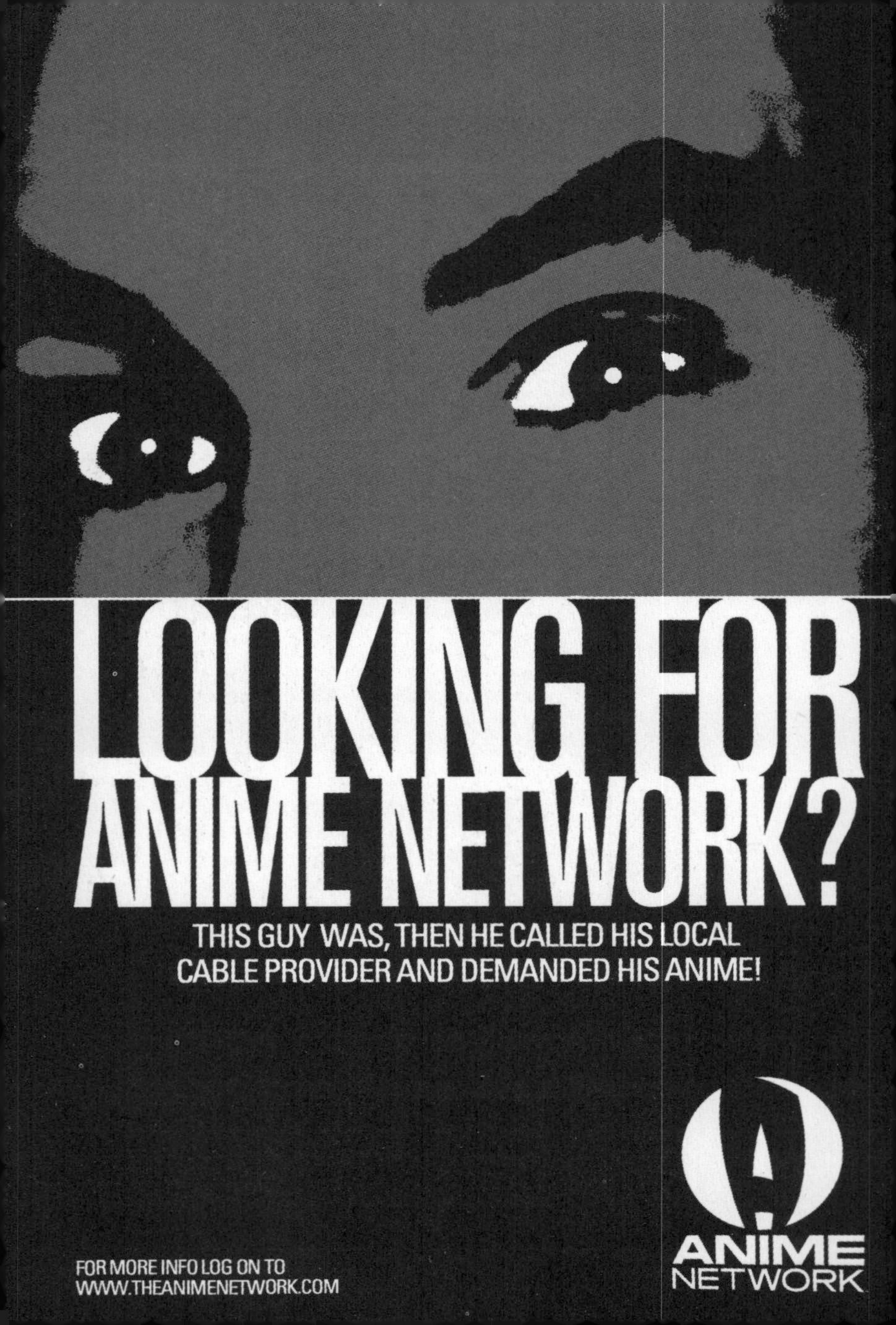
LOOKING FOR
ANIME NETWORK?
THIS GUY WAS, THEN HE CALLED HIS LOCAL
CABLE PROVIDER AND DEMANDED HIS ANIME!
FOR MORE INFO LOG ON TO
WWW.THEANIMENETWORK.COM
ANIME
NETWORK

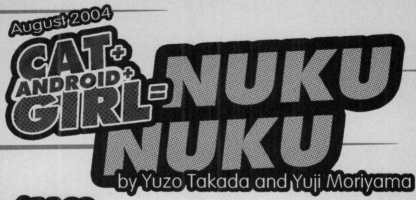
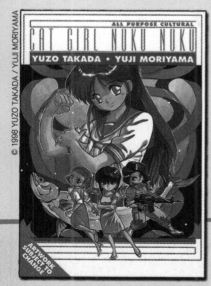

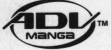

MANGA SURVEY

PLEASE MAIL THE COMPLETED FORM TO: EDITOR – ADV MANGA
c/o A.D. Vision, Inc. 10114 W. Sam Houston Pkwy., Suite 200 Houston, TX 77099

Name:_____

Address:_____

City, State, Zip:_____

_____

E-Mail:_____

Male ☐   Female ☐   Age:_____

☐ *CHECK HERE IF YOU WOULD LIKE TO RECEIVE OTHER INFORMATION OR FUTURE OFFERS FROM ADV.*

All information provided will be used for internal purposes only. We promise not to sell or otherwise divulge your information.

1. Annual Household Income (*Check only one*)
- ☐ Under $25,000
- ☐ $25,000 to $50,000
- ☐ $50,000 to $75,000
- ☐ Over $75,000

2. How do you hear about new Manga releases? (*Check all that apply*)
- ☐ Browsing in Store
- ☐ Internet Reviews
- ☐ Anime News Websites
- ☐ Direct Email Campaigns
- ☐ Online forums (message boards and chat rooms)
- ☐ Carrier pigeon
- ☐ Other:_____
- ☐ Magazine Ad
- ☐ Online Advertising
- ☐ Conventions
- ☐ TV Advertising

3. Which magazines do you read? (*Check all that apply*)
- ☐ Wizard
- ☐ SPIN
- ☐ Animerica
- ☐ Rolling Stone
- ☐ Maxim
- ☐ DC Comics
- ☐ URB
- ☐ Polygon
- ☐ Original Play Station Magazine
- ☐ Entertainment Weekly
- ☐ YRB
- ☐ EGM
- ☐ Newtype USA
- ☐ SciFi
- ☐ Starlog
- ☐ Wired
- ☐ Vice
- ☐ BPM
- ☐ I hate reading
- ☐ Other:_____

MNA/001

4. Have you visited the ADV Manga website?

- ☐ Yes
- ☐ No

5. Have you made any manga purchases online from the ADV website?

- ☐ Yes
- ☐ No

6. If you have visited the ADV Manga website, how would you rate your online experience?

- ☐ Excellent
- ☐ Good
- ☐ Average
- ☐ Poor

7. What genre of manga do you prefer?
(*Check all that apply*)

- ☐ adventure
- ☐ romance
- ☐ detective
- ☐ action
- ☐ horror
- ☐ sci-fi/fantasy
- ☐ sports
- ☐ comedy

8. How many manga titles have you purchased in the last 6 months?

- ☐ none
- ☐ 1-4
- ☐ 5-10
- ☐ 11+

9. Where do you make your manga purchases? (*Check all that apply*)

- ☐ comic store
- ☐ bookstore
- ☐ newsstand
- ☐ online
- ☐ other:________________
- ☐ department store
- ☐ grocery store
- ☐ video store
- ☐ video game store

10. Which bookstores do you usually make your manga purchases at?
(*Check all that apply*)

- ☐ Barnes & Noble
- ☐ Walden Books
- ☐ Suncoast
- ☐ Best Buy
- ☐ Amazon.com
- ☐ Borders
- ☐ Books-A-Million
- ☐ Toys "Я" Us
- ☐ Other bookstore:
____

11. What's your favorite anime/manga website? (*Check all that apply*)

- ☐ adv-manga.com
- ☐ advfilms.com
- ☐ rightstuf.com
- ☐ animenewsservice.com
- ☐ animenewsnetwork.com
- ☐ Other:________________
- ☐ animeondvd.com
- ☐ anipike.com
- ☐ animeonline.net
- ☐ planetanime.com
- ☐ animenation.com

All information provided will be used for internal purposes only. We promise not to sell or otherwise divulge your information.

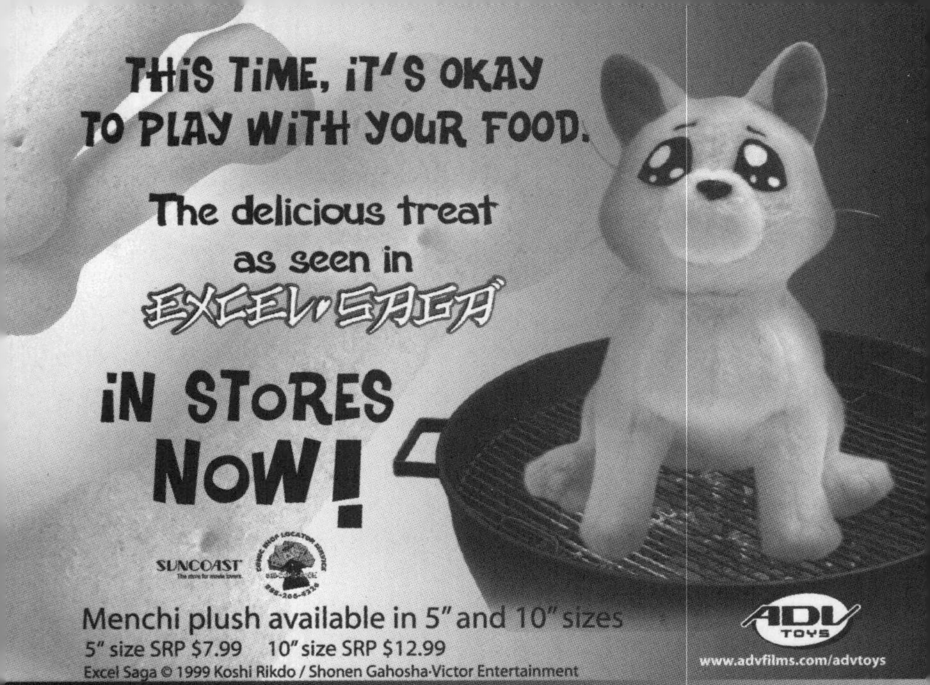
THIS TIME, IT'S OKAY
TO PLAY WITH YOUR FOOD.
The delicious treat
as seen in
EXCEL SAGA
IN STORES
NOW!
SUNCOAST
Menchi plush available in 5" and 10" sizes
5" size SRP $7.99 10" size SRP $12.99
Excel Saga © 1999 Koshi Rikdo / Shonen Gahosha·Victor Entertainment
ADV TOYS
www.advfilms.com/advtoys
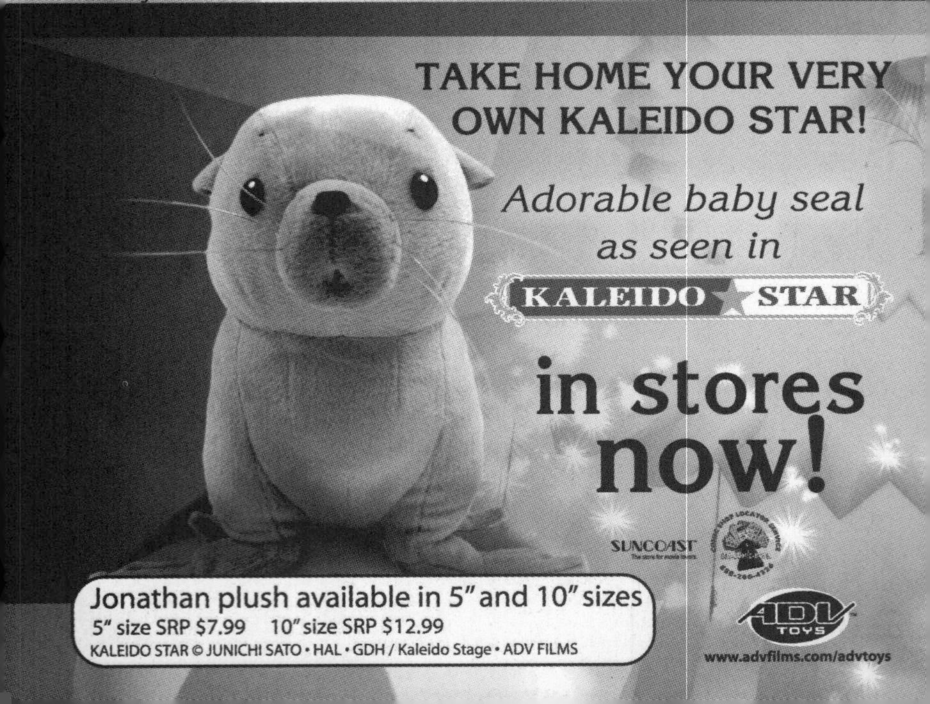
TAKE HOME YOUR VERY
OWN KALEIDO STAR!
Adorable baby seal
as seen in
KALEIDO STAR
in stores
now!
SUNCOAST
Jonathan plush available in 5" and 10" sizes
5" size SRP $7.99 10" size SRP $12.99
KALEIDO STAR © JUNICHI SATO • HAL • GDH / Kaleido Stage • ADV FILMS
ADV TOYS
www.advfilms.com/advtoys

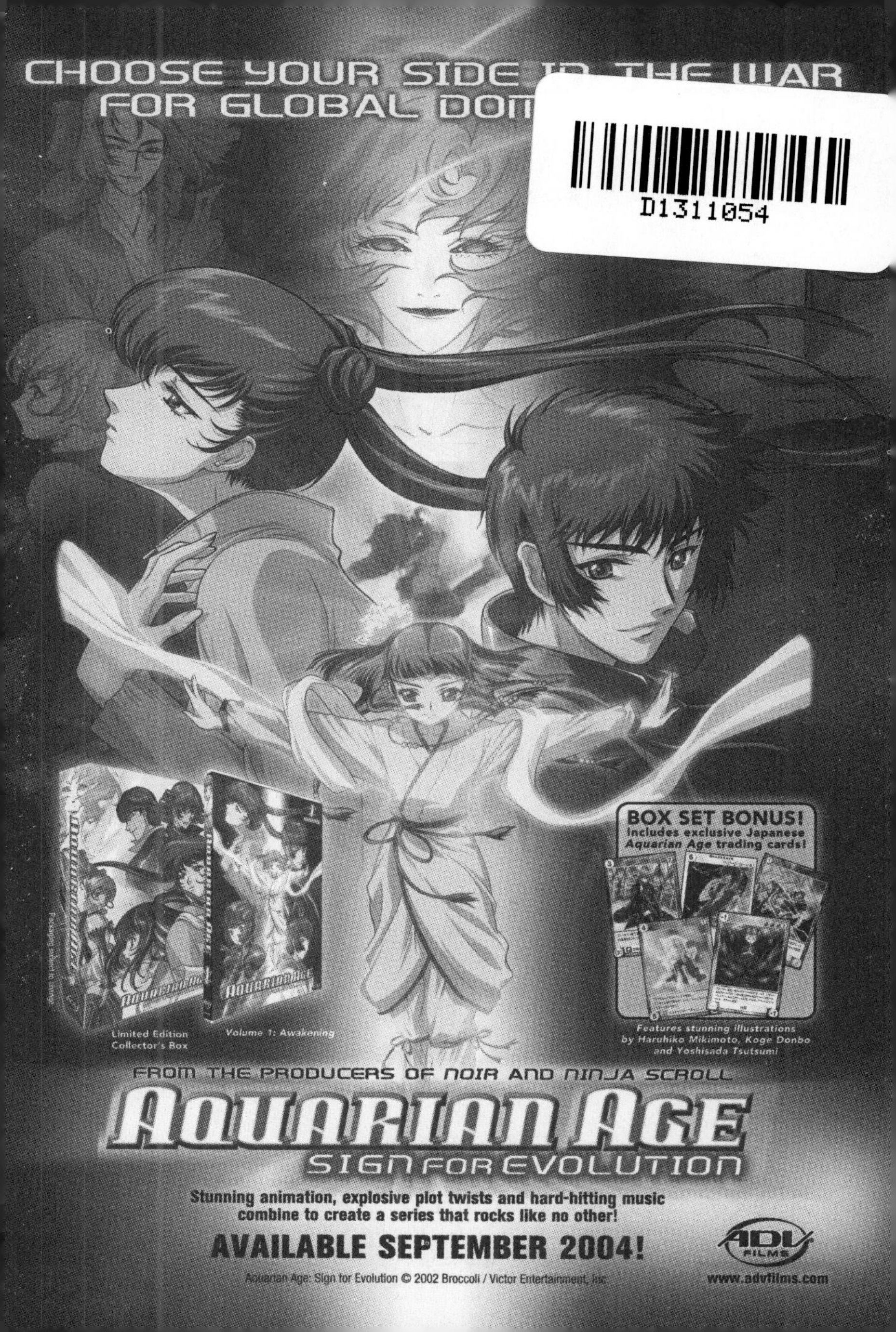
CHOOSE YOUR SIDE IN THE WAR
FOR GLOBAL DOM
BOX SET BONUS!
Includes exclusive Japanese Aquarian Age trading cards!
Features stunning illustrations by Haruhiko Mikimoto, Koge Donbo and Yoshisada Tsutsumi
Limited Edition Collector's Box
Volume 1: Awakening
FROM THE PRODUCERS OF NOIR AND NINJA SCROLL
AQUARIAN AGE
SIGN FOR EVOLUTION
Stunning animation, explosive plot twists and hard-hitting music combine to create a series that rocks like no other!
AVAILABLE SEPTEMBER 2004!
ADV FILMS
Aquarian Age: Sign for Evolution © 2002 Broccoli / Victor Entertainment, Inc.
www.advfilms.com